Clarity and Im

Clarity and Impact

Inform and impress
with your reports
and talks

Jon Moon

Oberon Publishing Limited

Published by Oberon Publishing Limited

First published 2016

ISBN 978-0-9935851-0-4

A catalogue record for this book is available from the British Library.

A catalog record for this book is available from the Library of Congress.

Typeset by Ian Kingston Publishing Services – www.iankingston.com

Printed in the United Kingdom by Lavenham Press Ltd, Suffolk

Brief contents

Contents

Acknowledgements

I now know what they mean by a rock band's 'tricky second album'. This book has taken five years to write. Not helped by a crashed hard drive and a stolen one.

But I had to do this 'second album'. In 2007, my first book introduced WiT, and since then, people have asked me questions about it. Shared experiences. Emailed me mock-ups (some great, some dreadful). I've taken WiT further since then too. Which is a big reason for this follow-up book: to capture all that.

But this book is more than just a WiT update, hence I've had lots of help from others. I owe a big thank you to Catherine Galvin, Chris Jones, Barry Leighton, Gary Peacock, Ed Percival, Alison Readman, Mike van de Water, and Simon Walters. They all reviewed a selection of Chapters and gave their insights. Then there's Ian Hinckley and Stephen Smith. I shouldn't single people out, but they deserve it. They painstakingly went through every single page and Figure. A remarkable effort, and a massive help. Thank you.

I am hugely grateful to other authors who were kind enough to let me borrow their ideas. Robin Williams has written many books on document design, including her brilliant *The Non-Designer's Design Book*, and Andy Maslen wrote the fantastic book *Write to Sell*. The greatest amount of borrowed material, though, comes from another author. Me. My first book *How to Make an Impact* is published by FT Prentice Hall (FTPH), and Richard Stagg of FTPH kindly agreed to let me use lots of its material. Six of this book's Chapters are stuff from that book. Then there's Chris Cudmore. If it wasn't for him, I would never have thought of self-publishing.

Talking of self-publishing, I've been lucky to work alongside people who have made the tough seem effortless: Amanda Tromans (editor) and Ian Kingston (typesetter). Together, they ensured my manuscript ended up as a proper book. No mean feat. Also, there's Michael Casey. He's been my web-chap for almost a decade, and long may it last.

Finally, my wonderful wife, Joan. She's been a fantastic sounding board for new ideas. She's kept my feet on the ground when I've got overconfident – and, much more often, picked me up when doubts crept in. She has coped magnificently whenever I retreated into the study to blast out a few more pages. I owe her a huge holiday. And if you read the acknowledgements of my first book, you know I said the same thing in 2007.

Which means I'm now in hock to her for two huge holidays.

Introduction

I once helped a confused CEO. His company had done lots of due diligence to decide whether to buy a company, yet he was unsure if he should proceed with the deal. The problem wasn't too little information – he'd received loads of reports. Nor too much – he'd been given lots of 'executive summaries'. The problem was: it all lacked clarity and impact.

The CEO asked me to review it all and arranged for us to meet. However, the meeting clashed with my son's sports day, so I instead put my thoughts in a three-page note. The thoughts weren't new, he'd seen them in previous reports. But for the first time they were clear. They had impact.

It galvanised. Within two days, he'd called off, then drastically renegotiated the deal – and I saw my son win the hoop race. Clear information saved the company a lot (millions) and saved me enough time to go to sports day. Clarity is great. Unfortunately, it's also rare.

Why so much information is poor

Every day, we struggle with poor information. It wastes time and leads to bad decisions. Apparently, bosses post-rationalise decisions. They use intuition to reach them, then look for information to support their hunch. I'm not surprised they do this – they can't grasp the reports they're sent.

Often when we're confused, we don't admit it. It's the Emperor's new clothes: we don't want to look stupid. We rationalise away our confusion. We blame ourselves: "I'm no good with numbers". Or we blame the topic: "It's complex, it takes time to grasp". So we ask report-writers to "pop over to my desk and talk through it". But if it's clear, it stands up on its own. I've written reports on complex frauds, yet didn't have to "talk through" them. Journalists write about complex issues, and I've never invited one to my home to "talk me through" their article.

People don't realise how much better it can all be. Before Mr Beck straightened the London Tube map in 1932, it was a literal diagram of where trains went and everyone thought it was fine. His new layout showed just how average earlier maps had been. So too at work – until bosses see something better, they don't realise they're being short-changed with poor reports.

To add to the problem, many people think it's all common sense. Got a lot of numbers? Hey, do a pie chart – we learnt them at primary school, albeit now we use computers, not crayons. Got a complex point to make in writing? Easy: put bullets in front of every paragraph. (Computers really do fool us into thinking that our reports and talks are good.)

Because people think clarity is common sense, we don't take time to learn about it. Many of us strive to master hobbies such as golf and bridge – we buy books, have lessons, etc – yet don't strive to master something that affects our job, our promotion, our pay. Companies are no better either. They spend lots on new systems to spew out management information, yet spend nothing learning how best to show it all.

If we do strive to improve, many of us misguidedly sign up for PowerPoint, Excel or MS Word courses. We learn to do groovy bullets, zany graphs, fancy fonts. We learn what we can do, not what we should do. Style triumphs over content: "Pimp your work," the mantra seems, "and people won't notice it's not clear". We let clarity play second fiddle to a less worthy but more fun goal: making dull work seem funky. It's such a shame, given that we've all got computers that can produce great work.

Some people claim there aren't underlying tips and principles for clarity; rather, it's all subjective. "Surely," they say, "we can't claim that a particular graph or table is better or worse than others – there aren't absolutes." They say this to mask their ignorance. They reckon it's better to claim subjectivity than admit they don't know the principles. But there are absolutes. After all, there are principles for everything from surgery to sales, so why not for clarity?

Some people learn how to write better, but as the saying goes, if you've only got a hammer, every problem looks like a nail – and if you learn only better writing, every problem is solved by better writing. Except it isn't – what about graphs, tables, flowcharts and more?

Some people resort to one-page notes. And yes, a confusing one-pager wastes less time than a confusing ten-pager – but it still confuses. Brevity doesn't guarantee clarity. Many CVs are just two pages, but are still dreadful.

Some people believe we merely need to think more about our objectives and messages. But knowing these won't help much if we can't convey them well.

There's one last reason why lack of clarity prevails – people can't find tips to improve. Hence this book. It provides them.

What's in this book and on my website

There are four Parts to this book (and each has an Introduction that outlines in more detail what it contains):

Part A: core content – most of it helps both reports and talks.
Part B: more on writing.
Part C: more on talks.
Part D: more on charts, numbers.

Read Part A first: other Parts refer to its ideas, and if you don't know them, they won't make sense. These other Parts can then be read in any order.

About 60 pages are from my other book, *How to Make an Impact* ('*Impact*'). As the text box in the margin explains, these pages are ring-fenced.

There's also free stuff on my website:

1. **Computing tips**: they help you put this book's ideas into practice. (This book has only a few tips – that's to keep the book short(ish) and to avoid it quickly going out of date.)
2. **Articles**: they delve further into some of the more fringe topics in this book.
3. **Templates to save you time**: some Figures in this book have a 🖥 next to them. They're downloads that help you adopt the book's ideas, plus you see the Figure in colour. All Figures in this book were done in MS Word, Excel and PowerPoint – none have been spruced up by a designer with a fancy design package.

These templates are important, because some ideas in this book create extra work for you. You may need to reformat your reports, plus it always takes longer to do something new. Fear not, for you get faster over time. Also, this book saves you time elsewhere – many of us waste time on stuff that doesn't help (e.g. pimping with funky fonts), and after reading this book, you'll no longer indulge in such nonsense. Finally, even if this book's ideas create a bit of extra work for you, it's worth it. Maybe you're working on a tender or board proposal – you spend ages getting your work to the final stage, so any extra time created by ideas in this book is a drop in the ocean. It's such a shame to do all that work, then fall at the final hurdle by conveying it badly, when with a bit of extra effort, it can have so much more clarity and impact.

However, be warned: this book is different to other business books. So here's what to expect – the good news and bad news.

It is good sense	*But* don't dismiss it as common sense. If it was, we'd all be following its ideas. Few do.
It has lots of ideas (part 1)	*But* many don't make that much difference by themselves. Collectively though, they make a huge difference.
It has lots of ideas (part 2)	*But* don't adopt all of them all the time – there are too many. Instead, adopt enough to get your work fit for purpose, then ignore the rest, save for something vital such as your CV. Adopt the tips intelligently, not slavishly.
It has lots of pages	*But* it doesn't take one big idea and s–t–r–e–t–c–h it out for a whole book. It covers a wide range of topics.

Overlap with *Impact*?
First, the headline: if you've read *Impact*, skip the first six Chapters of this book – and if you're thinking of buying *Impact*, you needn't, for it's all in those first six Chapters.

Let's explain: about 60 pages of this book are tips from *Impact*, and to avoid you constantly stumbling over stuff you might have already read, it's ring-fenced – it's in those first six Chapters. OK, this isn't 100% true – other Chapters include paragraphs here and there from *Impact* – but it's near enough (other than three of the pages on decision trees in Chapter 32).

Also – and as importantly – the first six Chapters consist only of stuff from *Impact*. That is, if you've read *Impact*, skip these and you won't miss any new tips. Again, this isn't 100% true – there are brief bits of new stuff in these six Chapters, but not much (other than the three-page Big Redo at the end of Chapter 4).

It gives illustrative words for you to use	*But* choose words that suit your style and organisation. For instance, if my words aren't assertive enough for you, butch yours up. Take my words and season to taste.
It hasn't much 'proof', i.e. formal evidence to support my tips	*But* proof is often flawed – see the one-page article on my website. So instead of evidence, I state reasons for my tips – and if my reasons resonate with you, good. If they don't, see the next row.
It has views you won't agree with	*But* I hope you agree with most, otherwise it's a waste of your time and money.
It shows how to convey clearly	*But* it doesn't help you decide what to convey – I assume you already know that. You just want help conveying it.
It improves the work you do for your clients, bosses, staff, etc	*But* it refers throughout to *bosses*. That's to avoid constantly referring to 'clients, senior managers, staff, colleagues, suppliers, etc'.

This book has many *before* and *after* examples. The *before*s are based on real work and are typical, not unusually bad. As for my *after*s, I avoid the trickery of diet ads in which someone not only loses weight, but also gets a new dress, teeth and hairdo. Rather, I keep *before* and *after* comparable.

Finally, I often show football league tables (to demonstrate how to do tables) and Latin text (to show page layouts). I don't follow football, but their tables help me make a learning point. Also, I don't know Latin, but it helps you see layouts without being distracted by exact words.

The benefits of clarity and impact

Clarity and impact saves time and money. People no longer spend ages grappling with indecipherable reports or listening to unclear talks. Instead, they understand instantly, then discuss consequences and more quickly reach better informed decisions. Meetings are *much* shorter.

But clarity and impact is more than bosses saving time and making better decisions. It's about you. You do work that's better than you thought possible. You win business. You inform, influence, impress. You do work that others praise and envy. After all, clear information shows clear thinking, and clear thinking impresses. Decision-makers look more favourably on proposals they quickly understand. You get results.

Also, you look more professional – and there's a halo effect to this. People will trust you more. Imagine delivering a report or talk that's a bit shabby – not thought through, poorly presented. It's akin to a typing error: it unnerves people, and they start to question everything you've done. Now imagine your work is sharp, concise, clear, well thought through. It reassures. People ask fewer questions.

There's more though. You do work you're proud of – and are more confident too. When you get it right, you know you're in control. You've thought it through properly and are putting your best foot forward. Your confidence will shine for people to see. Now that's something to aim for.

Final thoughts

Whenever there are economic or business crises, people call for change: tighter regulation, better governance, greater transparency. However, it's all meaningless without clarity. Without it, directors can't direct, regulators can't regulate, governments can't govern. As for transparency, 20 pages of contractual small print might be transparent, but it lacks clarity.

It's like *The Day of the Jackal* when the Police Chief explains that his security forces are powerless because, without knowing the Jackal's name, they're unable to chase, arrest or kill the assassin – and so solemnly concludes: "The first task, without which all other proposals become meaningless, is to give this man a name". For me, that name is clarity, for without it, all other proposals become meaningless.

Yet business gives so little attention to the topic. I'm an MBA, yet not once did my business school teach me anything in this book, and as an accountant, I learnt to crunch numbers, but not how to show them clearly. Instead, business schools teach sexy topics like leadership and strategy. Accountancy institutes do likewise: they teach their students how to do other people's work (strategy), but don't fully teach them how to do their own work (bring numbers to life). Who can blame them though? Leaders seem to ignore clarity – when CEOs write memoirs, they call them: "Smith on leadership!", not: "Smith on clarity!".

But without clarity, everything is "meaningless". The glib cliché is "Information is power" – but it isn't. Information without clarity is useless. Maybe even dangerous. As the text box explains, the credit crunch was triggered not by defaults, but by lack of clarity. Clarity *matters*, so this book shows how to convey information clearly. And with impact. I conclude by paraphrasing Robin Williams (she's a fantastic designer I mention later): "You won't agree with everything in this book, but you'll never look at a table, bullet, slide, graph or report – and you'll never listen to a talk, presentation or speech – in the same way".

Clarity and credit crunch
In August 2007, the giant French bank BNP Paribas said that, because of uncertainties in the sub-prime mortgage market, it was unable to value three of its investment funds. As Robert Peston, the BBC Economics Editor, said in his book: "All of a sudden, huge banks, hedge funds and professional investors woke up and recognised that they too did not know the proper value of hundreds of billions of dollars of assets they owned."

OK, the sub-prime mortgages were toxic, but toxicity itself isn't dangerous. Lack of clarity about toxicity is, for people then unknowingly consume something toxic. And the finance industry consumed it. By the billion.

Core content

Part A is relevant to almost everyone, and nearly all of it helps both reports and talks. Its first six chapters are from *How to Make an Impact*, my first book. Chapter 1 changes forever your view of bullets and is my signature dish: **WiT** – Words in Tables. WiT visually lifts ideas from reports and sharpens your thinking. Chapter 2 is on **graphs**. If you think graphs should be memorable and make instant sense, think again, then read Chapter 2. Then we look at **numbers** – if they confuse you or your readers, read Chapter 3. Many people dislike **tables**, but that's because they see bad tables. Chapter 4 shows five simple steps to ensure you do tables that people love, not loathe.

Often, we must compare alternatives (do joint venture, outsource or keep in-house?), but we then convey comparisons badly. Bosses struggle to have informed discussions about alternatives. Hence Chapter 5 (**making comparisons**). Ever wondered why some work looks *sharp*? Ever wasted time tinkering unsuccessfully to make yours sharp ("Try it in bold and blue")? Chapter 6 has **design** tips to help.

Worried you bore people with the words you use? Chapter 7 (**words for reports and talks**) ensures yours engage. Chapter 8 (**what people need – myths**) is a bit different – discover why you should be negative, random and more. Also, see how to write great talks in minutes, not hours.

So far, so good, but it all means nothing if we don't **achieve outcomes**. Hence Chapter 9. Sounds good – but how to start your reports and talks? Chapter 10 tells you (**your first 30 seconds**).

Chapter 11 takes us back to the written word – it gives tips **specific to writing**. Ever had the feeling you're not **getting to the nub** of what you wish to convey? Then read Chapter 12. It's one of the most useful bits of this book; it has a trick to ensure you hit the right buttons.

Visuals and photos are a great way to waste time at work ("Now… what autoshape shall we put here?") Do they help? Chapter 13 reveals all.

Lastly, we look at two hot topics: **infographics** and **story-telling**. If tempted to do them, Chapters 14 and 15 tell you when you should and shouldn't. If you like irony, both topics are overflowing with it.

1 Bullet points ('WiT')

Figure 1.1

Findings of interest were as follows:
- There has been a problem with staff turnover – 30% of staff left last year, up 10% from the prior year. Many leavers were from "Global Solutions" department.
- The market value of its Leeds site is £3m more than shown on the balance sheet.
- Last month, Regulators formally announced the company has been cleared of the mis-selling accusations that hung over it for the last 2 years.
- Its computer system is inadequate and needs replacing at a cost of £2m. This will also add £500k a year extra to running costs.
- Its pension deficit has worsened in the year from £10m to £30m. The company is increasing contributions by £7m a year to remedy.
- Its new business initiative has been a success and income is up 20% on last year. Every department has increased income by at least 12%.
- Because of poor hedging, the dollar weakness will hit profit by £3m next year (they've recently recruited a new Treasurer).
- It's finished clinical trials on the major new drug and Medical Authorities have indicated they should approve it next week.

This Chapter is on my signature dish: WiT. It's a seriously better alternative to bullets. It stands for Words in Tables. It gives immediate impact to reports, and it helps talks too. First though, let's see why bullets rarely work. Assume we've a complex piece of analysis to communicate in writing. In the old days, we'd have a good hard think and work out an effective way to do it. But nowadays, we dispense with hard thinking, for computers give us the answer – we pen a few words, then divide them into bullets. Or rather:

- We pen a few words
- Then divide them into bullets

These black dots are everywhere. Which is a shame, because bullets get us into bad habits. As we soon see, they're a big reason why many reports are incomplete, inconsistent, wordy and lack clarity. Also, bullets are visually unappealing – when we see bullet-riddled reports, our hearts sink. Bullets don't break up dull text. They are dull text. And because we see bullets everywhere, they've long lost any impact they had. Bullets no longer impress. They depress.

Time for an alternative: WiT. It solves all problems mentioned above. Readers love it too, it makes reports easier to read, visually lifting points from the page. Let's see our first WiT.

Turning bullets into WiT

Rather than going straight to a WiT, let's get there over four steps (WiT is the last step). Each step illustrates something new. Figure 1.1 (the *before*) shows findings from a company review – and it's a typical layout. Let's improve it.

Step 1: put the conclusion first

The *before* starts with the comment: "Findings of interest were as follows". Not helpful. It forces people to read the list and draw their own conclusions. Figure 1.2 has a lead-in comment that gives the conclusion ("overall in good shape"). It *starts at the end*. Much better. Chapter 10 has much more on this.

Step 2: segment, order, maybe strip out

In the *before* (Figure 1.1), bullets are in a random order. Never leave that way. Segment. Order. Strip a few out. Maybe do all three.

Segment them. Between good and bad, for instance. Or important and unimportant, or whatever. With five or more bullets, readers grasp them much more easily if we segment them. When you next send bosses a two-page note on your unit's 12 action points for next year, don't just list 12 points. By the time bosses reach the last point, they've forgotten the first 11 and are none the wiser. As Homer Simpson said: "Every time I learn something new, it pushes some old stuff out of my brain… when I took that home wine-making course, I forgot how to drive". Instead, sort your 12 action points between, say, costly and cheap. Or must-do and nice-to-do. However, as always there's an exception: don't sort minutes of meetings. Minutes are meant to be objective records, and if we sort and group, it introduces subjectivity. Leave that to the covering memo ("Here are the minutes; point 18 is vital because etc").

Order them. Avoid alphabetical. If we've segmented points between good and bad, put good ones in order of 'goodness'. Then tell readers we've done this, otherwise they waste valuable brain space putting them in some order so they can better grasp them, only to eventually realise we've already done that.

Strip out less material stuff. If we've, say, 30 good findings, some are probably less important, and these lessen the impact of stuff that matters. Relegate them to a secondary table, and write a lead-in comment that signposts this to readers ("below are less material findings included for completeness"). Or put in the appendix and tell readers where to find them – and again, lead into them with a comment. Maybe we don't wish to relegate any to an appendix, for we fear they won't get read. In which case, it's even more important to segment and order.

Some people object to removing stuff. "I may think something's unimportant," they say, "yet readers may think it critical." Or maybe subsequent events prove it to be critical. Surely it's safer not to filter. No. Everyone filters.

Figure 1.2

There were mixed findings, but overall the company seems in good shape:

Good findings
- Its new business initiative has been a success and income is up 20% on last year. Every department has increased income by at least 12%.
- It's finished clinical trials on the major new drug and Medical Authorities have indicated they should approve it next week.
- Last month, Regulators formally announced the company has been cleared of the mis-selling accusations that hung over it for the last 2 years.
- The market value of its Leeds site is £3m more than shown on the balance sheet.

Bad findings
- Its computer system is inadequate and needs replacing at a cost of £2m. This will also add £500k a year extra to running costs.
- Its pension deficit has worsened in the year from £10m to £30m. The company is increasing contributions by £7m a year to remedy.
- There has been a problem with staff turnover – 30% of staff left last year, up 10% from the prior year. Many leavers were from "Global Solutions" department.
- Because of poor hedging, the dollar weakness will hit profit by £3m next year (they've recently recruited a new Treasurer).

The HR director filters when she neglects to tell bosses about her pencil purchases. Fail to filter and bosses quickly tire of you.

OK, we've tidied a list… which doesn't sound enthralling. But lists are great, they distil and summarise. We talk about five steps for sending invoices, six lessons from our project, the Ten Commandments to live by. Even Santa Claus makes a list (and he checks it twice). We use lists a lot. Often, there's a lot of thinking behind them, so it's worth presenting them well.

Let's return to our findings (Figure 1.2). By starting at the end and segmenting, they're already much better. I didn't reorder any – or strip any out – but let's assume their order is fine and they're all material. Next is step 3 – and from here on we see just the good findings, for they're sufficient on their own to illustrate the learning points.

Figure 1.3

> **Good findings**
> - **New business drive successful**: income is up 20% on last year and every department is up by at least 12%.
> - **Major drug to be approved**: clinical trials have finished and Medical Authorities have indicated they should approve it next week.
> - **Cleared of mis-selling**: last month, Regulators formally announced the end of the two-year review.
> - **Property £3m undervalued**: the market value of its Leeds site is £3m more than shown on the balance sheet.

Step 3: 'start at the end' for each finding

In Figure 1.3, the first point now starts with the phrase: "New business drive successful", and it's in bold. Key points stand out more. It helps readers. However, next is the big change, and it makes key points *really* stand out.

Step 4: put Words in a Table ('WiT')

In step 3, we showed the first point as follows:

- **New business drive successful**: income is up 20% on last year and every department is up by at least 12%.

Instead, create a two-column table, and put the opening bit on the left and supporting detail on the right – see Figure 1.4. Opening bits are no longer in bold – they don't need to be, they now stand out anyway. Findings are in a WiT, and there are many benefits to this (notice they are shown in a WiT):

Figure 1.4

New business drive successful	Income is up 20% on last year and every department is up by at least 12%.
Major drug to be approved	Clinical trials have finished and Medical Authorities have indicated they should approve it next week.
Cleared of mis-selling	Last month, Regulators announced formally the end of the two-year review.
Property £3m undervalued	The market value of its Leeds site is £3m more than shown on the balance sheet.

It's less dense and intimidating	It looks smarter, sharper. Some people say they absorb information visually. WiT is visual.
It's more readable	Words are in narrower columns, and that's easier to read than if stretched across a page. Chapter 6 (*Design*) explains more.

Key points lift from the page	They stand proud in the left column, not hidden undercover amongst detail.
Readers can navigate around and skim-read and scan	They read more selectively – if familiar with something, they can skip detail. They can also refer back to stuff more easily.

Result: bosses have more informed discussions. After all, think about what often happens at work: when reaching decisions, bosses ignore the very reports they commission to help them reach decisions. That's because, in most reports, key findings are hidden within wordy paragraphs. It's difficult to discuss findings when you can't find them. With WiT, it's different. Findings leap from the page. Much better.

So WiT is great for readers, but there's much more to it. Hence the rest of this Chapter. We see WiT on slides and in CVs. We see it transform not just bullets, but continuous text. We also see its really big benefit. By the end, you'll use WiT to give your work real clarity and impact. First though, we see how WiT helps ensure completeness.

WiT helps ensure completeness

Figure 1.5 is from a report that pitches for business. The comments are typical ("We recruit the best staff"), and so too is the layout: a bunch of bullets. All rather uninspiring.

Because we've seven bullets, we need to group them. But how? Try this: group by vacuousness. Five comments are fine, and two are vacuous – "We recruit the best staff", and "Our clients are King". These two fail the *Not* test – no-one ever says they do *not* recruit the best staff, so there's no point in saying we do. OK, maybe we do recruit the best, but if we can't prove and demonstrate it, it's just hot air. Waffle doesn't help win business. Rather, it hinders – it makes it tougher for readers to see the comments that do help, and hence lessens the impact of stuff that really matters. So strip it out. If we must keep it, at least relegate it to a secondary table, then give a lead-in comment that flags to readers that the points are, well, just waffle.

Do that, and we're left with five bullets. Let's do a WiT of features and benefits (Figure 1.6). But now we've a problem: three points mention a feature, but no benefit. OK, we've a strong parent, but how's that help clients? Which brings us to the point of this section: WiT helps make writing more

Figure 1.5

Why choose us

- We recruit the best staff.
- Being the biggest, we get the best deals from the market for you.
- Our clever web system gives you 24/7 service.
- Our parent is Multinational Inc, the third biggest conglomerate in the world.
- We have been serving clients for over 150 years.
- Our clients are King – we put them first.
- We won the Employer of Choice award last year.

Figure 1.6

Why choose us?

Feature	Benefit
The biggest	You get the best deal from our market leverage
Clever web system	You get 24/7 access
A strong parent	?!?!?!
150 years' experience	?!?!?!
Employer of Choice	?!?!?!

complete. Most writing is incomplete, and unwittingly so. It's a random list of whatever writers remember to mention, and often they forget stuff and don't realise it. Readers don't realise it either, and everyone is happy in their ignorance. That's because bullets don't highlight omissions. WiT does – there's a blank cell in the table. When I edit reports, I turn bullets into WiT, then email the report's author and ask them to fill in the gaps, gaps they didn't know existed. WiT helps ensure completeness.

But there's more – WiT gives readers *choice.* That's next.

WiT gives readers choice

Figure 1.7

Locals prefer other shops' products	Lorem ipsum est gloriatur expetendis an. Con gue contentiones conse quuntur et eos, autem vocibus in nam. Agam conc eptam mel cu, eum.
We're in a poor location too	Eu sit cetero appareat accusata. Per et dicam tempor praesent, eripuit nonu mmy volu mus cu sea. Per tantas altep .
We can't relocate because of planning restrictions	Eum luptatum contentiones cu, eu mei fabellas medio critatem. Vivendo antio pam nec te, malis ullum epicut curipro fibsisrawa.

Assume a manager in a retail group writes a report on one of its stores. Figure 1.7 is part of the report, done as a WiT. On the left are key points, and on the right is detail that supports them (albeit in Latin). The WiT clearly argues why the store is in a bit of a fix. The first row starts with the thought: "Locals prefer other shops' products". The second row adds more: "We're in a poor location too". The third row gives the final thought: "We can't relocate because of planning restrictions". At this point, the conclusion is probably: "Close the store", but ignore that for now. Rather, note that WiT gives clarity and impact to the narrative – key points leap from the page – and there's detail too if readers want it.

Notice the left column gives answers. It could instead pose questions, e.g.: "Do locals prefer other shops' products?". Perhaps this would help arouse readers' curiosity and engage them. Here, though, posing questions is cruel because it forces people to read the right column to find answers. Don't do that. Wherever possible, make the left column a self-contained story – if people read only that column, that's all they *need* to read. Write so that, if readers cover up the right column, they still get the main thrust of your points. Hence don't say on the left: "Locals' views on other shops' products". Or: "Other shops' products". Those are just headings. Instead, do headlines: "Locals prefer other shops' products". That spells it out.

This is such an important point, I'll repeat it. Loudly. On the left, **do headlines, not headings**. It ensures reports work for everyone. People tell me they write 30-page reports for ten bosses – and five love detail, five hate detail. "How can we keep them all happy?", they ask. Easy. Do WiT. Those who don't want detail read only the left column, and in just six or seven seconds, they get the broad gist of an entire page. Those who want detail read the right column as well. Readers can even dip in and out throughout reports

– an HR boss might skim the treasury bit because it's only of background interest, but dive into detail in the HR bit. WiT allows people to do this.

Readers can even dip in and out row by row. In Figure 1.7, if readers know that locals prefer other shops' products, they don't read the detail on the first row. But if the second row arouses curiosity – maybe they don't know we're in a poor location – they read the details on the right and learn more. And if they know about planning restrictions, they can skip the detail on the third row.

Which is fantastic. It's as if every reader gets a report whose page length is perfect for them. They each get the word count they crave. Those who want detail read every word. Those who want some detail read some right columns. Those who want no detail read just left columns. In effect, WiT tailors reports for every reader.

Which means WiT does something that other reports don't: it gives readers *choice*. People read only what they want to read. WiT is great for readers. And next we see how it's great for writers too.

WiT removes waffle and shortens reports

"WiT shortens reports"…? It seems counterintuitive. WiT has unused space on the left, so if we turn a page of text into a WiT, surely it becomes more than a page. No. With WiT, it nearly always turns into less than a page. To understand why, think what typically happens when people start to type. They've a rough idea of what they wish to convey, yet their thoughts are neither well structured nor ordered. No worries, the act of typing brings it all together… doesn't it? In a blur of keyboard taps, five paragraphs appear.

Unfortunately, ideas rarely come out well. Yes, we've five paragraphs, but what's the key point of each? Often, the report-writer isn't aware of them. Rather, words just *emerge*. And even if the writer is aware of them, they're hidden deep within paragraphs. In the middle of the first paragraph. The start of the second. The end of the third. And so on.

So we've two problems: writers aren't aware of key points, and points are hidden in wordy paragraphs. WiT solves both. With WiT, we ask ourselves a simple but powerful question: how can we summarise this paragraph in a few words? We then put those five or ten words prominently in the left column. And when we do this, we realise many paragraphs say nothing. So we remove them. I once asked a sales team to take their one-page summary and redo it as a WiT. They removed seven out of eight paragraphs. They realised most paragraphs were just waffle. Figure 1.8 is similar to their opening paragraph, and if you're involved with tenders, it probably resonates. All it says is: "Thanks for letting us pitch". So they removed it.

Figure 1.8
How not to start a tender…
"Thank you for the opportunity to pitch for your business. You are a great firm. We are too. We both employ world-class, leading-edge professionals who would – if the suggestions in this report were to be adopted – work together to deliver benefits to you that would sustain your pre-eminent position in the 21st century trading environment in which we currently trade in this age of austerity." Cor…

But there's more:

We end up with shorter paragraphs	Bullets let us waffle on. WiT doesn't – our WiT would be lopsided (too much on the right, too little on the left). WiT gives us less room to waffle, so we waffle less.
We waffle less *between* paragraphs	We avoid all those joining-up phrases that link one thought to the next – Figure 1.9 illustrates one such link.

With WiT, we have fewer paragraphs. Shorter paragraphs. Less waffle between paragraphs. WiT shortens reports. People regularly tell me that WiT turned a 30-page report into a 14-pager. Or a ten-pager into a four-pager. Or a three-pager into a one-pager. They then add: "I had to think a lot harder when writing though". We see why next.

Figure 1.9

Wordy links between paragraphs

"However, after that most important point, there is another key point in this analysis that needs to be taken into consideration by all the decision-makers in this process going forward, and that key point is as follows…"

WiT orders ideas and takes them further

The British TV comic Eric Morecambe once said about his piano-playing: "I'm playing all the right notes, but not necessarily in the right order". Many of us write that way too. We use the right letters of the alphabet – we may even make the right points – but not necessarily in the right order. Result: most reports are disordered. They go from future to past to problem, then onto solution, back to past and onto another solution, etc. They're random walks and there are two reasons why:

Many reports have multiple authors	Our boss. Our boss's boss. Group legal. Group compliance. They all tinker. No wonder most reports are all over the shop.
Editors often tackle the wrong stuff	When words are hidden deep in continuous text, editors struggle to see the wood for the trees. They can't see the story for the words. So they don't do what they should (reorder), but do what they can (tinker). "We're fine" becomes: "We're mostly fine"…

Tinkering doesn't help though. Reordering does, and WiT helps us reorder. With WiT, it's not just readers who more easily see our points. We do too. There are two great benefits to this:

1. **We put things in the right order**: we see our points more clearly, so are better able to ponder their order. WiT helps us assemble reports.
2. **We take our thinking further**: people often write vacuous stuff like: "The situation must be managed," yet fail to say who to do what by when

and how. If empty remarks are hidden in the middle of text, they're not too shameful or embarrassing. Put them on the left of a WiT, and they're exposed. As writers, we see them more clearly for what they are – half-baked – and so we take our thinking further to avoid embarrassment. WiT prevents us falling back on empty business-speak.

So WiT isn't just about clear layout. *It's about clear thinking*. Next we see how WiT helps us write consistently. Hardly sounds thrilling, but stick with it, for we see how WiT helps us do a great CV.

Figure 1.10

WiT, consistency, and great CVs

Figure 1.10 is the career-history page of a CV. It's usually page two, and it shows where the person has worked and what they achieved in those jobs. The layout is typical: a repeating pattern of rows – date, position, company, achievements – laid out down the page in reverse date order. It's visually unappealing, plus read-ers struggle to find information. To see achievements, eyes flick down the page, skipping over stuff they don't want: "*Date* – nope… *Position* – nope… *Company* – nope… ah, at last – *Achievements*". After reading the first set of achievements, the hunt starts afresh as read-ers look for the second set, again skipping over stuff they don't want. And to see positions held over the years, it's the same unwieldy procedure.

Figure 1.11 shows it in a WiT. It looks sharper, and it's easier for readers to move around and find stuff. Achievements? The right column. Positions held? Column two. What was happening in 2009? The second row. Easy.

Also, Figure 1.11 shows how WiT makes writing more consistent. Imagine that the CV's author is a bit flaky in their thinking and writes as an achievement: "Ran marketing for two years". But it's a responsibility, not an achieve-ment. In traditionally laid-out CVs, this error might go unnoticed because of the stop–start staccato way people read achievements – read an achievement, then hunt down a few rows to the next, read another, then hunt down a few more rows, read another, etc.

Date: '13 - now
Position: Group Marketing Director, full plc director reporting to plc CEO, 40 staff
Company: LJZ Group plc, FMCG group, income £3bn
Achievements
- Agam conceptam mel cu, eum et por ro recteque interesset. Ea fugit ullum assentior duo.
- Ex ius idque corrumpit demo crit um, ad sit ponderum.

Date: '09 - '13
Position: Marketing Director, reporting to MD, 20 staff
Company: ITS Solutions Ltd, IT software distributor, income £500m, subsidiary of ITS plc
Achievements
- Agam conceptam mel cu, eum et por ro recteque interesset. Ea fugit ull um assentior duo.
- Ex ius idque corrumpit demo crit um, ad sit ponderum.

Date: '07 - '09
Position: Group Marketing Manager, reporting to Group Sales director, 10 staff
Company: Cableco Ltd, industrial cabling, £300m income, privately owned
Achievements
- Agam conceptam mel cu, eum et por ro recteque interesset. Ea fugit ullum assentior duo.
- Ex ius idque corrumpit demo crit um, ad sit ponderum.

Figure 1.11

Year	Position	Company	Achievements
'13 - now	**Group Marketing Director** Full plc director reporting to plc CEO 40 staff	**LJZ Group plc** FMCG group Income £3bn	Agam conceptam mel cu, eum et por ro recteque interesset. Ea fugit ullum assentior duo. Ex ius idque corrumpit demo crit um, ad sit ponderum.
'09 - '13	**Marketing Director** Reporting to MD 20 staff	**ITS Solutions Ltd** IT software distributor Income £500m Subsidiary of ITS plc	Agam conceptam mel cu, eum et por ro recteque interesset. Ea fugit ull um assentior duo. Ex ius idque corrumpit demo crit um, ad sit ponderum.
'07 - '09	**Group Marketing Manager** Reporting to Group Sales director 10 staff	**Cableco Ltd** Industrial cabling £300m income Privately owned	Agam conceptam mel cu, eum et por ro recteque interesset. Ea fugit ullum assentior duo. Ex ius idque corrumpit demo crit um, ad sit ponderum.

When CVs are in a WiT, people read achievements without interruption, so inconsistencies stand out more – "Ran marketing" wouldn't chime properly alongside genuine achievements. Also, WiT helps ensure consistent grammar. Assume that, whilst in different companies, the person developed gadgets, widgets, gudgets and wudgets – many CVs would say: "Developed gadgets", "I developed widgets", "Development of gudgets" and "Wudgets were developed". Grammatically different. But in traditionally laid out CVs, such inconsistencies are often not immediately apparent because of the stop–start way we read them. In WiT, we read achievements without interruption, so are more likely to spot inconsistent grammar.

And inconsistent grammar matters. It shows a lack of attention to detail – if we can't be bothered to get grammar right, what else have we got wrong? It sends out bad signals, unnerves readers and hinders our cause.

The WiT CV template is on my website as a free download in MS Word. There's the career-history page, plus a front page too. If you've only done a few summer jobs – or if you feel a CV shouldn't go beyond a single page – there's also a one-page version. They've been downloaded tens of thousands of times.

WiT saves time

WiT means our reports are shorter. Clearer. However, this might not save us time as writers – WiT forces us to think harder and that takes time. As the phrase goes: "Sorry this is such a long letter, I didn't have time to write a shorter one". No worries, for many other people save *lots* of time:

Bosses save time reviewing and editing	It's far quicker to review and edit reports that are already short and clear.
Co-authors save time debating	Often, a team of authors agonises over a paragraph – some say: "It's an obvious remark, remove it" and others retort: "It's vital to say it". The debate rages. With WiT, leave it in – readers skip it if they wish.
Readers save time	This is a no-brainer, enough said.
Meeting attendees save too	This is a huge benefit, I explore it more below.

Step back: often we attend meetings to discuss issues and reach decisions. To help this happen, we get sent 'pre-reads' – stuff to read beforehand. Often, they're bad, so in many meetings, delegates spend ages simply trying to *understand*. To overcome this, some bosses suggest longer meetings – it gives people more time to understand. But this tackles symptoms (confused people), not cause (confusing reports). Also, we've all only so much brain space. If we use too much – and spend too long – on understanding, we've no brain space left over for the important bit: discussing and deciding. Mental shutdown occurs before we reach the key part of the meeting.

With WiT, people grasp stuff much more quickly, which leaves more brain-space – and time – to discuss. Will that lead to better decisions? To decisions in our favour? If pitching for business, probably. If writing internal reports, maybe not. The text box explains more.

There is lots more to WiT – for instance, it's great for sub-sub-bullets – but that's for other Chapters. Next we see when to WiT.

Will WiT lead to better decisions? To decisions in our favour?

It depends. There are two bits of bad and good news.

Bad news (1): WiT helps people see if our idea is bad	So maybe obfuscate instead? No. Firstly, bosses rarely approve stuff they don't understand. Secondly, we *really* annoy bosses – we badly explain a bad idea.
Good news (1): WiT helps in sales	If our points stand out, it's easier for people to choose us rather than our competitors.
Bad news (2): WiT might not change internal decisions	Many bosses reach decisions long before they see the reports they commission to help them make decisions. Reports are a box-ticking, post-rationalising exercise.
Good news (2): bosses *like* us	Clear reports. Shorter meetings. Focused conversations. Bosses won't like us. They'll *love* us.

When to WiT

Use WiT if one of three situations arises:

If we have a repeating pattern to our words	The CV repeatedly mentions date, position, company, achievements. The client pitch repeatedly mentions features and benefits. If our text repeats captions – if we write about similar topics from one paragraph to the next – turn the words into a WiT.

| If we have comments or brief sections | The 'good and bad findings' example was just brief comments, so we redid them as a WiT. |
| If we have paragraphs | Take our page of text and turn each paragraph into a row of a WiT – key point on left, detail on right. |

Figure 1.12

> **What we will do**
>
> • We will focus on products and services where we are or can be in the top three.
> • We will grow organically, not by acquisition, unless we see an opportunity.
> • We will only include companies in our Group if they've synergies with other parts of it.
> • We will invest selectively to strengthen and build our business.

Figure 1.13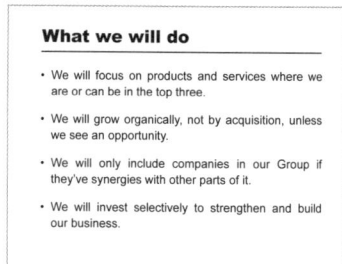

> **What we will do**
>
> | Market leader | We will focus on products and markets where we are or can be in the top three |
> | Organic growth | We will grow organically, not by acquisition, unless we see an opportunity |
> | Synergies | We will only include companies in our Group if they've synergies with other parts of it |
> | Investment | We will invest selectively to strengthen and build our businesses |

WiT is therefore good for minutes of meetings – they're brief sections and have a repeating pattern. My website has a template for minutes. Also, when we put bullets on slides, they're brief points, so use WiT. Figure 1.12 shows a typical bullet-riddled slide. Figure 1.13 is the WiT alternative. Much better. Key points lift from the page, and it's sharper and smarter too. Also, study the first letters of the words on the left of the WiT: MOSI. Not the snappiest acronym. Make it into a better acronym, and audiences are more likely to have unprompted recall of our points, and that helps our cause.

However, below are three cautionary comments on WiT in slides (and for more on the first two, see Part C, *More on talks*).

WiT is still words on a screen	On slides, WiT is better than bullets, but talks often benefit from hardly any words on slides. Or even none at all.
Don't overuse WiT on slides	Don't do 25 WiT slides on the trot. With talks, we need to ring the changes.
We've only room for headings	WiT is best when the left column has headlines. With slides, there isn't room though, so down the left of Figure 1.13, there are headings.

Figure 1.14

We assume:
• Interest rates are 5%
• Sterling is 50p to the $
• Prices are at £1.40/ kg

Figure 1.15

We assume interest rates are 5%, sterling is 50p to the $, and prices are at £1.40/ kg.

When bullets work and how to do them

Bullets are fine for lists of brief points. To list the five offices we'll visit next year – or the six parts to our talk – use bullets. To show assumptions behind forecasts, Figure 1.14 is fine. In fact, it's better than continuous text – Figure 1.15 is harder to scan. However, even when bullets are acceptable, here are three *do's*, two *don'ts* and two *maybe*s for them.

Do indent more than just the first line	• Compare these layouts, the one on the right is smarter and easier to read	• Compare these layouts, the one on the right is smarter and easier to read
Do be grammatically consistent – the right column shows how *not* to do it	We'll do the following: • Establish procedures • Implementation of procedures • Reporting back afterwards	
Do get the gaps right	•If we don't, it looks cramped… like this • This is too big a gap • This is about right	
• **Don't** do in headings	Headings don't need bullets to stand out.	
Don't do just one bullet, it looks like we've left some out	"They've offices in: • Marlow" Is that it…..? Just the one?	
Maybe number points instead	We're more likely to think about their order. Also, it's easier to refer to a particular point if it's numbered. To reduce typography, maybe number every fifth point only, as they do in drama books.	
Maybe put in columns?	If points are really brief, it's less space greedy (Figure 1.16).	

Figure 1.16

1. Cuba   10. Iraq
2. China   11. Ireland
3. Dubai   12. Italy
4. Fiji   13. Jersey
5. France   14. Norway
6. Greece   15. Peru
7. Haiti   16. Russia
8. India   17. Sweden
9. Iran   18. Wales

As for how to punctuate bullets, I can't get excited about it, other than: be consistent. If you think I obsess about bullets, many companies' style police obsess more, they tell staff which to use when (Level 1 = ●, Level 2 = ♦, etc). Somewhat ironically, it's pointless. Tips on how to format multiple levels of bullet are like tips on how to kill: don't give – or listen to – such tips.

Time for Final Thoughts – and they consist of a plea, a trailer, and another benefit. Firstly, the plea: on the left of your WiT, **put headlines, not headings**. This is the single most common mistake I see in people's WiTs. As for the trailer, read Chapters 16 to 18 for more on WiT.

Finally, another benefit: WiT gives you confidence. Not only do readers more clearly see what you convey, you do too. So you convey it with more confidence. You're more confident when you job-hunt – you can see what makes you different. You're more confident when you pitch for business – you better grasp what makes your pitch sizzle. WiT *empowers*.

2 Graphs

This Chapter looks at when graphs work and when they don't. It gives tips on formatting and looks at graphs on slides. First though, we need to pop a few myths. And just so you know: I love graphs. I just don't like bad graphs.

Weapons of mass distraction

Apparently, graphs paint a thousand words. And simplify the complex. And much more. But is it all fact or fiction? Over the next three pages, we find out. Let's start with this misconception: **graphs are instantly understood**. No. Readers must acclimatise even to simple graphs. Sometimes that's quick and easy to do. With Figure 2.1, we look at x- and y-axes, then the plot, and in just a few seconds, we see how prices have moved in recent years. The graph is simple, we grasp it quickly – and its lead-in title helps too. Assuming we seek patterns, not exact numbers, the graph is better than its equivalent table of numbers.

Now try Figure 2.2, it's a typical chart. Before reading on, work out what it conveys…. Got it? I bet it took 20 seconds to grasp that: *"We took 1.5% market share from our next biggest competitor"*. (OK, maybe we nicked market share from someone else, but go with the flow.) It takes time to acclimatise to this graph. As before, our eyes move around, taking in x- and y-axes, but now we've legends to decipher. We chant in our head: "Dark is them, light is us; dark is them, light is us" – and we do maths too. We take 13% from 15%, 15% from 16.5%, 11.5% from 16.5% and 11.5% from 13%. We're thinking: "Where's this taking me?" – and when we do work it all out, we're not sure if we got it right. Next time you plot a graph to help people "instantly grasp numbers", remember what you did to grasp Figure 2.2. Remember how much your brain had to process and how far your eyes had to move.

People say **graphs simplify the complex**, yet Figure 2.2 complicates the simple. People say **graphs paint a thousand words**. Figure 2.2 badly paints ten words (the italicised words above). Maybe the words would make a good lead-in title, but lead-in titles are to help good graphs, not clarify dumb ones. Here, the words *replace* the graph. This is a neat trick: before you plot a graph, ask: "Would words be better?". See how few words you can express it in.

Then again, maybe Figure 2.2 is a bad graph – but it's not stupidly bad. Rather, it's typical, similar to ones we often see. At work. But we don't do graphs for our friends. Why not? If graphs are so great, perhaps we should:

Figure 2.1

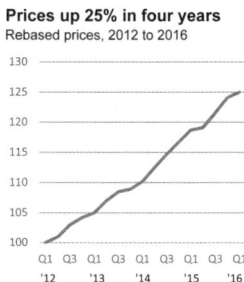

Prices up 25% in four years
Rebased prices, 2012 to 2016

Figure 2.2

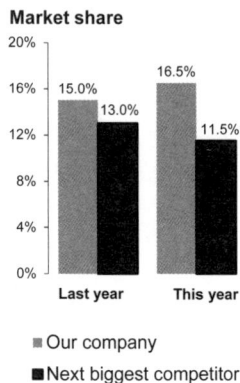

Market share

Pie charts: if our rent soaks up 45% of our salary, we don't do a pie chart to show friends how big '45%' looks as a slice in a circle. We just say it. Yet at work, we do a pie chart of income by client to convey that: "45% of income is from just three clients". This pie chart 'paints' just eight words.

Columns: how many points do City and Rovers have? We'd tell friends: "City 9, Rovers 10". Yet at work we do Figure 2.3 to compare £9m actual with £10m budget. The graph 'paints' just six words: "2016 income, actual £9m, budget £10m". Graph-lovers tell me that such graphs help people who are bad with numbers – the right column, they tell me, is bigger than the left, so it shows that '10' is bigger than '9'... Crazy, really. We've all seen Figure 2.3 at work. Maybe not *Actual versus Budget*, but *2015 versus 2016*. Or *Actual versus Benchmark*.

Line charts: to tell friends we've lost four kilos, we don't show a graph of weight loss over time. Yes, the graph is on our fridge to inspire us to lose weight, but we don't need it to convey progress to others. Yet we plot a graph to show we've lost £4m income. Yes, trend lines are great... if we want trends. Figure 2.4 shows interest rates over time better than a table of numbers. *But often we just want outcomes* ("I lost four kilos"). If it's 2017 and we have £100 to invest – and had £100 in 2012 – we don't need Figure 2.4. We just say: "Rates are the same as they were last time we had £100 to invest".

Pies, columns, lines. We can replace many of them with just a few words... assuming, that is, we know the message we wish to convey. Often, we don't. It's ironic – people say **graphs are good for conveying messages**, yet many of us plot graphs because we don't know what messages to convey. We have lots of numbers and aren't too sure what they mean – so we plot a graph and show it to bosses. "We don't know what it means," we say in effect, "maybe you can work it out – and because all the numbers are in the graph, we've covered our backsides. *You can never say we didn't show you everything.*"

When we work out what we wish to convey, we do fewer graphs. Think again about the 'four kilos weight loss': to tell friends about it, my words are just fine. Granted, they don't say whether I lost more at the start of the diet than the end, but my friends don't need that detail. And if they do, I simply say: "One kilo in the first three months, three kilos in the last". In other words, we tell others not what we know, but what they need to know. We don't show our workings, although we have them to hand just in case.

Sometimes though there isn't one overarching message. If we have profit figures for 12 divisions, maybe people want the detail, so why not do a graph? After all (cue myth), **graphs are great because people aren't good with numbers and tables**. Really!? These people that don't like tables – are they the same people who pore over sports and school league tables? As for being

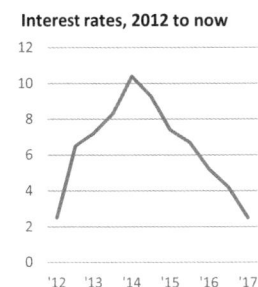

Figure 2.3

2016 Income (£m)

Figure 2.4

Interest rates, 2012 to now

uncomfortable with numbers, give them a numerical bonus scheme and they grasp it. OK, some people struggle with maths rules – in (0.6 × 5 – 1), do we multiply or subtract first? – but few people struggle with arithmetic (and if they do, they shouldn't do work that involves numbers). People are better with numbers than they admit. Here's why they feign innumeracy:

1. **It's cooler**. Which sounds funkier? (1) "I like logic, tables, numbers" (*nerdy*). Or (2) "I like visuals, I'm a creative right-brainer" (*cool*). Many people aren't right-brainers, they just like to think they are.
2. **It's convenient**. It legitimises laziness and lack of engagement: "Hey, don't give me detail, I'm strategic and big-picture".
3. **It's understandable**. At work, we're confused by bad tables and incorrectly conclude: (1) we aren't good with tables; and (2) tables aren't good. So we ask for bad tables to be replaced with… bad graphs.

People are quick to complain about bad tables, but slow to complain about bad graphs. When people see graphs – even bad ones – their hearts often lift:

We feel relieved	"At last," we think, "a bit of colour to break up dull text."
We feel reassured	Someone seems to have analysed and processed it for us. (Often though, they've just clicked on an Excel Wizard.)
We feel relieved (again)	We needn't face up to any summary or interpretation. (With tables, we feel obliged to *think* about them.)

Yet graphs often confuse – and we don't admit it either. Given the myths, though, who can blame us? Surely graphs are simple, intuitive, easy to grasp, so no-one wants to admit they don't understand them. We don't want to look stupid. So we convince ourselves that graphs give insight.

But it gets worse. People like *doing* graphs, it beats doing real work. Creating funky 3-D charts is fun. There's a huge confidence trick: "I do graphs and believe I give you insight; you look at my graphs and believe you get insight". Graphs really are weapons of mass distraction

Graph-lovers cry foul though. They say that **graphs are memorable** – yet how many can you remember? Hardly any, I bet. Then again, don't **graphs break up dull text and draw readers' eyes**? Maybe, but why break up dull text with something bad? Break it up with something good. Such as WiT. Finally, people say **we engage with graphs**. Don't confuse *glancing at* and *engaging with*. We give many graphs a cursory glance. We don't engage with them.

OK. Enough. We haven't popped all the myths – we see more later, plus we derive statements to ponder before we do a graph. But we've popped enough to look at specific graphs. That's next.

Figure 2.5

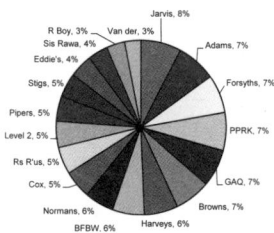

Figure 2.6

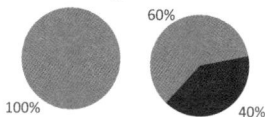

Figure 2.7

Income and share of group income: 2015, 2016

2016 total - £250m

2015 total - £150m

Graphs to avoid, graphs to use
Avoid pies, stacked bars, paired columns

Pies are badly laid-out tables that force readers' eyes to do a circular motion to read figures. And when readers finally understand the badly laid-out table, they fool themselves into thinking that it helps – they say it gives insight and a general impression of distribution. But what exactly gives insight? Is it the numbers around the outside, numbers that perhaps give a new view on, say, income distribution? Or the slices in the middle? We don't do pies at home, so avoid them at work. If people want numbers, do a table. Or, if there's a story to convey, just say it ("Three units are 60% of income").

Some pies look like bicycle wheels (Figure 2.5). Preposterous. Some take a lot of space to show three numbers badly. Or just two or one (Figure 2.6). Also, pies can't cope with negative numbers – if showing profit by division, what if one division made a loss? I once saw a pie try, it put the loss-making division as a little triangle by the side of the pie. Very odd.

Two adjacent pies are even worse, they're two badly laid-out tables. Figure 2.7 shows share of income by country for 2015 and 2016. Work out how many countries grew their share of income, how many shrunk their share, and which country grew the most. It's not easy.

Stacked bars are no better (Figure 2.8 – two graphs of income and share of income by country). They're both awful. The top one is less ugly – gone are the horrible, ubiquitous default colours that look awful even in black-and-white. Gone too are the thick black borders around each shaded rectangle. It's still useless though. *The Economist* says stacked bars are so bad, they're a great way to hide a bad number amongst a set of good ones. As for the bottom graph in Figure 2.8, it's merely two pies with corners.

What about a paired column chart (Figure 2.9)? People think it's intuitive, but it's not. From the graph, work out how many countries grew their share of income. It's not easy, you have to concentrate. Also, readers must twist their necks to read country names (names are at an angle so as to fit under the x-axis). Figure 2.10 sorts these out. It's still tricky to see patterns though. But what to do instead? That's next.

Use 'China surges'

To convey trends, not exact numbers, try Figure 2.11 (overleaf). It's an unusual graph, not everyone will have seen it before. The 2015 positions are on the

Figure 2.8

Income by country 2015 and 2016

Share of Group income 2015 and 2016 %

Figure 2.9

Share of group income, 2015 and 2016

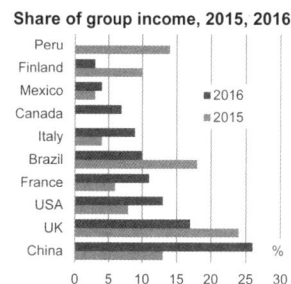

Figure 2.10

Share of group income, 2015, 2016

Figure 2.11 🖥

China surges
Share of group income, 2015 and 2016

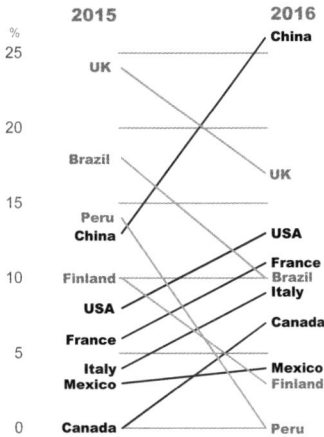

2015		2016
% 25		China
UK		
20		
Brazil		UK
15		
Peru China		USA
		France
10 Finland		Brazil Italy
USA		
France		Canada
5 Italy		Mexico
Mexico		Finland
0 Canada		Peru

left, 2016 positions on the right. Dark lines and dark labels go up, light lines and light labels go down. Look at it and ask yourself four questions. (1) How many countries increased their share of income? Simply count dark lines – six. (2) How many decreased their share of income? Count light lines – four. (3) Which country grew the most? Find the steepest dark line – China. (4) Which shrunk the most? Find the steepest light line – Peru. It's intuitive. If a line goes up, it means it's… well, going up. In the time it takes to answer four questions from Figure 2.11, most people struggle to answer one question from the pie and column charts. It's quite an indictment of those other graphs.

But Figure 2.11 gives even more. Read the names on the left – the 2015 'column' – it's the 2015 ranking. The 2016 'column' is the 2016 ranking. Then again, a table does that, no? Yes, but Figure 2.11 gives easy insight not just into ranking but also into relative size. In the 2016 'column', the big gap between the words *China* and *UK* signals that there's… well, a big gap between their shares of income. The graph works in detail and overview.

Finally, notice the lead-in title. It picks out something of interest in order to draw readers into the graph.

The 'China surges' graph isn't an Excel default, and takes ten minutes to do, not 30 seconds. My download explains how.

Granted, some people say Figure 2.11 looks odd, but that's because it's unfamiliar. Then again, Figure 2.9 – the paired columns – looked odd when we first saw such a chart all those years ago. The teacher pinged one on screen and said: "It's a paired column chart. I know it looks odd, children, but grown-ups do them at work, so you'd better get used to it…".

To convey detail as well, add figures alongside each country name, e.g. **China** 26% £65m. I assume people want trends first, detailed numbers second, so I de-emphasise numbers and put them in a small, grey font. If people primarily want numbers, ditch the graph and do a table.

Here's a final thought on the 'China surges' graph: would I do it at home? Imagine I'm a teenager – would I plot something like it to show how my exam results changed from last year to this? Of course not. But that's because of *time taken to do* versus *time saved by doing*. It takes me ten minutes to do the graph. By doing it, my parents save 30 seconds each, i.e. just one minute in total. Conclusion: not worth doing it.

What about at work? If it goes to 20 bosses, time saved by doing it is ten minutes (20 bosses × 30 seconds), and – as before – time to do it is ten minutes. A score-draw, perhaps? No. My time is cheaper than my bosses', plus I want to impress them by saving their time. Conclusion: worth doing.

Avoid multiple clustered columns for trends over time

Figure 2.12 shows numbers for five people for 2012 to 2018 – assume it is average hours worked a week during the year. It's a visually competing jungle of faceless anonymous blocks. Also, there's a legend, the box that defines each column. Legends create puzzles – readers' eyes flick back and forth between legend and columns to decipher the graph. Also, many legends rely on colour, yet 5–10% of people are colour blind or colour deficient, plus many reports are printed in black-and-white, so the colour cross-references are lost.

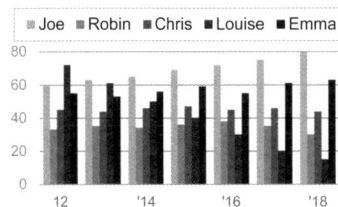

Figure 2.12

Figure 2.13 plots the data again and is much better. Use lines, not columns, for changes over time. Also, there's no legend, each line is labelled directly. Readers more easily see what's what. However, in this example, I fixed figures so that lines aren't a criss-crossing mess.

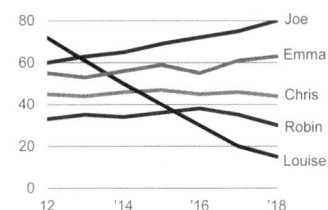

Figure 2.13

Figure 2.14 *is* a criss-crossing mess. What can we do now (and assume that our readers want rough trends, not exact numbers)? We could combine items – if we combine Joe and Emma into one line, combine Chris and Robin too, and leave Louise on her own – we've just three lines, and the graph might work. But what if we want to show all items – and for all periods too?

Try Figure 2.15: a series of small graphs. They're simpler and less daunting. They're laid out across the page with identical scales, so people can compare. A lead-in title would help – either one for the graphs as a whole, or five, one for each graph. Also, maybe put the graphs in some sort of order – I'm unsure what order though; it depends on what we wish to convey. Maybe in order of current position. Avoid alphabetical order though. Notice the plot lines are in grey. It's a softer colour than black, and looks smart.

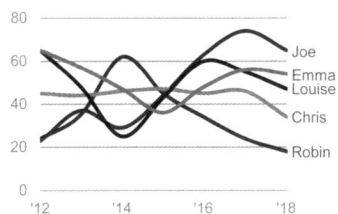

Figure 2.14

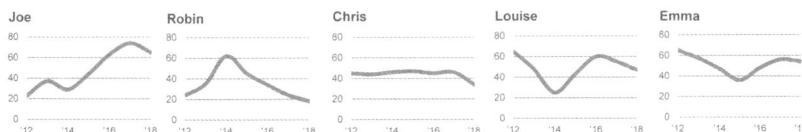

Figure 2.15

Some people complain that the graphs look like mountains or worm-traces. Maybe, but that's better than looking like a plate of spaghetti (Figure 2.14). Others say they're similar to sparklines, a type of graph we see in Chapter 30 (*Graphs – more*). Similar, yes. The same? No, as we see later.

These 'mini-graphs' are also a great alternative to a graph I often see: for the last 12 months, people show five criss-crossing lines, one for each of *Actual*, *Forecast*, *Last Year*, *Reforecast*, and *Budget*. The graph strives to convey several different messages, but by showing everything, it conveys nothing. Instead, strip apart into four separate graphs – each with just two lines – that each conveys a single message. E.g. *Actual versus Budget. Actual versus Last Year. Actual versus Forecast. Forecast versus Reforecast.* Alternatively, maybe convey in words ("Actual is 10% up on last year, albeit not as high as Forecast (15% up on last year) – so we've reduced the forecast etc").

To add commentary, put words under each graph (Figure 2.16, shown for just two graphs). If we wish to add lots of words, maybe put the mini-graphs not side by side but one under the other (Figure 2.17, again for just two). We've more room for words – but the graphs are less comparable if laid out one under the other, rather than side by side.

To recap, avoid pies, multiple pies, paired columns, multiple clustered columns. Which sounds negative, but there are positives too – try 'China surges' and mini-graphs. Next is another graph to try, one I call a 'logo chart', simply because I first did it with company logos.

Figure 2.16

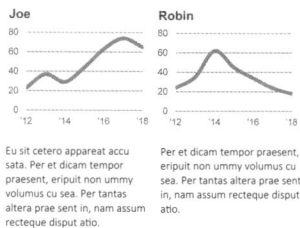

Eu sit cetero appareat accu sata. Per et dicam tempor praesent, eripuit non ummy volumus cu sea. Per tantas altera prae sent in, nam assum recteque disput atio.

Per et dicam tempor praesent, eripuit non ummy volumus cu sea. Per tantas altera prae sent in, nam assum recteque disput atio.

Figure 2.17

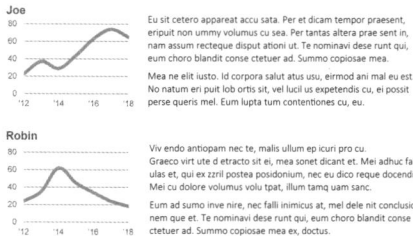

Use logo charts

We've researched customers' views on the Products, Service, After-sales and Delivery of four companies (Harvey, Smith, Forsyths and SKGP). A high score means customers like them, a low score means they don't. Figure 2.18 is how such results are often conveyed. It's another visually competing jungle of anonymous blocks. However, unlike the columns we saw in Figure 2.12, we can't replace these with lines: they aren't trends over time.

Figure 2.19 plots the companies' logos. The first column shows scores for Products, and as seen, Harvey scores about 78%, Smith 72% and so on. The graph starts at 50 to help differences stand out – and I highlighted this by putting '50' in a box (I don't want readers to think I'm deceiving them).

There are several benefits to this layout. Firstly, it's engaging. It shows logos, something that people recognise and are familiar with. Also, we avoid a legend. There's less clutter too, it's not a jungle of columns. Each category is in order – study Delivery. In the clustered column chart, columns go up, then down, then up, whilst in the logo chart, logos are in strict descending order. Result: it's easy to see patterns by company. Look at Harvey – it's mostly near the top, save for After-sales where it did poorly. We easily see patterns by type – scores for Products are closely grouped, whereas other scores are spread out. Compare this to Figure 2.18's columns: we spot patterns if we look hard enough, but we don't. We lazily skim over it. We glance at columns, but don't engage with them. Finally, if

Figure 2.18

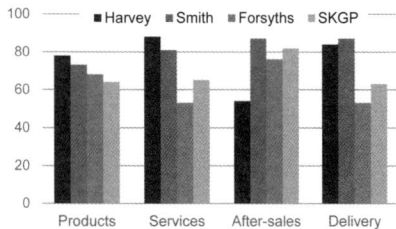

Figure 2.19

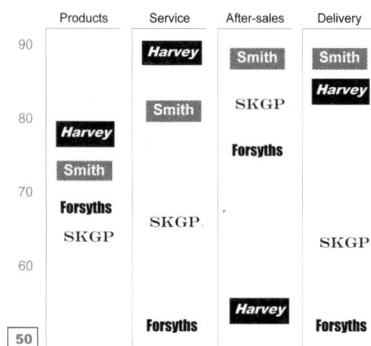

we want exact numbers, do a table, although it won't surrender patterns as easily as the logo chart.

There are two ways to prepare the logo chart. Firstly, simply drop text boxes on the page roughly where they should be. Steam-driven, yes, plus it takes longer than clicking on an Excel Wizard. But think how long we spent doing the market research, only to then ruin it with a bad graph. Alternatively, create the chart using the free download on my website.

Plot the labels – my 'get-out-of-jail' card

The logo chart and 'China surges' both do something similar: they plot labels. This is my 'get-out-of-jail' card. Many times, I've stared at a bunch of numbers, grappling with how to convey them (other than in tables), and many times, the answer is: plot the labels. It conveys both detail and overview – and next is another example of this.

At the start of 2007, Unicef issued a report on youths across 21 countries. It looked at 12 aspects of youths' lives: how often they got drunk, had a fight, smoked drugs and so on. Figure 2.20 is how one UK newspaper showed the findings, albeit it shows results for just 4 out 12 aspects. The top table, for instance, shows that 34.9% of Britain's youths used cannabis in the last 12 months, compared to 21.4% on average for all 21 countries (of which highest was Canada, lowest was Greece).

The tables struggle to convey patterns and ranges. Readers must scrutinise each number. It's repetitive too – the word *highest* is mentioned again and again. Instead, let's plot the labels (Figure 2.21). It has four 'silos', and each represents one of the four aspects, e.g. silo 1 is *Been drunk*. The worst performing country is at the top, best performing at the bottom, and average somewhere between them. The word *Britain* stands out, so we easily see the pattern created by Britain's results.

Also, the four silos are in order – as we move from left to right, Britain improves compared to its peers. Maybe we should invert the chart to make it more intuitive, with worst at bottom, not top – people tend to assume top is best and bottom worst. For details on how to plot this chart, see my website. It also talks through potential problems, e.g. what if two scores are identical?

We've one last graph to review: the single-series column chart. That's next.

Avoid columns that compare just a few items

Figure 2.22 shows income by country (represented by letters). It's well formatted, but beyond that, there's not much going for it. It's not memorable – not, that is, unless we memorise the letters down the left. It's not good at

Figure 2.20

Figure 2.21 🖳

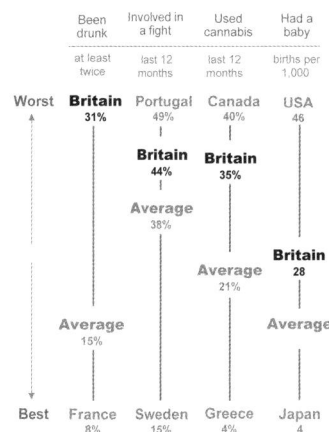

Figure 2.22

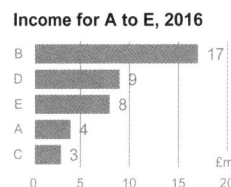

detail – numbers and letters are physically apart. A table would be better. It's not great at overview ("Columns get smaller… wow"). Also, we wouldn't do it at home – to show who scored goals for our team, we wouldn't plot a column chart. We'd do a table of numbers in descending order. I describe Figure 2.22 as: "Less unacceptable than a pie chart". Which is why I've *never* put anything like it in a report – and no boss has ever has asked me to redo my report with columns instead of tables. Yet graph-lovers do sometimes say to me: "But Figure 2.22 helps bosses to see which is biggest". So too does a table in descending order…

But there are exceptions. Very occasionally I put column charts on slides, but that's because graphs in talks are different – we see why soon. Also, I once saw Figure 2.23 – columns that work. It shows income by company in a duopoly. Two huge columns, several smaller ones. Distinctive, memorable. Sometimes, the best way to convey information depends on the data.

Next is when to do graphs. Before then, Figure 2.24 answers the question: if such graphs are bad, why do they appear in Annual Reports and on TV?

Figure 2.23

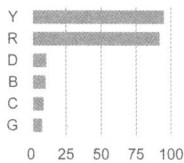

Figure 2.24

Annual Reports and TV

Why do bad graphs appear in both of these? Firstly, with Annual Reports there's a herd mentality – everyone does graphs, so everyone does graphs. And a circularity too – companies do graphs because investors want them. Or do investors expect them because companies do them? I can never remember. There's an exception: Warren Buffett. No graphs. Check out his Letters to Shareholders.

Then there's TV news. They do trend lines, but eschew pies, columns, etc. That tells us something. OK, on election night, they go a bit crazy with fancy graphics, but that's to keep us awake until dawn. As for newspapers and websites, see Chapter 14 (*Infographics*) – it briefly looks at visuals and graphics in print media.

When to do graphs

Here is when graphs help:

1. If exact numbers aren't critical (if they are, do a table).
2. If we can't replace the graph with just a few words (often, we can).
3. If the graph is better than the next best alternative.
4. If people take less time to grasp the graph than we spent creating it.

The third point begs the question: how do we know if a graph is *better*? Well, we know it needn't be instantly understood or memorable. It needn't have one clear message either – the logo chart doesn't, nor does 'China surges'. Both are more akin to 'look-up' charts – people look up to see what's of interest to them. Rather, for a graph to work, *it must help readers more easily grasp the significance of the data*. For example, maybe it helps readers spot if data rise or fall. Or spot how many territories grow or shrink (as the 'China surges' does). To put it another way, *a good graph answers readers' obvious questions*.

As for the fourth point – time taken to grasp – it shows just how warped it has all become. The logic should be: we spend time turning numbers into graphs so our readers save time grasping what the numbers mean. We spend time, they save time. But it's gone pear-shaped. We click on an Excel Wizard and do Figure 2.25 in just 30 seconds – then readers each take two minutes to work it out. It's the wrong way round.

There's one last question to ask if thinking of doing a graph: would you do it at home? It's a good sanity check. However, remember: we wouldn't do 'China surges' at home.

Figure 2.25

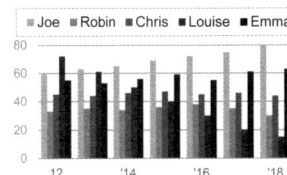

How to format graphs

Formats matter. Poor formats can ruin even good graphs. We've already seen some tips, e.g. avoid legends and avoid labels that make us twist our necks to read them. Here are more. Most tell you what not to do. That's because Excel offers frippery that distracts readers from the very thing we want them to see: the data. Don't let formatting compete with the plot.

Figure 2.26

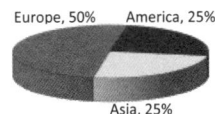

1. **Avoid 3-D**: it distorts. In Figure 2.26, America and Asia are both 25%, but Asia looks bigger because we see the front of its slice. In Figure 2.27, what are the values of *Actual* and *Budget*? It's tricky to work out. In Figure 2.28, one sofa is twice the height of the other because sales doubled, but it also looks twice as wide and twice as deep and so looks eight times bigger. Deceitful.

Figure 2.27

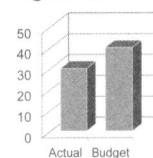

2. **Avoid as many grids as possible**: graphs are to show shapes and patterns, not detailed numbers, so avoid horizontal grids unless we've a good reason to include them. Avoid vertical grids, other than for transposed charts, i.e. where columns are horizontal, not vertical, such as Figure 2.29 which we saw earlier. For grids we do keep, make them unobtrusive. The graphs in this Chapter have thin grey grids. Grids should be like ones on a map – there when we need them, not in the way when we don't.

Figure 2.28

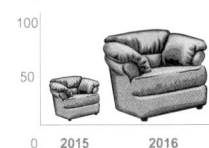

3. **Avoid background shading**: it looks bad when printed or copied.

4. **Avoid unnecessary axes**: e.g. Figure 2.29 has no y-axis. For axes we keep, grey them down.

Figure 2.29

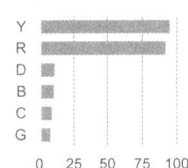

5. **Avoid too many tick marks**: these are the dashes on the axes. Figure 2.30 has too many on the y-axis, plus some cross the axis. The x-axis is better – fewer ticks, and they sit outside the axis. They're greyed down too.

Figure 2.30

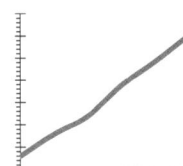

6. **Avoid data markers**: they're the little triangles, circles or squares that sit on trend lines to mark the position of the data (Figure 2.31). If exact numbers are of interest, do a table instead.

7. **Avoid garish colours**: go for soft colours. Granted, colour-blind people can distinguish garish colours more easily, but strive to avoid graphs that rely on colour to interpret them (i.e. avoid ones with legends).

Figure 2.31

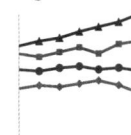

8. **Avoid too many labels, and keep them short**: if a graph covers, say, 1995 to 2015, label every second year on the axis, not every year. Or even every fourth year. Also, label as '95, '97, etc, not 1995, 1997, etc. If an axis is in '£', don't label as 100,000,000, then 200,000,000, etc with £ at the top. Label as 100, 200 and have £m at the top. If the axis is periods 1 to 5, don't label as

Figure 2.32

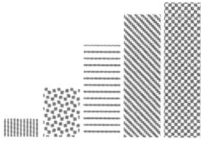

Figure 2.33

Period 1, *Period 2*, etc; label as *1*, *2*, etc and state *Period* once. Finally, grey down the labels too, it looks smarter.

9. **Avoid funky hatches** (Figure 2.32): they shimmer like a TV newsreader's check jacket. It's like Figure 2.33 – how many dots are in it?

That's what not to do. Here are tips on what to do:

1. **Use a 'sans serif' font**: if confused by this, Chapter 6 (*Design*) explains.
2. **Put graphs next to text**: don't relegate them to the appendix, it interrupts the flow. Newspapers don't shove everything in the appendix ("For the by-election result, see page 15, it's got all of today's graphs and tables"). If we can't put graphs alongside text, at least put them on the same page.
3. **Keep graphs small and compact**: in reports, avoid big graphs that are the size of a page. We hold such graphs at arm's length in order to take them in. Study newspapers and *The Economist*: their graphs are small and neat.

In summary, don't pimp graphs to 'give them more impact'. Would the *Mona Lisa* be better if we added blusher and makeup?

Graphs in talks

Lead audiences into our graphs. Don't just put a graph on screen and blurt out: "As you see from the graph, our industry's had five tough years". As presenter, we know the graph, we've seen it before. But delegates see it for the first time, so must acclimatise to it. They say to themselves: "So the x-axis is …2011 to 2015. The y-axis is… industry profit. The graph slopes down… so yup, it's been tough". Instead, show the graph, briefly explain axes, pattern, and conclusion. Keep people with you.

Also, use colours that you can name and that people know (red, green, blue, not auburn, azure, etc).

What about graph complexity? Some people think complex graphs are fine in talks – after all, we can talk delegates through them, explaining axes, illustrative points and more to ensure they grasp them. Some people think the opposite, that graphs in talks must be simple. After all, audiences expect instant gratification in talks, whereas with reports, readers are more prepared to engage intellectually and take time to understand.

Which is right? It depends on presenter and audience. Good presenters can make the Telephone Directory seem interesting, so a minute explaining a complex graph is no problem. But what are the talk's objectives? If it's to entertain and inspire, it's a bit of a downer to take time out to explain the intricacies of a complex graph. As I said, it depends.

Having said that, avoid too many graphs in quick succession in talks (and these comments apply also to tables and even WiT). Showing graph after graph is agony for audiences, so ring the changes a bit. Here's a suggestion for conference organisers: limit each speaker to just two or three graphs (and ditto for tables). OK, it's a didactic guideline, so follow it intelligently, not slavishly. Also, think of convention. When CEOs present results to analysts, they show 20 tables on the trot, and everyone expects and accepts it. Try something different and the stock would fall.

Time for Final Thoughts. In corporate life, I'd send bosses a 20-page benchmarking report, comparing our results to our competitors'. It had commentary, tables… and just one graph. The bosses were a diverse bunch – some were logical and loved detail, some creative and hated detail – yet they were fine with it. No-one said to me: "That table of competitors' profit – the one in descending order – I just didn't get it. Redo it as horizontal shaded rectangles…".

Also, think back to when we said: "Would words be better?". We found they often would be ("Income up 10%"). But don't assume that words are better only for simple graphs. Often, words are better for complex-looking graphs *because* they're complex-looking. I once saw a graph with a shed-load on it. Six sets of figures for up to nine years (four trend lines, two sets of columns – their legends alone had 35 words); 44 labels and markers (5.0, 10.0, 15.0, etc, and FY14 to FY22); 40 words for assumptions; 11 words for the heading. Confusing. It transpired that 29 words replaced it all – see Figure 2.34. People claim that graphs simplify the complex. Here, words simplify the complex graph.

Finally: (1) Figure 2.35 pops some more myths, and (2) if you want more on graphs, see Chapter 30. It's called *Graphs – more*.

Figure 2.34
The complex graph – what it said
"We need more income-generating projects. Lately, we've done mostly internal projects, which in the short term add expense, not income – ratios are projected to worsen by 8% by 2016"

(Words changed a bit to preserve anonymity.)

Figure 2.35
More things people say
"We got used to the graph over time." No. If that's the case, why not do the information pack in Latin? Bosses will probably get used to it over time...

"Graphs help if there's lots of strange accounting jargon." No. People must still face up to jargon even if it's in graphs. In fact, this remark reflects yet again that people don't engage with graphs, but glance at them. "Do a graph," the logic goes, "and people won't care that they don't know what it shows."

"Graphs help people trust my numbers." No. If friends don't believe we lost four kilos, will they believe us more if we show our weight-loss graph? If people don't trust us, we've a bigger problem than can be solved by merely showing a graph.

3 Numbers

This Chapter shows how to present numbers so they're understood. First, we see why numbers often confuse.

Why numbers often confuse

Often, people show too many digits. "Income grew £119,591,234 to £624,512,645, an increase of 23.6851%." We want to do mental arithmetic on those numbers – it helps us grasp them – but all those digits hinder us. Try computing last year's income – it's £624,512,645 less £119,591,234. Tough.

Also, long numbers intimidate. No wonder people get accountants to "look after the figures" – only accountants can understand numbers that long. A true story: a firm had revenues of £250m, and its management pack showed numbers to the nearest pound, e.g. "Q2 income: £82,392,967". When I redid it all to the nearest million with one decimal place (£82.4m), a long-standing director said of a particular page: "I've never understood it – can you talk me through it?" He'd seen that page every month for ten years.

Also, long numbers aren't memorable and they lack impact. An investment bank wrote that average revenue in a particular industry was $999.7m for the top ten players and $98.7m for players 11 to 20. They should instead have rounded to $1,000m and $100m. Finally, long numbers give a false sense of accuracy – people do five-year forecasts to the nearest pound. Dumb.

Instead, round numbers, e.g.: "Income grew £120m to £625m, an increase of 24%". Easier to mentally juggle. Less intimidating. Easier to remember. More engaging. However, there's more to rounding than showing numbers to the nearest one decimal place or the nearest million pounds. Next we look at different ways to round and see which work when.

How to round

Figure 3.1 shows income for five competitors (Xy, Pq, etc). There are too many digits. We need to round. Figure 3.2 shows the numbers again, but to the nearest million, plus it rounds them five different ways.

Column B – to one decimal place: there are still too many digits, even for Gh's income of £22.9m. Remember: this is competitor income, so we seek general indications of magnitude, not exact figures – £23m would be fine.

Figure 3.1

£	Income
Xy	3,623,145,794
Pq	753,419,756
Mn	123,759,456
Kl	115,643,179
Gh	22,876,431

Figure 3.2

£m	1 dec place	No dec place	3 digits	2 digits	Variable rounding
A	B	C	D	E	F
Xy	3,623.1	3,623	3,620	3,600	3,600
Pq	753.4	753	753	750	750
Mn	123.8	124	124	120	124
Kl	115.6	116	116	120	116
Gh	22.9	23	23	23	23

Column C – to no decimal place: better, but still too many digits for Xy whose income is £3,623m.

Column D – to three digits: Xy's income is now £3,620m, not £3,623m, and it is better still. But still not ideal – many of us can't mentally juggle three digits. For instance, to see how much bigger Xy is than Pq, we struggle to compute 3,620 less 753 – so we instead shorten and simplify, and compute 3,600 less 750. Much easier.

Column E – to two digits: it's better for some numbers – Xy's income is now £3,600m, not £3,623m. But now we have big rounding errors. Study Mn and Kl's income – in column D, they're almost 10% different to each other, but in column E, they're both £120m. It's an unacceptable rounding error. (What's 'acceptable'? See later.) To conclude, rounding to three digits retains too many digits, but rounding to two digits can introduce rounding errors. What now?

Column F – variable rounding: that is, round to two digits to aid mental arithmetic, but when big rounding errors arise, round to three digits.

It's tricky to variably round in Excel (see my website for how). In Power-Point and Word though, it's easier than *not* rounding. It's easier to type *3,600* in a table than *3,623*. It's easier to type that income ranges from '£3.6bn to £23m' than from '£3,623,145,794 to £22,876,431'. Easier for us when preparing the report. Easier for others when they see it. Variable rounding is great – yet it causes people grief. That's next.

Objections to rounding; when not to round

People often object to rounding. Let's deal with the objections:

1. **£3,600m is inaccurate**. So is £3,623m. The real number is £3,623,145,794 – and a few pence. So the issue isn't: "Should we show inaccurate numbers?", but: "How inaccurate is OK?". Answer: it's better to be approximate and understood, than accurate and confusing. I've read that rounding errors of 3% or less are usually acceptable – but I'm not totally convinced. It depends on context. We explore this soon.

2. **£3,600m and £23m are inconsistently rounded**. One is to three digits, the other to two… inconsistent, no? No, it's more consistent. Consider the rounding errors. For a number shown as £3,623m, the maximum rounding error is about 140 parts in a million (when the actual number is £3,622,500,000). Compare that to the maximum rounding error for a number shown as £23m: 22,000 parts in a million. That is, showing to no decimal places produces widely diverse rounding errors. Yet with

Figure 3.3
Effective rounding
This is similar to variable rounding. Assume we had the following numbers: 142, 153, 159, 166. The leading '1' is common to all, so isn't *effective*. Hence, to round to two *effective* digits, we show all three digits. We also show all three digits with *variable* rounding. Two digits would give 140, 150, 160, 170, which is too much rounding. Therefore, rounding to effective digits produces similar results to variable rounding.

Figure 3.4
Why people don't round
Bosses want clear information and will willingly sacrifice accuracy for clarity. So why don't people round? Firstly, they don't understand the numbers – they aren't sure of the significance of the margin being 10.364% – so they report all digits just in case. Also, they fear bosses might make a wrong decision from rounded numbers.

No. Bosses rarely make decisions based on a single statistic (e.g. "Margin is 10.364%"). They look also at prior years' margins, the impact of the new IT system, the economy, competitors' margins, etc. And when faced with all this information, bosses don't want to be confused by long, unrounded numbers.

variable rounding, maximum rounding errors are much more similar – for a number shown as £3,600m, it's 14,000 parts in a million (when actual = £3,550,000,000) which is much closer to the 22,000-parts-in-a-million error for £23m.

3. **£3,600m looks estimated – and numbers won't add up**. Surely £3,623m looks more... *definitive*. In which case, put a note alongside: "Numbers rounded for clarity; small rounding differences may arise; exact numbers available". Tell readers that we sacrifice accuracy for clarity, that we think about their needs. Does this help? I presume so – no-one's ever accused me of making up my numbers, or asked me for exact figures. As for not adding up, sometimes that doesn't matter. For the five competitors' income (Figure 3.2), I'd show the *Total* as £4.6bn. Rough – but wrong. The real total is £4,638,844,616. And a few pence.

There are times when not to round. Firstly, don't round if you want to confuse people. Below are other times not to round. They're from the book *A Primer in Data Reduction* by A. Ehrenberg.

If dealing with small differences	If you're a foreign-exchange dealer, you'd lose lots if you round.
If doing repeated multiplications	Don't round in the middle of compound interest computations, otherwise large rounding errors accumulate. Do your computations, then round when presenting.
If you've a control check to make	If accountants round numbers too soon, the trial balance won't balance. Ensure it balances first, then round after.
If the numbers are to be used by others for analysis	People use figures from the Office of National Statistics (ONS) to produce 'derived' figures (e.g. one divided by another). The ONS can't round numbers too much, otherwise derived numbers are wrong.

Avoiding problems with percentage changes

Figure 3.5

	2015	2016	Incr/ (decr)
	£m	£m	%
Income	100	110	10%
Costs	(99)	(101)	2%
Profit	**1**	**9**	**>99%**

First, two tests: what's the percentage change from 100 to 350: 250% or 350%? And what's a 600% increase on £100: £600 or £700? People struggle with large percentage changes, so avoid them. Instead, fix formulae to show > 99%, or < (99%) (Figure 3.5). It avoids big percentage changes that confuse readers. It flags to readers that the change is a bit different to others, it isn't a 'plus 5 or 10%' number. Readers then refer to the actual numbers and see the story first-hand – that we went from £1m to £9m. Much better.

But there's more. Percentages can be tricky to compute. This might come as a surprise – after all, aren't year-on-year changes simply: [(This Year)/(Last Year) minus 1] percent? That is, if *This Year* is 110, and *Last Year* is 100, we get 10%. Good. But what if *This Year* is £2m profit, and *Last Year* £4m loss? The formula gives minus 150%. Minus? But the result improves in the year?! The formula struggles with negatives. It also struggles if *Last Year* is nil – we get '#DIV/0!'. And, of course, we've problems if changes exceed +/–100%.

Percentage changes are tough. In fact, Figure 3.6 shows 17 different variants of changes to profit or loss (go up a little, go up a lot, down a little or a lot, stay the same, loss to profit, etc), and the formula gives a decent number only four times out of 17 (rows 1, 2, 3 and 7.)

If your variances are in Excel, see my website for a formula that solves it all.

Figure 3.6

Row	Last year	This year	(This yr/ Lst yr)-1
	£m	£m	
1	5	5	-
2	5	4	(20%)
3	5	6	20%
4	5	(3)	(160%)
5	5	(7)	(240%)
6	5	12	140%
7	(4)	(4)	-
8	(4)	(6)	50%
9	(4)	(2)	(50%)
10	(4)	2	(150%)
11	(4)	6	(250%)
12	(4)	(10)	150%
13	-	(2)	#DIV/0!
14	-	2	#DIV/0!
15	(2)	-	(100%)
16	-	-	#DIV/0!
17	1	-	(100%)

Numbers need context

This month's marketing spend was £650k, but is that good? Who knows? How does it compare to last year? Or budget? How many leads were generated? The number needs context – and don't assume people know it. The CEO of a big company once told me his second biggest division had just reported a margin of 15%. As I stood in front of him vainly thinking of something wise to say, he said rhetorically: "Hmmm…is that good? Not sure. What did it make last year?".

If we can't give context, at least strive to bring numbers to life. Not with an infographic (Chapter 14 explains why). Rather, do what Radio 4 did one morning in 2009 – in two separate features on truancy and race hatred, it said:

1. Every two weeks, someone goes to prison because their kids play truant.
2. Every two days, someone gets turned away at our borders because they'd been stirring up race hatred.

There's no context in the statements – how many went to prison last year? How many are turned away at other countries' borders? Yet the statements work, and to see why, consider how Radio 4 could have presented them:

1. Twenty-five people a year go to prison because their kids play truant.
2. About 200 people a year get turned away at our borders because they'd been stirring up race hatred.

The statements refer to a length of time – a year – then mention numbers: 25 and 200. Listeners feel compelled to compare them with something else: how does *25* compare with the UK population? How does *200* compare with the annual visitors to the UK? Listeners struggle to connect.

Instead, Radio 4 related a single unit ('one person') to time. Every two weeks for truancy. Every two days for borders. We easily grasp the context of a passing day, so the numbers settle more readily within our consciousness. They're brought to life, even though there aren't comparatives.

I don't countenance deceit and spin though, and have written a one-page article exposing numerical sophistry – Figure 3.7 has details.

There's no Final Thoughts. I've said all I need to say, other than: see the text box for how to show numbers in text.

Figure 3.7
Exposing numerical sophistry
Visit the *Articles* page of my website for a one-page article that lists six numerical deceits in a 2008 Budget Speech by the UK Chancellor.

> ### Showing numbers in text
>
> **Write numbers as words if ten or fewer**: "We've 150 staff in six units". The exception: use numbers even if less than 11 if part of series, e.g. "Scores were 15, 6, 2 and 11". Or if a reference, e.g. "See section 2, chapter 3". And if a percentage – margins are 5%, not five percent.
>
> **Don't start a sentence with a number**: avoid: "15 days ago, we finished". Type the number in full: "Fifteen days ago, we finished". Or rejig to avoid the problem, e.g. "We finished 15 days ago".
>
> **Don't omit the leading zero**: the rate is 0.5 to the Euro, not .5. We received 0.8% replies, not .8%. The exception: fire a Colt .45, not a 0.45.

Tables get a bad press, but that's because people do bad tables. Tables can be fantastic, and this Chapter shows how. The first half shows Five Steps to tidy your tables and the second half has more tips and ideas. Individually, the tips don't help much. Collectively, they make a huge difference. By the end, you'll do tables that people love, not loathe.

Already read *How To Make An Impact?* Still read the last three pages of this Chapter (The Big Redo) – it's new material.

Five Steps to better tables

To see the first three Steps in action, see Figure 4.1 (the *before*). It shows staff numbers for eight offices, along with how they changed from the prior year (*Diff* column). The three Steps turn it into Figure 4.2 (the *after*), and whilst there's more we can do, it's already much better.

Step 1: remove as many grids as possible

We	don't	imprison	words,	so	don't	imprison	numbers

In the *before*, every number is imprisoned by a grid. Grids look ugly, visually dominate, and hinder our ability to scan tables – they create barriers for our eyes to leap across. They fragment information. In the *after*, most grids are gone, and the ones that remain don't visually intrude.

However, surely grids help us keep our place as we scan across rows. It depends. Scanning across rows isn't a problem if just a few columns – in Figure 4.2, we don't lose our place as we scan, say, Fleet's row. But if many columns, scanning across is tougher. Maybe we could add shading every second row – but don't. As we see soon, strive to remove typography from tables, not add it. Also, shading looks poor when copied. Instead, try these:

1. **Add horizontal rules to each row**: but make them unobtrusive. Grey and thin. There when we need them, not in the way when we don't.
2. **Add an empty row after every, say, four or five rows of data**: the UK's Office of National Statistics does this in its tables. Make the height of the empty row smaller than normal – about a half or a third the height of other rows.
3. **Repeat the row labels on the far right**: Figure 4.3 does this, and also has an empty row after every five rows. Alternatively, maybe show

Figure 4.1

Staff	2016	Diff
Bath	94	8
Calne	112	10
Diss	22	(7)
Fleet	132	15
Hull	33	(5)
Leek	76	4
Rait	46	(2)
Ware	56	1
Total	**571**	**24**

Figure 4.2

Staff	2016	Diff
Bath	94	8
Calne	112	10
Diss	22	(7)
Fleet	132	15
Hull	33	(5)
Leek	76	4
Rait	46	(2)
Ware	56	1
Total	**571**	**24**

Figure 4.3

	Month			Year to date			Full year				
£	Act	Bdgt	Fav/(adv)	Act	Bdgt	Fav/(adv)	Bdgt	F'cst	Re 'fcst	Last yr	£
Staff	81	75	(6)	300	306	6	900	850	904	956	Staff
Travel	74	76	2	304	303	(1)	912	894	872	926	Travel
Drinks	71	70	(1)	280	287	7	840	801	749	773	Drinks
Rent	69	68	(1)	272	279	7	816	846	822	767	Rent
Rates	65	62	(3)	248	262	14	744	779	790	739	Rates
Phone	60	63	3	252	265	13	756	744	708	734	Phone
Post	57	61	4	244	256	12	732	723	674	644	Post
Rates	51	53	2	212	213	1	636	617	604	649	Rates
Tax	44	43	(1)	172	180	8	516	515	489	456	Tax
Fines	39	37	(2)	148	153	5	444	436	460	444	Fines
Food	31	32	1	128	127	(1)	384	373	352	338	Food
IT	25	24	(1)	96	100	4	288	288	282	294	IT
Chairs	22	23	1	92	95	3	276	283	268	251	Chairs
Tips	19	18	(1)	72	69	(3)	216	232	245	231	Tips
Taxis	11	10	(1)	40	41	1	120	122	128	133	Taxis

row labels once in the middle of the columns of numbers, e.g. between the *Year to date* and *Full year* columns.

Step 2: avoid too much typography

The *before* has shading, white-on-black (reversed font), italic, bold. But if we highlight *everything*, WE emphasise **nothing**. The *after* is typographically simple. Numbers stand out more.

Which is why we should avoid reversed fonts for column headings (Figure 4.4). Yes, it's funky, but it hinders. It draws readers' eyes away from the table's main story (the numbers in the middle), and towards something more for reference (the column headings). We struggle to focus. After all, imagine reading a report while someone stands next to you waving a big flag. Distracting. So too with funky column headings. Instead, go the other way: grey them down and do in a slightly smaller font than the rest of the table.

Whilst on font sizes, have data and row labels about 10–15% smaller than any surrounding continuous text. It looks neat and creates visual distinctions between table and text. So if my surrounding text is font size 10, my table's numbers are font size 9, and column headings font size 8. (Or rather, they are… except for stuff like Figure 4.3 – it's for illustration, not detailed study, so its font is much smaller.)

It begs the question though: how to highlight a number of interest? Figure 4.5 shows two ways: either put a box around it (the top table), or put it in, say, Arial Black to make it pop from the page (the bottom one). Maybe reduce the size of the Arial Black number because that font comes out bigger. Also, highlight sparingly, otherwise it loses impact. Or see Chapter 31, it shows how to highlight whole groups of numbers. Finally, alongside our table, comment on why we've highlighted the number.

Figure 4.4

Staff	2016	Diff
Bath	94	8
Calne	112	10
Diss	22	(7)
Fleet	132	15
Hull	33	(5)
Leek	76	4
Rait	46	(2)
Ware	56	1
Total	**571**	**24**

Figure 4.5

£	A	B	C
Pig	5	7	8
Ape	4	2	2
Dog	3	4	4
Cow	4	3	6

£	A	B	C
Pig	5	7	8
Ape	4	2	2
Dog	3	**4**	4
Cow	4	3	6

Step 3: make compact

The *before* is too spaced out, its rows too high, its columns too wide. Readers' eyes make a big journey to take in numbers. After all, it's easier to compare:

175 and 162,

than 175 and 162.

The *after* is compact. Everything is in a common eye line. Much better. Don't make too compact though, otherwise it looks cramped. What's too cramped? It's when we lose the descenders (the bottom bits of *y*, *g*, *p*, etc). In Figure 4.6, *pig, ape* and *dog* come out poorly.

Figure 4.6

£	A	B	C
Pig	5	7	8
Ape	4	2	2
Dog	3	4	4
Cow	4	3	6

Step 4: sort out column and row order

There are four sub-steps to this Step. The first three are on columns.

Sub-step 1: put the most important column next to the labels

Figure 4.7 is how most UK newspapers show soccer league tables. The two most important columns – team names and points to date (*Pnts*) – are distant from each other. Between them is other stuff – games played (*Plyd*), then wins, draw, losses (*W, D, L*), and finally goal difference (*GD*). Often, there's even more (goals for and against, etc). To see how teams are doing, our eyes flick back and forth from far left to far right. It's like watching a game of tennis. Figure 4.8 puts the points to date next to the team names. The most important column is next to the labels. Chapter 1 says to 'start at the end' with words. Here, we start at the end with numbers. Maybe we could do even more. If teams have equal points, goal difference matters, so maybe put the *GD* column after the *Pnts* column.

Figure 4.9 shows sales by region and product (*Co, Ab, Be*). Total sales are on the right – and why not? It's how we crunch numbers in Excel. No. Put the *Total* column first (Figure 4.10). Then there's Figure 4.11, costs by division (*AB, CD, EF*) for four months. The *Total* is far right. Instead, give readers the big picture first – put the *Total* column first (Figure 4.12).

Sub-step 2: put comparable columns next to each other

Figure 4.13 shows profit before tax (PBT) for three firms (Red, Tan, Blue) for three years. The PBT is shown as both a value (£m), and a ratio (%, of income). Columns are grouped by year, not type, so 2015 figures are together, as are 2016 and 2017 figures. To see how PBT (£m) changes over time, eyes must leap the percentage columns. It's like a game of draughts.

Instead, put comparable columns next to each other. Group columns by type (Figure 4.14). We more easily compare the comparable. We more easily see patterns over time and do mental arithmetic between years.

Sub-step 3: avoid alphabetical order for comparable columns

Revisit Figure 4.10. The order of products is Co, Ab, Be. Not alphabetical, but descending order of *Total* (50, 31, 17). It helps us more easily grasp the numbers. Having said that, Figure 4.10 is a small table, so this sub-step doesn't make much difference. Soon, we see it make a big difference.

Also, revisit Figure 4.12. Columns aren't in order of *Total*, but go 48, 47, 50, 49. It's not alphabetical order either (**A**pr, **F**eb, **J**an, **M**ar…), but is month order. That's fine, of course. It helps us see patterns over time.

Sub-step 4: put rows in some order other than alphabetical

The final sub-step is on row order. We put columns in some order other than alphabetical, and must do likewise with rows. Look at the *after* table of staff numbers (shown again overleaf – Figure 4.15). It's in alphabetical order. To see how an office compares to others, we must mentally reorder rows. Instead, put rows in numerical descending order (Figure 4.16). Much better.

Figure 4.7

	Plyd	Home			Away			GD	Pnts
		W	D	L	W	D	L		
Derby	38	9	9	1	7	5	7	9	62
Hull	38	12	4	3	5	3	11	15	58
QPR	38	8	7	4	3	9	7	6	49
Leeds	38	8	7	4	4	5	10	-11	48

Figure 4.8

	Pnts	Plyd	Home			Away			GD
			W	D	L	W	D	L	
Derby	62	38	9	9	1	7	5	7	9
Hull	58	38	12	4	3	5	3	11	15
QPR	49	38	8	7	4	3	9	7	6
Leeds	48	38	8	7	4	4	5	10	-11

Figure 4.9

£k	Co	Ab	Be	Total
North	19	11	5	35
South	16	6	6	28
West	9	8	4	21
East	6	6	2	14
Total	50	31	17	98

Figure 4.10

£k	Total	Co	Ab	Be
North	35	19	11	5
South	28	16	6	6
West	21	9	8	4
East	14	6	6	2
Total	98	50	31	17

Figure 4.11

£k	Jan	Feb	Mar	Apr	Total
AB	20	20	22	20	82
CD	16	15	13	15	59
EF	12	12	15	14	53
Total	48	47	50	49	194

Figure 4.12

£k	Total	Jan	Feb	Mar	Apr
AB	82	20	20	22	20
CD	59	16	15	13	15
EF	53	12	12	15	14
Total	194	48	47	50	49

Figure 4.13

	2015		2016		2017	
PBT	£m	%	£m	%	£m	%
Red	87	23	91	23	94	22
Tan	53	17	51	18	57	21
Blue	32	2	32	6	39	10

Figure 4.14

	£m			%		
PBT	'15	'16	'17	'15	'16	'17
Red	87	91	94	23	23	22
Tan	53	51	57	17	18	21
Blue	32	32	39	2	6	10

Figure 4.15

Staff	2016	Diff
Bath	94	8
Calne	112	10
Diss	22	(7)
Fleet	132	15
Hull	33	(5)
Leek	76	4
Rait	46	(2)
Ware	56	1
Total	**571**	**24**

Figure 4.16

Staff	2016	Diff
Fleet	132	15
Calne	112	10
Bath	94	8
Leek	76	4
Ware	56	1
Rait	46	(2)
Hull	33	(5)
Diss	22	(7)
Total	**571**	**24**

OK, it's not alphabetical, so we take a moment longer to find a particular office – but the benefit of grasping numbers much more quickly far outweighs the benefit of finding something a bit more quickly. After all, imagine sports tables in alphabetical order. We'd find our team a little more quickly, but would have no idea what's going on.

Note that descending – rather than ascending – also helps mental maths. It's easier to subtract one number from another if the big number is above the small one. And mental arithmetic gives us a feel for spread and distribution within a group of numbers ("Gosh, the biggest office has 20 more staff than the second biggest"). It helps us internalise and grasp it all.

When many rows create problems

Newspapers show tables of exam pass-marks for 500 schools – 500 rows, one row per school and several columns of data for each school. The best school is the top row, the worst is the bottom. So far, so good. But with 500 rows, finding a particular school is tricky, so what to do? We could do the following:

1. **Reorder alphabetically.** Don't. OK, finding schools is easier, but it's impossible to see how schools do. We can't mentally reorder 500 rows.
2. **Retain alphabetical order** and add an extra column. The extra column gives overall position, so we can look up, say, St Leo's (rows are alphabetical), and the extra column tells us it's 374th. But we then struggle to compare the comparable. It's tricky to spot patterns and abnormalities. Is there a link between results and geography? Or size? Or gender? We struggle to get insight.
3. **Retain descending order and do a smaller second table.** The second table shows the 500 schools in alphabetical order and gives just one figure: each school's position in the master table (e.g. St Leo's: 374). Much better.

Step 5: give a lead-in title

Tables – like graphs – need lead-in titles. Look again at Figure 4.16 and study the *Diff* column: 15, 10, 8, 4, 1, (2), (5), (7). *Big offices get bigger, small offices get smaller*. Did you spot that in the *before* at the start of the Chapter? I bet not, it's impenetrable. However, remove unnecessary grids and typography, make compact, restructure – and all becomes clear. Clear layout helps clear thinking. Titles often emerge only after we've done Steps 1 to 4. (Notice to avoid wordiness, below I use *title* to mean *lead-in title*.)

Titles help us as writers. They force us to think: "What does our table convey?". They then convey that message for us and so help our cause. Maybe the table supports a point we wish to make, but if we don't state it, readers might not spot it, or might spot a different point.

Titles also help us as readers. They draw us in. When our eyes land on a table in a report, we're unsure where to start – do we look at headings, labels, totals or numbers? Without an obvious start point, we amble aimlessly around the table, unsure what to read into it. We eventually give up and turn the page, hoping to find a graph to stare at.

A title gives us a jumping-in point. We validate the title with the table and this helps us acclimatise to it. We become familiar with the structure of the table, and are comfortable to scan around it and explore. Much better. This is especially true for big tables: daunting without a lead-in title (so many numbers and labels), much better with one.

Titles are great, so here are more tips on them:

1. Keep brief, don't describe the table in full.
2. Give literal titles too. Under the lead-in title, have a strapline that says in a more subdued font: "Staff numbers 2016, plus change from prior year".
3. If we think something looks odd, others will too – so comment on it, otherwise people may doubt our data. I'm not suggesting this be our title, it might not be that critical, but ensure we refer to it somewhere.

Also, do a title that's supported by the table. For instance, in the table of 2016 staff numbers, we could say: "The two largest offices have over three times more staff than the two smallest". Yes they do, but the table doesn't show the sum of staff numbers for the two largest and two smallest offices, so readers must get out calculators to validate our title. So write a different comment. Or, if this is the key message, structure a table that shows it clearly, not one that requires arithmetic to see it. Or do two different tables of the same data – each can show and comment on different aspects of it.

And give titles to tables in slides. When presenting, it behoves us to give insight, not show data. If our table shows Oslo's results, don't head it up as: "Oslo's results". Instead, write: "A record year for Oslo".

Not all tables need titles. So-called reference tables don't, e.g. train timetables and pages produced by statistics offices. However, most tables at work are less for reference and more for insight. OK, we don't know why bosses want a table of profit and staff numbers for all offices – we don't know they'll close the worst office – but we can guess they wish to compare office performance. So do a title that helps them compare.

What about a benchmarking report – should we do a title for the big table of competitor stats in its appendix? Assume that the main report talks through items of interest, and the big table is for readers to review to find whatever is of interest to them. In which case say so – alongside it, write: "There's no summary to this table; it's for you to browse and find whatever is of interest to you". It avoids doubt as to the table's purpose.

Finally, here's one last oddity: avoid titles in a Chapter on tables. This Chapter's tables each illustrate a point, and I want you to focus on the point, not on my interpretation of the table's data. Hence its lack of titles.

That's the Five Steps. Before moving onto new tips, we've one more example, one that shows the power of Step 4 (which sorts out row and column order).

Figure 4.17 is the *before*: it shows four 'provisions' – staff, tax, etc. The first column of numbers is year-start values (*Jan*), the last column is year-end values (*Dec*), and the six columns in between are how we go from one to the other – individual movements in the year. These six columns are usually finance jargon, e.g. 'Adjustment to gross basis', – but that confuses here, so there are UK towns instead. Note that the *before* complies with Steps 1 to 3: (1) not many grids; (2) simple typography; (3) compact. However, apply Step 4, and it becomes Figure 4.18 (the *after*):

Figure 4.17

£k	Jan	Rye	Diss	Holt	Clun	Leek	Deal	Dec
Staff	12.9	0.1	(3.8)	-	0.5	0.3	-	10.0
Tax	22.7	0.1	1.4	11.9	1.0	-	-	37.1
Legal	20.0	0.6	(6.3)	-	-	0.1	1.6	16.0
Fines	1.3	-	(0.1)	-	-	-	-	1.2
Total	56.9	0.8	(8.8)	11.9	1.5	0.4	1.6	64.3

Figure 4.18

£k	Dec	Jan	Inc/(decr)	Movement made up as follows					
				Holt	Diss	Deal	Clun	Rye	Leek
Tax	37.1	22.7	14.4	11.9	1.4	-	1.0	0.1	-
Legal	16.0	20.0	(4.0)	-	(6.3)	1.6	-	0.6	0.1
Staff	10.0	12.9	(2.9)	-	(3.8)	-	0.5	0.1	0.3
Fines	1.2	1.3	(0.1)	-	(0.1)	-	-	-	-
Total	64.3	56.9	7.4	11.9	(8.8)	1.6	1.5	0.8	0.4

We put the most important column next to the labels. In the *before*, January is next to the labels, even though it's over 12 months ago. In the *after*, December is next to the labels because it's more up-to-date.

We put comparable columns next to each other. What's comparable to December? Answer: January, so in the *after*, it's next to December.

We avoid alphabetical order for comparable columns. Study the towns' columns. In the *before*, they're in random order. In the *after*, they're in descending order of their *Total*, regardless of whether it's positive or negative, i.e. in order of absolute value. The *minus £8.8m* number is big, I don't want it hidden away far right. I want it near the action on the left. Reordering this way is counterintuitive, but it really helps here.

We put rows in some order other than alphabetical. In the *before*, row order is random. In the *after*, it's in order of the December numbers because that's the most important column. This is why reordering rows is the last sub-step – often, we can't reorder rows until we choose the most important column.

Also, the *after* has an *Incr/(decr)* column. It's the difference between the January and December numbers.

These sub-steps really help. The *after* is much easier to grasp because it groups the numbers. When readers first alight on a table, they hunt out big numbers to get an overview of it. The *after* helps readers do just that because rows are in descending order, and the most important columns are near the labels. Big numbers on the left, small numbers on the right. Compare this to the *before* – big numbers are all around the place. Readers' eyes make a huge criss-crossing journey to find them. Small numbers get in the way too, they compete equally for attention. It's tricky to see the wood for the trees.

Also, consider what people usually do if they're asked to improve the *before*: they pimp it. They add colour, shading, logos, red for negatives (red for negatives is a blunt instrument that often fails – in Figure 4.17, it would highlight the tiny figure of minus £0.1m, and that's dumb). But pimping hinders. It distracts. Sort out structure though, and we dramatically improve the table.

Next are more tips for tables. Individually they're less critical than the Five Steps, but collectively they make a good table great.

Why we should reorder our tables every month

Some people worry that readers will struggle if we reorder a table every month. If something was row 10 last time but is now row 8, will they not spot it? Fear not. Sports tables change every week, and it's fine.

Maybe we don't have time to reorder. A shame. The time taken to reorder tables is often a fraction of the time spent preparing numbers up to that point. Fail to reorder them, and we don't do justice to all our work.

Maybe our system can't reorder. Unlikely. Most can – and without manual intervention. Excel can via its *Large* function, as my website explains.

But if we reorder, maybe people will all too clearly see which units do well and which don't (showing yet again that, when we reorder rows, people more easily grasp numbers). Bosses of poor-performing units may create ructions, so we've internal politics to consider. But here's one thing I guarantee: reorder our table of unit performance every month, and unit-bosses will beat a path to it. They'll ache to see where they are in the latest pecking order.

Finally, if we really can't reorder every month, try this workaround: put tables in order of *forecast for year*. This ensures the table has an underlying and visible order, yet doesn't need reordering every month.

Going from good to great

1. Removing even more typography
2. Formatting numbers
3. Tidying column headings
4. Perfecting grids

Removing even more typography

The more we remove, the easier it is to grasp the numbers.

Figure 4.19

	A	B	C	D	E	F
Jan	9	0	1	0	0	0
Feb	9	0	0	0	1	0
Mar	10	0	0	0	0	0
Apr	9	0	1	0	0	0
May	10	0	0	0	0	0
Jun	8	0	0	1	0	1

Figure 4.20

	A	B	C	D	E	F
Jan	9		1			
Feb	9				1	
Mar	10					
Apr	9		1			
May	10					
Jun	8			1		1

Figure 4.21

	A	B	C	D	E	F
Jan	9	-	1	-	-	-
Feb	9	-	-	-	1	-
Mar	10	-	-	-	-	-
Apr	9	-	1	-	-	-
May	10	-	-	-	-	-
Jun	8	-	-	1	-	1

Figure 4.22

£m	'16	'15
Salaries	(321)	(337)
Rent	(96)	(101)
Travel	(66)	(69)
Utilities	(24)	(25)
Bad debts	(24)	10
IT	(20)	(19)
Other	(15)	(10)
Total	**(566)**	**(551)**

Figure 4.23

£m	'16	'15
Salaries	321	337
Rent	96	101
Travel	66	69
Utilities	24	25
Bad debts	24	(10)
IT	20	19
Other	15	10
Total	**566**	**551**

Figure 4.26

	Length of service (years)		
	0<1 year	1-5 years	10+ years
North Ltd	41%	32%	27%
South Ltd	35%	32%	33%
West Ltd	29%	27%	44%
East Ltd	19%	24%	57%

Replace zeroes with a dash: Figure 4.19 shows end-of-month exam grades for ten students – they're a bright bunch, most get A. The zeros make it tougher to spot non-zeros. Remove them (Figure 4.20) and non-zeros stand out more. To help readers scan across, maybe have a dash for a zero (Figure 4.21 – the dash is greyed down). The dash also removes uncertainty ("Are empty cells missing a number or a zero?"). Perhaps readers don't know that a dash means zero, so maybe explain it in a note to the table ("– means Nil").

Remove unnecessary brackets: accountants like to show costs in brackets (Figure 4.22, a table of costs). But the brackets visually intrude. Remove them and numbers stand out more (Figure 4.23). Which makes it easier to spot the figure that's the 'wrong way round' – the bad debt write-back. "But," accountants retort, "surely we need brackets for a sub-table of costs in a profit and loss account." (Figure 4.24). No. The sub-table is clearer without them (Figure 4.25). It won't confuse readers either ("Hey… no brackets on *Staff* costs – staff must now pay to work here"). I once removed 250 brackets from a cost sub-table, and readers could actually see the numbers.

Remove unnecessary labels: Figure 4.26 shows the number of years that staff have been with parts of a group, e.g. 41% have been with North Ltd less than a year, 32% between one and five years, and so on. There's repetition though – the word *Ltd* occurs four times (do we really need to state the legal status of our business units?), % 12 times, and *years* four times. Remove repetition and numbers stand out more (Figure 4.27 – notice the average row and column; the text box explains more). Maybe I could show % just once, top left of the table. But it might confuse readers, for they see the top left number (*41*) and think it's to do with years ("North is 41 years? What's that mean?"). The % astride each column helps avoid that confusion.

Figure 4.24

	'16	'15
	£m	£m
Income	200	160
Costs		
Staff	(43)	(39)
Property	(21)	(19)
IT	(15)	(17)
Other	(10)	(8)
Total costs	(89)	(83)
Gross profit	111	77
Rent income	15	20
Operating profit	126	97
Interest	(10)	(7)
PBT	**116**	**90**

Figure 4.25

	'16	'15
	£m	£m
Income	200	160
Costs		
Staff	43	39
Property	21	19
IT	15	17
Other	10	8
Total costs	89	83
Gross profit	289	243
Rent income	15	20
Operating profit	304	263
Interest	(10)	(7)
PBT	**294**	**256**

Average columns and rows can give extra insight

In Figure 4.27, the far right column shows the average years' service for each unit, e.g. North's average is 3.6 years. This *3.6* isn't a percentage but is *years*, and the box around that column helps signal to readers that its numbers are unlike others in the table. It helps avoid possible confusion. If this *average* is

Figure 4.27

	Length of service (years)			
	0<1	1-5	10+	Aver-age
	%	%	%	Yrs
North	41	32	27	3.6
South	35	32	33	4.7
West	29	27	44	5.8
East	19	24	57	7.3
Avrge	31	29	40	5.4

the most important column, maybe we could move it so it's next to the row labels.

There's an average row too, it's for the group as a whole. It's a simple average; a weighted average would probably be better, one that reflects staff numbers in each unit. Investment banks often do average rows. They show profit margins for, say, 20 quoted companies in an industry, and have extra rows for average, highest, median and lowest profit margins.

Formatting numbers

Chapter 3 looked at numbers in general. Here are tips on numbers in tables.

Right-align numbers: it makes mental maths easier. In Figure 4.28, column A is left-aligned, and column B centre-aligned. Similar-sized digits are out of whack. The 8 of 218 and 1 of 31 don't align. Column C is right-aligned and numbers now line up. Better for mental maths, and easier to scan down too.

Figure 4.28

A	B	C
218	218	218
31	31	31

Show negatives in brackets: earlier, I said: don't show costs as negatives – but what if our table shows, say, a value for something that's *minus 31*. How to show this? Don't show just in red, for 5% to 10% of people are colour blind or colour deficient. We could show with a leading minus sign – but readers can all too easily miss the small dash and not realise the number is negative. And never use the dreadful Excel format where the minus sign is on the left of the cell (Figure 4.29) – it's *very* easy to miss. Instead, show in brackets, e.g. (31). No-one'll miss that. If our readers might not realise that brackets means *negative*, the way round that is easy. Tell them.

Figure 4.29

-	31

Correct misaligned brackets: study Figure 4.30 – in column A, the closing bracket shunts the negative number to the left and misaligns digits. Column B corrects this – bracketed numbers are shunted to the right (or unbracketed numbers are shunted left, if you prefer). Similar-sized digits now align. See my website for how to do this in Word and Excel. Also, the Excel formula gives us a dash for a zero.

Figure 4.30

A	B
6,218	6,218
(31)	(31)

Tidying column headings

'Tidying column headings' – hardly sounds riveting. But it makes a huge difference. When I redo tables, I spend more time on column headings than anything else. Figure 4.31 does what many tables do – it shoehorns each column's heading into a single cell that sits astride the column. Result: we haven't room to write much, and so resort to acronyms. Such as *YTD*. "Big deal," I hear you say, "most people know it's *Year to date*". But when we

Figure 4.31

£m	YTD 2016 Act	YTD 2016 Bdgt	Full yr 2016 Bdgt	Full yr 2015 Act
Fees	297	246	479	482
Costs	68	72	125	117

shoehorn headings into single cells, we create another problem: readers struggle to grasp a table's structure. Let me explain: at first glance, readers see that Figure 4.31 has four columns of numbers. Eventually they twig there's more to it than that… four columns but in two groups. One group for *Year to date*, one for *Full year*. Figure 4.32 resolves this. Headings stretch over columns to which they relate, and this helps signal the groupings to readers. And there's a by-product to this: we notice that the table might need another column: *2015 Year to date*. Sometimes when we tidy a table, we realise we need to do it differently. As we've seen before, clear layout helps clear thinking.

And, of course, when we stretch headings over columns, we avoid acronyms. Whilst this isn't a big deal for Figure 4.31, it is for Figure 4.33 (and it really existed). Its far-right column is acronym hell. Figure 4.34 stretches headings over columns to which they relate – and we see that *CQTD* is *Cumulative quarter to date* (now you know). Much clearer. There are several other points to note about Figure 4.34 (some of which apply equally to the YTD table (Figure 4.32)):

Figure 4.32

£m	Year to date		Full year	
	2016		2016	2015
	Act	Bdgt	Bdgt	Act
Fees	297	246	479	482
Costs	68	72	125	117

Figure 4.33

	CQTD 2016 Act	CQTD 2016 Fcast	CQTD 2015 Act	% change over PY CQTD Fcst 16 v Act 16	% change over PY CQTD Act 16 v Act 15
	£m	£m	£m	%	%
Fees	382	375	365	1.9	4.7
Costs	(234)	(232)	(222)	(0.9)	(5.4)
Profit	148	143	143	3.5	3.5

Figure 4.34

Cumulative quarter to date

	2016		2015	% change fav/ (adv)	
				Act 16 v Fcst 16	Act 16 v Act 15
	Act	Fcast	Act		
	A	B	C	D = B to A	E = C to A
	£m	£m	£m	%	%
Fees	382	375	365	1.9	4.7
Costs	(234)	(232)	(222)	(0.9)	(5.4)
Profit	148	143	143	3.5	3.5

It still has abbreviations	E.g. *Act*, not *Actual*. *Actual* is clearer, but *Act* is compact. It's a trade-off, and one that I view as acceptable.
It has labels (A, B, C)	We more easily comment on stuff ("see column C"). Make labels unobtrusive. Labels really help big tables (ones bigger than Figure 4.34).
Labels help us more quickly grasp the maths	In the fourth column of numbers, how is *1.9%* computed? It takes a couple of seconds to work it out. Hence the labels. They say: D=B to A. Easy.

For Excel users: its column headings use *Alt Enter* (this won't change your life, but it's a neat trick)	Study the heading in column D. The words *Act 16 v Fcast 16* are all in one cell, yet *Fcast 16* sits under the *v*. That's because I typed *Act 16*, then hit *Alt Enter* on my keyboard – and when I then type *v*, it sits under *Act 16*. I then hit *Alt Enter* again, and words again shunt down in the cell. *Alt Enter* gives us the word-wrap we want, not the word-wrap that Excel's column widths give us.
The horizontal lines have gaps to help signal structure – and they aren't all the same size	There's a bigger gap between C and D than between B and C, because B and C's content is similar (£m figures) whereas C and D's isn't (one's a value, one's a percentage). Gap size helps signal proximity of meaning. Which is another reason not to pimp column headings – they often lack grids and hence have no gaps (Figure 4.35).

Figure 4.35

£m	Year to date		Full year	
	2016		2016	2015
	Act	Bdgt	Bdgt	Act
Fees	297	246	479	482
Costs	68	72	125	117

Labels also help prevent questions. Figure 4.36 has labels, albeit now on rows. As before, it helps commentary ("problems with row 8"), but it also avoids questions on the maths – how's trading margin derived? Profit divided by fees? Or divided by (fees + gains)? Row 13 tells us: it's trading profit divided by fees.

Figure 4.36

	£m	
IFA fees	562	1
IFA gains	72	2
IFA revenue	634	3
IT income	276	4
Total revenue	**910**	5
IFA trading profit	115	6
IFA gains	72	7
IFA operating profit	187	8
IT operating profit	54	9
Total operating profit	241	10
Goodwill	(82)	11
Profit before tax	**159**	12
Margin		
IFA trading margin	20%	13=6/1
IFA operating margin	33%	14=8/1

Perfecting grids

Step 1 of the Five Steps looked at grids, but here's a bit more. In Figure 4.37, Table 1 is compact – which is good for data rows (C to K), but not good for the grids at the top and bottom. They inelegantly butt up against stuff they're next to. Table 2 attempts to resolve this – row heights are bigger – but it's worse. Data rows aren't compact (not good), and stuff still butts up to grids. That's because the Excel default is to bottom-align. At the top of Table 2, *'16* sits on the grid under it, as do Σ and *108* at the bottom. Also, *108* has a grid above and beneath it, and because it's bottom-aligned, it looks a bit low in the water.

Table 3 sorts all this out with several small changes.

Vertically centre-align numbers. It avoids the 'low-in-the-water' look.

For data rows, have narrow row heights. Rows C to K are nicely compact.

Before and after the data rows, insert small empty rows. Table 3 has an empty row between C and the grid above it – and one after K too. The empty rows are about a third the row height of data rows. They help tables look less dense, plus create visual distinctions between the three parts of the table – headings, data, totals. They also help avoid problems with formulae when adding rows at the top or bottom.

Where content sits between grids, have a bigger row height. The Σ row has a bigger row height. It stops grids cramping down on content.

Figure 4.37

Table 1		Table 2		Table 3	
	'16		'16		'16
C	176	C	176	C	176
D	153	D	153	D	153
A	124			A	124
R	94	A	124	R	94
G	67			G	67
K	34	R	94	K	34
Σ	108				
		G	67	Σ	108
		K	34		
		Σ	108		

Figure 4.38

	Staff	Staff t'over	Fees	Gross profit
	Nos	%	£m	£m
Bus	443	8%	322	34
Quad bike	341	15%	188	15
Jet	206	10%	102	17
Total	**990**	**11%**	**612**	**66**

Figure 4.39

	Staff	Staff t'over	Fees	Gross profit
	Nos	%	£m	£m
Bus	443	8%	322	34
Quad bike	341	15%	188	15
Jet	206	10%	102	17
Total	**990**	**11%**	**612**	**66**

Figure 4.40

Figure 4.41

	'17	'16
ABC	21	17
DEF	17	14
GHI	15	12
Total	53	43

Whilst on row heights, strive to make them consistent – and column widths too. In Figure 4.38, row heights aren't all the same, nor are the widths of the data columns. That's because we word-wrap a row label when we shouldn't (*Quad bike*), and don't word-wrap a column heading when we should (*Staff t'over*). All in all, visually distracting and inelegant. Figure 4.39 corrects this.

Finally, if you use Excel or take my Excel downloads, see the text box.

Cell alignment in Excel

Excel goes weird when vertically aligning. Figure 4.40 shows seven dashes (-------) in nine different ways. Study the three cells along row 1 – dashes are top-aligned in the left cell, centre-aligned in the middle, and bottom-aligned in the right. And yes, scan along row 1, and dashes shunt down. So far, so good.

Now study row 2. Same formats as row 1, but a lower row height. Now, dashes hover at the same height, even though one is top-aligned, one centre, and one bottom-aligned. Weird.

It gets weirder. Study row 3. Same formats as rows 1 and 2, but an even lower row height. Now the top-aligned dashes (bottom left) are *lower* in the cell than the bottom-aligned dashes (bottom right). This strange behaviour occurs when row height is small compared to font size.

That's when Excel goes weird. However, I admit I go weird in Excel – it's when I prevent grids butting up to content (and the following comments assume you use Format Painter). In Figure 4.41, the thick lines are the table's grids. The thin lines are its non-printing cell boundaries. Notice the table has six extra rows – see the arrows. These extra rows enable me to use Format Painter to format numbers without altering the format of nearby grids. And to use Format Painter to format grids without altering the format of nearby numbers. The extra rows keep numbers and grids separate.

Should numbers be in rows or columns?

Figure 4.42

Jan	Feb	Mar	Apr	May	Jun
94	97	92	96	98	93

Figure 4.43

Jan	94
Feb	97
Mar	92
Apr	96
May	98
Jun	93

In Figure 4.42, scan along the row. The eye reads a number, jumps a gap, reads another number, jumps another gap, and so on. The gaps between numbers hinder. Figure 4.43 redoes it, but this time in a column. By transposing the table, it's better. We find it easier to scan down columns of numbers than along rows. Also, the brain can screen out 9s that are common to all numbers, and scans in one quick sweep of the eye: 4, 7, 2, 6, 8, 3.

To conclude, *by putting comparable numbers in columns, we more easily compare the comparable.* Let's apply this to a debt-ageing report (Figure 4.44).

The column for unit A shows that 34% of its debtors are between 0 and 30 days late, 32% are between 30 and 60, and so on. However, look at the bottom row of numbers – they're all between 11 and 18. They're comparable, so Figure 4.45 transposes it all. Now scan the first column of numbers, it's easier to compare the comparable. We screen out the leading *1* and read: 8, 4, 2, 1. Also, notice two other changes. Firstly, it assumes readers are interested in old debt, so old debt is the first column. Compare that to most debt-ageing tables where the *>90* column is on the far right, and readers' eyes flick back and forth to see units' old debt. Secondly, rows aren't in alphabetical order, they're in descending order of the *>90* column (the column reads: 18, 14, 12, 11).

Also, study train timetables. In Figure 4.46, departure times run along a row. Figure 4.47 transposes them. Much better.

A warning though – transposing can create more problems than it solves. Figure 4.48 is a table of results by month (*PBT* and *PAT* are profit before and after tax). Don't worry that there's no *Total* column. Rather, notice that comparable numbers are in rows – so let's transpose them (Figure 4.49). And yes, it's now easier to compare the comparable, but the table lacks something vital: the horizontal rules that signal sub-total and total. The *before* is better.

Finally, what about TV guides (Figures 4.50 and 4.51)? Is it better with the channels in columns (Figure 4.50)? Or in rows (Figure 4.51)? A tougher call. What do you think?

Figure 4.44

Days	A %	B %	C %	D %
0-30	34	33	31	32
30-60	32	31	21	30
60-90	22	25	34	20
>90	12	11	14	18

Figure 4.45

Days				
	>90	60 -90	30 -60	0 -30
	%	%	%	%
D	18	20	30	32
C	14	34	21	31
A	12	22	32	34
B	11	25	31	33

Figure 4.46

Here	Leave	10.08	11.04	14.11	16.15	17.02
There	Arrive	11.18	12.14	15.21	17.25	18.12

Figure 4.47

Here	There
Leave	Arrive
10.08	11.18
11.04	12.14
14.11	15.21
16.15	17.25
17.02	18.12

Figure 4.48

£m	Jan	Feb	Mar	Apr
Fees	82	87	91	99
Costs	(45)	(47)	(53)	(49)
PBT	37	40	38	50
Tax	(15)	(17)	(16)	(19)
PAT	22	23	22	31

Figure 4.49

£m	Fees	Costs	PBT	Tax	PAT
Jan	82	(45)	37	(15)	22
Feb	87	(47)	40	(17)	23
Mar	91	(53)	38	(16)	22
Apr	99	(49)	50	(19)	31

Figure 4.50

	BBC1	BBC2	ITV	Ch 4
6pm	XXX	XXX	XXX	XXX
7pm	XXX	XXX	XXX	XXX
8pm	XXX	XXX	XXX	XXX
9pm	XXX	XXX	XXX	XXX

Figure 4.51

	6pm	7pm	8pm	9pm
BBC1	XXX	XXX	XXX	XXX
BBC2	XXX	XXX	XXX	XXX
ITV	XXX	XXX	XXX	XXX
Ch 4	XXX	XXX	XXX	XXX

Several years' figures: what column order?

Figure 4.52 shows five years of Fees, and the most important year is probably the most recent, so – according to the Five Steps – it's next to the labels. Prior years' numbers stretch to the right in reverse order.

But a time-series usually runs left to right, not right to left, so Figure 4.53 reverts to this convention – but it has a big gap between *Fees* and the most recent year's numbers. So we've two ways to show it. Which is best?

It depends. To show trends over time, put 2013 first – but if this year's number is the main focus (and comparatives are there in case people want them), put 2017 first. As it is though, we can improve both ways. For trends over time, show numbers in columns, not rows (as we saw earlier in this Chapter). Or, if exact numbers aren't vital, do a graph. And if this year's number is the focus (and older numbers are there just in case), put 2017 first, but tweak it slightly. That is, add a column that shows the year-on-year change, then have a gap and grey down the earlier years' numbers to signal that they're less important (Figure 4.54).

Figure 4.52

	'17	'16	'15	'14	'13
Fees	78	81	76	82	85

Figure 4.53

	'13	'14	'15	'16	'17
Fees	85	81	76	81	78

Figure 4.54

	'17	'16	Diff	'15	'14	'13
Fees	78	81	(3)	76	82	85

When to put the most important row first

We know we should put the most important column first, but should we also put the most important row first? Figure 4.55 shows staff numbers by office, with country and group totals at the bottom. Big and small numbers compete for attention. Country totals (mostly big) interweave with office numbers (some are tiny). Readers struggle.

Figure 4.56 shows the numbers again, but with the most important row first. Group total at the top, then country totals, then offices. It inverts the table. Readers easily see the big picture and drill down to whatever level of detail they want. Inverting tables is like 'starting at the end', and it's great when you've a series of sub-tables. If you're an accountant, do this for the cash flow in your monthly pack. Ditch the statutory format and invert the table.

Maybe we should invert all tables, not just ones with sub-tables? No. Figure 4.57 is sales by region and product – we saw it earlier, but now it's changed slightly. The *Total* row is first. Does it help? Not really. It's a small, simple table – not a series of sub-tables – so putting the most important row first isn't necessary. If we've many rows though, it helps. If showing population for every country, put the world population at the top.

Notice in Figure 4.56, the *Totals* have only an underline, not an 'overline'. When tables have lots in them, rigorously remove typography. A variance column would help, but I left it out because it's not relevant to the point in this section.

That's the individual tips. Next is the Big Redo.

Figure 4.55

Staff nos	'16	'15
England		
Oxford	127	104
Preston	92	96
Telford	58	58
Romford	42	32
Total	**319**	**290**
Wales		
Harlech	118	112
Cardiff	87	94
Mumbles	35	27
Swansea	28	24
Total	**268**	**257**
Scotland		
Fife	91	95
Gretna	88	85
Perth	10	14
Kilbride	1	2
Total	**190**	**196**
Ireland		
Dublin	53	56
Cork	15	22
Ballina	9	7
Limerick	7	12
Total	**84**	**97**
Group		
England	319	290
Wales	268	257
Scotland	190	196
Ireland	84	97
Total	**861**	**840**

Figure 4.56

Staff nos	'16	'15
Group	**861**	**840**
England	319	290
Wales	268	257
Scotland	190	196
Ireland	84	97
England		
Oxford	127	104
Preston	92	96
Telford	58	58
Romford	42	32
Total	**319**	**290**
Wales		
Harlech	118	112
Cardiff	87	94
Mumbles	35	27
Swansea	28	24
Total	**268**	**257**
Scotland		
Fife	91	95
Gretna	88	85
Perth	10	14
Kilbride	1	2
Total	**190**	**196**
Ireland		
Dublin	53	56
Cork	15	22
Ballina	9	7
Limerick	7	12
Total	**84**	**97**

Figure 4.57

£k	Total	Co	Ab	Be
Total	98	50	31	17
North	35	19	11	5
South	28	16	6	6
West	21	9	8	4
East	14	6	6	2

Highlighting hierarchy in tables

Above, we looked at staff numbers by country. Figure 4.58 shows staff numbers again, albeit they're now by region. There are four versions – each shows a different way to highlight hierarchy. Which way is best?

Versions 1 and 2 don't work well. The first puts region names in bold, and it's a bit flat and timid. Version 2 adds a slight indent to make region names stand out, but it lacks alignment and looks a bit messy. Version 3 reverts to tighter alignment and adds contrast – Arial Black. The table is stronger, bolder. Hierarchy is more apparent and alignment retained. And in version 4, region names have their own column. It avoids messy overlaps. Version 4 uses more horizontal space, yet less vertical space because region names are alongside town names, not above them. Version 4 – like version 3 – also has contrast.

Versions 3 and 4 are both fine. They highlight hierarchy well and look smart, strong and confident.

Figure 4.58

Version 1		Version 2		Version 3		Version 4		
	'16		'16		'16			'16
Wales		**Wales**		**Wales**		**Wales**	Holt	145
Holt	145	Holt	145	Holt	145		Usk	134
Usk	134	Usk	134	Usk	134		Flint	121
Flint	121	Flint	121	Flint	121		Risca	112
Risca	112	Risca	112	Risca	112		Bala	108
Bala	108	Bala	108	Bala	108		Total	620
Total	620	Total	620	Total	620			
						West	Bath	142
West		**West**		**West**			Ash	123
Bath	142	Bath	142	Bath	142		Ilton	98
Ash	123	Ash	123	Ash	123		Vole	17
Ilton	98	Ilton	98	Ilton	98		Total	380
Vole	17	Vole	17	Vole	17			
Total	380	Total	380	Total	380	**Bucks**	Aston	148
							Fern	106
Bucks		**Bucks**		**Bucks**			Grove	98
Aston	148	Aston	148	Aston	148		Nash	89
Fern	106	Fern	106	Fern	106		Total	441
Grove	98	Grove	98	Grove	98			
Nash	89	Nash	89	Nash	89			
Total	441	Total	441	Total	441			

The Big Redo

The second half of this Chapter has many tips. This section shows them in action all at once. Figure 4.59 (the *before* overleaf) is the *Income* page from a board pack. It's not too horrible, plus it follows Four of the Five Steps we saw earlier, i.e. (1) not many grids; (2) no intrusive typography; (3) compact; and (4) decent structure. There's no lead-in title (that's Step (5)), but let's not worry about that. All in all, it's better than many tables.

Figure 4.60 is the *after*, and it's distinctly better. It follows tips in the second half of this Chapter, plus some from the *Numbers* Chapter – and even introduces some new ones. The changes are listed two pages on. They're grouped, but not in order of importance. Notice the *after* doesn't have logos, shading, pimped headings. Thank goodness.

This Chapter doesn't have any Final Thoughts. It doesn't need it. Figures 4.59 and 4.60 say it all. The difference is dramatic. Follow the tips in this Chapter and people might just congratulate you on your tables.

Figure 4.60

ABC Inc   **Income**   **Period 8, Nov 16**

		Year to date				Budget	
£ millions		Actual A	Budget B	Variance good/(bad) C=A-B	D=C/B x100	Annual E	To go F=E-A
North	Below	15.9	18.7	(2.8)	(15%)	32.8	16.9
South	Below	14.2	12.7	1.5	12%	27.8	13.6
West	Below	1.5	1.5	(0.1)	(8%)	-	1.2
Head office	B72						
Group total		**32.1**	**33.1**	**(1.0)**	**(3%)**	**63.3**	**31.7**
£ thousands							
North							
Digital widgets	B47	9,240	10,275	(1,035)	(10%)	20,281	11,041
Wigital digits	B48	2,759	3,098	(339)	(11%)	5,350	2,591
Fluorescent gadgets	B11	2,394	2,701	(307)	(11%)	4,019	1,625
Fancy gadgets	B57	1,487	2,639	(1,152)	(44%)	3,154	1,667
Total		**15,880**	**18,713**	**(2,833)**	**(15%)**	**32,804**	**16,924**
South							
Browns	B03	11,955	10,405	1,550	15%	24,336	12,381
Blacks	B02	2,185	2,171	14	1%	3,287	1,102
Greens and yellows	B46	57	121	(64)	(53%)	161	104
Total		**14,197**	**12,697**	**1,500**	**12%**	**27,784**	**13,587**
West							
Ern Movies	B21	477	687	(210)	(31%)	1,176	699
Erly Wind	B20	645	566	79	14%	899	254
Minster	B45	391	389	2	1%	611	220
Total		**1,513**	**1,642**	**(129)**	**(8%)**	**2,686**	**1,173**

By Pat Smith. 5 December 2016 (0208 840 4555) v2

Figure 4.59

ABC Inc
FOR THE MONTH ENDING NOVEMBER 2016 (PERIOD 8)
Summary income - budget, actual, remaining to year-end + variances

£k		Year to date				Budget	
		Actual	Budget	Variance good/(bad)		Annual	Remaining to year end
North							
Digital widgets	B47	9,240	10,275	(1,035)	(10%)	20,281	11,041
Wigital digits	B48	2,759	3,098	(339)	(11%)	5,350	2,591
Fluorescent gadgets	B11	2,394	2,701	(307)	(11%)	4,019	1,625
Fancy gadgets	B57	1,487	2,639	(1,152)	(44%)	3,154	1,667
Total North		15,880	18,713	(2,833)	(15%)	32,804	16,924
South							
Browns	B03	11,955	10,405	1,550	15%	24,336	12,381
Blacks	B02	2,185	2,171	14	1%	3,287	1,102
Greens and yellows	B46	57	121	(64)	(53%)	161	104
Total South		14,197	12,697	1,500	12%	27,784	13,587
West							
Ern Movies	B21	477	687	(210)	(31%)	1,176	699
Erly Wind	B20	645	566	79	14%	899	254
Minster	B45	391	389	2	1%	611	220
Total West		1,513	1,642	(129)	(8%)	2,686	1,173
Head office	B72	512	0.0	512	#DIV/0!	0.0	0.0
Group total		**32,102**	**33,052**	**(950)**	**(3%)**	**63,274**	**31,684**

Page 10 of 16

Cell grids

1. Removed the upper grid for the *Total* rows.
2. Put a slight gap between grid and number – they no longer butt up to each other.
3. At the top of columns, improved the gaps in the horizontal grids. The *before* has gaps (good), but they're all the same size (bad). To signal structure better, the *after* has a bigger gap between columns D and E than between B and C.
4. **New** Tidied the box on the right. In the *before*, it intersects the horizontal grids. Messy. The *after* avoids intersects. If that column is key, maybe put it as the first column.

Page heading (all new)

5. Made the page title more prominent (*Income*). When people alight on a page, they want to know what it covers. The *before* makes it tough for them, its *Summary income* title is in the smallest font size of the headings, and underlined too (that hinders readability).
6. Shortened the heading – the *before* goes on so long, it bores.
7. De-emphasised the company name. We don't need to remind bosses who they work for.
8. Greyed down *Period 8* – the entire report is Period 8.

Column headings

9. Used a smaller font than in the rest of the table.
10. Greyed down a bit.
11. Tidied the far-right heading – in the *before*, it's *Remainin* (new line) *g*. To make it fit, it's now *To go*.
12. Put column labels at the top of each column (A, B, etc) – it helps commentary and shows maths.

Rows and columns – other

13. Made row heights consistent – in the *before*, the row height for *Fluorescent gadgets* is bigger.
14. **New** Right-aligned row labels. I prefer to left-align, but if there's a mix of long and short labels, left-alignment struggles – short labels are far removed from the numbers to which they relate. So I instead right-align.
15. Put most important rows first – there's now a summary table at the top. I could put the *Group total* first, but decided it wasn't vital.
16. Made column widths consistent.

Numbers

17. Rounded the summary table to the nearest £m.
18. Replaced zeros with a dash.
19. Removed *#DIV/0!*. The *after* says na in small and grey.
20. Stopped brackets misaligning numbers.

Other

21. Used a smaller font throughout.
22. Greyed down the codes (B47, B48, etc) and moved them out of the way – they're accounting codes, so aren't that critical.
23. **New** Put author name, contact details, date. It's an audit trail, plus shows pride and ownership. Bosses now know whom to ring to thank for the great table.

Design changes (all new – see Chapter 6 for more)

24. Created contrast. Used Arial Black sparingly. Greyed down less important stuff.
25. Avoided upper case and italics. They slow reading speed.
26. Lined stuff up. In the *after*, stuff lines up along the left and right edges of the page (and the left edge looks sharper – its alignment tighter – because I moved the codes there). In the *before*, bits stick out here and there – and other bits are centred (e.g. *page 10 of 16*). It's all a bit misaligned.
27. Bottom-aligned headings within cells. The *before* vertically centre-aligns, and that creates something called 'trapped white space' – Chapter 16 explains this. However... in the *after*, column labels (A, B, etc) are *top-aligned...*? In the design world, they say: "If you've a strong source of alignment, use it". And here we've a strong source: the horizontal grids at the top of the columns. So I butt stuff up to it – I bottom-align stuff that's just above that grid and top-align stuff that's just beneath it.

5 Making comparisons

Figure 5.1

Cheap compact
Pros
- Cheap
- Easy to use
- Fits in pocket

Cons
- Can't control settings
- Bad for enlargements
- Cannot do videos

Medium-priced
Pros
- OK for enlargements
- Tidy size
- Can shoot videos
- Can control a few settings

Cons
- Existing lenses incompatible
- Controls bit intimidating

Pricey fancy
Pros
- Great for enlargements
- Great flexibility for settings
- Can use existing lenses

Cons
- Expensive
- Needs a suitcase to carry
- Intimidating set of controls

Figure 5.2

	Cheap compact	Medium-priced	Pricey fancy
Price	✓	-	✗
Enlargements	✗	✓	✓✓
Easy to use	✓	✗	✗✗
Fits in pocket	✓	✓	✗
Video'ing	✗	✓	✗
Flexibility/control	✗	✓	✓✓
Existing lenses	✗	✗	✓

Should we outsource IT or keep in-house? Should we enter a new market by joint venture, acquisition or setting up a local office? To help decide between alternatives, bosses read reports and listen to talks. Yet – as we see – many reports and talks compare options badly. Bosses struggle to have informed discussions about alternatives. And they don't even realise it.

This Chapter brings clarity and comparability to analysis. First though, a quick warning – this chapter doesn't look at: (1) how we make decisions (e.g. are we risk-averse or risk-seekers?); (2) how we take decisions (e.g. behind closed doors or via consensus?); (3) how accountants quantify outcomes (e.g. NPV or IRR?). First, we see how people often compare alternatives.

Ticks and crosses

Assume bosses wish to buy a camera (unlikely, but go with the flow), and must decide between a cheap compact one, a medium-priced one and a pricey fancy one. We analyse the pros and cons of each – is the camera easy to use? Can it take videos? Etc. We then present three slides on the pros and cons: slide 1 = cheap compact, slide 2 = medium-priced, slide 3 = pricey fancy (Figure 5.1). But, because pros and cons are spread over three slides, bosses can't easily compare alternatives unless they've a photographic memory (excuse the pun). Reports similarly fragment the information – pros and cons are spread over three paragraphs or even three pages. Comparisons are tricky.

Instead, do a table of ticks and crosses (Figure 5.2). For each of the three alternatives, it compares their key criteria. There are even double ticks and double crosses for seriously good or bad items. Readers more easily compare alternatives. It's less repetitive too – the list of pros and cons mentions the word *enlargements* three times, the table just once. Also, there are other benefits to this tick-and-cross table:

It's more likely to be consistent: with pros and cons, people are casual with terminology. They unwittingly use different words to describe the same thing and similar words to describe different things. For instance, the slides use the word *control* in two different ways – the cheap compact won't let people control settings (it's a verb), but the other two cameras have intimidating controls (now a noun). It hinders comparison. The table of ticks and crosses says *control* just once, so there's no confusion.

It's more likely to be complete: lists of pros and cons are nearly always incomplete. The slides in Figure 5.1 have three omissions (e.g. they don't say if fancy cameras do videos), and in lists, it's not obvious that stuff is missing. With a table of ticks and crosses, it is – the table has empty cells.

It's more granular: the table gives scores out of five (double tick to double cross), whilst lists of pros and cons divide answers into just two, and that can create problems. A medium-priced camera is neither cheap nor expensive, so is that a pro or con? The list misses it out anyway (it's incomplete…). In the table, it's easy – it's a dash.

To get these benefits, ask questions properly. If we ask, "Is it easy to use?" and "Is it expensive?", we get a tick and cross for the cheap compact (easy, not expensive), yet both are good news for purchasers. For a consistent visual overview, phrase questions so *Yes* is good ("Is it cheap?").

Also, draw readers into the table with a lead-in comment. It could be a sentence that summarises trade-offs ("Cheap compacts save money, but if we subsequently want decent enlargements, we spend more overall – as they say: buy cheap, buy twice"). Or maybe write a recommendation: "We need decent enlargements, but don't have a big budget, so medium-priced is the best compromise". Join dots for readers. Tables of ticks and crosses help us reach conclusions, but often aren't the best way to convey those conclusions to others.

There are two other ways people summarise findings. Firstly, a table of pros of cons (Figure 5.3). It's better than comparing over three slides, but is still poor. To find out how each camera is for enlargements, readers' eyes must float around the table looking for the word *enlargements*. Not easy. Also, it's repetitive, offers little granularity (just a pro or con), has no underlying structure that imposes consistency or completeness, and all too easily suffers from inconsistent terminology.

Then there's a table of numbers (Figure 5.4). It gives scores from 1 (previously a double cross) to 5 (a double tick). Take care though, for two reasons. Firstly, numbers aren't as intuitive as ticks and crosses – compare Figures 5.4 and 5.2. Ticks and crosses give a quick visual overview of scores, whereas with numbers, readers must concentrate more. Secondly, people often add up the numbers, and this can mislead – the most appropriate camera depends on purchasing priorities, not mathematical averages. For instance, cheap compacts score 20 overall, medium-priced 23 and pricey fancy 21, so medium seems best. But if bosses want the cheapest, get a cheap compact, and if they want the most flexible, get a pricey fancy (albeit if we know

Figure 5.3

Type	Pro	Con
Cheap compact	Cheap	Can't control settings
	Easy to use	Not good for enlarging
	Fits in pocket	Cannot do videos
Medium-priced	OK for enlargements	Existing lenses incompatible
	Tidy size	Controls bit intimidating
	Can shoot videos	
	Can control a few settings	
Pricey fancy	Good for enlargements	Expensive
	Good flexibility for settings	Needs a suitcase to carry
	Can use existing lenses	Intimidating set of controls

Figure 5.4

	Cheap compact	Medium-priced	Pricey fancy
Price	4	3	2
Enlargements	2	4	5
Easy to use	4	2	1
Fits in pocket	4	4	2
Video'ing	2	4	2
Flexibility/ control	2	4	5
Existing lenses	2	2	4

that bosses want the cheapest or most flexible, we eschew the comparative table and simply find the cheapest or most flexible). And if bosses seek a mix of requirements, e.g. reasonable enlargements, plus video too, we get a medium-priced. As I said, averages can mislead.

Comparative tables not only help us choose cameras, they help us decide how best to enter new territories (three options: joint venture, acquisition or set up a local office?). First, decide the key criteria. E.g. cost? Time? Ability to overcome regulatory barriers? Availability of key staff? Etc. Then do a table of ticks and crosses for the options and criteria.

Finally, what if readers want more granularity than offered by ticks and crosses? We're left with little option but a table of numbers. The *Which?* magazine does comparative tables a lot – *Which?* is an outfit in the UK that sticks up for consumers and compares products. It often does tables that score criteria out of 100 – and equally often does tables of ticks and crosses. It never compares with bullets of pros and cons.

Two-by-two grids; cluster charts

We've analysed our overseas offices: some are in high-growth countries, some aren't. Some have a strong ability to compete, others don't. Figure 5.5 shows our findings in bullets, Figure 5.6 shows them in a two-by-two grid. The grid uses its physical space to show both overview and detail. Groupings are easier to pick out – three countries are top right (and the double tick signals to readers that top right is best), and only one is bottom left (bad news, it's a double cross). These ticks and crosses make the grid more intuitive – if they weren't included, readers would have to think a bit harder: "Now… which is good – top right or bottom left?".

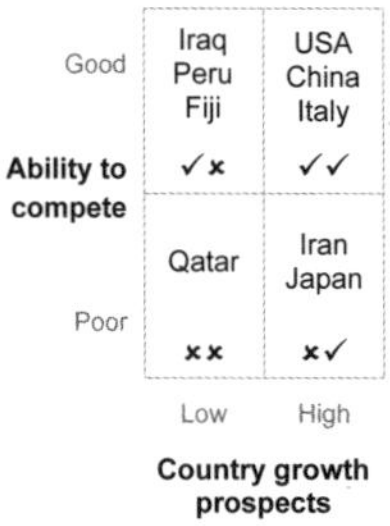

Introduce greater granularity: to score growth as high, medium or low – as opposed to just high and low – do a two-by-three grid. Or a three-by-three grid. You get my drift. We could strive for even greater granularity and score out of, say, 100 and maybe even plot a scattergram of country names – arguably useful if many names. However, it can introduce spurious accuracy that hinders, not helps. If we tell bosses that an office's ability to compete is a weighted average of its management, results, market position, and so on, they may spend too much time on whether *results* warrants more weighting than *management*, and too little time on the bigger picture.

Introduce a third question: to comment on political stability, for instance, use different typography. In Figure 5.7, stable countries are in Arial Black, unstable ones light grey (it's illustrative). Maybe we've a fourth question, e.g. labour supply, in which case we could try differently sized fonts – big fonts

Figure 5.5

- Good growth, good ability to compete: USA, China, Italy.
- Poor growth, good ability to compete: Iraq, Peru, Fiji.
- Good growth, poor ability to compete: Iran, Japan.
- Poor growth, poor ability to compete: Qatar.

Figure 5.6

	Iraq Peru Fiji	USA China Italy
Good	✓✗	✓✓
Poor	Qatar ✗✗	Iran Japan ✗✓
	Low	High

Ability to compete

Country growth prospects

Figure 5.7

	Iraq Peru Fiji	USA Italy
Good	✓✗	✓✓
Poor	Qatar ✗✗	Iran Japan ✗✓
	Low	High

Ability to compete

Country growth prospects

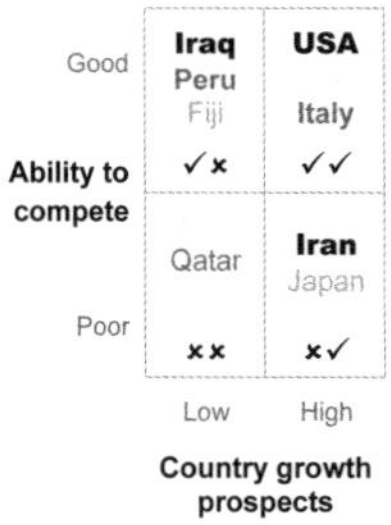

for good supply, small fonts poor supply. Don't. It confuses. Readers have too many typographical cues to decode. If more than three questions, do a table of ticks and crosses. When we compared cameras, we had seven questions. Which begs the question: why not do a table even if just two questions? See Figure 5.8. It's not bad, but not as intuitive as the two-by-two grid. It doesn't use its physical space as effectively.

Clusters – where answers are in a range

Grids struggle if answers aren't discrete, but in a range. Imagine we rank *product quality* and *management experience* for each of seven UK regions in our business. However, each region consists of several offices, and product quality varies by office – in the South, for instance, it ranges from dreadful to great. We can't show that on a grid; the words *product quality* would straddle two grids. So do a cluster chart instead – see Figure 5.9. Ovals and circles represent ranges, e.g. in the South, all offices have good management, but product quality varies. Cluster charts help readers see ranges, and the more they show, the more they help. If we try to convey Figure 5.9 in words, it would be lengthy and impenetrable.

What if we've a third question for our clusters? Assume we wish to convey audit scores – did a region pass or fail? What we do next depends on how this third question affects groupings – and here's a quick warning: the following few paragraphs are a bit of a brain-teaser.

Assume the third question doesn't affect groupings: that is, within a region, every office fared the same in the audit, e.g. assume that all South offices failed, and all East offices passed. In which case, we've seven groupings before we ask the *audit* question (the seven regions), and seven groups after we ask it. So use typography to signal the answer to the third question, e.g. light font for region name = fail, dark font = pass. Explain this in a key to the chart.

Assume the third question does affect groupings: not all offices in a given region fared the same, e.g. in the North West, three offices failed, three passed. Perhaps we could show two ovals for North West – one for offices that failed, one for offices that passed – and typographically signal them with light and dark fonts. But it's unhelpful to have an oval that says: "Offices that passed" – it's as unhelpful as saying: "I've two lists: people to promote, and people not to", but then not name the individuals. Instead, get more granular and show not regions but offices: see Figure 5.10 (again, light font = fail, dark font =

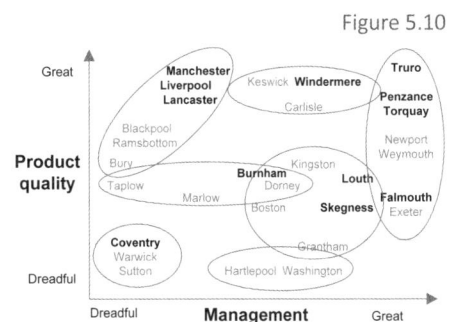

Figure 5.8

Country	Ability to compete	Country growth prospects
USA China Italy	✓	✓
Iraq Peru Fiji	✓	✗
Iran Japan	✗	✓
Qatar	✗	✗

Figure 5.9

Figure 5.10

Figure 5.11

Great
Manchester
Liverpool Keswick **Windermere** **Truro**
Lancaster **Penzanze**
Carlisle **Torquay**
Blackpool
Ramsbottom Newport
Bury Kingston Weymouth
Burnham
Taplow **Dorney** **Louth**
Marlow **Falmouth**
Boston **Skegness** Exeter
Coventry
Warwick Grantham
Dreadful Sutton Hartlepool Washington

Dreadful **Management** Great

Product quality (left axis)

Figure 5.12

Loose
Japan
Regulatory controls
Tight **Peru**

Low **Growth prospects** High

Figure 5.14

Testing the grid

Let's apply the grid to itself and use it to answer the question: what's the best way to compare the different ways to make comparisons? First, see the question down the left side of the grid – "How many questions are you asking?". Well, to decide how best to make comparisons, we must answer two questions – one question down the left of Figure 5.13, one along the bottom.

Next, see the question along the bottom: "Are answers discrete or a range?". They're discrete – in the grid, no answers sprawl over two or more adjacent parts of it. So we've two questions, and discrete answers. Now look on Figure 5.13: it says the best way to show the information is a grid.

Which is what Figure 5.13 does. Which is reassuring.

pass). We could remove ovals and keep just office names in light and dark fonts (Figure 5.11), and yes, it's less cluttered, but it's not as easy to see patterns by region. Therefore, retain ovals and circles if: (1) they don't overlap much (otherwise it will look cluttered); and (2) regional patterns matter to your readers. And if they do overlap a lot, maybe simply show the information in a table. A table doesn't use its physical space so well, but it avoids messy overlaps. Also, refer to Chapter 31 (*Signalling performance*) for other ideas.

So cluster charts convey ranges that arise from *variety*, e.g. the South has seven offices, and product quality varies across them. Cluster charts also convey ranges that arise from *uncertainty*, e.g. Figure 5.12 is a simple chart that shows for two countries their expected growth and regulatory control – for each country there is a range that we expect might arise.

Time for Final Thoughts. We've seen various ways to compare alternatives. To decide which to use when, see Figure 5.13 below. Simply answer the questions on the bottom and the left, then look up on the grid to find the best way to convey the information. The grid helps us make more informed decisions about how to compare alternatives so others can make more informed decisions about the alternatives…

Figure 5.13

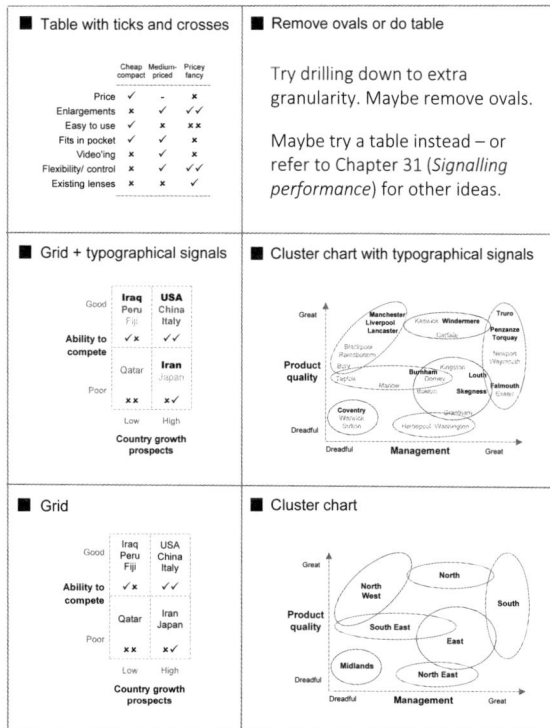

Are the answers discrete or a range?

Design 6

Or: how to do work that looks sharp. Figure 6.1 is page 1 of a CV – the *before*. Unusually, it has testimonials: they're included so I can comment on their design. Also, there's no list of jobs in date order. They're usually on page 2 of a CV, plus Chapter 1 has already shown how to do them as a WiT.

Figure 6.2 redoes it (the *after*). The *before* is shabby, the *after* is sharp – and this Chapter explains why. Before then, a suggestion: to avoid flicking back to these Figures as you read the Chapter, visit my website and print them off.

Figure 6.1

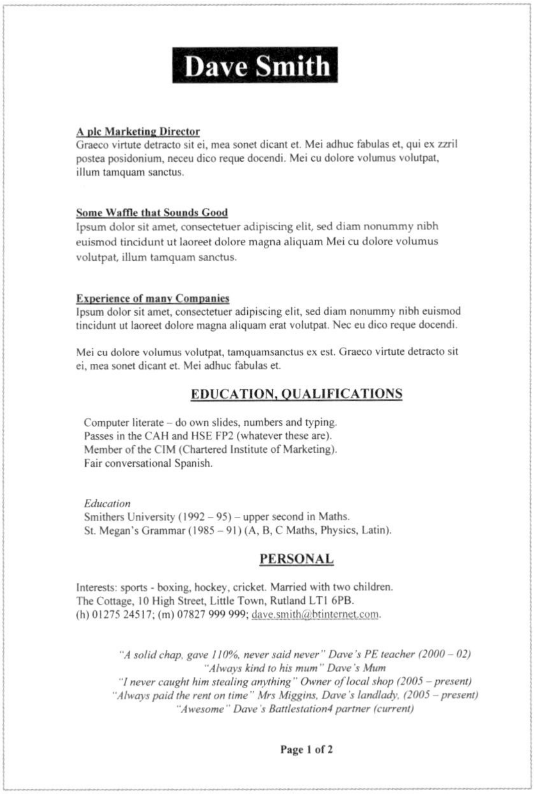

Dave Smith

A plc Marketing Director
Graeco virtute detracto sit ei, mea sonet dicant et. Mei adhuc fabulas et, qui ex zzril postea posidonium, neceu dico reque docendi. Mei cu dolore volumus volutpat, illum tamquam sanctus.

Some Waffle that Sounds Good
Ipsum dolor sit amet, consectetuer adipiscing elit, sed diam nonummy nibh euismod tincidunt ut laoreet dolore magna aliquam Mei cu dolore volumus volutpat, illum tamquam sanctus.

Experience of many Companies
Ipsum dolor sit amet, consectetuer adipiscing elit, sed diam nonummy nibh euismod tincidunt ut laoreet dolore magna aliquam erat volutpat. Nec eu dico reque docendi.

Mei cu dolore volumus volutpat, tamquamsanctus ex est. Graeco virtute detracto sit ei, mea sonet dicant et. Mei adhuc fabulas et.

EDUCATION, QUALIFICATIONS

Computer literate – do own slides, numbers and typing.
Passes in the CAH and HSE FP2 (whatever these are).
Member of the CIM (Chartered Institute of Marketing).
Fair conversational Spanish.

Education
Smithers University (1992 – 95) – upper second in Maths.
St. Megan's Grammar (1985 – 91) (A, B, C Maths, Physics, Latin).

PERSONAL

Interests: sports - boxing, hockey, cricket. Married with two children.
The Cottage, 10 High Street, Little Town, Rutland LT1 6PB.
(h) 01275 24517; (m) 07827 999 999; dave.smith@btinternet.com.

"A solid chap, gave 110%, never said never" Dave's PE teacher (2000 – 02)
"Always kind to his mum" Dave's Mum
"I never caught him stealing anything" Owner of local shop (2005 – present)
"Always paid the rent on time" Mrs Miggins, Dave's landlady, (2005 – present)
"Awesome" Dave's Battlestation4 partner (current)

Page 1 of 2

Figure 6.2

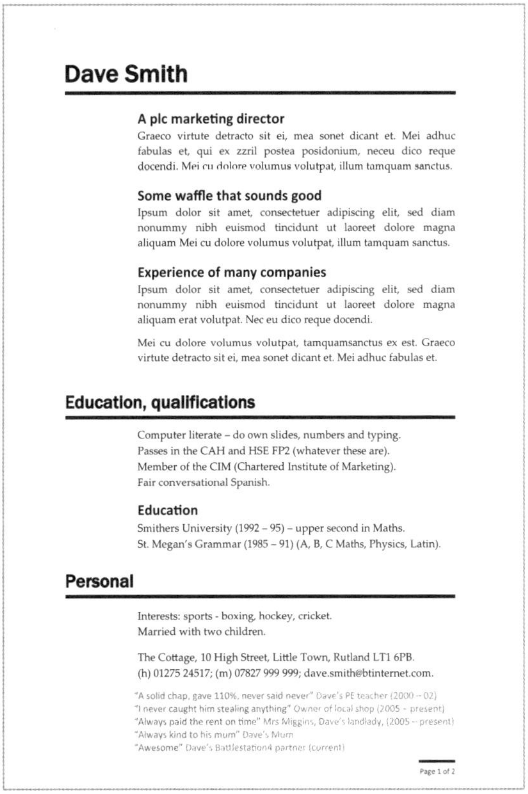

Dave Smith

A plc marketing director
Graeco virtute detracto sit ei, mea sonet dicant et. Mei adhuc fabulas et, qui ex zzril postea posidonium, neceu dico reque docendi. Mei cu dolore volumus volutpat, illum tamquam sanctus.

Some waffle that sounds good
Ipsum dolor sit amet, consectetuer adipiscing elit, sed diam nonummy nibh euismod tincidunt ut laoreet dolore magna aliquam Mei cu dolore volumus volutpat, illum tamquam sanctus.

Experience of many companies
Ipsum dolor sit amet, consectetuer adipiscing elit, sed diam nonummy nibh euismod tincidunt ut laoreet dolore magna aliquam erat volutpat. Nec eu dico reque docendi.

Mei cu dolore volumus volutpat, tamquamsanctus ex est. Graeco virtute detracto sit ei, mea sonet dicant et. Mei adhuc fabulas et.

Education, qualifications

Computer literate – do own slides, numbers and typing.
Passes in the CAH and HSE FP2 (whatever these are).
Member of the CIM (Chartered Institute of Marketing).
Fair conversational Spanish.

Education
Smithers University (1992 – 95) – upper second in Maths.
St. Megan's Grammar (1985 – 91) (A, B, C Maths, Physics, Latin).

Personal

Interests: sports - boxing, hockey, cricket.
Married with two children.

The Cottage, 10 High Street, Little Town, Rutland LT1 6PB.
(h) 01275 24517; (m) 07827 999 999; dave.smith@btinternet.com.

"A solid chap, gave 110%, never said never" Dave's PE teacher (2000 – 02)
"I never caught him stealing anything" Owner of local shop (2005 - present)
"Always paid the rent on time" Mrs Miggins, Dave's landlady, (2005 – present)
"Always kind to his mum" Dave's Mum
"Awesome" Dave's Battlestation4 partner (current)

Page 1 of 2

Robin Williams' four design tips

Robin is a designer from New Mexico and author of the brilliant book *The Non-Designer's Design Book*. Her tips are a big reason why the *after* is sharp – and below I quickly introduce them, albeit I don't give many examples. Fear not though, for my book has lots – study its Figures and typesetting. Time for her first principle: **Contrast**.

Principle 1: Contrast

The *before* has a bit of bold and slightly bigger fonts. And that's it. It looks visually flat and uninteresting. Timid. The *after* has contrast. Its fonts stand out more. As Robin Williams says: "Don't be a wimp" – go for it. Use fonts three or four points bigger or that have more 'oommph', e.g. **Arial Black** or, if you prefer, **Franklin Gothic** – the CV uses it for its three main headings. Contrast creates visual interest, looks confident, and helps readers navigate around and find stuff more easily. We see contrast in magazines and newspapers. We often see lack of contrast too – flat-looking pages in Arial 11. A shame, for adding contrast to a page takes just seconds.

Use contrast sparingly though, don't overdo it. Highlight everything and we contrast nothing. In particular, *please* use **Arial Black** sparingly, otherwise it visually overwhelms. And don't do it in bold, for it looks smudgy.

Principle 2: Alignment

In the *before*, some bits are indented, some aren't. Some bits are centred across the page, some left-aligned. It's all a bit out of whack. The *after* is tightly aligned. Aligning stuff can be time-consuming and fiddly – my website explains the computing tweaks to do it in MS Word. But it's worth doing. It brings order out of chaos and makes stuff look sharp.

Notice in the *after*, I indent detail within each section. Doesn't that misalign stuff? No. Documents can have more than one line of alignment, and by indenting detail, I create a second strong line. This also creates decent white space, visual interest, and helps readers navigate – section headings stand out more.

Finally, see Figure 6.3 for a detailed point on alignment: hanging the punctuation.

Principle 3: Proximity

Think of seven-year-olds spouting lines in junior school plays – they don't pause when they should and do pause when they shouldn't. So too with typography – people put gaps between items when they shouldn't and don't put gaps when they should. Just below the middle of the *before*, details of school and university are closer to the *Personal* section than the section to which they relate (*Education, qualifications*). It's poor proximity. Also, near the top of the *before*, study the second paragraph of *Experience of many Companies* (the one starting *Mei cu dolore*) – it's as close to the section that follows as it is to the preceding paragraph.

Proximity matters. It creates visual distinctions between parts of a page and helps readers more easily see structure. Also, if there aren't decent

Figure 6.3

Hang the punctuation
Below is the same quote, shown twice:

"Hanging the punctuation keeps stuff nicely aligned from one row to the next"

"Hanging the punctuation keeps stuff nicely aligned from one row to the next"

In the first, the opening quote mark misaligns the first letter of the first row with the first letters of subsequent rows. The second one 'hangs the punctuation' – the opening quote mark is shunted slightly left so that first letters align. Do this if you've a page of quotes in, say, market survey reports. It makes the page look sharp.

Rather like the long table in St George's Hall in Windsor Castle. It seats 160 guests for banquets – and Castle staff set the cutlery with rulers. If cutlery isn't set quite right, it looks a bit messy, but if set exactly right, it looks superb. It wonderfully illustrates the binary switch we can get with alignment when we go from 'not quite right' to 'spot-on'.

gaps, stuff runs endlessly down the page without pause or break. Gaps give readers 'breathing space' between sections.

Figure 6.4 is another example, it shows how bullets on slides often suffer from poor proximity. Gaps between lines of the same bullet are the same as gaps between different bullets – and that's wrong. Figure 6.5 has better proximity. Gaps where we need them, no gaps where we don't.

Principle 4: Repetition

We know about consistency. Headings must look like other headings, sub-headings must look like other sub-headings. This helps readers see the hierarchy of text – is it a heading, sub-heading, text box, etc? Reports benefit from consistent typography, just as maps benefit from consistent symbols.

It's not enough though. We've all seen reports that are consistent… but consistently bland. They need repetition. It's a unified look and feel that runs through a document – maybe headers and footers have a particular style. Or there's a strong font (used sparingly, of course). Or a flash down the side. Think of newspapers. Each paper has its own unique look and feel. Remove a newspaper's name from the page, and we still know which paper it is. The look of the page would tell us. That's repetition.

Which is why this principle is the toughest to illustrate with the CV. Repetition helps unite separate pages, but our CV is one page. No worries though, for hopefully you'll now see repetition in newspapers, magazines, reports, corporate slides – and even this book.

Those are Robin's tips: Contrast, Repetition, Alignment, Proximity. Notice the acronym… OK, let's move on. Next is typography. First up are fonts.

Figure 6.4

- Graeco virtute detracto sit ei, mea sonet dicant volutpat magna et.
- Mei adhuc fabulas et, qui. Ex zzril postea posid onium docendi est.
- Neceu dico reque docendi. Mei cu dolore volumus volutpat.

Figure 6.5

- Graeco virtute detracto sit ei, mea sonet dicant volutpat magna et.
- Mei adhuc fabulas et, qui. Ex zzril postea posid onium docendi est.
- Neceu dico reque docendi. Mei cu dolore volumus volutpat.

Fonts and formatting fonts

We need to define terms: Arial is a *typeface*, a family of fonts, whilst 'Arial Black, 10 points' is a *font*. For most purposes, there are two groups of typeface: serif and sans serif.

Serif (Figure 6.6): Times New Roman and CG Times are serifs. They've thick and thin bits (as if written with a quill pen), and squiggly bits too. The *serif* is the bit at the letters' end, the tail.

Sans serif (Figure 6.7): Arial and Calibri are sans serifs. 'Sans' is French for 'without' – no tails. No thick or thin bits either. They're monoweight.

Figure 6.6

Serif

Figure 6.7

Sans Serif

Figure 6.8

ill

Figure 6.9

ill

Which to use when? Serifs are good for **continuous text** because they're **readable**. They appear in newspapers and fictional books. According to typographers, the tails lead readers' eyes across a page. After all, in Figure 6.8, *ill* is in Arial, and even though we read left to right, nothing goes in that direction. Figure 6.9 shows *ill* in Times New Roman (I'll call it 'Times' from hereon), and at least the serifs go left to right. If you're not convinced – and many people aren't – put it to the test. Mock up two versions of a page of easy-to-read text. One in Arial, one in Times. Do the Times page in a slightly bigger font (it always comes out slightly smaller), and print them both out (don't read on screen). Then compare. At first glance, the Arial page may look easier to read, there are fewer twiddly bits. But read it, and the Times page will almost certainly be easier.

So why do sans serifs exist? They're **legible** and good for **glancing** at. They're good for road signs, car number plates, London Underground maps. And good for labels on graphs, numbers in tables, commentaries on slides. This may be why some people hate Times. They see it on slides and rightly hate it, but wrongly assume it's always bad. It isn't. It's just bad on slides.

Sans serifs are good also for headings, section headings and sub-headings – they're stuff we glance at. Now you know why this book has serifs for continuous text, sans serifs for headings. As does the *after* CV. Note:

Take care if we've more than two typefaces on a page	If we've two similar but different typefaces (two serifs or two sans serifs), readers may think it's an error. "Ha!" they think, "you've got Arial and Calibri mixed up!". When I use two sans serifs on a page, they're so different to each other, no-one would think it's an accident. The *after* CV uses **Franklin Gothic** and Calibri.
Avoid serifs for small fonts	If using font size 8 or lower, use sans serifs. With small fonts, the serif tails can look a bit fiddly.
Try Palatino Linotype ('PL') instead of Times	It's nice. Less squished too – below, the first is PL, the second is Times. The serifs in this book are PL. - Times looks a bit too squished; PL less so - Times looks a bit too squished; PL less so
Use sans serifs for stuff that's read on screen, even if it's mostly continuous text	For instance, most emails are read on screen, and the resolution of a computer screen is far worse than that of a printed page. The thin bits of serifs look bad with a poor resolution.

This last point – emails on screen – creates problems: what if some readers print out and some read on screen? Should we use Arial or Times? My suggestion: keep the important people happy, e.g. if our boss reads on screen, use Arial. But what if half the bosses print out, and half read on screen? If we use Times, 'on screen' bosses struggle, whilst 'print out' bosses are fine. On balance, we lose out though – we annoy the 'on-screen-ers' more than we please the 'print-out-ers'. So, avoid Times unless we're confident our bosses are mostly 'print-out-ers' – or technology improves even more and serifs always look good on screen. Talking of bosses, Figure 6.10 speculates as to why corporate fonts in the UK are usually sans serifs.

Then there's formats (and again, the *before* and *after* CVs illustrate).

1. **Avoid upper case**. IT SLOWS READING SPEED BY BETWEEN 13% AND 20%. WE READ WORDS NOT JUST BY THE LETTERS THAT MAKE THEM UP, BUT BY THEIR SHAPES TOO. Upper case has no ascenders or descenders (as in b, g), so every word is shaped like a rectangle. There are no distinctive shapes. The brain must concentrate harder to read words. ALSO, UPPER CASE SEEMS A BIT SHOUTY. However, it's OK to use upper case where words are surrounded by space (e.g. a heading such as PART 4). Then again, why not write it as Part 4? Or **Part 4**?

2. **Avoid Random upper Case**. People do This on Slides. Don't. Upper case isn't A lifestyle Choice. Use it When You should, Don't use It when you Shouldn't. It's Distracting to Read, plus it creates defined Terms that Change meanings. As it says in the book *This is Spinal Tap, the Official Companion*: "A closer look at the itinerary revealed that this was not to be our third world tour, but a Third World tour. And, really, there's not a lot of logistics involved except: 'Where's the electricity?'".

3. **Mostly avoid italics**. *They aren't easy to read, so use sparingly. Don't do whole paragraphs in italics.*

4. **Avoid underlines**. They merge letters together, hindering readability. Also, they bump into descenders and look ugly.

5. Avoid reversed fonts for continuous text. They hinder reading. Also, don't put serifs in reversed fonts – their thin bits come out poorly with a strong background. Avoid doing reversed fonts for words entirely in upper case – every word is shaped like a box, so we've a BOX IN A BOX.

HENCE AVOID ITALIC UPPER CASE REVERSED FONT UNDERLINED SERIFS, IT'S VERY TRICKY TO READ. SEE WHAT I MEAN?

Figure 6.10

Why UK corporate style police rarely choose serifs Simple. They don't want to be sacked. Over the years, I've asked thousands of people if they hate Times – and about a third say *Yes*. Result: if the style police choose Times as the corporate font – and if their CEO is one of the third that hates Times – they're in trouble. Yes, the style police can intellectualise about how Times is more readable, but to no avail. The CEO will still think they're idiots. It's safer to advocate Arial.

But there's a postscript: after I ask who hates Times, I then say: "You know that layout I showed three hours ago? The one you really liked? Its main font was Times". At which point, 75% of the Times-haters say: "Goodness, I didn't notice… I thought the layout looked great". If we choose the right font, people don't even notice it. They aren't consciously aware of the fonts. Which is how it should be.

Typography – more tips on the CV

Line spacing: the *after* CV has 1.1×. The *before* had MS Word's default spacing of 1.0×. For words that stretch across a page, 1.1× to 1.2× is better. If

Figure 6.11

Figure 6.12

This row of text isn't wide enough to justify, so I shouldn't – we get distractingly large gaps b e t w e e n words.

Wide rows of text are tricky to read. Readers' eyes get weary scanning along. Also, on reaching the far right, readers take too long to scan back to the far left to continue reading – and there's a good chance they accidentally move onto the wrong row.

words stretch part way across a page, 1.1× works well, and if we've narrow columns, 1.0× is fine. With really big fonts (e.g. font size 80 or more on a slide), use 0.9×, otherwise consecutive lines seem too far apart.

Row width: shorter and hence more readable. Wide rows of text are tricky to read – see Figure 6.11. The optimum width of text is about 70 characters. About 10 or 11 words. Except on a computer screen when it's about 50 characters. Or in a reference document when it's about 40 characters. In the *after* CV, I indent detail to create a second strong source of alignment. This also creates narrower rows of text which are easier to read.

Alignment: justified, not left-aligned. In the *before* CV, words are left-aligned (also called ragged-right). The *after* justifies text – words stretch to meet left and right edges – and this creates sharp lines of alignment on the left and right. However, don't justify narrow rows of text, otherwise we get visually distracting gaps between words (Figure 6.12), and that hinders readability. As a rule of thumb, justify if the row width in centimetres is more than the font size divided by 1.2. Eh?!?! Let me illustrate: with font size 10, justify only if row width exceeds 8 cm. But with words like *supercalifragilisticexpialidocious* or a long web address, this rule of thumb can break down. See two rows above.

Font size: smaller. With narrow rows of text, smaller fonts aren't just acceptable, they're preferable. In newspapers, font sizes are usually 8.5 to 9, a size that's too small if words spread across the page, but fine if in narrow rows. Also, fonts that look fine when spread across the full width of a page look a bit big and inelegant when put into narrow columns.

Font colour: some bits are greyed down. The *after* CV has quotes at the bottom, and the words that follow each quote are greyed down. This de-emphasises the less important (the person making quote), and highlights the more important (the quote). Grey is a great colour, it creates visual distinctions, plus stops pages looking so black and white. Note that in the *after*, quotes are in descending order of length. Long ones first, short ones next. This makes them easier to read and more elegant too. But only do this if no other order is preferable.

Emails: formatted pleasantly. E.g. abc@gmail.com, not abc@gmail.com.

We're there. Typographically, we're set up nicely for the rest of the book. However, design is a big topic and we've devoted just six pages to it. Do read Robin Williams' book *The Non-Designer's Design Book*. It's fantastic.

Words for reports and talks 7

This Chapter gives quick tips for words in reports and talks. Below, I just say we're writing reports. It avoids repeatedly saying the phrase: "Imagine we're writing or talking". For tips specific to reports, see Chapter 11.

Replace nouns with verbs

Study the following, it's typical of what people write in reports:

> "We do the procurement and installation of your IT; we also do the management and development of your staff."

It crawls with *nominalisations*. Abstract nouns derived from verbs. *Procurement* is from the verb *to procure*. *Installation* from *to install*. *Management* from *to manage*, and *development* from *to develop*. Abstract nouns are anodyne and bureaucratic. They obscure meaning and slow reading because they're, well, abstract. The clue is in the name. Instead, replace nouns with verbs.

> "We procure and install your IT; we also manage and develop your staff."

Shorter. More immediate. Abstract nouns are a plague. Reports talk about identification, instigation, mitigation, etc. Replace them with verbs, it's a quick, big change you can make to most writing. Compare: (1) "Quality improvements occur", and: (2) "Quality improves". Much better.

Many abstract nouns end in *tion*. *Recommendation* comes from *to recommend*. *Clarification* and *clarify*. Some don't end in *tion* – *provision* and *provide*; *avoidance* and *avoid*; *hindrance* and *hinder*; *delivery* and *deliver*. Abstract nouns can even be the same word as the verb: "We suggest the use of IT" becomes: "We suggest you use IT".

Sometimes we have a noun, but struggle to find the corresponding verb. *Efficiency* is a noun, but what is the verb? *Efficientise*? Use the adjective instead. Don't write: "Strive for more efficiency". Write: "Be more efficient". So, for enhancements in writing, ensure the reduction of abstract nouns...

Use *we* and *you*

To persuade bosses to spend £100k on a new bit of kit, we might write:

> "It will lead to reductions in our waste and enhancements in our quality."

OK, we don't know if quality improves by 1% or 100%, but don't worry about that. Let's rewrite it. First, we replace abstract nouns with verbs:

"It will reduce our waste and enhance our quality."

Better, but impersonal. So try this:

"We will reduce our waste and enhance our quality."

Much more human because of the *we* word. *We* is great. Don't say: "The situation will be monitored". Who will do that? A robot? Instead, say: "We will monitor the situation". In other words: "Leave it with us, it's on our patch – trust us". It shows pride, ownership, accountability, commitment. *You* is great too, it helps connect us to our audience. It reminds us who we're writing for. Politicians use *you* a lot – ask politicians what'll happen to interest rates, and they'll say: "You'll see your mortgage increase". Adverts use *you*: "Do your children go to school looking really clean?". Use *you* in talks too, it's great in rhetorical questions: "How many of you remember how you felt when you joined this firm?". Or: "You're probably wondering how this affects your costs". Our messages resonate more.

And it helps us avoid the passive voice (if unsure what that means, see Figure 7.1). Study this:

"Waste will be reduced and quality will be enhanced."

Yes, it uses verbs, not nouns, but it's in the passive voice. It's impersonal and unengaging. Wordy, bureaucratic, robotic, plodding, self-important. Instead, use *we*, *you* and the active voice.

Some people object to using *we* and *you*. They say it's too informal, it's not what we're taught to do at school and not what bosses do. I address these comments in Chapter 11. Also, there's another objection: "It's wrong to say: '*We* reduce waste' because *we* don't… *the new bit of kit* does". What?!?! These people who say this… when they hear: "Fancy a cuppa? I've boiled some water", do they reply: "You didn't boil it; a kettle did"? Do they say to CEOs: "Your Annual Report is wrong when it says: 'This year, we took ten million orders online'. You didn't. Your online system did". Give me strength.

Back to our sentence. There's more we can do:

"We'll reduce waste and enhance quality."

There are two changes, albeit both are quite small. Firstly, I remove the word *our* twice. Readers know from context it's our waste, there's no need say it. Secondly, there's now a contraction – *we will* becomes *we'll*. Contractions help our words to flow, and most readers won't mind. (There's a contraction in that last sentence, and one in this one too.) Avoid contractions for formal documents though, and avoid contractions that just ain't going to work.

Figure 7.1

Active versus passive

Active: Jim sent a note

Passive: A note was sent by Jim

Active: I kick a ball

Passive: A ball was kicked by me

Notice the sentence is in the future tense ("We'll reduce waste"). The benefits – less waste and more quality – will happen one day. In the future. After we put in a new system. If it works. It all sounds like hard work and an uncertain glimpse of the future. Instead, try the present tense:

"We reduce waste and enhance quality."

It's more confident. Readers can almost see and touch the benefits, they're more immediate. Yes, some people say that it wrongly implies we've put in the kit already, but no, it's a writing style and it's fine:

We're fine with it in TV ads	They seductively purr at us: "You're on a beach, sipping Bacardi". No we're not, we're at home on a sofa.
We trade precision for persuasion	The present tense persuades more, so use it when persuading. I do ("WiT transforms reports").
Anyway, the *before* is wrong too	It says: "We'll reduce waste and enhance quality". Which implies it *will* happen. But it might not. We lie when we say *will*, so why not lie and use the present tense?

Let's recap. We made five changes.

1. Replace abstract nouns with verbs.
2. Use *we* (and *you* too, when possible).
3. Remove unnecessary words (*our*).
4. Use contractions.
5. Use the present tense.

The first two will massively improve most reports and talks, so please adopt them. Arguably, the last two make the smallest difference, so if you don't adopt them, it's not such a big deal. As for the third – remove unnecessary words – here, it made a small difference, but in many reports, it helps massively, so Chapter 20 looks more at editing.

Those are the five changes. Compare *before* and *after*.

"It will lead to reductions in our waste and enhancements in our quality."

"We reduce waste and enhance quality."

The *after* is more concise, without loss of meaning. It's impactful too, it engages, persuades and helps us in our cause. It's also great for readers and audiences – study the stats: the *before* has 71 characters spread over 13 words; the *after* has 37 characters in six words. A 50% reduction. Our 12-page note becomes a six-pager. Our ten-minute talk shrinks to five. Fantastic.

Figure 7.2
Exceptions to this Chapter
The passive voice can be OK:
**When the subject is unim-
portant:** "Kate's baby was
delivered at 3.01pm". Who's
the midwife? Who cares?

Or not known: "Waste was
dumped in the lake last
night". Who dumped it? We
don't know.

**When we wish to avoid
pinning blame or being ex-
plicit:** the letter to staff says:
"Pay won't be increased
this year", but doesn't say
who's to blame for the lack
of increase. Politicians say:
"Lessons have been learnt"
– but not who learnt them.

**When it helps give more
bite:** Compare: (1) "We
will sack people who make
racist remarks"; and: (2)
"People who make racist
remarks will be sacked".
Because (2) is in the passive
voice, its 'impact' word
comes right at the end
("*sacked*"). It has more bite.

As for other exceptions:
**Use nominalisations when
they create rhythm:** "It trades
precision for persuasion" has
more rhythm than: "Be less
precise and we persuade
more". Chapter 20 has more
on this topic.

**Avoid a contraction to add
emphasis:** "We won't be
complacent, we won't give
up – and we will not miss
our sales target".

Avoid *we* and *you* to soften:
the letter says: "This year
sees a salary freeze". It
never says: "*We* won't
increase *your* pay".

Some quick examples

These *before* and *after* examples are all based on real-life stuff.

Before: This report has been written to help your decision-making process.
After: We wrote this to help you decide what to do.

This one is easy. We replace *decision* with the verb *decide*, we use *we* and *you*, and we avoid the passive voice. Next is a slide to staff on what we've done in the year:

Before	*After*
Action points this year	**We've been busy**
Major new product developed	We launched a new product
Key acquisition undertaken	We acquired ABC plc
Group organisation restructured	We restructured our Group

I won't detail the changes, you can see them for yourself. Note three things. Firstly, the *after* has a higher word count. This sometimes happens, but don't worry – low word count achieves nothing if words are inaccessible. *Contemporaneously* is fewer words than *at the same time*, but I know which I prefer.

Secondly, the *after* sounds like we've done something, it's more action-oriented. Finally, the *after* uses *we* three times – isn't that repetitive and wordy? Maybe not. Sometimes it adds impact. Think of Churchill's speech: "We shall fight on the beaches, we shall fight on the landing grounds, we shall fight in the fields…". To we or not to we? Which is best? It's down to personal taste.

There are no Final Thoughts, albeit see Figure 7.2 for exceptions to some of the advice in this Chapter.

What people need – myths 8

Too often we're seduced by flawed 'tips' on how to communicate. "Give people what they want," we're told, "and what they expect". And to keep them happy, give them a narrative. Be positive. Be brief. All seemingly sound advice, yet it often steers us in the wrong direction. Hence this Chapter's tips: don't give people what they want or expect. Be random. Be negative. Don't strive for brevity. This Chapter explains why, plus you also see:

- How to roll out ideas in ways people accept, not reject.
- A fantastic sanity check on all the time-wasting stuff we do at work.
- How to write speeches in minutes, not hours.
- A neat three-letter word to excite interest – it's not known by many.

Myth 1: give people what they want

Or: how to roll out ideas in ways people accept, not reject

Apparently, we should think of our audiences – their wants, needs, preferred styles. And yes, it makes sense. If we want to spend £100k on IT, bosses want to know why. If we've done market research, people want to know what we found. So yes, anticipate and address questions, reactions, concerns (it would be foolish not to), but don't fret too much about how people want to receive it all. Most bosses aren't wedded to the talks or reports they endure, and certainly aren't wedded to the 3-D exploding pies, sub-sub-bullets, and autoshapes they suffer. Just because bosses accept them all, it doesn't mean they like them that way. They just don't know what to ask for instead. Their minds have been corrupted by all the rubbish they've seen over the years.

You know what to do instead. This book tells you. So ignore what you think they think they want and try something new. Imagine that, after reading this book, we wish to redo our weekly five-pager that goes to bosses – and every week they spend 15 minutes asking us questions, all the answers to which are in our report. Below are ideas to help bosses accept our redo, not reject it. The first four are on when we should attempt a redo, the rest are on how to roll it out.

Look for opportunities to try new ideas.	After bosses bug us yet again for 15 minutes, offer to help them: "This report doesn't give you what you want the way you want it – would you like me to save you 15 minutes of your time every week? Shall I try to redo it?"

Or contrive opportunities	At a place I worked, I got the mandate to redo the packs via a bit of theatre – I asked bosses: "Last month, how did we do we against budget?". To their surprise (not mine), the pack didn't tell them. They asked me to redo it.
Wait for a company restructure	It alters reporting lines, comparatives and more, so tweak templates then. Sneak through changes while everyone is distracted with internal politics.
Or just go for it	It's easier to get forgiveness than seek approval. Anyway, if something is conspicuously better, people will probably simply say: "Fine". Or even: "Thanks!".
But dip in a toe gently, don't pilot on something high-profile	Don't redo a 100-pager that goes to 700 people once a year. If they don't like it, it's a visible muck-up, plus we must wait a year to revert to the prior version. Instead, pilot on a weekly five-page note to five people.
Do it piecemeal, perhaps	I took ten months to redo the pack where I worked – and got ten months of brownie points from bosses ("Great, Jon, you've redone three more pages this month"). I had fewer late nights at work. I tested the water as I did it all. Much better than doing it all in one month.
Do two versions – the *before* and *after*	Changes look better when contrasted with the earlier bad five-page *before*. If possible, briefly talk through the changes.
Or do three versions – the *before* and two *afters*	Give bosses the bad five-page *before*, a great two-page *after*, and a half-page *after* that's too brief. Bosses will approve the great two-pager. PS: make the *before* slightly worse than normal, but not so much that bosses notice…

Also remember that we can't be a prophet in our own land. If we've a new idea, bosses view it that way: our idea. Their junior's idea. Instead, maybe claim it was a guru's – it gives it credibility. When I wanted to tell bosses something a bit off-the-wall or controversial, I'd claim I learnt it from a business professor or FT article. Bosses were more likely to accept it.

So we've seen what bosses want. Soon we see what they expect. Before then, the text box has thoughts on 'trouble-makers': those middle-people who burden us with their 'insight'.

Trouble-makers: "It depends on your audience"

At work, there are two groups. Group 1 are people for whom we prepare reports and talks. They're bosses and clients and are open to ideas. They want an easier life, so if we save them time or effort, they're delighted.

Group 2 are middle-people. They burden us with their 'insight' into bosses' preferences. "Don't change it to that," middle-people tell us, "bosses want it *this* way." Middle-people are trouble-makers who pretend to like new ideas, but rail against them. This book's *Introduction* lists some counter-arguments they use ("There's no right or wrong way to convey information"). Middle-people resort to exaggeration too – if we suggest doing a table, they say: "No-one wants to read 100 pages of dense tables". Annoying.

When all else fails, middle-people resort to their final pushback: "It depends," they patronisingly say, "on your audience". At first glance, it's true – will we be opinionated or cautious? Will we use jargon? Yes, what we say or write depends on our audience, but not to the extent people believe. After all, if it did, why bother reading this book? Why not simply email bosses, ask what they want, then serve it up to them? No. With many reports and talks, we can't survey people to establish preferences – and even if we could, they won't reply. And if they do reply, they won't agree on what they want, other than: "Make it easy for me to grasp". Which is what this book strives to do.

Trouble-makers don't give up easily though. "Someone once told me," they say, "that they like it the way it is." However, don't let a single 'someone' be our guide. Cater for the vast majority, not a one-off... unless that one-off is our boss. But even if he or she is, remember that bosses aren't wedded to what they get, they just don't know what to ask for instead.

Finally, how to get past trouble-makers? Try the *three-version* trick mentioned above – the normal bad five-pager (which is slightly worse than normal, but not so that they'd notice), a great two-pager, and an over-the-top half-pager. If it's an internal report, maybe even suggest that all three go to the bosses. I bet that bosses choose the two-pager.

Myth 2: give people what they expect

Or: would I do it at home?

At work, if we must prepare a talk to tell six people about a plan we've made, most of us would dive into a frenzy of business-like activity – we'd blast out slides, charts, bullets and more. After all, it's what our audiences expect, and surely we must meet their expectations.

Now imagine we're at home and we want to tell six friends about the plan for the upcoming golf holiday. We're less business-like. More cavalier. No slides, charts, bullets. We don't over-engineer. That is, we think about what we want to say, then say it. We keep it simple, we take the shortest

Figure 8.1

Three topics in 60 words
"Hi dear, I've three quick things to bore you with! Firstly, I won 91–85 in last night's game – which was good. Bad news on the building work though – it'll take seven weeks. We do need to sort out our teenage kid – we should tell him he should show more effort, honesty and respect. Sound OK? Good – let's watch telly."

Figure 8.2

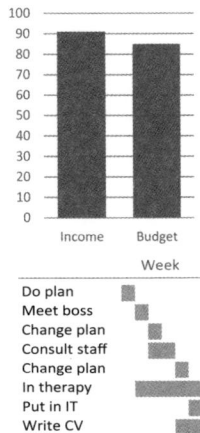

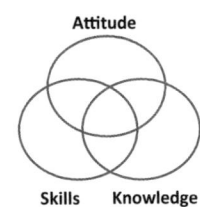

Figure 8.3

distance between two points. And the benefits? We save so much time. We save our 'prep' time – and when our friends hear our golf plan, we save their time too.

Not convinced? OK, try another example. Imagine I wish to convey three points to my wife: (1) I won 91–85 in last night's game; (2) the building work will take seven weeks; (3) we seek more effort, honesty, respect from our teenage kid. At home, I just talk her through it (Figure 8.1). Just 60 words, and that includes opening and closing niceties ("Hi dear" and "Let's watch telly"). The words are quick to say and easy to understand. Now imagine we're at work, and: (1) income is 91, budget is 85; (2) putting in new IT will take seven weeks; (3) we want staff to up their skills, attitude, knowledge. In our report and talk, we do Figure 8.2: a graph, a Gantt chart, an auto-shape. Or – as I like to call it – we do *bumf*.

Bumf comes in many forms, it's more than graphs of two numbers, Gantt charts, and overlapping circles. Bumf includes funky front pages adorned with photos. Slides that outline the agenda (why not just say it?). Chevrons (Figure 8.3). And much more. If we eschew bumf, we save so much time and communicate better. If tempted to do bumf, ask yourself a simple question: **"Would I do it at home?"**. It's a great sanity check on all the crazy stuff we do at work.

However, people express concerns with this question, e.g.: "At home," they say, "we don't do reports". Let's deal with the concerns.

At home, we don't do reports	We do. We just don't call them reports. They're emails, texts, etc. To tell people in writing about the above three topics in Figure 8.1, we simply text or email the 60 words. No bumf.
At home, we don't write 50-page reports – and long reports need bumf	A circular argument: we add bumf because reports are long, but they're so darned long because we add bumf. Remove it, and they're not as long. Of course, bumf-free reports might still be 50 pages – but don't add bumf back. Rather, use WiT, write clearly, etc.
At work, reports are often dull	So what? When we discuss dull topics with friends, we don't enliven the chat with photos and autoshapes.
Bumf gives the veneer of good governance, e.g. in big IT projects	No. Bumf hinders governance – bosses can't see the wood for trees. Bureaucracy trumps control: "We can't grasp this big report," bosses surmise, "but it lets us tick the governance box". For better governance, remove bumf. Shorten. Simplify.

Bosses expect bumf, my partner doesn't	Yes, bosses expect it, but as we saw in the previous section, it doesn't mean they want it.

What about tables? "We don't do tables at home," people say, "so are you saying we shouldn't do them at work?!". Actually, we do create tables at home. Scoresheets for card games and Scrabble. Shopping lists, maybe with costs against items. Also, we devour tables for sports and elections.

Then there's infographics. We increasingly see them outside work. It's a big topic though, so see Chapter 14 for more.

OK, I suppose bumf beats doing real work. Also, maybe it helps if reports are poor. And many are – poor content (bad logic and writing) and ugly layout (nasty look and feel). Their authors know it too, so they strive to improve it all. But improving logic and writing is tough. Improving look and feel is easy though – just add colourful bumf. And my, doesn't it help mask all that tiresome flawed logic! Bosses will surely admire our report. But their admiration will wane when they realise its content is poor. Eventually they realise that bumf is no more than a futile attempt to mask ineptitude.

If still unconvinced, read Warren Buffett's Letters to Shareholders (www.berkshirehathaway.com). No bumf and no need either, for the Letters are wonderfully written.

To conclude, ignore what we think audiences expect. Be less business-like. Do as we would at home. We save time and money – which perhaps explains why we don't do bumf at home: it's *our* time and money we'd waste. At work, it's the company's, so we care less if we waste it doing bumf.

Myth 3: provide a narrative, be logical

Or: how to write talks in minutes, not hours

Ever had to give a 30-minute talk, e.g. a lunch-and-learn, training event or conference talk? Tough to write. You need a narrative – something that ensures coherence. A bit of levity too. That's why this tip is so great: it gives both. Easily and instantly. You write great talks in minutes, not hours, and as we see later, this tip helps reports too.

Step back: we're taught to be logical, yet it's occasionally good to be a bit random. Such as in the wonderful list entitled "Eleven things they don't teach you at school" – and how this oversight creates kids with no concept of reality and sets them up for failure. The list is from the book *Dumbing Down Our Kids* by Charles Sykes (and rumour has it that Bill Gates said them in a speech to kids). Below are just the first four – the rest are on the internet.

1. Life is not fair – get used to it.
2. The world won't care about your self-esteem. The world will expect you to accomplish something BEFORE you feel good about yourself.
3. You will NOT make $40,000 dollars a year right out of high school. You won't be a vice president with a carphone until you earn both.
4. If you think your teacher is tough, wait until you get a boss. He doesn't have tenure.

Charles' list shouldn't work, it has several faults. Items aren't grouped, they're random. Grammar is inconsistent from one point to the next. And so on. Yet it's brilliant. Lists like this are fantastic. Do a list of numbers for your lunchtime talk on HR ("HR in ten numbers"). Or your conference talk ("Our industry in six numbers"). For your training event, try: "The five myths of compliance". Or: "Six things you don't know about IT". And: "Ten things you wish you didn't know about lawyers". Lists are wonderful:

They're quick to write, we fret less over order	When drafting speeches, people agonise over the right order for the points they wish to make. With lists, yes, we must still decide an order, but it takes far less time because our points are *meant* to be a bit random.
We fret less over 'links' too	'Normal' speeches need links that lead audiences through the talk – and as presenters, we agonise over such links. Lists don't need links, we just spit points out one after the other.
They're quick to deliver	Lists are high in content, low in waffle, devoid of links. Just study Charles' list. A model of succinctness.
They create coherence	Lists have a quirky, random charm – yet paradoxically, they give coherence to isolated facts and figures.
They create interest	"IT: the five myths". Or: "IT: five things you don't know". It throws down a gauntlet. People read them to see how many they *do* know.

Three caveats though (sounds like a list…):

1. **Remember to achieve our outcome**. It's not the list that changes attitudes or behaviour, it's what we say within the list. The list is a means to an end, the vehicle by which we convey the points we wish to make.
2. **Maybe avoid for board updates**, especially for bad news ("Cost overruns in five numbers!"…). A bit too idiosyncratic.

3. **Use cautiously in sales**. "Ten sure-fire ways to pick stocks!". In theory, it arouses curiosity, but irritates if overdone. (And avoid exclamation marks! People use them to show how witty and wacky they are!!!!)

Here's another list: six tips on creating and delivering lists. All apply to both reports and talks, although for brevity I refer only to talks:

Don't admit if we've more than, say, ten points – it frightens people	"The 18 myths of sales," the audience thinks, "we'll be here all day." Instead, introduce them as 'The nine myths of sales'. List them, then say: "Hmm… I've still 12 minutes left… no worries, I've nine more". Then carry on.
Don't fear discontinuity between points	It's part of a list's charm. Study Charles' list, it flits discontinuously from one topic to another.
Have a mix of short and long bits	Again, study Charles' list. Some points are brief, some a bit longer. An abrupt one alters the rhythm, wakes people up and avoids talks seeming so metronomic.
Maybe have a mix of core and 'off-the-wall' stuff	'My team in six numbers': our fourth could be: "Ian uses four staples a day – ask me about it later if interested". Then move to the fifth. It mixes things up. (It's true too. Ian did – and delegates did ask me about it after.)
Try an occasional misdirection (part 1)	If presenting, say, six myths on IT, include one that isn't a myth. E.g. say to delegates: "Myth (3): IT is costly", then talk through it, but then conclude – surprise, surprise – that IT *is* costly. That is, it's a myth that it's a myth… Again, it mixes things up.
Try an occasional misdirection (part 2)	For the 'six myths of outsourcing', we might say: "Myth (3): it saves us £5m next year. It's a myth though… it saves us £10m". Yes, £5m is a myth, but the audience expected the real figure to be lower, not higher.

Lists are great in writing too. Need to do a note on what our unit did last year? Want to make it memorable? Try: "Ten things we did last year". Lists are also good for sales tenders. Most tenders include egocentric blurb somewhere within a page of text: "We're third in the industry and have 900 staff in 85 countries, etc". Instead, do as a list in a text box (Figure 8.4), maybe at the bottom of the summary or in the margin. It de-emphasises it, plus readers aren't forced to read it; they ignore it if they want. They probably will read it though, because its heading arouses curiosity, plus it looks idiosyncratic. But – and this is the key point – people read it because

Figure 8.4

ABC Group in numbers

3	Position in industry
900	Staff
85	Countries we're in
27	Clients in FTSE 100
83	Years trading
£2bn	Market value

they *choose* to, not because they have no choice not to. They don't begrudge reading it. Also, it's less egocentric. We're listing numbers, not saying: "Me! Me! Me!". It's quick to read too – it's a table, so is easier to skim and scan, plus it uses fewer words than its continuous text equivalent. All in all, Figure 8.4 is great for boasting without boring. One last comment though: it lists features. Benefits would be better. Also, here are some *do's* and *don'ts* on how to lay out such tables:

1. Express numbers impactfully. Don't say: "1.5m: schools that use us". Say: "One in four: schools that use us".
2. Don't pimp it (shading every second row, funky reversed fonts, etc). We want to de-emphasise it, not draw attention to it.
3. Avoid ambiguous statistics. "Six: the territories in which we operate" – but what's a territory? North of Taplow? Or Europe?

Also, avoid numerical descending order. Yes, numerical descending helps readers do mental arithmetic – if a table shows 12 sports teams' points, we more easily compute the points difference between teams. However, in Figure 8.4, each row is unrelated to the others – readers won't want to deduct one row's number from another. Arguably, random order is not just acceptable, it's preferable, given it's meant to be idiosyncratic. However, try this: put the most arresting stuff at the top and bottom – they stand out more. In the days of CDs and vinyl, record companies did this with *Greatest Hits* albums – big hits first and last, minor hits tucked away unobtrusively in the middle. Sneaky.

Use this layout also for internal documents. Our IT plan brags: "We run 10,000 computers in eight time zones and deal with 500,000 queries a year". Instead, do something like Figure 8.4.

Lists are good outside work. For my father's 90th birthday, I did "Ten things you don't know about Dad – one for each decade he's lived in". I wrote it in 15 minutes, memorised it easily because of its structure, then delivered it in four minutes. Job done. Lists are also a popular journalistic trick. The day before the 2012 Royal Wedding, UK newspapers had: "The Royal Wedding in numbers" – how many months older Kate is than William, and so on. And if we want kids to know the 11 things they don't get taught at school, a list does the job wonderfully.

One final cautionary comment: lists are idiosyncratic and good for speeches or articles, but don't overdo them. Don't bang on about your 18 business capabilities (3 relate to core business identity, 3 underpin strategy, and 12 are corporate), your 21 goals (13 of which are IT-related), etc. And I once read all that in a report. It didn't clarify and inspire. It confused.

There are two more pages on lists, albeit they apply to talks, so are in Part C.

Myth 4: be positive

Or: use the 'not' word to clarify, generate interest, persuade and more
Here are four positive reasons to be negative.

We clarify: "We *won't* buy companies operating in the USA because we're concerned by its litigious culture." That spells it out. Saying what we won't do narrows down alternatives and clarifies plans. Also, bosses are being negative when they talk about barriers to entry, for they're the conditions when we *can't* easily enter a market. Negative? Yes. Clear? Definitely.

We engage and generate interest: journalists often take the negative view to create reader interest. In 2013, a UK broadsheet wrote about modern manners. Compare three possible headings: (1) How to Behave in 2013; (2) The Guide to Modern Manners; (3) How not to Behave in 2013. The last version draws readers in more. So when you next deliver compliance training, maybe headline it as: "How *not* to pass your audit".

We address concerns: imagine telling staff that we're rolling out budgets down to unit level. Don't just tell them what budgets are. Also say what they aren't. It addresses staff's concerns and juxtaposes them with points we wish to make. For instance, budgets don't compute *the* profit, they compute *a* profit – the point being: it's impossible to compute *the* profit; all we do is compute something close to it.

We don't need a slide, but if we want one, try something like Figure 8.5. The first row juxtaposes *the profit* and *a profit*. As for row 2, it manages expectations – budgets will evolve. And so on.

This construct – *What It Isn't, What It Is* – creates a quick and easy theme for talks. It also helps talks succeed intellectually. By juxtaposing two contrary views, it forces us as presenters to address not just what we want, but what contrarians think. Result: we do more than trot out corporate truisms ("Hey, everyone, budgets help!") and instead address obvious objections and concerns.

We persuade: by being contrary, it helps the obvious seem less obvious. I once read a seemingly dumb sentence: "Communication must be targeted to meet the needs of people to whom it's sent". Surely, it doesn't pass the *Not* test that we saw it in Chapter 1 – no-one would say: "Communication should *not* be targeted to meet the needs of people".

But it's not dumb, as we realise when we ponder the opposite thought: "We'll send everyone the same thing, regardless of what they do and who they are". Now that sounds dumb. It also gives clues on how to avoid saying stuff that, on the surface, seems dumb but which isn't:

Figure 8.5

The myths of budgeting	
What it isn't	What it is
The profit	A profit
Cast in stone	Evolving
The way we compute bonuses	An input into bonuses
Etc, etc	Etc, etc

1. Mention a seemingly sensible, but ultimately dumb idea.
2. Expose the flaw in it.
3. Propose the opposite – which now seems really rather sensible.

For the 'communication' example, we'd say: "To update staff, we could do a newsletter that outlines progress. *We won't though*. Staff aren't homogenous, so one size does not fit all. We'll do three different newsletters, plus emails and posters, each tailored to – and meeting the needs of – different audiences." Much better. Our words are more compelling and persuasive.

So next time, don't write in a tender: "To design your new IT, we'll work closely with your staff". Instead, try this: "We've designed IT like yours many times, so can design it for you. But we won't. Not without first talking to your staff. It's your IT and must meet your needs, etc".

Note the following about being negative:

It's like strawman arguments – but isn't: by looking at the opposite of what we seek – "Let's not be targeted in our comms" – we see that targeted comms are better. Valid, helpful. In strawman arguments, we look not at the opposite of what we seek, but at a deliberately misrepresented, exaggerated version of it. We saw one earlier: "Do a brief table", to which the retort is: "No-one wants 100 pages of dense tables". Invalid, unhelpful.

It's like magicians' misdirection – but it isn't: misdirection is when magicians wave around their left hand to prove they've nothing up their sleeve, whilst surreptitiously sneaking coins into their right hand. The 'communication' example is actually a *paraprosdokian* – we take the conversation one way, but reveal it to be something unexpected. It's a comic's best friend – Groucho Marx said: "I've had a perfectly wonderful evening – but this wasn't it".

Negatives can backfire though, so here are cautionary comments.

We might demoralise: "Currently, we can't do this, can't do that, and can't do the other, so give us cash for new IT please". Depressing. Instead maybe paint an upbeat picture of the future, not a downbeat picture of the present.

Bosses might not like them: a boss of mine often told me: "Don't tell me what we shouldn't do, don't bring me problems." His remark was laughably ironic – but also helpful. It told me how to do work he liked.

We might unwittingly insult: say: "As you probably know," as opposed to: "As you probably don't know". Assume people are informed, not ignorant.

We might confuse: positives are easier to grasp, plus they can seem less bureaucratic and bossy. "Don't invoice if it's not a widget" – it creates a riddle. Instead, use the positive: "Invoice only if it is a widget". Also, avoid confusing openings: "We shouldn't accept this won't happen". Instead, say: "This could happen".

I often see such riddles. A market-research note said: "When respondents view a neutral result as negative, the number of replies that falls below the target rate of 65% dramatically increases as compared to when they view a neutral response as positive". Eh?! Readers get taken in opposite directions too often, too quickly – "… neutral… negative…falls… increases… neutral… positive". It reminds me of the line in the movie *Airplane II*: "Dunn was over Unger, and I was over Dunn". Rewrite, taking care to avoid too many directional changes: "When people view 'neutral' as bad, we miss our 65% target more often".

I saw something similar in a budget report: "There was an underachievement in breakdown reductions, despite an overachievement in servicing costs – which seems odd". Again, too many directional changes. Instead, try this: "We spent more on servicing, yet still had more breakdowns – which seems odd".

Two last points on being negative. Firstly, there's the movie *It's A Wonderful Life*. George Bailey (James Stewart) wants to commit suicide, but his guardian angel, Clarence Odbody, intervenes not by talking up the present ("Things aren't as bad as they seem"), nor by looking at the past or future ("You've had a great life/will have a great life"). Instead, he shows George what his hometown would be if he hadn't existed. It's negative in two ways – negative news because he did not exist. And it worked. George saw how his actions had touched many lives in great ways over the years – and he went home and sang songs with his family. Heart-warming stuff.

Secondly, there's the marvellous advice given to Homer Simpson by his life-coach: "NDC – Never Don't Concentrate". And, as I sometimes say to people, never don't avoid clarity by not using negatives properly…

Myth 5: be brief

Or: don't strive for brevity; strive for clarity

Many bosses insist on one-page summaries to spare themselves from bulky reports. "Give me SOAP," they say, "Summary On A Page" (what a horrible acronym). They insist on brevity. However, it's flawed thinking. Yes, they get shorter notes, but the notes are still dreadful. For good reason too – if someone can't write a decent ten-pager, they won't write a decent one-pager. Writing isn't a test of duration like, say, jogging ("Can't do five miles? Just do one instead"). It's more akin to singing – I have a poor voice, so it matters not if I sing one song or five: I sound awful. Also, it's tough to write short notes.

When bosses ask for brevity, they confuse cause and effect. Brevity doesn't produce clarity. Rather, clarity produces brevity. Ask for clarity and we often also get brevity. It's a by-product of clarity. (And if wondering how to get clarity, read the rest of this book.)

But whilst it's easy to gauge brevity (three pages is shorter than six), it's tougher to gauge clarity. So think not of *reading time*, but of *understanding time*. Imagine we have a confusing two-pager on topic ABC and a clear four-pager on XYZ. We read the two-pager more quickly than the four-pager, but we then must read the tough two-pager again. And again. Then we ask its author to pop to our desk to talk through it. On *understanding time*, the clear four-pager wins by a mile. Don't judge reports on brevity or *reading time*. Judge them on clarity or *understanding time*.

Here are Final Thoughts:

1. If readers' needs were all that mattered, you wouldn't need this book to find out how to do something different for them: you'd just ask them.
2. Do you show bumf – graphs, slides, visuals – to friends in the pub?
3. Lists even work for Chapter recaps.
4. Don't always be positive.
5. This list is quick to read and understand. Brevity and clarity. Neat.

Achieving outcomes 9

Apparently, people act on facts. So, to persuade people, surely we simply drown them with facts. Tables, analysis, graphs and more. And if the facts relate to our audience, we're home and dry, no? No. This Chapter explains why. It takes you from conveying information to achieving outcomes. Let's start with something seemingly mundane. Competition law.

Logic and analysis – a short half-life

We've three tasks on our desk – we want to do the following:

1. Get blasé staff to comply with competition law that prevents price-fixing.
2. Convince sceptical bosses to spend more on soft-skills training.
3. Roll out to cynical staff yet another quality initiative.

Of course, not everyone is blasé about laws, sceptical about training, cynical about quality. But some are. We must overcome lethargy and suspicion. Here's how we typically proceed with these tasks.

Comply with competition law: we gather staff in a room, then bore them for 20 minutes. We talk through rules, contrive half-baked communal benefits ("We avoid time-consuming litigation"), and suggest staff visit the firm's intranet to find out more. But they don't.

More soft-skills training: we benchmark ("We spend less than competitors"). We cite studies that 'prove' £1 on training reaps £3 in extra profit. We hope sceptical bosses now believe in training. But they don't.

The quality initiative: we give a talk, replete with statements of the obvious: "Errors cost money, harm reputation, create work, etc". We hope people make more effort to avoid them. But they don't.

Sound familiar? Despite facts and evidence, nothing changes. That's because logic – and analysis – helps us generate ideas and reach conclusions, but often isn't the best way to persuade others to go along with them. It struggles to get under people's skin and win hearts and minds. We nod along to it – but don't go along with it. That's because:

We can all too easily dismiss it if we want: we convince ourselves the analysis is flawed. Or different to our circumstances and not applicable. We dismiss it as theoretical. Or 'logical', as if that's an insult.

Often we struggle to remember it: result: even if it convinces us when we first hear it, we don't remain convinced. How can we stay convinced if we don't remember why we were in the first place? Logic and analysis has a half-life. Often, it merely beats us temporarily into submission.

Which means we're unlikely to tell others we're convinced: after we read a report, imagine we bump into our bosses who ask us: "Was the report good?". We won't say it is if we can't recall its specifics – we'd look foolish. "You say it's good," our bosses would think, "but can't remember why?!?".

This last point – not telling others – is key. Even if people like our thinking, they won't say they like it if unable to recall the detail as to *why* they like it. In fact, it's worse. People will say they don't like it even though they did when they first heard it. It's a huge reversal of fortune: people like our thinking, but tell others they don't.

But what to do instead? That's next.

Revisiting the three tasks

Competition law, training, quality – here's what I've seen people do instead.

Comply with competition law: at corporate away-days, group legal often gives a dull half-hour compliance talk. No-one listens. Except when Keith Packer talks. He travels the world as a speaker at such events. Halfway through the day, a boss introduces him: "Keith will speak for 30 minutes on competition law". Yawn. People start surreptitiously texting and emailing. Keith starts: "I was commercial general manager as part of the leadership team of a Big Company – until a career change four years ago: I spent eight months in America. In prison. For not complying with competition law." Stunned silence. Mobiles get turned off. Jaws hit the floor. Delegates listen. He continues: "I lost my job, reputation and money – I had to pay a big personal fine. Please listen… competition law matters."

Keith doesn't talk about rules (he didn't really know them, but does now…). Rather, he says how prison affected him, his wife, kids and career. He scares people. Group legal loves it – it raises awareness massively and is the best training they've done in years. Impactful. Behaviour-changing. Afterwards, people beat a path to group legal to ensure they haven't unwittingly crossed a line – "At an industry conference recently," they say, "I chatted with a mate who works for a rival. I've not broken rules, have I?". They don't want to go to prison.

Soft-skills training: when bosses asked an in-house analyst to look into this topic, he found the firm spent just £19 per person per year on it. His Big Idea was therefore simple: spend more. Surely no-one would argue against that, especially if he presents evidence: "Just £19 a year". No. Some bosses would debate the £19 figure to death: "What was last year's spend? What do rivals spend? Is the spend effective?". They'd ask him to benchmark and come back in two months – then ignore his report. The analyst needed more. So when presenting his Big Idea to bosses, he started with two words. "Pot plants." After a pause, he said: "We spend three times more per person per year on office pot plants than soft-skills training."

It hit home. Bosses felt embarrassed – is this how we look after staff?! No-one debated the figure ("Do we get value from plants…?"). The analyst silenced opposition, and – as we see later – did much more too.

The quality initiative: to persuade people to reduce errors, a manager told staff about a $220m typo – in 2005, a client asked its stockbroker to sell one share for 610,000 yen (£3,000), but the broker entered numbers wrongly and offered to sell 610,000 shares for one yen each. Result: online investors placed orders until the broker spotted the error. It honoured the deals, losing $220m.

OK, this story hasn't the same shock value as Keith or pot plants, it doesn't scare or embarrass. But it does amuse and intrigue. It makes staff think: "Something like that could happen to us".

A scare story. A ludicrous comparison. A crazy typo. All three eschew analysis. No competition rules. No benchmarking stats. No 'sensible' reasons to avoid errors. Instead, they all have something else. That's next.

Repeatability – a chain reaction

Tell people about Keith, pot plants or a $220m typo, and they tell others. Our ideas spread because we've given them *repeatability*. And when we do that, there's a great outcome: we start a chain reaction. People are willing and able to repeat our ideas to others. They even go into bat for us because we've given them the ammunition and vocabulary to do so. If, a few months after we start the training, someone asks why we "waste money" on it, colleagues can retort: "Shall we spend it on pot plants instead…?".

Repeatability breathes life into ideas. They soar. We change attitudes and behaviour. And how to get repeatability? Answer:

Don't think like an analyst. Think like a journalist.

Journalists turn boring facts into riveting reads. In the 1980s, Kelvin Mackenzie was editor of *The Sun*, the UK's biggest newspaper, and he somewhat chauvinistically told his journalists to give stories the *Cor Doris* factor. He wanted people to read a story, then turn to their colleague and say: "Cor, Doris, read that!".

Repeatability. Cor Doris. Call it what you want – your choice. And to get it, you need an *arresting angle*. Keith, pot plants, and a $220m typo are all arresting angles on dull topics (compliance, training, quality). They bring the topics to life.

Whilst angles work in both talks and reports, they're often better in talks. You've more opportunity for theatre or dramatic pauses ("I've two words to say… pot plants" (pause)). In talks, you can milk ludicrous comparisons more effectively. And the word *prison* is scarier when spoken.

So for repeatability, use angles. But how to find them? That's next.

How to get repeatability

Keith tells me he raises awareness, but I know he does something else: he scares people. He makes his audiences feel something. He presses the *feel* button so well, people rush off to learn the rules. When you next draft reports or talks, step back and ask yourself: "What do I want my readers or audiences to *feel*?". When we do this, it's fantastic. We think about the reactions we seek. About buttons to press – and words to use – to get those reactions. We hence make it more likely we achieve our outcomes.

And what might we want people to feel? Nervous? Happy? Miserable, suicidal, confused, angry? Try the Seven Deadly Sins: pride, lust, greed, envy, gluttony, anger, sloth. Fear's not a deadly sin, but it's why people buy insurance ("What if you die soon?"). I'm not advocating 'fear' and 'scare' as a new business fad. Rather, if used judiciously, they have impact.

There is more to say on the *feel* button (common mistakes, frequently asked questions, etc), but that's for later. Instead, we've another source of repeatability to look at. Years ago, I listened as an in-house analyst explained to bosses why they should not proceed with an acquisition. "In our industry," he said, "there aren't first-mover advantages." To support this statement, he presented analysis (by Michael Porter, the Strategy Professor). I liked it. Bosses didn't – they weren't going to let 'MBA guff' stand between them and a juicy deal. His comments weren't landing punches.

Then he said: "After all… the second mouse gets the cheese". Memorable. Persuasive. Bosses dropped the deal. Of course, it wasn't entirely due to the mouse–cheese comment – it was canned for several reasons – but I know two things: (1) the comment made bosses sit up and listen; and (2) when bosses spoke about why the deal was canned, they spoke about mice and cheese. The comment worked.

But why? Not because it presses a *feel* button – for it doesn't. Ask yourself: how does the sentence make you feel? What emotion does it evoke?

Not much. On hearing about mice and cheese, I can't imagine you feel angry or pleased or whatever. OK, maybe you *feel* persuaded, but that's not emotive.

Rather, the sentence prompts agreement. It's a statement of logic, not emotion. However, it's *accessible logic*. Which means it engages – study these two opening sentences:

"There aren't first-mover advantages – let me explain why."

"The second mouse gets the cheese – let me explain why."

On hearing "first-mover advantages", we hunker down, fearing a blizzard of MBA-speak. On hearing "mice and cheese", we almost sigh with relief. "Phew," we think, "we won't be blinded with science." Our ears are open, not closed. And if the presenter then lapses into some MBA-speak, we give it the benefit of the doubt – that it was said only because there was no alternative.

To conclude, for repeatability, try: (1) accessible logic – which mostly works on the head; and (2) the *feel* button – which mostly works on the heart (and Figure 9.1 explains where I first stumbled across this *feel* idea). Head and heart. A complementary double-act. So far, so good. Next we see problems that arise when people put it into practice.

Repeatability: some do's and don'ts

There are many misconceptions and mistakes about repeatability. Here are two *do's* and four *don'ts*.

Do strive for more than unprompted recall. It's not enough to be memorable or for something to stick	Yes, tell me "£19" repeatedly and I remember it – but I'll still debate it to death. Yes, create an acronym for your strategy ("B-R-I-L-L!"), and yes, I remember it – but that doesn't mean I agree with it or follow it. Also, tell me something outlandish ("I went to Mars"), and yes, it's memorable – but I won't repeat it to others, for it's neither credible nor believable.
Do ensure you have your analysis	Analysis and angles are complementary. Analysis helps us reach conclusions, so have it to hand too, just in case.
Don't worry about slides and visuals	People say: "Make slides visual to give talks more impact". No. Find a decent angle. That's how to achieve outcomes.

Figure 9.1

Andy Maslen and KFC

Andy Maslen's book *Write to Sell* is wonderful, but tucked in the middle is something truly magical: Andy says to put *KFC* in our work. What do we want people to Know, Feel, Commit to?

When I read it, I was stunned, I'd never thought along those lines before. Within a week, I'd rewritten my entire website. I removed facts ("I've a great alternative to bullets") and wrote to get reactions ("Imagine doing work others praise and envy. That gets results"). Much better.

Andy says that KFC is great for sales pitches (his book teaches how to write so people buy stuff from us). He's partially right. KFC is great not just for sales pitches, it's great for *any* talk and report.

Finally, one last comment: a client of mine liked this KFC tip. It was KFC.

Don't worry if you don't hit home runs (part 1)	Mention pot plants, and bosses don't instantly spend more on training – but it does prevent dumb debates on whether £19 is enough. Keith doesn't tighten compliance – but he makes people want to learn the rules.
Don't worry if you don't hit home runs (part 2)	Sometimes two bits of accessible logic go head-to-head, and neither wins. Think of mice and cheese – someone might counter: "The early bird gets the worm". Neither comment triumphs. But at least our opponent's accessible logic doesn't prevail.
Don't think it's 'Telling Stories'	Telling Stories is trendy, and as Chapter 15 describes in more detail, Stories need roadblocks, villains, heroes emerging triumphant, etc. Repeatability doesn't. Keith went to prison. If he'd emerged triumphant, his story fails. The broker that lost $220m cancelled the Christmas party. Hardly happy.

Also, don't confuse repeatability with elevator pitches (let's call it 'pitch'). Imagine I'm a procurement expert and you ask me in the elevator: "What do you do?". I reply (cue cheesy sales voice): "I save firms money when they buy stuff – I saved your rival £10m, I can save you £10m". Memorable. Enticing. You might just reply: "Wow! I want to find out more – let's have a coffee for 15 minutes". My pitch teases. Entices us to meet. A good pitch.

But it's not repeatable because, as it stands, it lacks credibility. If you repeat it to your bosses, they might patronisingly say: "Surely you didn't fall for that baloney…?". But no worries, for pitches aren't aimed at your bosses – they're aimed at you.

All of which means pitches overlap with repeatability – but aren't the same. Successful pitches needn't have repeatability. Some do, of course – if I add credibility to my '£10m-saving' claim, my pitch will be top drawer. For more on elevator pitches and credibility, see later in this Chapter.

That's repeatability. Next we see misconceptions of the *feel* button.

The *feel* button – misconceptions, mistakes

Isn't the *feel* button merely a resprayed *objective* button? That is, if we think more clearly about our objectives, wouldn't we arrive at the *feel* bit anyway? Often no, for several reasons:

There are many different *questions* we could pose...	We agonise. "What's my objective?" we ask ourselves. Or: "What's my purpose?". Or: "What outcome – or behaviour or future – do we seek?" We go round in circles.
... and many different answers we could ponder	If thinking about a conference talk to improve compliance, group legal could grapple with many possible objectives – see Figure 9.2. A mix of general and specific. Also, some are subsets of others. Not easy.
There's often more than one objective	Yes, there's an overarching objective – if pitching, it's: "Win the account". If rolling out rules, it might be: "Impress my Boss!". But often there are sub-objectives ("Achieve A, B, C").
They've a hierarchy and are diverse too	E.g. we must achieve A before B and C. Also, objective A requires staff to agree with us, B requires them not to disagree, and C requires they do something.

Figure 9.2
1. To reduce errors by 50%
2. To reduce fines by 10%
3. To increase office audit scores by 10%
4. To get every office to pass their audit
5. To tighten compliance
6. To raise awareness
7. To motivate staff to find out more
8. To scare staff
9. To reward staff for better compliance
10. To show my boss I'm ready to promote
11. To show up other speakers

Because objectives are so broad and multi-layered, people can spend ages debating them. The *feel* button is more specific. It ignores facts and actions, and focuses solely on feelings. Which is great – but, I admit, it won't always get us the right answer first time:

We dream up something too high level: think of compliance – when group legal wonder what to do at the conference, they might think: "I want staff to feel *motivated* to learn rules". A feeling, yes, but too high level to help much. That's because, to motivate, we can reward (greed) or punish (fear), so group legal need to decide which button to press.

We dream up something dull: when I helped a small charity that saves lives, its boss was completing an application form to get funding. I asked him: "When people read your application, what do you want them to feel?". He replied: "That we're competent". How underwhelming. "Can you imagine them," I said "saying to their bosses: 'This lot are *competent* – let's fund them'?" The conversation won't happen. *Competence* lacks repeatability.

We dream up something too nebulous: I was talking to someone about his mailshots to his group members. "When reading them," he said, "I want members to feel engaged." *Engaged*?! It didn't give me much to work on, so this time, I ignored the *feel* button and instead said: "What do you want them to *do*?". "Feel engaged," came the reply. I tried again. And again. Until I got the answer: "Attend our weekly local events". Bingo. When members read about events in his mailshot, we want them to think: "I must attend". The mailshots should *entice*. Tease. That's the *feel* button to press. Much better.

But when striving to make people feel something, don't just spout adjectives. "Our great talk!" "Our Fab New Idea!" Also, don't reel off adjectives to denigrate Old Ideas. "My New Idea," I read in business books, "is better than *dull* bullets and *monotone* speeches". Chapter 11 talks more about adjectives.

Next we see how the *feel* button achieves a bit more than just repeatability.

The *feel* button – more to strive for

When thinking about the *feel* button, don't just think about what we *want* people to feel. Think about what we *expect* them to feel. It helps us **join dots** and **anticipate problems**.

We join dots: most monthly finance packs start with a one-paragraph summary that goes on about cash, net assets, profit, ratios ("That's up, this is down, etc"). When people read these isolated facts, what do they feel? Miserable? Happy? Who knows. They must work it out themselves. Instead, join the dots for them. The best opening line I've seen in a pack is: "We've had a good month". That spells it out.

So, when we list the five changes needed to comply with new industry rules, do a lead-in that addresses how people should feel about it all.

We anticipate problems: imagine we want bosses to approve a ten-page list of new tighter rules. Don't just do a covering note that says: "Please approve them". Instead, think about what we *expect* bosses to feel – strive to anticipate and head off problems. With tighter rules, bosses have conflicting emotions. They fear everyone will drown in admin. They worry that local bosses will rebel against the rules. However, they're also relieved that frauds are now less likely to happen on their watch. So address it all: "The new rules are tighter, but create little extra admin. Local bosses are fine with them, save for Widget Boss who thinks etc". It reassures.

Sometimes the problems we anticipate are mundane or obvious, but do still address them. If sending out a 100-pager and we know people expect five pages, address it: "Most is in the appendix". If it's five pages and they expect 50, make a virtue of it: "To save you time, it's five pages – I've more if you want it".

Then again, maybe there's no problem to anticipate because we're pushing on an open door – readers are fine with our plan. So keep our report brief, otherwise we risk saying something that unnerves.

However, do keep it in perspective. OK, we reassure and hence anticipate problems, but it hardly passes the *Cor Doris* test. Also, we join dots and summarise, but it won't necessarily persuade. "It was a good month," we say, yet bosses could all too easily decide otherwise when they see the numbers.

We're halfway through this Chapter. There's a bit more detail to cover – on angles, unprompted recall, pitches and credibility. But let's recap first.

1.   Often, logic has a short half-life. We struggle to remember it, plus if we don't like it, we find 'reasons' to reject it.
2.   On the other hand, repeatability starts a chain reaction. Ideas soar.
3.   Repeatability is more than being memorable or making ideas stick. It's giving readers and audiences something they're willing and able to tell others. And it's more than spouting adjectives ("Our exciting product!").
4.   To get repeatability, think not like an analyst but like a journalist. Strive for an arresting angle, i.e. something that passes the *Cor Doris* test.
5.   Accessible logic works on the head, the *feel* button on the heart. Also, the *feel* button focuses our thinking and prevents us agonising over objectives.
6.   Remember to summarise (join dots) and anticipate ("What do we *expect* people to feel?"). If we're telling people good news, say so. Don't leave them to work it out for themselves.

Of course, there are other ways for ideas to soar. Such as the tactics espoused by change managers, e.g.: find early-adopters. Form RATs (Rapid Action Teams). Publicise success. Contrive to let bosses think that our idea was in fact theirs. Etc. But this isn't a book on how to manoeuvre ideas through corporate jungles. Let's move on.

More on angles – finding and using

To ensure you've a good angle when you need one, build a library of them. Watch out for decent quotes and stories. Our stories needn't be real, they can be apocryphal. If they are, admit it – if the story is good enough, it still resonates. Figure 9.3 is a great story that mocks business-speak, and when I tell it to others, I always admit that it might be a myth.

Cartoons can be great angles. To persuade people to be patient with teething troubles during, say, an office relocation, try Figure 9.4: it's a cartoon of Moses holding back waves. Its subtext is: "Don't moan about tiny problems when I perform miracles". It's more effective than a slide of bullets, one of which says: "Please be patient with teething troubles".

Figure 9.3

Apocryphal or true?
An accountancy firm asked a marketing agency to do its corporate brochure, and the agency blasted out a draft. The firm loved it, they thought its words encapsulated how the firm was different. The agency then admitted that the words in the draft were from a competitor's brochure. "You obviously don't know what makes you different," said the agency, "so first you need to work it out."

In other words, many marketing brochures promote bland, not brand.

Figure 9.4

"What do you mean... 'it's a bit muddy'?"

The cartoon gives people a vocabulary to help us – if during the reloca-tion, someone moans that their PC fires up more slowly than before, the person at the next desk might say to them: "What do you mean… 'It's a bit muddy'?!?!". People go into bat for us.

Or try a quote. Pot plants help persuade some bosses to spend more on training, but what if other bosses don't want to spend anything? Try Warren Buffett's comment – he says his golf professional says to him: "Practice makes permanent". That is, practice cements bad habits. The statement is logical. And accessible. Accessible logic.

Think of your audience though; some may think cartoons trivialise. Also, don't breach copyright. If you can't get permission to show a cartoon, maybe describe it. Radio 4 does this a lot.

Think laterally; avoid clichéd ideas

If you need an angle and you've nothing to hand, think laterally. Often it doesn't take long to find one. The $220m story was found by Googling 'most expensive typing error'. If we want people to visit our website to find out more, give them a reason to do so, something more than just: "Visit the website to find out more". Instead, put a personality quiz on the web-site, one that people complete and which relates to our initiative – we all like stuff about ourselves. Or a competition with a prize. Or something we vote on. Maybe arouse curiosity – it's tabloid-y but try: "Discover the most expensive typing error". In other words, think like a journalist. Let your mind wander when sitting on the train. Or cleaning your teeth. Or in the car. Decent ideas often surface when we're offline.

Avoid clichéd photos though (rowing eights, mountaineers, etc) – Chapter 13 explains why. And avoid clichéd metaphors such as ostriches and sport. That is, to encourage change, don't talk about ostriches with heads in the sand – and to motivate staff to beat competitors, don't bang on about rugby tackles. If you must refer to a metaphor, do it quickly and in passing, plus don't expect much from it: it rarely sways people.

Do we need a budget to do all this? Yes, if we want Keith to talk at our conference. But if we're teaching compliance to some new joiners, that's not cost effective. So try DIY-scaring. Get them together for 20 minutes under the pretence of teaching them the rules, but casually chat away before the start. "Where's Ian? No, wait… he got fired for breaching rules." Turn to someone else: "How's morale in your unit? Oh… don't you know? They lost their bonus last year for not following rules". Of course, all these ad-lib lines are well rehearsed and designed to unnerve. Then as we start to talk through the rules, our phone rings (we arranged this to happen), we answer it and pretend a disaster's happened that we must attend to. As we leave the room, say to delegates: "I haven't told you the rules, but no worries – they're on the intranet…". If we've done our job well, staff beat a path there.

When you think you have found a good angle, test it on colleagues before going live with it. Ask if they think it naff or neat. Does it pass the *Cor Doris* test? Ensure it doesn't oversimplify or dumb down. The best aren't about spin and catchy headlines. Rather, they encapsulate and help us do justice to our work. They ensure we don't fall at the first hurdle ("MBA theory") or the last ("Great… but I can't remember it").

When to use angles

In reports, use in the first page. In talks, save the best for first and last. Think *Raiders of the Lost Ark*: the boulder scene at the start, and at the end, the ghostly spirits of the Ark wiping out baddies. Also, by starting with our angles, we prevent opponents using theirs first. I learnt this lesson from bitter experience, having got it wrong for several years. When discussing graphs on Courses, I'd start with logic – I'd test delegates on typical graphs, and conclude that the graphs were poor, only for someone to then say: "But a picture paints a thousand words". The phrase is so well known, people nod along with it. It puts me on the back foot. Not good.

Now I start with accessible logic. When I begin the *Graphs* section, I ask: "Who does graphs at work?". Hands go up. I then ask: "Who does them… to show friends in the pub?". Delegates stare quizzically. "Are you for real?" they think. I then give examples of how we might do them at home. Dumb examples, that is – page 15 in the *Graphs* Chapter has details. I then conclude: "If a graph paints a thousand words, we'd do them at home… but we don't". As an opening, it works. The *Graphs* part of the day is now a much easier journey for me. OK, some people still retort: "But a picture paints a thousand words", but because I've got my 'retaliation in first' – and because other delegates see we eschew graphs in the pub – this 'thousand words' phrase isn't as compelling. It faces an uphill struggle to gain acceptance, so people say it more diffidently.

More on unprompted recall

Below are three ways to help people have unprompted recall. But note that even if people remember our comments or ideas, they might not necessarily agree with them.

Repeat, repeat, repeat. Say something enough times in talks or reports and people remember it. If we want staff to remember the key message within our shiny new change initiative, repeat it. On posters, mouse-mats, stress balls, etc. Make it the corporate screen-saver. The options are endless.

Use big fonts (this one's more for talks than reports). Want bosses to remember a figure in our talk, e.g. that staff turnover is 30%? We could show bullets on screen (Figure 9.5). However, 30% is hidden, submerged by words. Bullets don't help unprompted recall – of all the bullets you've seen on slides, how many can you remember? Hardly any, I bet.

Instead, show just '30%' on screen. On its own. In font size 200. OK, it's not repetition, we show the number just once. But we show it LOUDLY. It's big, memorable and gives unprompted recall. Also, we don't spend long preparing slides, it takes ten seconds to prepare. It doesn't make a good handout though. We look at handouts in Part C of the book (*More on talks*).

Big fonts also work for words. To ram home the need to plan, just write 'Plan' on screen, again in font size 200. Focus on the one message we wish to convey, then convey it in a way that's understood and remembered.

DANA ('Do A Neat Acronym'). Acronyms help us remember stuff. For music, Every Good Boy Deserves Food. For document design, try C-R-A-P, as Chapter 6 explains. Sometimes, minor tweaks turn isolated lists into something memorable. One client had five action points to beat its rivals; by changing "Investigate" to "Find", they became "FIRST". And I'll always remember a stockbroker's review of a company just before it went bust: "Can't Recommend A Purchase".

However, yes, acronyms remind, but they don't help persuade or convince. If your strategy spells B-R-I-L-L, don't delude yourself. B-R-I-L-L doesn't argue the strategy's merits with either emotion or logic.

Sometimes, however, acronyms can impress and influence. I once saw a manager's report on his 'change' project – the report was to reassure bosses he was on top of it all, but it was full of facts, dates, long words. Bosses struggled to see the wood for trees, so the report did the exact opposite of what it was meant to: it unnerved. But by tweaking a word, the three bits of the project became: being Aware, being Ready and doing Training. The ART of change: Awareness, Readiness, Training. Better. The manager now looked on top of it all – he rose above detail and summarised it in a way people grasp. Also, the ART acronym helps bosses look clever – they could use it in front of others, and so look like they know all about change. And making bosses look good is always a neat move.

But – and this is key – the acronym doesn't persuade bosses that ART is right. Rather, it helps persuade them that the manager is up to the job.

Finally, which fonts are best for recall? To understand which, step back. There are two types of font. Firstly, there are *monospaced* fonts – e.g. Courier

---

Figure 9.5
Key findings
- Staff turnover a concern
- It's currently 30%
- Above industry average
- Near a tipping point
- Blah, blah, etc

New – in which letters are equally spaced, as if done on a typewriter. Figure 9.6 shows *ill* and *wow* in Courier New, and they're the same width. Then there are so-called *proportional* fonts – e.g. Times New Roman and Arial. Figure 9.7 shows *ill* and *wow* in Arial and they're different widths. Researchers found that people remember written stuff more if it's in Courier New. They reckon it's because the font slows reading, and if we take longer to read something, more sinks in.

I have two conflicting thoughts on this.

Ignore the research: I suspect those being tested had to read it so they could then be tested on it. Reality's different. If it's tough to read, we don't read it.

Don't ignore the research: direct-mail people do tests on mailshots to see which get better response rates. Headlines that cite benefits or that arouse curiosity? Long or short emails? Monospaced or proportional fonts? And they find Courier New gets the best results. Direct mail isn't something we have to read, so there must be something in it.

On which side of the fence do I sit? Study this book – there's no Courier New. I'm sorry, but even if it helps recall and mailshots, it's still achingly ugly.

Figure 9.6

```
ill.
```
wow.

Figure 9.7

ill.
WOW.

More on credibility

I do wonder if this section is a bit off-piste for this book. Also, a lot of it seems a bit obvious. But given what I see – given what people put in pitch documents – maybe it isn't. So here goes: what should we say when we meet people and wish to establish credibility? Tricky, for it's a case of different strokes for different folks. Some people are fine if we really go for it ("I'm the best!!"). Others would hate listening to such immodesty. Here's a page of thoughts on what to say or write:

Think of the *BID*: Buyer, Influencer, Decision-maker. To convince my father of something, I need first to get to his golf mates.

Don't just claim; prove: make it real. Talk through an example, or quote a client testimonial. Figure 9.8 illustrates the difference between a claim (weasel words that leave little imprint) and a real example (which entices).

Build a library of examples that covers all bases: if we say we're creative and knowledgeable, get a couple of testimonials and stories for each. After a while, we've an armoury of credibility-enhancing material.

Remember: people are cynical: "Involved with…"? Or: "Made the tea…"?

Reassure: tell people that our ideas have worked before. No-one wants to feel they're a guinea pig.

Figure 9.8

Don't claim. Prove

Here's some weasel words from a CV: "I grasp the commercial, strategic and financial issues, then design innovative structures that resolve issues."

Yawn. Instead, try this:

Innovating structures

The CEO asked for my thoughts on a dead-locked deal. I created an earnout structure that was new to the industry, and the deal progressed. My structure became the Group template for future deals.

Strategic analysis

I was brought in on a deal near completion and did commercial, strategic and financial analysis that highlighted previously unknown problems. The deal was re-negotiated, saving millions.

It's more words, but also way more enticing. It doesn't give too much away either, and so arouses curiosity. And it's from my CV from the 1990s.

Different strokes for different folks (again): how might someone react if we mention we've worked with Goldman Sachs? Impressed? Unnerved (after all, Goldmans is the 'vampire squid')? Indifferent? I once told a prospect about my clients (IMF, World Bank, etc) to which she idly said: "Shame no airlines – they're one of our clients, so it would have impressed my staff".

Be brief (10 to 20 seconds maybe): few people want to hear egocentric monologues. Rather, entice quickly. If people want more, they ask for it.

Think journalistically: at the start of Courses, I rattle off four names of huge companies where I've given Courses (it takes just three seconds to do this) – then say they all went bust afterwards. It impresses, yet also shows authenticity and humility.

Make your rehearsed lines sound natural: avoid sounding over-rehearsed.

Type of purchase? Elevator pitches and *feel* buttons work better on consumer purchases, not corporate ones. Chapter 15 (*Story-telling*) explains more.

Finally, see Figure 9.9 for a bit more on elevator pitches.

Figure 9.9
More on elevator pitches
There are many types of pitch. The brief and blunt: "I save firms millions – would you like that?". The evidence-based: "I help companies buy stuff – last year ABC's systems were blah, and then I did blah, and they saved millions". And the stupid: "I deliver web-enabled paradigm shifts". Some are less than ten seconds, others are up to two minutes.

But two minutes is too long for most elevators – and for monologues too. It would bore. Limit to ten seconds. Leave people curious and wanting more. Also, don't have an elevator pitch – have several. Maybe a blunt one and a more evidence-based one. I've three. One for bosses, one for staff, and one if chatting socially. I then have follow-up spiel – usually a mix of the elevator pitches I've not used, plus some name-dropping (client names), etc.

More on the stories (Keith, pot plants, etc)

This Chapter is on achieving outcomes – yet ironically it rarely tells you them. Yes, you hear about Keith, pot plants, typos – and yes, you hear short-term outcomes (bosses don't debate the £19 figure, etc) – but what happens next? Does compliance tighten? Training spend rise? Errors plummet? To be honest, I don't know – but even if I did, I wouldn't tell you, and that's because I've read too much business-book nonsense. "When launching the new product," the book declares, "the CEO adopted my Seven Steps for Great Speeches and sales took off."

There are 101 reasons why a new product sells (great R&D, doubling of sales force, huge advertising, discounting, etc). "Heck, though," a CEO thinks, "let's claim it's because of the guru's Seven Steps. If I big up the guru, and the guru bigs up me, it's win–win". So – with the CEO's permission – the guru writes: "It sold in huge numbers because of the brilliant CEO's brilliant speech – and that speech followed my brilliant Seven Steps".

"Yeah, right," I think. If you've read this far in this book, perhaps you think a bit like me, so maybe you feel likewise about such claims. And you'd think worse of me if I made such claims. So I don't. Instead, I tell you why I believe something works. If it resonates, good. If it doesn't, I've given it my best shot, but to no avail. And no spurious claim of mine will convince you otherwise – as I say in this Chapter, if we don't like an idea, we decide it's wrong, flawed, irrelevant. So if I then make a spurious claim about an idea that you think is dumb, I've doubled my trouble – I try to justify my dumb idea with a dumb claim. Not good.

Final thoughts

A thought, a Figure, a postscript.

The thought: when we use logic and analysis, I reckon we convince people. Temporarily. When we use arresting angles and strive for repeatability, we leave people convinced. Much more permanent.

The Figure: Figure 9.10 is another example of accessible logic and is from a brilliant business book about the takeover madness of the mid-1980s.

The postscript: when I talk about Keith on training days, people often ask incredulously: "Did he really go to prison? Or is it just a fictional story, made up for dramatic effect?". People can't quite believe it happened. It did. I flew across the Atlantic to visit him in prison. We've known each other since the age of 14, and are godfathers to each other's kids. And the success he's had since coming out of prison has been great to witness.

But whisper that quietly, it's not part of the story he tells at conferences.

Figure 9.10

Accessible logic from the book *Barbarians at the Gate*

The author describes how Ross Johnson, a senior manager in a drinks company, eschews analysis for something more impactful:

"Other directors were even more taken (with Johnson). His easy charm contrasted sharply with the prickliness of his boss (Wilson). Wilson plowed through a five-point discourse on why the soft drink Canada Dry didn't fit into the strategic plan and therefore must be divested. Johnson simply told directors: 'You could walk on water with that business, and holy hell! There's the boys from Coke and Pepsi waiting for you on the other side'."

Barbarians at the Gate by Bryan Burrough and John Helyar, page 103

10 Your first 30 seconds

What should we write at the start of reports and say at the start of talks? Answer: jump straight to the heart of the story. Hit people with messages, conclusions, recommendations. Interest in seconds, not bore in minutes.

Sounds obvious – surely we all do this anyway. No. In reports, half of so-called Summaries don't summarise; we see why later. As for talks, many presenters start with agenda, objectives, methodology and more. Result: within one minute, delegates are bored rigid, eating their fists in frustration.

Hence this Chapter. We look at reports first, then talks.

Start at the end in reports

In reports, state the conclusion at the start. It gives readers context with which to more easily judge findings that follow. Years ago, I heard a great phrase: "Start at the end". Newspapers start at the end, they summarise stories in the very first sentence ("Yesterday, peace broke out"). The rest of the article then adds detail to this opening sentence.

It sounds obvious, yet here's what happens in many reports:

Many are like Agatha Christie novels: imagine a report that assesses three alternatives (e.g. in-house, joint venture, outsource). The report introduces the three alternatives, gives background to each, throws in red herrings, kills one off halfway through, then – at last – gives the big reveal on the final page ("It's the joint venture!"). It's a 15-page magical mystery tour.

Many Summaries don't summarise, they introduce: they say:

"We've done a due diligence. We spoke to people, asked questions, reviewed documents. Please see the report for what we found."

That's not a summary, it's a methodology. Also, many Executive Summaries merely signpost (and this one really existed):

"This paper gives updates on responses to the consultation paper, outlines developments in the market, analyses options going forward and seeks approval for the proposed decision outlined in this paper."

So uninformative. Its last bit ("seeks approval") is also pointless – no-one would say: "We recommend (B)… but *don't* want you to approve it".

At the start, don't tell people what we've done. Don't tell them what we're going to tell them. Instead, tell them. State the conclusion at the start, then add key details. E.g. the first bit of a due diligence report might say:

"We should buy the firm. We can protect against its few bad points with warranties in the contract. We should pay £30m, spread over four years. The next step is blah, blah, and the timetable is… etc."

This helps readers better judge the rest of the report. We appear focused and action-oriented – we look ahead at outcomes, not backwards at analysis. "However," people retort, "surely readers need background." Such as:

Specific context: in 2014, I read a report that looked at what the firm should do about the internet – and its entire first page told us about the internet: "You can look stuff up on it, download stuff from it, people use it at work, at home, etc"... Pointless. Boring.

General context: i.e. tired clichés such as: "Pace of change quickening… only constant is change… global competition… change to survive". They're all 'NSS' remarks – they make people go: "No Sh*t, Sherlock".

Elmore Leonard was a crime writer who had ten rules for fictional writing (Figure 10.1). His tenth rule is a bit tongue-in-cheek, but it's great and applies also to business writing: "Try to leave out the part that readers tend to skip".

If we really think readers need context, be brief. Two or three lines at most. Maybe merge it with the opening sentence: "We want to buy a French rival and merge it with our existing French unit so we become market leader, and I recommend we buy this one, etc…". It makes our reports pacier – within one sentence, they're up and running.

There are two *do*'s and five *don't*s to starting at the end:

Do start with outcomes, not findings	If presenting market research, the outcome isn't: "Here's what we found". It's: "Here's what we should do". We do surveys not to find what people think, but how we should change. Start with that.
But **do** say if outcomes are beyond our remit	Maybe we do the survey, and others decide what to do about its findings. No worries – still start wherever our 'end' happens to be, albeit highlight early on that we stop short of making suggestions. However, maybe have one or two up our sleeve in case someone puts us on the spot.
Don't delude yourself – really start at the end	People tell me: "My report starts at the end – on page 1, I give context, outline options, then recommend". No. The recommendations don't arrive until halfway down page 1, and that's not starting at the end.
Don't worry if our very first words aren't: "*We should do* blah blah"	Yes, put recommendations in the first two or three lines, but don't fret if it's not the start of the first line. In the 'buy-French-rival' example above, the recommendation comes after 21 words and it's fine.

Figure 10.1

Elmore Leonard rules for fictional writing

1. Never open a book with weather.
2. Avoid prologues.
3. Never use a verb other than "said" to carry dialogue.
4. Never use an adverb to modify the verb "said"… he admonished gravely.
5. Keep your exclamation points under control. You are allowed no more than two or three per 100,000 words of prose.
6. Never use the words "suddenly" or "all hell broke loose".
7. Use regional dialect, patois, sparingly.
8. Avoid detailed descriptions of characters.
9. Don't go into great detail describing places and things.
10. Try to leave out the part that readers tend to skip.

Don't fall for the argument: "Readers know that conclusions are at the back"	Readers can flick to the back and read conclusions if they wish, so surely it's fine to leave them there, no? No. Flawed logic – some dog-owners leave dog-mess on pavements, and even though we learn to sidestep it, it doesn't mean it's OK to leave it there.
Don't worry that people might skip the rest of our report	Fear not. Counterintuitively, it's the other way round – if we put conclusions first, people are more likely to read on. We've made it easier for them to engage with our content.
Don't feel you must call it 'Executive Summary'	Why not just Summary? Or something that gives the headline (e.g. "Buy the French rival for £30m").

What if we can't give recommendations? Some people say to me: "We can only give options, not recommendations – bosses don't think we're bright enough to give an opinion". Personally, I think that is a crying shame, but if that's you, see the bottom half of page 117 for what to do.

Then there other bits to a report. There are paragraphs – start at the end for them too. People often write stuff like this (albeit with longer words and sentences – I've shortened and simplified so it works better as an example):

"Interest rates are down from the start of this month. Our cash balances are lower too. Also, we're taking on less investment risk. Therefore, our interest income is lower this month".

When we read the three bits on rates, cash and risk, we don't know where it's going, and so must remember it all. It's a strain on our memory. When we reach the punchline ("income's lower"), we reread it all to ensure it all fits together. Instead, it should start at the end: "Income's fallen because etc". This also helps writers limit themselves to one idea per paragraph – which is good. When we put the paragraph's conclusion at the start like this, some people call it a 'topic sentence'.

Then there are lists. As we saw at the start of Chapter 1, start at the end for them too. Finally, start at the end for sections in big reports – Chapter 19 explains more.

> **Why we don't start at the end**
>
> At school, we're taught *not* to start at the end. Teachers tell us to start with objectives, then give methodology, analysis, and finally conclusions. Which is fine for school – teachers already know the answer and merely want to see how

close we get to it. In business though, people only know the answer when we tell them, and they much prefer we tell them sooner rather than later.

But there's more. Often we put the conclusion at the end because that's where the cursor is blinking when we type it. Imagine we're typing a list of eight good and bad findings – we type the eight points, then come to a grinding halt. What should we type next? In a flash of inspiration, we decide to summarise ("That helps," we realise). So we read the list and conclude that overall, it's good. As we start to type that into our report ("It's good"), guess where our cursor is sitting? It's winking seductively at us right after the last thing we typed: the eighth bullet. So that's where we type the conclusion. Don't leave it there though. Put it at the start.

Start at the end in talks

In many talks, underlings present to bosses, maybe seeking approval for plans or giving updates on projects. Bosses have the upper hand. If they don't like what they hear, they interrupt, object and more. Imagine our unit has taken on extra work and needs two more staff – we must present this plan to bosses for them to approve. I've seen this scenario, and I've seen the slides presented in a 15-minute talk. First, slides analysed extra work every which way – how much (about 350 hours per month); where, how, when and why it arose; how it harms internal controls, work-life balance, etc. Slides then talked through the options: (1) work smarter; (2) do less; (3) recruit more, etc. Finally, the preferred option emerged: recruit two more staff.

Awful. It's like the *Agatha Christie* reports we saw earlier. Delegates settle down for a journey of discovery that puts a strain on their short-term memory and forces them to wait 15 minutes for the answer.

Here's how we should start our talk:

"We need more staff to deal with 350 hours of work we've taken on. We could instead work smarter, do less or hand work back to other departments – but none solves the problem properly. So I need £35,000 to recruit two people each at £17,500 a year. It'll take three months to recruit and one month to get them up to speed, etc", then we say: "That's the overview… shall I tell you more about the 350 hours… or options we rejected… or the new recruits perhaps?"

"Etc" means we briefly mention whatever resonates with delegates. If they're into compliance, maybe we say that controls improve. If they're into work-life balance, perhaps we talk about that instead.

That's it. In 30 seconds, we get to the heart of the story. Earlier we saw the benefits of starting at the end in reports – we give context which helps people better judge details that follow, and we appear more focused and forward-looking. All those benefits apply equally to talks. However, with talks we've even more benefits:

If pushing on an open door, we save time	We no longer unilaterally decide to talk at people for 15 minutes. Instead, we have a conversation with people for however long is needed – and if everyone's fine with our idea, we all pack up after one minute. It's not rude to cut to the chase so quickly. It's considerate. Meetings needn't last as long as they're scheduled to. No-one complains if we finish early.
If the door isn't open, we avoid burning bridges	If there's a big gap between what we seek and what bosses will give, it's better if we all realise this sooner rather than later. That way, we've more time to explore alternatives, discuss assumptions, etc. Otherwise, we spend 25 minutes digging a hole for ourselves, and leave only 5 minutes to dig ourselves out of it.
We don't unwittingly undermine our case. When we've made the sale, shut up	If we talk longer than necessary, we may say something that unnerves bosses and jeopardises our case (plus we waste time and bore people). It's not what we know. It's not what audiences need to know. It's what we need to say to achieve our outcome.
We give people unprompted recall of our ideas	People are more likely to remember our key points if we come straight out with them – and Chapter 9 explains the benefits of this.
We avoid irony	We do lengthy talks to persuade bosses we're overworked and need more resources. No wonder we're overworked, we do lengthy talks.
We give people choice	Regardless of whether the door is open or closed, don't assume bosses want to see all our workings. If they want it, give it. If they don't, don't. Let them decide.

The last point – *choice* – is a huge benefit. Starting at the end in talks is the equivalent of WiT in reports. It gives people choice. And in talks, it's fantastic. Bosses have set aside 30 minutes to discuss our report – 20 minutes for us to present, 10 minutes for questions and answers. And in those 20 minutes, we'll show Gantt charts bosses don't want to see. Give background they don't need to hear. And so on. But when we start at the end, we short-circuit it all. After our opening statement, bosses steer the conversation where they wish.

However, give them something else too: the chance to save face, for many bosses don't want to admit they don't know something. So after our brief summary, give them an 'out': "You probably know the context, but so we all start from a common understanding, shall I quickly recap?". A boss may retort: "I know it" (yeah, right…), "but others might not, so go for it".

Let's revisit the 'two new recruits' example we saw earlier: the original slides didn't say the cost of the recruits or what they'd do – but that's what happens when presenters focus on what they know (the past) and not on what bosses need to know (outcome, consequences, future). As it was, bosses knew there was lots of extra work, albeit they didn't know the '350 hours' statistic. Of course, the talk mentioned that figure, but it was hidden deep amongst other stuff. Afterwards, bosses wouldn't remember it.

However, here's the big punchline to this story: bosses were already happy to recruit two more staff. The presenter was pushing on an open door. The presentation could have been wrapped up in two minutes. And would have been, had the presenter started at the end.

There's one final benefit to starting at the end in talks, but to understand it, we must first see how most talks start. That's next.

How most talks start

Starting at the end has so many benefits, it sounds obvious… yet the vast majority of presenters start with agenda, objectives, methodology and scene-setting. It makes the opening minutes eye-wateringly dull – consider the talk to bosses on why we need two more staff:

> "Pat will talk through the analysis – what we spend our time on and how and why it's changed in the last year. Pat also shows our pinch-points – which parts of our department are struggling the most. Les then outlines options going forward and looks at their pros and cons. I then talk through our preferred option, its resource implications and time to implement. Over to you, Pat."

As if that's not dull enough, presenters shove this on a slide (Figure 10.2). It conveys a strong message: "This talk will bore you stupid".

There are reasons why we start talks this way. Firstly, we copy the mistakes of others – they start with the agenda, so we do too. Also, many people know the tip for talks: "Tell 'em what you are going to tell 'em; Tell 'em; Tell 'em what you told 'em". Seemingly sensible, but it makes talks horribly linear. Soon we see a different, more engaging structure for talks.

However, that doesn't fully explain people's reluctance to start at the end in talks – for they are reluctant. Many people are happy starting at the end in reports, yet aren't comfortable doing it in talks. That's because talks have an annoying ingredient: audiences. They interrupt, and that can unsettle

Figure 10.2

Unit ABC resources

1. Introduction, objectives
2. Audit of current situation
3. Options, incl pros and cons
4. Recommendation
5. Benefits
6. Timetable
7. Next steps

presenters. However, if presenting to bosses, it's even worse because some *like* to interrupt, it's their power trip. Interruptions – or the expectation of them – can tip nervous presenters over the edge.

No worries. Start with the agenda, the logic goes. It's a great security blanket, a safe way to start. Presenters get a few minutes of uninterrupted talking under their belts before they reach the trickier bits of the talk.

Dream on. Even if we spell out our agenda, bosses interrupt. And if presenting to malicious bosses, an agenda makes it more likely they interrupt. Such people look for ways to impose their power, and railing against a presenter's agenda helps them do just that. And when they do – be it benignly or maliciously – agendas make interruptions even worse for presenters. We've all seen it happen. Presenters outline the agenda and put it on screen, but a boss then hijacks the talk. He or she interrupts and fast forwards to something that's later in the agenda or moves to a topic not even on it. It's cringing to witness. In effect, it says to the presenter: "You thought long and hard about what we want to see and the order we want to see it… your first slide even spells out the order – *but you got it wrong*." Humiliating. And – unlike with reports – the humiliation is public. If, in reports, someone skips to section 2 before reading section 1, no-one knows.

Now imagine presenting to bosses, but this time we don't hide behind our analysis but instead start at the end. Now, it's different. When bosses interrupt – when they object, fast forward or raise a topic not on the agenda – they're not hijacking our talk. They're doing the very thing we want – and invite – them to do. Earlier I said that, because audiences interrupt, many of us don't start at the end – yet it should be the other way round: because audiences interrupt, we *should* start at the end. It keeps talks flexible.

Some people have questions and concerns though:

Surely we need to tell audiences our agenda *sometime*	Yes, but do it after we start at the end, otherwise our audience doesn't have context to assess it. If discussing an investment and we earmark 15 minutes to discuss it, they don't know if that's too long or too short. If the investment is £100, it's too long. If £10m, it's too short.
What if bosses hate our opening remarks?	We covered this already – better to realise this sooner rather than later. We leave ourselves longer to try to resolve it all. Or – if our talk really isn't salvageable – it's better that bosses kick us out after two minutes, not 22.
Shouldn't we pitch people *before* we present?	Smooth operators already know the outcome before they present – they've lobbied and cajoled beforehand. They know objections, concerns, hostile delegates, etc. If you can lobby beforehand, good. Many of us can't.

So far, so good. But we've assumed we're presenting to bosses. Often we're not. We look at such talks next.

Where presenters have the upper hand

Sometimes, presenters have the upper hand. Such as in conference talks. Or lunch-and-learns to staff on the IT function. Or on HR's staff survey. Then there's the new product launch to Sales. Or the CEO's roll-out of the new strategy. And training events, of course. In such talks, delegates are more deferential and less likely to interrupt. There are other differences too:

A wider mix of delegates	Often there are senior and junior bods (when presenting to bosses, delegates are all, well, bosses).
Different delegate enthusiasms	Some don't want to be there. Others don't mind, but will quickly decide otherwise if we bore them.
A different atmosphere	Project updates to bosses tend to be earnest and humourless (at least, they were in my day), whereas with a lunch-and-learn, delegates hope for a bit of levity, even style. The pressure is on.

So how to start? For an update to staff on some recent market research, here's how it often starts:

> "Today we present our latest market research. First, I look at its objectives and how we revised them in the light of last year based on feedback from key stakeholders. Les then talks through methodology – who we surveyed and how we chose them. Robin talks you through the questions – what we asked and what we chose not to. Sam canters through key findings, then I return to look at lessons and themes."

At which point delegates think: "Kill me now". Starting at the end is better, yet it still might not be enough. Remember: audiences hope for a bit of style.

So try this idea that I learnt years ago: the Three Ks. Kapture 'em, Keep 'em, Konvince 'em (yes, the spelling is a bit off). I like them. Or rather, I *really* like the first one. I'd be fine if it was just the One K (Kapture), for it sums up what we should strive to achieve:

> At the start of our talks, what will we say to make people think: "OK… you have my attention. I'm listening"?

Your Kapture can be quick. Try a teaser ("Guess which office spends longest on the internet…?"). Maybe go straight to your theme: "Morning all. Here are six things you don't know about IT" (this is the 'list' theme from Chapter 8). When I talk, my Kapture is the WiT CV layout from Chapter 1. That wakes delegates up.

Alternatively, try a quote or even a story. Maybe repeat an anecdote that a client told you, for instance (but keep it short – anywhere between 10 and 30 seconds perhaps). With talks, we can indulge a bit in tangents or theatre, more so than in written reports – it's odd to start formal reports with quotes or anecdotes. However, if you're tempted to indulge more – to be a raconteur who takes audiences on a narrative journey – read Chapter 15 (*Story-telling*).

But will *Kapture* and *start at the end* combine to create problems? What if we say stuff people disagree with? I've addressed this for talks to bosses (better to realise problems sooner rather than later), but what about other types of talk (lunch-and-learns, staff survey findings, etc)? If people disagree with our thoughts or findings, might they then just switch off?

No. Play our cards right and they do the opposite: they hang onto our every word. If our material is counterintuitive, use it to make our opening even more arresting. Make the audience think we're going one way (the way everyone expects), then reveal we're going the other way. That grabs them. Rather than illustrate this with a highfalutin example, here's a minor one from my Courses: it's when I talk briefly about jargon, and my message is: "Jargon's fine" (Chapter 21 explains why). But I know people expect me to say the opposite. So, when starting, I pause, then say: "Jargon… sheesh". People expect me to say: "Isn't it awful?" – but I say: "It's great". I can almost hear delegates thinking: "?!?". So I explain. They listen.

Such openings work for several reasons:

We show a bit of panache	Delegates see that we're not just spouting stuff. We've had the style to indulge in misdirection.
We empathise and acknowledge differences	After all, when people say stuff that runs contrary to what everyone thinks and don't even acknowledge it, it seems a bit arrogant. Discourteous.
We've awoken their curiosity	Delegates want to know why we think what we think. "Surely you can't be serious?" they ponder.

Some people fear that this approach gives an opening to those who disagree with us. That it invites them to disagree. No. Firstly, such people often don't need invites, they ache to disagree. Also, because we acknowledge that our comment is a bit contrary, we take the wind out of their sails. They no longer need to disagree with us. We've already done it for them.

Note four points on Kaptures:

Maybe use several Kaptures in a talk	Don't just keep Kaptures for the start. Use them as often as is necessary within a talk.
Experiment to find one that works	If you don't get the reaction you seek, try something else next time. And the next until you do.
Have a face-saver for the disagree-ers who just won't give up	Not a stand-up comic's put-down, of course. But have something that enables us to carry on. Chapter 29 talks more about hostile delegates.
In talks to bosses, use Kaptures cautiously	Kaptures are great for talks that need some levity. However, for talks to bosses, it's safer to play it straight, unless we're sure they like our style and Kaptures.

Kaptures help us impress. Of course, it's easier to impress if delivering good news. That's not always possible though. That's next.

Bad or tricky news

When we make someone redundant or tell the board we won't renew the credit line – that's bad news. When we tell bosses we pencilled in frothy sales forecasts for the 'New Store' proposal (because it was the only way to make our numbers work), it's not so much bad news. It's tricky news.

No worries. Start at the end for both. After all, we prefer that people start at the end when telling such news to us, so start at the end when delivering it to others. Not convinced? Imagine one of our staff is telling us something and after a while we realise they're pitching us because there's news they haven't 'fessed up to, although it looks like they're about to. It annoys us. We resent them wasting our time to manage our expectations. We demand they 'fess up. Not good.

It's no different if we receive tricky news not from staff but from bosses. It's time for the bonus chat, and unbeknownst to us, our bonus has been cut. Which do we prefer from our boss? Five minutes of scene setting, prior to the bonus reveal? Or the boss telling us the reduced bonus figure at the start? Everyone says: at the start.

However, some people believe there are better alternatives:

Shouldn't we manage expectations? Maybe you're the Great Persuader. Think of the 'frothy forecasts' example above – before revealing their frothiness, maybe it's better to tell bosses about the great local demographics, management and more, thereby making it more likely they accept our forecasts. No.

Of course, anticipate reactions, but still start at the end. Get it out in the open. Mention the high forecasts early on, then move instantly to well-prepared reasons ("That's high, but it's what we did in Oslo, a place that's similar, etc"). If our reasons are valid and bosses trust us, we'll be fine. If they aren't valid, we're stuffed anyway, albeit with one consolation – at least we waste only two minutes of the bosses' time.

Can't we bury or hide the bad news? Risky. Bosses might hear it from others – maybe from their boss or from bosses of rival units. Not good. So own up. But bring not just the problem but ways to solve it. Try to turn it into a positive. And remember Nick Leeson. When he tried to hide and trade his way out of bad news, it cost Barings Bank £800m and Nick his freedom.

What if bosses rant at bad news? If we start with bad news and the bosses go on a rant, we won't be able to talk about our ideas to solve it. Therefore – so the logic goes – talk first about what we'll do, then at the end explain that we're doing it to sort out the bad news that we finally 'fess up to. There's a problem with this: when we tell bosses what we'll do, they listen with perplexion, for they don't know why we're telling them all this – not, that is, until we finally confess. It's a trick we get away with just once. For when we try it again, alarm bells ring in bosses' heads: "I've seen this before – Pat's telling me his plan, but I don't know why … bad news is on its way".

But my talks are different…

People tell me they can't start at the end because their talks are different. Below are three examples – the left column gives the reasons why people claim their talks are different, and the right explains why they're wrong. Yes, presenters have valid concerns, e.g. will delegates trust me? Will they understand me? But no, don't address the concerns by making audiences wait for the punchline. Address it properly. And still start at the end.

Why I can't start at the end	What to do about it
The audience know me and won't trust my thinking	Maybe there's a conflict of interest, e.g. we're an investment bank pushing a client to do a big deal. So start at the end ("Do a big deal"), then address it: "We're a bank, so we need to justify that remark or we look foolish – so here goes".

The audience don't know me – and are unsure whether to trust my thinking	They don't know if we talk rubbish. Again, address it. Say something to establish credibility. On training days, I mention I train the IMF, the World Bank, etc. That usually works.
My topic is complex, so I must talk through it S..L..O..W..L..Y (In other words, the audience isn't bright enough to understand it – how patronising)	It's actually the other way round: the more complex the topic, the more we should start at the end. If we don't – if we instead go through the analysis, for instance – we put a huge strain on people's short-term memory; they have nothing on which to hang the facts we tell them. Also, the topic may be complex, but recommendations rarely are ("Buy ABC"), so state that up front. Finally, see Chapter 21 for tips on explaining complex stuff.

Start at the end – training events

We're delivering training on *Advanced Excel*. Or *Better Selling*. But how to start? Not with the agenda – we saw that earlier – but what to do instead? Below are five ways. Which works best?

1. Introduce ourselves (big ourselves up perhaps).
2. Define what we mean by *Better Selling*.
3. Get delegates to introduce themselves.
4. Get delegates into a break-out session.
5. Clarify the event's objectives.

Answer: none of the above. None is a decent Kapture. Instead, start with something that wakes people up, that makes them think: "OK, you got my attention". If it's *Advanced Excel*, show a little-known Excel trick that makes people go: "Cor!". If *Better Selling*, think of something that everyone does (the *before*), then explain why they shouldn't – and show what to do instead (the *after*). In other words, start at the end. Make them feel something.

But to really start at the end, surely we show the *after* first, not the *before*. Strictly yes, but earlier in this Chapter, I said that the recommendation can come after three lines of our report. So too with talks: the *after* needn't be the very first thing we show. It just needs to be close to it – so do the following:

Choose a *before* that delegates relate to quickly	Avoid something that needs too much introduction. We want to move to the *after* in seconds, not minutes. We seek an arresting opening.

Figure 10.3

**Start with sales price
in pitches?**

(Don't expect a definitive
answer, you will be disappointed.)

If it's a written report, it
depends. If answering questions in a tender, retain the
order in which they're asked
– if the 'price' question is
first, answer it first. If it's
last, answer last.

If not part of a tender,
we've more freedom, but
don't put at the end. State
it in the first two paragraphs
of our summary – or at least
on the first half page.

If it's a talk, again it
depends, albeit this time I
don't say where it should
go. There are too many
variables. Is it a one-hour
talk to a panel? Or a half-
hour chat with a person?
Or a ten-minute phone
call? Do we know them
well or not at all? Do they
know our stuff, even if
they don't know us? Are
we incumbent? Insurgent?
Favourite? Outsider? Near
the expected price? Or very
different?

One size won't fit all. It's
disproportionate to devote
the next 11 pages of this
book to dealing with every
permutation. Instead, try
other books.

Don't explain or talk through theory	At this stage of the event, the idea isn't to educate, it's to inspire. Delegates don't yet need to know all the details that make the *after* better.

Let's return to the five alternative ways to start a training event. Yes, do the introductions after the arresting opening, but as for the others on the list:

Don't formally define objectives or define what we mean by *Better Selling*	If we really must cover those topics, slip them casually into the conversation later, almost as an afterthought. Cover them by stealth.
Do breakouts *very* sparingly	I've only one in the entire day, it's not until the afternoon and is brief.

Time for some honesty and an epiphany. In 2005, I set out to earn a crust delivering all-day training on clarity and impact. I had material, but also a problem: I'd never delivered a training day in my life. OK, I'd done training talks before. For one hour. Internally. To people I knew. I was attempting a huge leap – a whole training day with strangers. Tough. That's the honesty bit.

So I thought about all the training I'd attended over the years… then ignored what they all did (that's the epiphany). I hate how most training events pan out: agenda, objectives, definitions (what do we mean by 'clarity and impact'?), timetable, breakout, bullets, breakout, etc, culminating in a poor handout (usually the slides). Trainers do this because of 'perceived wisdom'. Apparently, we remember better if we see it on screen – so use bullets. People can't focus for more than 30 minutes – so have breakouts. Tell 'em what you're going to tell 'em, etc – so start with agenda. People don't know why they're attending – so start with objectives.

I ignored it all. I'm glad I did. As are my delegates.

Time for Final Thoughts. If I wrote a thriller, it wouldn't be thrilling. It would start: "Pat was the murderer. Want more? OK, she had the victim's wallet in her pocket. Still not convinced? She was sleeping with her victim's spouse." Not much suspense.

At work, we want answers, not suspense. So start at the end (or as I've heard it called: BLUF – Bottom Line Up Front). It's fantastic… assuming, that is, we know what we wish to say. Many don't. Many of us *agonise*: "What do I wish to convey?". Chapter 12 helps us get to that nub.

Finally, Figure 10.3 looks at starting at the end in sales pitches.

Words – specific to writing 11

WiT won't guarantee clarity. That's because if we put turgid words in a WiT, they're still turgid. We can put a pig in a palace, but it's still a pig.

Hence this Chapter. It gives tips to help the written word. And my goodness, we need help. At work, many of us speak normally, but write weirdly. We use business-speak. Do you use words like *facilitate* and *implement* at home? I don't say to my wife: "Let's implement a TV strategy".

People write business-speak in slides too. I once saw someone stride on stage and show a slide that described how great last year had been – an easy message to deliver, no? Yet delegate depression set in instantly. The slide had just ten words, but was turgid. We see it soon.

It can easily be so much better. The first half of this Chapter gives tips to make our reports a joy to read. They sharpen our thinking too. The second half then addresses people's concerns (e.g. "Simple words oversimplify").

Business-speak: a modern-day curse

Chapter 7 gave tips for better words – let's apply them to this:

"If there's a successful implementation of our innovative widget, it will ensure optimisation of your operational resources and an enhancement of collaboration."

If we rewrite it with verbs, the present tense, and *you*, it becomes:

"If you successfully implement our innovative widget, you optimise operational resources and enhance how you collaborate."

Better – but still poor because of long words and business-speak: implement, innovative, optimise, operational, etc. Often, we use such words to hype:

1. "We're excited to announce our new team of highly motivated, experienced, dedicated executives."
2. "ABC is a unique sizeable market player with unmatched marketing and entrenched relationships with a diversified and quality customer base."
3. "Our aim is to enhance the competitiveness of your business by exploring innovative solutions for risk reduction."

The last two really existed. Such nonsense is wrong for so many reasons.

It bores and leaves little imprint	People see it and give up. Eyes glaze over, brains shut down. Did you properly read examples (1) to (3) above?
It wastes times and annoys	When we decode it, we realise it says little. Example (3) above just says: "We help you reduce risk".
And so lacks impact	It's said that if we need to explain a joke, it's failed. And if a reader needs to decode our words, we've failed.
It fails to convince – and often that's because it's devalued from overuse	No-one ever says: "Let's award the contract to them – they say they're innovative". True story: when a colleague of mine reviewed websites of 156 competitors, he found they were all 'innovative' and had 'unique' relationships with their markets. Their websites said so.
It dehumanises	It sounds as if it was written not by a human, but by a corporate robot (a corpbot, perhaps).

Figure 11.1

Our successes:
- Assessment, evaluation
- Commercial, procurement
- Logistics, implementation
- Resource management

Earlier I mentioned a slide that induced delegate depression – it's Figure 11.1. It bores, not inspires. Delegates had to decode it to work out what on earth it said. However, it gets worse, for business-speak does more than failing to convey or convince. Often, it hides and hinders decent thinking.

It doesn't properly reflect writers' thinking	Often, when I translate someone's business-speak into simple words, the person who wrote it says: "OK, yes, it does say that… but that's not what I meant it to say". Business-speak confuses not just readers, but writers too.
It encourages lazy thinking – "We're excited to launch our new widget!"	Just because we're excited about it, it doesn't mean others are. No. Think of the readers' emotions, not ours – think of a reason why they should be excited. Then again, I suppose it's easier to trot out tired hyperbole than bother with thinking. Yet when we do think, we unearth stuff far more convincing – in example (2) above, it transpired that ABC was market leader by a long chalk with great historic and forecast figures.
It masks decent thinking	Hidden within five bits of waffle, there's often a compelling sixth point that's struggling – and failing – to be heard.
It masks bad thinking – often hidden within business-speak is flawed logic	So much business-speak to choose from, so little time to use it properly. Think properly though, and we see its flaws. As Warren Buffett says, we only learn who's been swimming naked when the tide goes out. And we only spot flaws when business-speak goes out.

This last point is important. Business-speak can seem sensible. Worthy. Translate it though, and often it's less benign, as these real examples show:

The boast that backfires: the tender says: "We deliver brilliant service," but if service is a hygiene factor, the comment backfires. Brilliant service costs money, and people object to paying extra for stuff they don't need or value. Instead, deliver the *right* service – no more, no less.

The impossible plan: its objectives were the promotion of innovation, enhancement of efficiencies, maximisation of revenues, and improvement of quality. Sounds grand, but several are mutually exclusive. We can't meet them all – so which takes precedence when there's a clash? Who knows? The report's authors didn't know when I asked them.

The wrong investment plan: the boss's plan was to buy a big competitor. It would be *paradigm shifting* and deliver *enhanced customer experience*, etc. After 40 minutes of talking to him and decoding jargon, I finally saw that his industry suffered from diseconomies of scale. After 80 minutes, I saw the deal was to make him market leader. So I asked: "If there are diseconomies, why be biggest?". A pause. "We will," he eventually replied, "*create* economies of scale." He was winging it. I asked: "How?". Another pause: "IT," he said unconvincingly. He knew he was swimming naked. (And if interested in when we can create economies of scale, see Figure 11.2.)

I could continue, it's easy and fun to mock business-speak. Many places do. The Plain English Campaign has its annual Golden Bull awards. The internet has Buzzword Generators to help us create strings of waffle ("enhanced synergistic deliverables"). The joke consultancy website www.huhcorp.com parodies business words. And for a slightly different take on this topic – one that mocks buzzwords in films – watch *Comedian Movie Trailer* on YouTube.

Let's move on. Short words are like WiT. WiT exposes our thinking, and if it lacks merit, we think harder. That is, WiT is about clear thinking. So too with short simple words. They expose our thinking, and if it lacks merit, we think harder until we dream up something more compelling. Simple words aren't just about clear reading. They're about clear thinking.

However, people have concerns. "Surely," they say, "simple words make me look simple, and long words make me look clever." After all, at school we get extra marks for long words. Interestingly, a Professor has proven the opposite – that simple words make us look clever (Figure 11.3). But proof is often flawed, biased or both (my website has a one-page article on this), so let's not put too much weight on academic findings. Instead, think about who impresses you more: someone who explains stuff in ways you struggle to grasp? Or who explains stuff in ways you instantly understand?

Figure 11.2

Fragmented industries
Michael Porter's book *Competitive Strategy* has several brilliant chapters, and one of them gives the conditions under which we can consolidate a previously fragmented industry.

Figure 11.3

Use short words to look clever
According to a Harvard Professor, we should use short words... and streaky toner. Here's why: in 2005, he found that readers make a link between their reading speed and author intelligence – and if we write short words, people read faster and assume we're brighter. So far, so good.

He then redid reports in less readable fonts, then with nasty streaks as if toner is low. Both times, readers struggle to read, but with the streaks, readers know why they struggle and compensate accordingly. Or rather, they seemingly overcompensate and think authors are even brighter. Conclusion: use short words and put streaks in reports.

The Professor won an Ig Nobel Prize for his findings. My website has his 18-page report. The 'less readable font' and 'streaky toner' bits are experiments 4 and 5 – read their introduction and 'discussion' for more.

It's a no-brainer. Any idiot can make the simple seem complex. Many idiots do this constantly. When people use long words, many of us assume it's a smokescreen to hide ignorance. We assume the person doesn't know what's going on themselves. As Einstein said: "If you can't explain something simply, you don't understand it well".

Instead, strive to do the opposite. The more complex the topic, the more simply we explain it. Do this, and we shine. We all see people who rise above jargon, complexity, detail and dross, and make the complex seem simple. Maybe they're pundits on radio or TV, maybe they're people at work – whoever they are, they've such mastery of their topics, they explain tough stuff in ways we understand. And we admire them.

The next section looks at the *do's* and *don'ts* for using short, simple words. Also, the text box looks at some popular but awful words. Please avoid them.

Business words I despise – please avoid

Below are words that are beguiling – they seem acceptable, and many people use them. I never do.

Stakeholders: are we human? Or are we stakeholder? (Thanks to *The Killers*.)

Collaboration: in other words, we talk to people. (Sometimes. If we feel like it.)

Process: increasingly, this word is sandwiched between the words *the* and *of*, e.g.: "Vans begin *the* process *of* removing waste". Instead, try this: "Vans remove waste". Often people use the phrase *the process of* to hide inactivity. "We're doing stuff, even if it's plate-spinning activities that precede real work – we plan, risk-assess, give briefings." However, if you think that the 'process' can give more insight than the output, see my website for some thoughts. Or rather, a rant. Then there is *process to*, e.g.: "Learn the process to do it". Again, rewrite and shorten: "Learn how to do it". However, *process* the verb is fine ("We struggle to process it"). As is *process* the noun, if not followed by *of* or *to* ("Tell me the process"). But given my dislike of the word *process*, I'd still rewrite to avoid it ("Tell me how you do it").

Solutions: should I call this book *Clarity and Impact Solutions*?

Framework: there is a great *Dilbert* cartoon where the boss says to staff: "(We've) a model for developing a process to create a framework" – but then adds: "Or it might be a process for creating a framework to make a model". Sums it up, really.

Invest(ment): at home, imagine I had to pay my cleaning person a bit more, plus replace my knackered car. I wouldn't say: "I'm investing in my cleaning person and a new car…". We don't pretend they're investments – yet we indulge in that

---

pretence at work. But surely at work we sometimes 'invest', e.g. we recruit a new team now because it will generate income for us in the future. Yes, but the future income isn't copper-bottomed. Not inevitable. The new team, I suppose, is a bit of a *punt*. Also, when our firm buys a new costly e-system, often that's not an investment either. Our rivals are also buying one, so we must too – it's the price we pay to stay in business. To conclude, when someone next says *investment*, ask whether it's a replacement (car). Or paying people more (cleaning lady). Or a punt (new team). Or the cost of staying in business (new e-system). I'm not against spending money; I'm against euphemisms.

The do's and don'ts of using short words

1. **Do strive for a short word if tempted to use a long word**. If about to type *commencement*, stop and think: "What about *start*?". The Plain English Campaign's website has a great free PDF download: "The A-Z of alternative words". It lists long words, then gives a shorter, better alternative (e.g. *adjacent to = next to*).

2. **Do use short sentences**. The full-stop gives readers' brains a rest before reading on. Short sentences help when the going is tough. They also stop us piling multiple thoughts into one sentence.

3. **Do think of your Fog Factor**. It measures how readable our writing is. There are many different ways to compute it, but I like this way: it's the number of long words per sentence, where *long* is defined as three syllables or more. The more long words per sentence, the higher the Fog Factor and the tougher it is to read. Strive for a Fog Factor of three or fewer. Three long words per sentence on average. Short sentences help your Fog Factor – cut a sentence in two, and we've the same number of long words but now spread over two sentences. Our Fog Factor halves.

4. **Do talk through your report with a colleague**. Most people use normal words when speaking. Chapter 12 explains.

5. **Do use the language of everyday speech**. Why use one word when speaking, and a different word when writing? Use the same word for both, our work will be clearer. Don't talk about high-net-worth individuals. Talk about the rich. After all, we don't go into a bar and say: "There necessitates the consumption of an alcoholic beverage"…

MS Word and readability
If we ask MS Word nicely, it gives us readability statistics every time we do a spell-check. I don't like their statistics though. My website has a one-page article that explains why.

After a while, short words become second nature. We're about to type *facilitation*, but realise it's an abstract noun and so replace it with *facilitate* – but then realise we don't use *facilitate* at home ("Darling, let's facilitate Johnny's birthday party"). So we write *help* or *make happen*. Easy.

Those are five *do's* of short simple words. Here are ten *don'ts*:

1. **Don't ever compute your Fog Factor**. It's not worth it. Rather, strive to use short sentences and short words.

2. **Don't be afraid to use a long word**. Use it if it's the best for the job and appropriate for our readers. (Or if it's apposite…) But don't surround it with other long words. Keep it in the company of short words and in a short sentence too.

3. **Don't have too many short sentences in quick succession**. They lose impact. It sounds clipped. Stylised. Annoying. Like this.

4. **Don't just strive for short words, strive for everyday words**. Don't say: "We'll retard payment" (I've seen this…). Say: "We'll delay payment".

5. **Don't worry if the final version sounds simple**. Our *before* bangs on about commitment, stakeholder buy-in, project deliverables, robust timetable, ongoing monitoring and so on, yet our *after* says: "We must all agree who is to do what by when, then check it happens". Some people fear it seems, well, a bit simple. That's because, when we cut the business-speak, it is – so keep it that way. Delight in its simplicity and clarity. Remember: readers won't thank us for complicating the simple.

6. **Don't worry about higher Fog Factors in lists**. "The benefits are: we turnaround faster, improve quality, reduce omissions, avoid litigation, enhance management reports, and reconcile more easily". Even without abstract nouns such as *enhancement*, it's still a high Fog Factor (8), yet just about gets away with it because it's a list of similar stuff – they're all benefits. Compare that to a sentence that ebbs and flows with nouns, adjectives, sub-clauses, adverbs, conjunctions and more – readers need a lower Fog Factor to survive such a journey. However, if you fear that the Fog Factor of your list is getting too much for readers, redo it all as a numbered list or in bullets (bullets are fine for lists of brief items).

7. **Don't assume that short words guarantee clarity**. UK politician Boris Johnson once said in jest: "I could not fail to disagree with you less".

8. **Don't patronise readers**. And *patronising* means talking down to people.

9. **Don't write the word *stuff***. Here's a little oddity. Many people say *stuff* when talking. "We saw lots of stuff." "We've still stuff to do." Which is fine. But it's probably best to omit such stuff from reports to bosses.

10. **Don't dumb down or use colloquialisms or slang**. Short words won't dumb down unless we let them. And if we use slang, our report might, like, be dissed, leaving our project, like, totally dead as a dodo.

We started slowly
"There was a slow commencement to the implementation process."

Mental Health Commissioner, Ireland, on radio, 24 January 2013

Adjectives and failed attempts at rigour

Good adjectives clarify. "Look in the red file, not the green one." "Meet in the big room, not the small one." They help. Many adjectives don't though.

Imagine our report outlines what the new proposed IT will deliver: "It will give us," we write, "numbers that are concise, relevant, timely, significant, understandable". We list five adjectives. By doing this, we hope to achieve two goals: (1) design a decent system; and (2) impress bosses ("Look, boss – a long list! How thorough we've been").

But there's a problem looming on the horizon: our new IT won't be adaptable. That wasn't in the list. Nor was accurate. Or scalable. No. If we want to be thorough, we need 15 or 20 adjectives, otherwise we omit something important. But 20 adjectives is nuts. So instead, try this: "The new IT will give us numbers that help us run our business better". Do this and there are fascinating by-products:

Bosses tinker less with our reports before circulating them: if we use five adjectives, our boss then adds four (he or she thinks this is progress) – then their boss adds another and puts them into two groups of five. Pointless.

Readers discuss issues, not adjectives: give people a list of adjectives and they critique it ("Is *thorough* the same as – or a subset of – *complete*?"). Omit the list, and people are no longer distracted by it. Instead they focus on bigger issues such as: "In what way does our existing IT fail to produce numbers that help us run our business?". They no longer grapple with 20 adjectives, but drill down to the two or three that really matter ("Well, boss, our numbers are late and incomplete"). Much more enlightening.

Two adjectives are particularly horrible. Firstly, *strategic*. Don't use it to justify an action, for it's usually the absence of a decent reason. When we ask people: "Why have you priced this so low?", they emptily reply: "It's strategic pricing". Or: "Why pay this new recruit so much?". "It's a strategic hire". Again, empty. Warren Buffett avoids the word – I searched through five of his 15-page Letters to Shareholders and didn't find the word once. Instead, think of decent reasons to justify actions. However, *strategic* is acceptable when it describes, not justifies, e.g. "Make your report more strategic". Then again, why not *high-level*?

Then there's *unique*. I've never used it. And *almost unique* is even worse. Similar, I suppose, to being almost a virgin.

Always consider context before removing adjectives though. The IT boss says: "We need to buy a good system". *Good* seems superfluous – would anyone buy a bad system? Here though, the current system is rubbish, so *good* clarifies. It draws a distinction between the bad current system and good new system. Which explains why there's the occasional adjective in this book. "Here's a great tip," I say. All tips are good. Some are great. And the next tip is fantastic, exceptional, creative and paradigm-changing.

Sometimes I cross-check adjectives between reports. In one unit, its report said the new Application should produce: "A consistent, reliable, collection of authoritative data, delivered in a cost-effective manner to support client-focused business solutions".

Yet the unit's Plan said they should: "Articulate, guide and deliver a targeted, agile, scalable and resilient Application that underpins and facilitates delivery of our strategy". Seemingly, the Plan didn't care about being consistent, reliable, authoritative, cost-effective or client-focused – and the Application wasn't bothered about being targeted, agile, scalable, resilient, facilitating or underpinning. ·

A rubbish Plan, a rubbish Application. If confused, see the Venn diagram below.

The Application

Consistent
Client-focused
Authoritative
Cost-effective
Reliable

What – no overlap?

Targeted
Scalable
Resilient
Facilitating
Underpinning
Agile

The Plan

Finally on this topic, see Figure 11.4 for the fun I once had when analysing two long lists of adjectives.

Nouns – a growing plague in business

Here is a typical introduction to an internal audit report: "Our audit ensures staff follow policies, processes and procedures". But I'm confused – what's the difference between policies, processes, procedures? And even if there is a difference, does it matter?

Sometimes, it's our bosses who add extra nouns to reports. Someone kindly sent me the *before-boss* and *after-boss* versions of a sentence they'd written:

Before-boss: "Goal: to understand how AFJ might develop"

After-boss: "Goal: to understand the workings, capabilities, and limitations of how AFJ might develop"

Bosses do this for two reasons. Firstly, they feel they've made a difference to the report (they have – they've made it worse). Secondly, it's similar to the lists of adjectives we saw earlier: doomed attempts at rigour. It seems more complete to say *workings*, *capabilities*, *limitations*. But it's not. For instance, we omitted *concerns*. How to be complete? Don't add. Remove. Try this: "Goal: to understand the AFJ". An all-encompassing catch-all.

Sometimes we add nouns not for completeness but for defence. "If we omit the bit about policies, processes, procedures," auditors tell me, "the boss of the unit I've audited will say I didn't define the audit scope and hence can undermine my findings". Misguided thinking. The three nouns don't aid clarity – if people don't know what audits are, the nouns don't help, and if they do know, the nouns aren't needed. Also, nouns won't defend us: if people want to undermine us, we have a problem, no matter what we write. And if we waste their time with lots of nouns, they're even more intent on undermining us.

But do I worry too much? It's only three nouns, and that's hardly a crime against clarity. Yes, only three here – but loads more elsewhere. "The audit ensures you comply with rules, regulations, directives, guidance, best practice and generally accepted custom. We review documents, reports, file notes, emails and written representations. We look at controls, checks and management oversight." A whole page to describe what audits do. Pointless. (And I bet you didn't read it all properly, but merely skimmed it.)

Instead, keep it simple. Try this: "We check to see if staff do what they should". Or: "We check to see if staff follow procedures". And if we must say more, bung it in the appendix. But clarity creates concerns – people fear that it now sounds a bit obvious (that's because it is…). So *concatenate*. Don't let obvious comments stand proud in their own sentences – they don't deserve that prominence. Instead, merge with other stuff, e.g.:

Unconcatenated (three sentences, the first of which is a bit obvious): "We checked to see if staff follow procedures. We reviewed deals from the trading desk in June. Based on our review, staff follow procedures."

Partially concatenated (now two sentences): "We looked at 20 deals from the trading desk in June to see if staff follow procedures. Based on our review, they do."

Fully concatenated (now one sentence): "Based on our review of 20 deals from the trading desk in June, staff follow procedures."

The final sentence states the obvious, but without making it look too, well, obvious. It moves seamlessly and quickly onto findings. Also, it has fewer words – 16, down from 24 and 23 for the *before* versions. One third shorter.

Don't just concatenate in audit reports. If writing something a bit obvious ("The strong survive"…), don't give it its own sentence, it doesn't deserve it. Concatenate it with whatever follows ("So we've a new training project").

However, some people have understandable concerns about writing short simple words. That's next.

Concerns with simple writing

Even if you're fine with short words, still read this section – you'll meet people who aren't, and this section helps you stop them in their tracks. Here are the main concerns, which I address in turn:

1. Audiences and bosses want long words.
2. Short words oversimplify and change meaning.
3. It's not appropriate in our organisation.
4. My topic has jargon – surely it's OK to use it.

Concern 1: audiences and bosses want long words

When you read stuff, what do you want? Reports with short words, I bet. Our audiences and bosses are no different. They don't want their time wasted. Think also about people's complaints – they're quick to complain if reports and talks have lots of long words, yet I've never known anyone complain about too *few* long words. OK, sometimes people say: "Add long words, *it's what bosses want*," but they're trouble-makers and Chapter 8 talked about them.

Concern 2: Short words oversimplify and change meaning

I rewrite stuff and people object. The *before* says: "We need evidence to justify our action". I change it to: "We must justify our action". People then say that my rewrite is incomplete because I removed *evidence*. To which I counter: the *before* is incomplete – it didn't say *credible* evidence.

Whenever we speak or write, we simplify. It would be impossible to do anything if we didn't, we'd be bogged down by detail. As the saying goes: "You can be accurate or clear, but not accurate and clear". So the question isn't: "Should we simplify?", but: "By how much should we simplify?". Here are two thoughts:

Readers aren't completely dim: consider the *evidence* example above. Even kids understand the need for evidence. They know it's not enough to say they've done their homework, they must prove it too. Everyone knows we need evidence. So don't waste words saying we need it.

"A difference is only a difference if it makes a difference" (from the great book *How To Lie With Statistics* by Daryl Huff): most of the time, it doesn't make a difference, so it's fine to simplify. When others talk about sustainable competitive advantage (SCA), talk instead about how we're different. Yes, it changes meaning – competitors can copy how we're different, but can't copy an SCA. However, a difference is only a difference... well, you know the rest.

Concern 3: It's not appropriate in our organisation

Study your firm's marketing literature. If it was written by a decent marketing person, it's almost certainly an oasis of short words. And if short words are fine for customers, they're fine for bosses. Also, read the following two paragraphs from internal reports – one's from procurement, one's from a departmental plan. The first is clear, the second gibberish:

From procurement: "We help colleagues buy and pay for goods and services they need in the quickest and easiest way possible, without exposing the company to serious risk."

From departmental plan: "For evolved export markets, we'll have to develop multi-location enterprise-wide transformational solutions while managing margin pressures through process excellence and innovative pricing."

As you've probably guessed, they're from the same company. Often, there isn't a long-words culture. We just mistakenly think there is.

Concern 4: my topic has jargon – surely it's OK to use it

Jargon is a big important topic, so Chapter 21 looks at it in detail.

Those are the big concerns with simple writing. See the text box for other more minor ones, albeit here's one last concern: "Short words," people say, "prevent me obfuscating". Exactly. Short words are easier to understand. No worries though – if you want to obfuscate, do the opposite of what this book suggests: bung in lots of long words and more.

Other concerns with short words

People will see how simple my job is	No. They'll be impressed with how well we explain it in a way they get. Remember: it takes intelligence to make the complex seem simple.
My reports will look different to others	Different – yes. Better too. Good news.
I like language	It's not about our preferences, nor even our readers' needs. It's about achieving outcomes. Which writing style helps us achieve ours? We won't persuade if people don't understand.
Short words make it obvious I've not much to say	The alternative is worse – spout lots of long words, then have people slowly decode it all only to realise we've actually said very little.

Time for Final Thoughts. At work, we've two parallel worlds, and to understand why, think of Buzzword Bingo. Before a talk, delegates get a page with 25 clichés on it ("add value", "blue-sky thinking", etc). They each circle the five that they think the presenter will say, then tick them if they're said. If a delegate ticks all five they've circled, they yell *Bingo*. It's a great game and significantly, most people play it without the presenter knowing – hence the parallel worlds. In one world, presenters trot out business-speak that bores, yet they believe that they persuade and inspire. Delusional.

In the other world, delegates are bored. Confused. As a survival mechanism, they play Buzzword Bingo. Who can blame them? When people use the wrong words, they don't connect. They disconnect.

There is an alternative though: explain stuff in ways people can grasp. It does wonders for your career.

12 Getting to the nub

Chapter 10 says we should start at the end. That is, at the start of reports and talks, give the main story. But what is the main story? When drafting reports and talks, we often struggle to rise above detail. Yes, we churn out tables, graphs, analysis and more, but can't quite put our finger on what it is we wish to convey. If that's you, this Chapter answers your prayers – and as you'll see, it's one of the most important bits of this book.

How to get to the heart of the story

The answer is: talk it through in a role-play. In other words, before we deliver reports or talks, ask a colleague to pretend to be our boss, audience, reader, client – whatever's appropriate. Let's call them the 'Boss'. We then try to give the Boss a 30-second summary of our report or talk. To tee up this conversation, we pretend we bump into each other in the corridor and the Boss says: "Thanks for the report you sent me. I haven't read it and can't make the meeting when you present it. No worries, walk with me now – give me a 30-second summary".

We role-play a 30-second summary. When we do this, two things happen. Firstly, we use simple English (which is better, as Chapter 11 explains). Many people talk normally, yet write weirdly – in our report, we write: "It's a strategic investment for the implementation of an enhancement of greater cross-divisional collaboration". Eh?!? But in our role-play we say: "I want £100k to help us work together better." Much better.

Secondly, we struggle. We ramble. So the Boss *grills* us. He or she prods, pokes and questions for a few minutes, and even repeats it back to us to ensure it makes sense. Eventually, clarity emerges. Our summary turns from base metal (rambling) into pure gold (clear, concise). We get to the nub of our story – and then we put this 30-second summary at the start of our report or talk.

Result: we **start at the end**, use **simple language** and give our thinking **repeatability**. Previous Chapters explain the huge benefits of all these – Chapter 10 (*Your first 30 seconds*); Chapter 7 (*Words for reports and talks*); Chapter 9 (*Achieving outcomes*). I won't repeat them, other than to remind you that simple language helps us spot flaws in logic. Here are new benefits:

We avoid a grilling from our real boss	Better to spend time being grilled by the Boss than waste time with our boss. Also, it's better if flaws in our logic are spotted by the Boss, not our boss.

We may just be asked to summarise in 30 seconds	Many bosses don't read reports or attend meetings, but instead ask for a summary. Also, meetings often over-run, and our 20-minute talk shrinks to two minutes. Including Q&A. So we must summarise in 30 seconds.

Role-play a 30-second summary. It's one of the biggest tips in this book. WiT often cuts reports by 40%, 50%, even 60%. Chicken feed. When we role-play, we often cut reports by 90%. We realise we needn't remind bosses of background and objectives, nor tell them 'the only constant is change'. We needn't tell them all about the alternatives we analysed but rejected because they turned out to be rubbish. We needn't show Gantt charts and flowcharts that make no sense except to those that created them. Instead, we realise we can remove it all (but we still keep it in reserve, in case it's needed).

On my training days, this is the one tip that produces the most 'light-bulb' moments. In the afternoon, break-out groups spend 30 minutes discussing how to improve, say, a 12-page report written by someone in their group. For the first five minutes, they skim-read its key bits in silence, then collectively spend ten minutes *tinkering*. They delete this, reorder that, tweak the other, and more. But alas, it doesn't help much.

Then someone remembers the 30-second role-play I'd mentioned earlier. Bingo. They do one – and the group has its light-bulb moment: "Why on earth does the report have all *this*?!?" They realise that the report should be 90% shorter (done as a WiT too), with maybe a one-page appendix. They slash and burn. Ironic, really – we improve writing by talking.

Role-playing sounds easy, but often Bosses ask the wrong questions and we give the wrong answers. Hence this Chapter. It has four steps. Seventeen tips. Fourteen illustrative questions. We also see why the 30-second summary isn't the same as an elevator pitch. First are the four steps for doing it all.

We speak for a bit, the Boss asks questions	If we meander or confuse, the Boss interrupts and forces us back on track.
The Boss repeats it back	This helps ensure our words make sense. If they do, the Boss repeats them easily. If they don't, the Boss doesn't. It needn't be from memory, the Boss can take notes.
If necessary, try again. And again.	At first, the story is incomplete, confusing, etc – so we both give it another go: we try another 30-second summary, our Boss tries to repeat it back. And so on.

| Stop when the Boss's 30 seconds roughly matches ours and makes sense | At which point we're there. We have distilled our report or talk into 30 seconds and got to the nub of it all. |

Seventeen tips

First are two tips on choosing the Boss:

Choose someone who accepts and questions jargon: they must have the confidence to question jargon and the wisdom to accept it in small doses.

Choose someone who doesn't mind being blunt: they must repeatedly ask us questions, so maybe don't choose someone who reports to you – they might find it uncomfortable grilling their boss.

The table below has 13 more tips. Some briefly repeat stuff seen in other Chapters (e.g. 'Agatha Christie').

Do a 30-second summary, not a 5-second one	"I want £10k to spend on new IT that helps us work together better." Not enough. The Boss needs to know the broad gist of what we want, enough to decide where to drill down next to find out more. So talk through risks, alternatives, timetable, benefits, etc.
Do start at the end – with what we *want* or *need*, or our *suggested changes*	E.g: "I want £100k and three extra staff etc". Don't do an *Agatha Christie* novel ("We've four options"), with the reveal on the last page. And don't give a long history lesson ("Two years ago, we put in new IT etc, etc").
Do give context if needed	But briefly. In two or three lines. Merge with the opening sentence.
Do use *you* as well as *we*	Don't just say: "We did this, we'll do that, etc". Try to include your audience, even if just a bit: "You'll notice this, you need to do that, etc".
Do think of the *feel* button	And accessible logic too. Remember: analysis helps us reach conclusions, but often isn't the best way to convey it to others.
Do reassure (part 1) – demonstrate thoroughness	Maybe briefly outline what we did to reach conclusions – we can describe work without showing it: "We spoke to 20 clients"; or: "Our Gantt chart has 400 steps".

Do reassure (part 2) – demonstrate credibility	Maybe say where our idea has worked elsewhere. Or name-drop about clients. Somehow let people know they're not guinea pigs in a strange indulgent experiment of ours.
Do reassure (part 3) – briefly mention alternatives too	"We could instead do A, B and C, but they're not suitable because etc (*briefly*)". Also talk about the 'do-nothing' option. It helps convey that we've been thorough.
Do think of Rudyard Kipling	Rudyard said: "I keep six honest serving-men, (they taught me all I knew); their names are What and Why and When, and How and Where and Who". Also, Figure 12.1 has 14 questions to ask.
Do add one more to Rudyard's list – "how much"	In role-plays, people often omit a key figure: cost. "I want new IT," they say – but will it cost £10 or £1m? Bosses don't know how much time to devote to the chat. If £10, the chat should stop instantly. If £1m, it needs longer.
Do give context to numbers	We say that the new system spits out reports "just eight hours after the month-end", but how long does it take now? Nine hours? Nine days?
Do cover next steps	Maybe we don't think there are any and that our work is just "for information" – in which case: (1) say so to avoid doubt; and (2) think harder. There must be something that can emerge from our efforts.
Do at least *encapsulate* if we aren't allowed to recommend	If bosses won't allow us to recommend, I think it a shame. But at least help them see tipping points. If your report looks at whether to do A or B, rise above long lists of their pros and cons. Instead summarise how A and B differ in a way that helps others see the wood for the trees. "A is high-risk, high-reward, B low-risk, low-reward". Or: "A is a cheap, short-term fix, B is costly, but sorts us out for the long-term".

Notice in that last point, we compare and contrast. When we review alternatives, it's unlikely that one option is better across the board – rather, we must assess trade-offs and make compromises. So identify and summarise them. When we juxtapose this way, we lift scales from people's eyes – including our own. Everyone better understands.

Figure 12.1
Fourteen questions
1. What if we do nothing?
2. What other ways might work?
3. What trade-offs? Compromises?
4. How much will it cost?
5. How long to do?
6. How long has the problem persisted?
7. Who else has similar problems (rivals) and what have they done about it?
8. How did the problem first surface?
9. Has it worked before?
10. What does it mean for me?
11. What do we need to change?
12. What risks if we do it? Or don't do it?
13. Who will dislike this idea?
14. What do you want me to do?

Then there are the last of the 17 tips: two *don't*s. Firstly, Figure 12.1 lists 14 possible questions – but **don't** degenerate the role-play into a run-through of the list. It won't work. The conversation must ebb and flow and be organic. Also, the 30-second role-play helps every report or talk – from ones that lead to decisions (close branch, buy IT, etc), to ones for information or compliance (market or regulatory updates, etc) – and the list strives to cover them all. You won't need all the questions all the time.

Secondly, **don't** confuse the 30-second summary with an elevator pitch. Firstly, it's longer – 30 seconds, not five. Secondly, it strives to do the exact opposite to most pitches. When I pitch you, I hope we meet after. When I give you a 30-second summary, I hope we don't. That is, if my summary is good enough, we can cancel that meeting we have in our diaries in two days.

Of course, maybe there isn't a meeting in two days, but pretend there is. It's a role-play. And if there actually is a meeting in two days, it still might happen even if my 30-second summary is fantastic – if it's a big topic, bosses may need more than 30 seconds to discuss it. No worries though, for the role-play ensures we get straight to the heart of it all in our reports and meetings. That is, we put our best foot forward and *impress*.

Time to do

Allow yourself between five and ten minutes to get to the nub. But it can take as little as 15 seconds, or as long as 80 minutes.

As little as 15 seconds: OK, it was for just part of a report, but it helps to role-play not just entire reports and talks, but individual bits too. And it's enlightening to study the 15-second role-play – I asked the author of a lengthy internal 'media audit' report: "What's a media audit and why do one?". Granted, the report's *Introduction* told me, it spoke of perception, sentiment, benchmark, reputation, strategy, evolution, communications, status, engagement, enhancement, programme, relationships, yield, journalists, corporate, improvement, investment, and more. More than 110 words over the report's first half-page. It bored and confused. Yet when we role-played, its author explained it in just five seconds: "We speak to others to see how others see us, and see if we need to change what we do". Brilliant.

As long as 80 minutes: imagine we're playing the role of the Boss and someone says their plan is a "strategic development of the gadget range". That confuses us, so we ask if it's a new gadget or better old gadget – but the reply is: "It's a paradigm shift". We try again: "New gadget or better old gadget?", but still no luck: "It's like an improved customer experience," we're told. After several minutes, we realise the old gadget now has a new button. And several more to realise the button lets us turn on the gadget from a different room. Eighty minutes later, we arrive at our 30-second summary. This happened to me once, it's the bit in Chapter 11 where someone wants to be market leader in an industry that has diseconomies of scale.

There are no Final Thoughts, other than a brief plea: even if you work from home a lot and you've no colleagues with whom to role-play, please still do it. Grab a neighbour, partner, parent (retain confidentiality, of course). Or do it over the phone with a colleague. Please.

13 Visuals and photos

People often use visuals at work – and I don't mean stuff like the London tube map. I mean frippery. Circles. Chevrons. Triangles. Etc. The frippery in Figure 13.1 all says *Skills, Knowledge, Attitude*. We refer to it often in this Chapter, so here's the context: it's part of the boss's message to staff: "Business is tough, so strive for these three things". The boss wants staff to have unprompted recall of this message.

The first half of this Chapter tells you when to use visuals and when not to. The second half looks at photos.

Figure 13.1

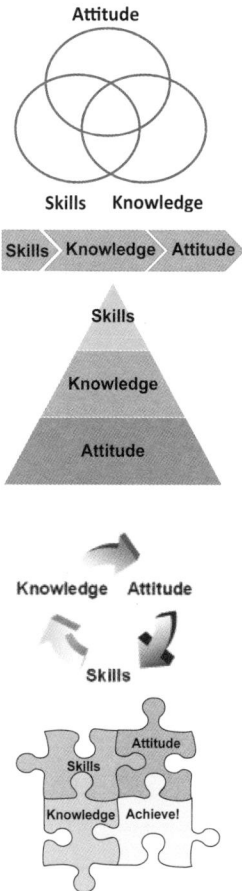

The myths of visuals

Why do we use visuals? Maybe it's because we live in a visual world. And apparently, visuals inspire, persuade and have impact. Also, people like to process information visually. And surely visuals are better than dull text and numbers. Finally we remember visuals. Let's stress-test all this.

We live in a visual world – every day we see and admire brilliant visuals	So avoid visuals unless yours are great, otherwise you look amateur. Are your visuals great? Do people compliment you on yours? Don't fool yourself by saying: "I've won pitches with visual-based talks". Maybe you won despite the visuals. As for liking visuals outside work… so what? We like songs too, but please don't sing any in talks at work.
Visuals inspire and persuade	Some do. To tug at heartstrings, show photos of sick children, sad pensioners, neglected animals. They make us feel something. Three overlapping circles don't (Figure 13.1).
Visuals have impact	This implies that visuals *automatically* have impact. It's as illogical as claiming that everyone with a voice can sing well. No. 'Visual impact' isn't a tautology.
Many people are creative right-brainers	No they're not, they just like to think they are. I covered this in Chapter 2 (*Graphs*).

Surely though, visuals **are better than dull words and numbers**. People often say this to me… yet ironically they convey it to me with words, not visuals. OK, OK, a cheap shot, but there are many cheap shots on this topic.

It's a cheap shot to say that visuals are better than *dull* words and numbers – if we compare something to a bad alternative, we can justify most things.

Anyway, words and numbers can be visual. The slide in Figure 13.2 shows the name of the new CEO (in font size 140 if slide-sized). It's visual. It's not practical to use font size 140 in reports, but we don't have to – below, it's font size 16 and 10, a bit of white space, and a typeface called Impact:

Figure 13.2

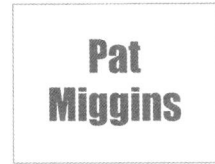

£680 trim wisteria and mend conservatory

It gives a clear mental picture and is memorable. OK, we don't know the context, but that's not important for now.

Then, of course, apparently **we remember visuals**. There's science to prove this too: according to an oft-quoted mantra, we remember 10% of what we read, 20% of what we hear, 30% of what we see, 50% of what we see and hear, etc, etc. These stats justify visuals and have launched an industry of slide-pimping consultancies.

However, back up a bit. Many people hear these stats – quite a few even quote them (PowerPoint trainers do) – yet few know where they're from. A tiny few say they're from Edgar Dale's *Cone of Learning*, but then say no more. Maybe they don't know that the Cone appeared in Edgar's 1948 book on how to teach children. I question whether its tips are relevant for what we do at work today.

However, it gets worse. I bought Edgar's book, and yes, it has a Cone of Learning, but no, there are no statistics. That's because, according to someone called Will Thalheimer, the statistics were made up by an office worker in Mobil in the 1960s[1]. Granted, other more recent research probably 'proves' visuals work. But as I said in earlier Chapters, be careful with what research proves. Instead, consider the following:

(1) see www.willatworklearning.com/2006/05/people_remember.html

Many autoshapes aren't memorable	Of all the autoshapes you've seen over the years, how many can you remember? Not many, I bet.
Many are just weird shapes with words around them	For most of us, when we see Figure 13.3, we remember the shape – and that's it. The myth needs restating – it's not: "Visuals help us remember," but: "We remember the visuals, not the words around them".
Even worse, they hinder unprompted recall	Figure 13.3 fragments words, so it's more of an effort to scan and absorb them. Also, funky autoshapes compete visually with words – and win. People's eyes get drawn to the shapes and colours. Autoshapes attract people in, but distract them from content.

Figure 13.3

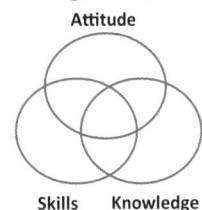

Figure 13.4

Skills
Attitude
Knowledge
or get the sack...

Attitude
Skills
Knowledge...
for promotion

Figure 13.5

Effort

Respect   **Honesty**

Figure 13.6

Ratio 1 (%)

◆ Company A

Ratio 2 (%)

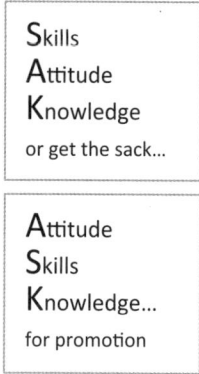

To get people to remember the three attributes, try acronyms (Figure 13.4 – *SAK* and *ASK*). They're akin to the stick and carrot – the first says: "Shape up or get out", and the second says: "Shape up and get rewarded". Which is best? It depends on your approach. Regardless, both are more memorable than the autoshape. Both are visual too, even though they're just text.

Maybe I'm being harsh on autoshapes. After all, when presenters show Figure 13.3, they can talk through its context. However, there's no great context to grasp other than: "Staff need these attributes". Just four words. In fact, let's give not just context but the whole story: "Staff need skills, knowledge, attitude". It is said that a picture paints a thousand words, yet these five words replace the entire visual. If we don't know the five words, the visual means nothing. If we do know them, the visual adds nothing.

Also, **we don't do autoshapes at home**. As we saw in Chapter 8, if we need to tell our 14-year-old son he needs more effort, honesty, respect, would we show those words around three overlapping circles (Figure 13.5)? It wouldn't take long to create, we could scribble it out in just ten seconds. But we don't. Instead we connect with our son in a way he feels: we talk sticks-and-carrots ("Behave well, we reward you; behave badly, we ground you"). Yet at work we show three overlapping circles. It's strange, really – we think more intelligently at home than at work.

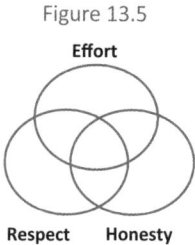

There are many illogical reasons why people use visuals (and I haven't even addressed a popular one: "Visuals are good, so we should use them" – a ridiculously circular argument). However, let's move on. I'm not against visuals; I'm against bad visuals. Next we see when visuals work.

When visuals work

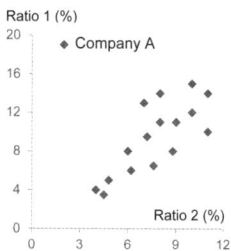

In Figure 13.6, the dot labelled *Company A* is set apart, and that's because there was a huge fraud in it – more on that soon. However, I did the graph not to tell you there's been a fraud – I do that easily enough in words (I just did). Rather, it's to show how accountants failed to spot it. To understand how, we need context. The graph plots two accounting ratios for 17 companies – x-axis one ratio, y-axis the other. Don't worry what the ratios are, just go with the flow. Each dot represents ratios for one of 17 companies. The ratios lie in a band that goes up at roughly 45°, except for Company A's where the fraud distorts its ratios. It really happened, I plotted a similar graph whilst investigating a multi-million pound fraud.

Now you know the context, the graph is far better than words or a table of numbers. People effortlessly see what accountants and auditors failed to spot – that something is awry with Company A. The graph isn't instantly understood though, it needs context – but then again, all visuals need context, even pictures of lonely pensioners. When context is known though, there's a virtuous circle. Context helps readers understand shape, and shape helps readers remember context. The shape is the story. Hence the graph would be fine even if its labels were in Latin. In a talk, we could still show the graph to demonstrate how the fraud distorts Company A's ratios.

Then there's the information pyramid (Figure 13.7). It shows the three types of information needed to run businesses (strategic, operational, tactical), and it shows how the volume of information decreases as we move up the company. At the bottom, there's shedloads of tactical stuff to help junior managers run teams. Then there's operational stuff to help middle managers run divisions, albeit not so much of it. At the top, there's a small amount of strategic stuff to help bosses run the group.

The visual works because its shape is significant – it reinforces the decreasing amounts of information as we move up a company. In fact, let's go one further and say: it's the only autoshape we could show for this hierarchy of information. We couldn't show overlapping circles, circular arrows or whatever, for their shapes aren't relevant.

Compare this to the *Skills, Knowledge, Attitude* we saw earlier (shown again in Figure 13.8). We could trot out any autoshape for it and it wouldn't matter. The shape isn't significant, it's just decoration. OK, some people say its middle bit – where circles overlap – highlights the intersection of Skills, Knowledge, Attitude. Big deal. It's a weak argument, partly because we know people trot out any autoshape for it. Also, if overlaps are significant, what about other overlaps then? Which is better: Skills, Attitude, but no Knowledge? Or Skills, Knowledge, but no Attitude? At this point, proponents of such autoshapes counter: "You're being too literal, too analytical… it's only symbolic". Which is a euphemism for: "The overlaps don't really mean much". (Of course, overlaps sometimes matter – but real Venn diagrams are rare.)

However, consider this: yes, the information pyramid works as a visual, but we can live without it. If the projector fails and we've no flipchart, we can talk through it in just 68 words with little loss of impact or understanding (Figure 13.9). It works as a visual, but works also in words. Compare that to the fraud graph we saw earlier. If we can't show it, it loses impact.

Let's draw threads together. Here are questions to ask before we do a visual – if we answer *Yes* to any of them, our visual has a reason to live.

1. **Does it work in Latin?** Good visuals work without words, bad visuals work only with words. Remember though: all visuals need context.
2. **Does it replace many words?** "Staff need skills, knowledge, attitude". Five words. The information pyramid needs more, but not many more.

Figure 13.7

Figure 13.8

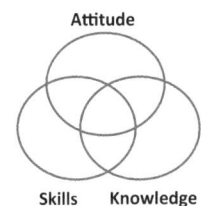

Attitude

Skills   Knowledge

Figure 13.9

A visual that paints just 68 words

"Bosses need information to run businesses – strategic, operational, tactical – and the volume of information decreases as we move up the company. At the bottom, there's shedloads of tactical stuff to help junior managers run teams. Then there's operational stuff to help middle managers run divisions, albeit there isn't as much of it. At the top, there's a small amount of strategic stuff to help bosses run the group."

3. **If it has a shape, is it significant?** In good visuals, the shape is the story (e.g. Company A's dot is different to others). In bad visuals, any auto-shape suffices – it's merely a weird shape with words on it.

4. **Would we do it at home?** Would we do 'overlapping circles' to explain effort, honesty, respect to our son?

Apply these questions to the visuals above, and the circles-for-staff-attributes gets four *Nos*, so we ditch it. The information pyramid and fraud graph both get at least one *Yes*, so they've reasons to live. None of them gets a tick for Question (4) though – we wouldn't do them at home. In fact, we struggle to say we'd do any work-related visual at home, so should we even bother asking Question (4)? Yes, for it reminds us that we get on fine at home without visuals. It's a reality check.

If we decide to ditch a visual, what can we do instead? It depends on the outcome we seek to achieve. Chapter 9 covers that topic.

Next are Final Thoughts on visuals. After that, we move onto photos.

Figure 13.10

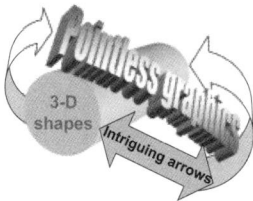

Figure 13.11

The US 'food pyramid'
For almost 20 years, the pyramid had taught Americans what to eat. It showed good stuff at the bottom (bread, rice, pasta), and at the top was a small triangle of bad stuff (fats, sweets).

But in 2011 it was scrapped – the Agriculture Secretary said it was "very complicated", plus some people had mistakenly interpreted it upside down: fats and sweets are at the top, so we should eat them the most. The US Admin-istration replaced it with another shape: a pie chart of food.

But pies can be bad for us so it said it was a **plate** of food: *MyPlate*. Maybe in 20 years, it'll bite the dust too.

Visuals – final thoughts

Ever since the 1980s, we've had a great time creating funky stuff to mask flabby thinking or paucity of content. Not got much to say? Worried our work looks a bit… *empty*? No worries, pad it out with triangles, chevrons – or even intriguing arrows (Figure 13.10). That fools people. It may even fool them into thinking that we're clever. After all, chevrons-in-a-line 'prove' our ideas are logical and linear. Venn diagrams 'prove' they're unified, inter-connected. Circle-of-life diagrams 'prove' they're iterative. Easy. Visuals spare us the tiresome task of logic and thinking. Yet:

1. In Chapters 1 to 12, how many times have I resorted to a visual to help explain my ideas to you?

2. When the US administration ditched a famous visual in 2011, it made front-page news. Figure 13.11 explains.

3. See my website for two articles that wade into visuals, one by the UK journalist Matthew Parris, the other from the Harvard Business Review (entitled *It's Time to Retire 'Crap Circles'*).

4. I haven't mentioned clipart, so here goes. Use only for people who are easily impressed. Such as junior-school children. Enough said.

Photos – choosing good ones

We've all been moved by photos of sick children, sad pensioners, neglected animals. So we use photos in our work. In talks, we show photos of mountain climbers ("Aspire!" bosses exhort us). Or rowers ("Teamwork!"). We shove them in reports – if pitching an oil company, we show photos of oil rigs ("Hey! You're in oil, so here's a rig!"). To break up dull text, we show photos of 'person staring at chart on laptop', or 'pen on watermarked paper'.

Such photos are worse than useless. Clichéd, unimaginative photos show we're clichéd and unimaginative. They don't inspire either: no-one ever says: "That *rowing eight* photo nailed it for me – let's work as a team". No. To encourage greater teamwork, talk about the consequences of good and bad teamwork (e.g. bigger bonus versus going bust). Strive to connect with people in a way they feel.

Also, photos waste so much time. People choose them, debate them, and try them out in different sizes and places on the page. Unproductive.

"But," people say, "photos help draw readers into reports." They do – but then distract them from content. Readers comment on photos, not words – and everyone seems to be a photo expert ("An aerial photo would be better…"). Maybe pictures aren't meant to inspire and convince, for our words do that. Maybe they're just something to stare at, and, if used quickly in, say, a talk, they're fine. Yes, but strive to show good ones:

Show photos that are different…	When a Sales Director gave a lunch-and-learn to staff on Sales, he started by showing a screen-filling photo of a frog. "Sales," he said, "is like kissing frogs. We must kiss lots of frogs to find a prince." Memorable, not clichéd. To find photos, try www.istockphoto.com. It has clichéd ones (avoid) and different ones (use if they work).
…and if possible, personal to delegates	If our talk is on work–life balance, find photos of some delegates doing their hobby – maybe some are in an office five-a-side sports team. It connects with delegates much more than library photos of handsome athletes.
But don't offend	Don't single people out ("Here's Pat looking geeky"), or come across as a stalker ("Here's a photo of Les's dog").
Maybe instead make them personal to you	Show a picture of you as a geeky kid or of your dog. I once saw a great 'geeky kid' photo – the presenter as a ten-year old. He said he was a nerd then and still is now, one who enjoys maximising actuarial risk–reward ratios for clients. Which was convenient, for that was his job.

Figure 13.12

However, take care with vanity photos, the mugshots of staff that companies include in slides, brochures and reports when they pitch for business:

In brochures, they're expensive mistakes	Someone in our brochure will resign, which means we must pulp our entire stock and print new ones.
On slides, they're ego trips	They tell prospects that our favourite topics of conversation are us, us and us.
In pitch reports, they won't help us win	If prospects know the people in the mugshots, photos aren't necessary. If prospects don't know them, photos don't help us win business.
If we must do them, maybe make them different – but think of your culture	Maybe show staff doing their hobbies – in sports kit or a Kiss tribute band. It engages, provides light relief, and if prospects like Kiss, it connects. Having said that, a friend tells me that, in his country, 'rugged jawline' vanity shots help. I'm surprised, but that's what he says.

Figure 13.13

Figure 13.14

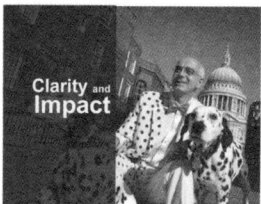

On Courses, I briefly show a photo (Figure 13.12). It accompanied a press release on WiT. The caption said: "'Dots are for Dalmatians, not documents,' says Jon as he launches his Campaign to make work pointless". OK, it's not personal to delegates, but it is to me. It doesn't connect with or inspire delegates, but that's not why I show it. Rather, I show it to intrigue and bring a bit of levity. It's relevant and different too – it's not been in a thousand other talks. Conclusion: it works.

That's how to choose photos. Next we see how to lay them out well.

Photos – laying them out

In one breathless paragraph, I will show how to put a photo on a slide. Figure 13.13 is how presenters often show a photo – in the middle of the slide, with words above it. Instead, if it's landscape, try covering the whole slide with the photo (Figure 13.14). If we've a good photo, it's more dramatic. Ensure its resolution is high enough to avoid it looking pixelated. If we need a title, lay it over the photo: Figure 13.15 has words at the side, Figure 13.16 at the top. Both titles are white font on top of a partially transparent black background that allows the picture to peak through slightly (in PowerPoint, it's *Format, Text Box, Colours* and *Lines, Fill, Transparency,* and set to, say, 30%). Maybe try a solid background, or a white one with a black font – it might be better, depending on the photo. Don't put the title at the bottom, those sitting at the back in our talk struggle to read it over other delegates' heads. Maybe put words on the photo itself (Figure 13.17).

Figure 13.15

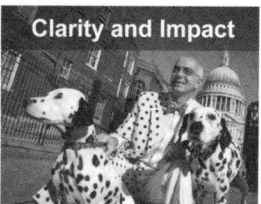

Figure 13.16

I couldn't do this with my *Dalmatian dogs* photo, the left side of the photo is visually busy (railings, houses, etc) and interferes with the words. The options are endless: what works best depends on the photo. Don't muck about for too long though – remember to do some real work.

But how to show more than one photo on a slide? Figure 13.18 (the *before*) is a typical layout. Figure 13.19 (the *after*) is smarter. Below are the reasons why, and they might seem familiar – they're Robin Williams' principles that we saw in Chapter 6 (*Design*).

We improve Proximity. In the *before*, different bits are splattered around the slide. When delegates' eyes first see the slide, they move all over the place to take it in. The *after* groups photos together.

We tighten Alignment. In the *before*, different bits of the slide don't align, it's all a bit random. The *after* lines stuff up with each other. Words line up with photos, photos line up with other photos, photos line up with the title above, and so on.

It has Contrast. The *before*'s heading is a bit timid and diffident. The *after*'s is bold and confident.

It has a style to it. If it was part of a slide pack, other slides would have a similar look and feel. That's Repetition.

That's how to lay out photos on slides. As for laying out photos in reports, follow the same principles (proximity, alignment, etc).

We're near the end of this Chapter, so maybe I should show a photo of 'beautiful-athlete-crossing-finishing-line'. Maybe not. Instead, here are two brief Final Thoughts. Firstly, www. huhcorp.com and www.despair.com have great parodies of business and motivational photos. Secondly, we've not looked at a popular type of visual: animations. We see them briefly in the next Chapter (*Infographics*).

Figure 13.17

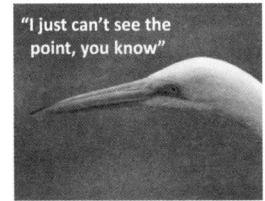

"I just can't see the point, you know"

Figure 13.18

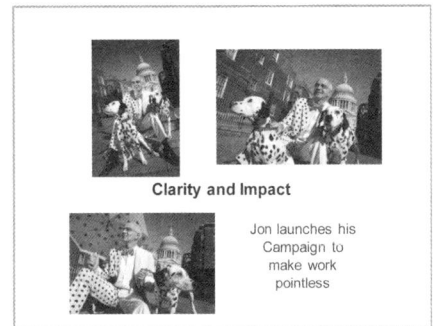

Clarity and Impact

Jon launches his Campaign to make work pointless

Figure 13.19

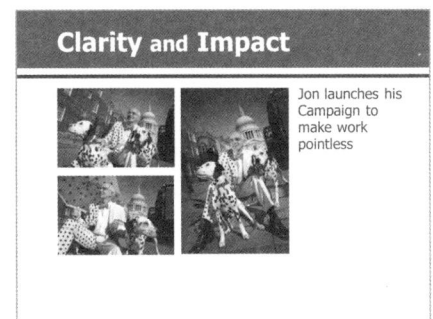

Clarity and Impact

Jon launches his Campaign to make work pointless

14 Infographics

First, let's define terms. I'm not referring to stuff like maps (ordinary maps, crime heat maps, London Tube maps, etc). They're great. Rather, I refer to arty ways to show information, crammed with frippery – funky images, icons, fonts, etc. Like Figure 14.1. And Figure 14.2, which is part of how Barnet Council showed its 2012/13 budget – as orbiting planets. We discuss it soon.

Figure 14.1

Infographics are popular, we see them in newspapers and on websites. Perhaps we should use them at work in our reports, packs, pitches, newsletters. Don't, except on very rare occasions. I am not an *infographista* (it's my word for people who love infographics) – which explains why this Chapter doesn't show any other than Figures 14.1 and 14.2. There's no point in showing examples of something you should rarely do. Instead, I address all the false arguments for doing infographics, plus look briefly at animation. We also see when infographics are just about OK.

The problems with infographics

Figure 14.2

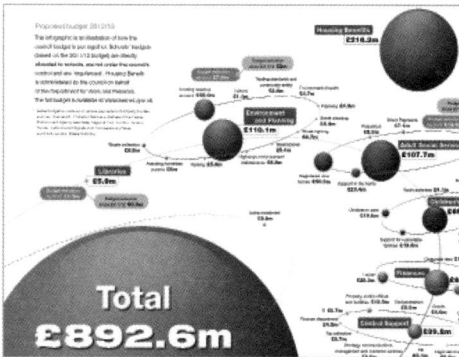

The planets in Figure 14.2 nicely illustrate the problems. Firstly, they fragment information and hinder comparability – to read it, readers' eyes float all over the place. Also, planets distract. Frippery and fact compete for attention, and frippery wins. It attracts us to the page, but distracts us from the content. People give up when reading it, for it's too much of a struggle to take in. It distorts too. Figure 14.2 relates spend to a planet's radius (r), even though its area is πr^2 (we saw something similar in Chapter 2 (*Graphs*) – the 3-D sofas that distort reality). Result: big spend looks bigger, e.g. £276m on Schools (worthy), and small spend looks smaller, e.g. £39m on Central Support (less worthy). Deliberate or accident? You decide.

The planets patronise too. Apparently, we're so innumerate and uninterested in detail, we need pictures. It's like colouring books for the illiterate. Finally, planets are costly. Infographics aren't cheap.

Instead, try a table of numbers. Numbers line up for easy comparison, and are in order too – big at top, small at bottom. And no distracting typography.

At this point, infographistas cry foul. "Barnet's budget is a bad infographic," they say, "and other infographics are better." No. Most suffer from the same problems – and more. Many lack context – in Figure 14.1, is

£972 good? I don't know. What was it last year? What was its budget? Also, many lack **consistency**, **completeness** and **readability**. For instance, an infographic might show lots of stuff, including income and staff over time, yet income is shoved top left of the page, and staff bottom right – and income is for 2012 to 2015, yet staff for 2013 to 2015 – and in reverse order. As I said, incomplete and inconsistent. As for readability, infographics love to take something linear and make it circular or curved (Figure 14.3 – *cool*). Result: readers crane their necks to read it. All of which begs the question: why are infographics so popular?

Figure 14.3

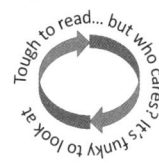

Why infographics are popular

Infographics seem new (albeit as Figure 14.4 explains, they're not), and people like novelty. We all want the latest toy. Also, marketeers fear missing out on the Next Big Thing. So infographistas justify doing them by flooding us with lazy soundbites and false argument. We've addressed much of it in previous Chapters – see Figure 14.5 for a list (overleaf). Here's new sophistry:

Imagine IKEA instructions in words, not diagrams	That's as dumb as saying: "Imagine fictional books that don't have words".
The digital age has redefined the way in which we view and absorb information (Wow!)	Don't confuse medium with content. Yes, medium is now digital (tablets, Kindles, etc). No, content hasn't changed that much – we still read articles, books and more, just like we did in the past.
Numbers never speak for themselves – infographics help them speak	Isolated images don't speak for themselves either. Nor does a graph. *Everything* needs context. The question therefore is: how to give context? Clearly? Or hidden by frippery within an infographic?
Our monthly pack needs infographics because, were we to stumble across it when browsing the newspaper, we wouldn't read it	Flawed logic, for we don't stumble across monthly packs in papers, but are sent them. It's our job to read them. Reading papers isn't. It's a fun way to while away a spare hour. As is watching TV. Playing sport. Sleeping. All these 'fun' activities compete with each other for our spare time. Which is why editors of newspapers lure us in with infographics. Or – rather – broadsheet editors do.

This last point – broadsheets luring us in – seems even more apposite when we think of tabloids. They rarely do infographics, if ever, but instead lure us

Figure 14.4
Infographics aren't new
Diagrams is a great book by Arthur Lockwood, published in 1969. He collated hundreds of diagrams, and many are similar to today's infographics (other than today's are often animated or can be filtered). A well known infographic is *Billion Dollar Gram* – similar to 'block diagrams' in Arthur's book. Another infographic is *In search of food deserts*. Similar to Arthur's 'ray maps'.

Also, *Diagrams* has stuff shown later by Edward Tufte (a guru on showing information), e.g. a beetle's life-cycle. Tufte also has a chart of Napoleon's march on Moscow, whilst *Diagrams* has a chart of traffic flow in Newbury, England. Similar, albeit not as historic or heroic.

Finally, an aside: Arthur's book kick-started my interest in this whole topic of showing information. Back in the 1980s, my brother bought *Diagrams*, and it lit a fuse in me. Thirty years later in 2014, I finally got to speak to Arthur and thanked him for his book. A wonderful moment for me.

Figure 14.5
**False arguments
we've addressed**

From the *Graphs* Chapter
It's cooler to say we're a creative right-brainer.

Graphs are instantly understood.

Graphs simplify the complex.

Graphs are memorable.

Graphs break up dull text.

People engage with graphs.

Graphs convey messages well.

Graphs help people trust our figures.

Graphs paint a thousand words.

From the *Visuals* Chapter
They're better than pages of dense text.

We live in a visual world.

Visuals beat dull text and numbers.

Visuals inspire and persuade.

We recall 10% of what we read, etc.

What we see in Chapter 31
(it looks at 'RAGs' etc)
We like to grasp information visually.

We need information NOW!

(1) www.theguardian.com/world/interactive/2012/may/08/gay-rights-united-states

(2) www.bloomberg.com/billionaires/2014-02-05/b8a

in with salacious pictures and stories. Conclusion: infographics are nothing more than the equivalent of titillating pictures for broadsheet readers.

To conclude, the arguments are flawed. However, don't take my word for it. Look at what infographistas do: ironically, they don't use infographics themselves to communicate. Here are examples I've seen:

1. **The email that was trying to sell us infographics**: it said that infographics sell anything ("So buy one now!") – yet the email didn't have any.

2. **The infographics' trainer**: he showed infographics that people had done to convey their messages to others, yet to convey *his* messages to us, he showed just one in three hours – and it was done partly for irony.

3. **The article**: it said that infographics are the new way to communicate – yet to convey that to us, it used words, not infographics. Also, it didn't show any, but merely referred to one 'good' one: "Infographic weather forecasts". Odd… in days gone by, we called them weather maps.

There's a saying: "The cobbler's children have no shoes". So too with infographistas: their 'children' have no infographics. Having said that, they do show us stuff that gives great insight. As we see next though, it's great not because of infographics, but despite them.

Insight, animation and more

Failure is always an orphan, yet success has a thousand fathers. So too with good analysis – and it often finds one group of people claiming parental rights: infographistas. If we do eye-opening analysis and shove a visual on it, infographistas claim it's the visual that's eye-opening. "A great infographic," they purr. No. The analysis is eye-opening. As for the visual, it rarely helps – and often hinders (it's incomplete, fragmented, etc).

For instance, there's a fascinating analysis of gay rights in America[1] analysed by state and region. The analysis is great *despite* the funky layout (thankfully, it doesn't force readers to crane necks too much to read words).

Then there's Bloomberg's list of the world's richest 200 people[2]. It reveals surprising stories when we filter by country. Or gender. Or inherited versus created wealth. It's a great list… unless, that is, we shove 200 photos on it, then it becomes an infographic – and a 'cool' animated one too, because faces move around on screen when we change filters. All very groovy, but it creates problems. Faces obscure each other if too close together, so we can no longer see who's who. Also, they aren't photos, but cartoons, so aren't useful if we don't know what someone looks like, and not needed if we do. And there aren't cartoons of everyone (Bloomberg didn't have them?!). To conclude, the faces make the whole thing worse, not better.

Hans Rosling's fantastic population analysis

Hans' four-minute clip has been seen by millions on YouTube, and surely it shows the power of visualisation. No. To understand why, first let's explain what his clip shows. It's on how prosperity and lifespan have changed since 1810. It summaries 200,000 numbers – over 200 years and countries, average income (x-axis), lifespan (y-axis). Over 200 circles on screen, one for each country (big circles for big countries). A scrolling meter shows the years roll by, and circles move and grow as prosperity and lifespan change over time.

Then there's Hans. He explains it all: "We see," he says, "the impact of the first world war and the Spanish flu epidemic...*what a catastrophe*!". He does so with a comedian's timing, a game-show host's enthusiasm and a TV pundit's insight. (If you watch it, notice he talks through the x- and y-axes before diving into the messages, as Chapter 2 advises.) And, of course, infographistas claim the clip shows the power of visualisation.

Except it doesn't. Hans says it's not the visualisation, it's the animation. Too true. Watch the clip, but imagine it without moving circles, but as a series of still images, each representing every, say, 50 years. Nowhere near as good. Also, it works because of Hans himself – his enthusiasm, person-ality, timing. I know this because I've seen someone attempt a voiceover to it all. Awful.

Animation and presentation. A powerful double-act. Column charts rarely float my boat, but because of decent animation and presentation, I really like how a TV presenter used one to compare two numbers. In February 2009, he explained how much the UK government stumped up for bank bailouts: £750bn (if I remember correctly). He then glanced just to the right of his feet and watched as a computer-generated '£750bn' column grew from the ground up until slightly taller than him, his eyes tracking the top of the column as it grew. Then he explained how much the government takes in tax a year: £500bn. He glanced down again, but this time to his left, and watched as another column grew from the ground up until shoulder height. Again, his eyes tracked the top of the growing column. Finally, he theatrically glanced up to the top of the right column ("£750bn," he said), then down at the top of the left column ("£500bn"). From start to finish, it took less than 15 seconds, and worked wonderfully. But not because of visualisation. Figure 14.6 visualises it, and it's dull. No. It powerfully contrasted two numbers because of animation and pres-entation: the presenter's words, and his upward and downward glances, theatrical pauses, and growing columns.

Figure 14.6

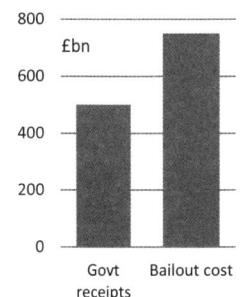

Animated columns can also fail miserably though. Unwittingly, the BBC shows how in two awful 15-second animations from its 2014 series *Mind the Gap – London versus the Rest*. I won't go into details here, other than to say the BBC used animation – and 3-D effects – to alter perspective and portray a skewed view of the statistics. The clips are on YouTube and the relevant bit comes about 19 minutes into Part 1 and 19 minutes into Part 2.

Then there are animations that are completely naff. Such as PowerPoint's zooming-in clipart and bullets. Never use them.

The next section looks at when infographics work. Before then, let's mention an animation that's utterly brilliant. YouTube has a wonderful 12-minute animation called *Changing education paradigms* that's been seen by millions. The topic isn't that thrilling – listen to it without looking at the screen and you'll see what I mean – but the animation keeps us totally engaged. Figure 14.7 is a still from the clip (with thanks to Cognitive Media Ltd for letting me show it – www.wearecognitive.com). Obviously, you need a budget to do this sort of thing, so it's not for the weekly unit update to staff.

Figure 14.7

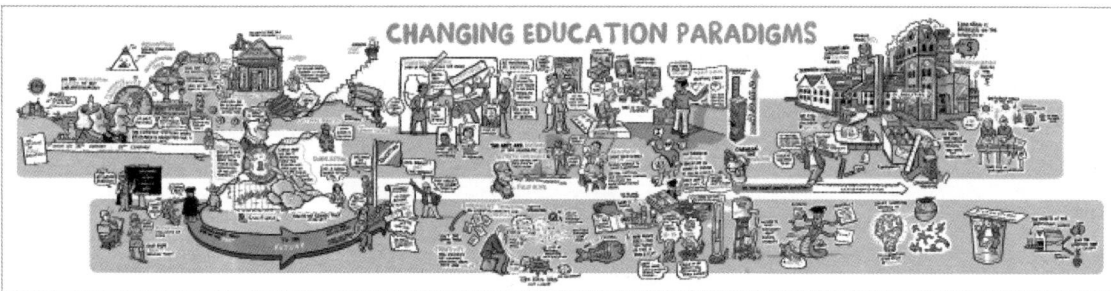

When to do infographics

A renowned infographista says there are two groups of people:

People who like infographics – journalists, graphic designers	These people, he says, cheat data if it better conveys messages. They use design to emphasise the story and make it visually appealing.
People who dislike infographics – academics and statisticians	These people, he says, never cheat data and keep design minimal or invisible.

Ignore the generalisation that journalists and designers like to cheat data. Rather, ponder this: what about people who are neither journalist, graphic designer, academic, nor statistician? The infographista didn't say.

So here's my suggestion: avoid infographics for reports to bosses. Bosses eventually tire of funky colours and fonts, and instead crave clarity. Many clients have asked me to redo their groovy packs that had been created by consultants a year or two earlier. They realise the Emperor has no clothes (Figure 14.8).

However there are exceptions to this default position:

Maybe use in newsletters to staff, clients, market practitioners, etc	Most newsletters are optional reading, so authors must compete for our attention and lure us in. Risqué pictures are risky, so maybe try infographics.
But don't cheat data	It's a dangerous path to go down – get caught cheating and we ruin credibility. Confidence is a fragile commodity that's easily broken and difficult to repair.
And realise we won't always impress	There's a good chance our infographics alienate as many as they impress.

What about when we see an infographic? If it seduces us, ask why. Are its facts and figures interesting? Does it give new insights that resonate or engage? Or inspire, amaze, anger, entice? Or is it the colours, fonts, frippery that capture our brain and heart? I hope not, otherwise it's like admiring the frame around the *Mona Lisa*. And maybe we can 'improve' the London tube map by adorning it with cute icons of trains.

Finally, I should describe two 'work' infographics that I've seen and which were good. One was a CV infographic done by someone applying for a job to do infographics – it was 100% fit for purpose. The other was by the infographista I mentioned above who said there are two groups of people – he did an infographic to compare them. OK, some fonts were illegible (he did this), but it was both ironic and apposite. Its creator seemingly thought so too, because as he pinged it on screen in his talk, I could swear he sported an ironic smile.

Time for Final Thoughts. An article by an infographista told a great story: in 2011, a Brazilian newspaper reviewed the telephone expense claims of 513 civil servants and discovered the amount reclaimed in eight months was $7m (US dollars). Based on call charges, the $7m was enough to speak nonstop for 298 years – so the newspaper printed its findings, alongside an infographic and a headline: "298 years of chatter". The story caused uproar.

So far, so good. However, in the article, the infographista then asked: "Would (the newspaper's findings) have been as effective without the playful headline, pictograms and summaries? I honestly doubt it". I disagree.

Figure 14.8
The Emperor's new clothes
Everyone said, loud enough for the others to hear: "Look at the Emperor's new clothes. They're beautiful!"

"What a marvellous train!"

"And the colours! The colours of that beautiful fabric! I have never seen anything like it in my life!" They all tried to conceal their disappointment at not being able to see the clothes, and since nobody was willing to admit his own stupidity and incompetence, they all behaved as the two scoundrels had predicted.

A child, however, who had no important job and could only see things as his eyes showed them to him, went up to the carriage.

"The Emperor is naked," he said.

Yes, the headline helps, but the story is so good, it doesn't need pictograms to be effective. It's fascinating without them – I hope you liked it... *even though you haven't seen the "298 years" infographic.*

Also, unbelievably, the article didn't even show the infographic. You couldn't script it. As I said earlier, the cobbler's children have no shoes.

Finally, visit the *Fun* page of my website for bad infographics (is that tautology?). Also, see the infographic I did to parody them. Enjoy.

Story-telling   15

I disagree with people who exhort us to tell stories in business, yet I tell stories in business. Confused? I was. Hence this Chapter. We look at what we're told to do by experts, then subject it to a reality check. We see how written stories differ from spoken ones. Along the way, we pop a few myths. By the end, we see when to tell stories and when not to.

A reality check on expert advice

Experts say we should tell stories in business. Here are the ingredients they say our stories need. A situation, complication, resolution. A 'relatable and likeable hero' (maybe 'flawed' too). 'Roadblocks' that a hero overcomes to emerge 'transformed'. An 'inciting' event that throws life out of whack. A 'protagonist' who digs deep and discovers truth. And a 'villain' too – someone for the audience to boo and hiss.

Experts say we need these because: "We follow people in whom we believe". Also, they say: "The best leaders are those who have come to terms with a dark reality". When we tell others about our roadblocks and dark realities, it helps us appear authentic – so experts say – plus it helps audiences empathise and engage with our messages.

Now we know. All those wonderful outcomes, and all for the price of a story about our trials and tribulations. It seems to make sense too. We all can list great orators who inspired and led with stories (JFK, Churchill, Lincoln). Such orators are an exclusive gang, and if we aspire to that exclusivity – if we wish to be seen as a great leader who gets people to follow our big idea – then Tell Stories. (From here on, capital letters denote anything that aspires to use Story-Telling ingredients.) Also, Telling Stories makes us look ambassadorial. Senior.

Most of us don't operate at those levels though. We deal with routine topics unsuited to sweeping narrative, roadblocks, etc. We present IT updates to bosses. New rules to staff. Office relocation plans. Tips for writing. This last one is me, of course – and it's why I don't Tell Stories. I tell stories, ones devoid of roadblocks and dark realities. They're short, simple illustrations, similar to those told by salespeople to show that their product is great ("Look! It works for others"). Of course, I want my stories to persuade, reassure, have repeatability, etc. But I don't Tell Stories. Perhaps I should… but if I'm tempted to do so, I should take care, for Telling Stories has – to borrow a phrase – a *dark reality*.

Raconteur... or crushing bore?	There's a fine line between them that's easy to cross. What we think are pithy morals of exciting stories, audiences might think are facile and a cure for insomnia.
Time well spent... or time we resent?	Even if our Stories are great, audiences may not want to listen to us indulgently talking about our life.
Narrating... or exaggerating? 'Telling Stories' also means fibbing	When politicians talk of 'inciting' events and show their human side, is it inspiration? Or manipulation? And when staff describe roadblocks to bosses, it's often to manage expectations. They stretch truth so bosses accept failure without penalty, or reward success with a big bonus ("Boss, I did the impossible for you"). *Life* and *Lie* are similar – is our life story just an F in lie?

If people think our Story is boring, indulgent or exaggerating, they slap us down.... if they're senior to us. If we're senior to them, they politely listen and sycophantically say our Story is great.

We've reached a tipping point. Seniority. When bosses Tell Stories to underlings, it seems acceptable. Normal. But if underlings Tell Stories to bosses, it's unusual. A bit bizarre. Potentially career-limiting – bosses might shout: "Get to the point!". There's an exclusivity to Telling Stories, akin to out-takes in movies: if lead actors muck up, it's funny. If extras muck up, they're fired. Or, if you prefer, it's about target market. When gurus exhort us to Tell Stories, their advice is meant for senior bods. Leaders. After all, think back to the expert's quote earlier: "The best *leaders* are those who have come to terms with a dark reality" (italics now added). Experts aim their advice at leaders. They neglect to say, though, whether underlings should follow or shun it.

Some underlings follow it. Some Tell Stories to bosses. Maybe they're sufficiently confident in themselves – or their Stories – to believe bosses want to hear them. Take care though, for most bosses don't, albeit there are exceptions. *Dragons' Den* is a TV show in the UK where entrepreneurs pitch investors (Dragons) for money, and entrepreneurs often Tell Stories. That's because Dragons invest not just in products and plans, but in people – and Stories help Dragons see the person. So there's more to this topic than just seniority. Hence the next section.

Trust – without it, every Story is a lie

Are you a leader? Concerned that people don't trust you? No worries, just resort to that panacea: *communication*. Do newsletters, deliver talks, write memos – then sit back, relax and enjoy the warmth of everyone's trust. And if we Tell Stories too, we won't just be warm with their trust, we'll positively overheat on it. After all, people say that Telling Stories adds authenticity. People trust us and engage with our messages.

Dream on. Our newsletters, talks and memos – and the Stories we Tell in them – achieve nothing if people don't trust us. They're as effective as if we say: "I don't lie". Fine if people trust us, useless if they don't. Yet books on Story-Telling rarely mention trust, except to come at it the wrong way: "We need Stories to build trust," they declare. It's the other way round though: "You need trust to build Stories". If little or no trust, avoid Stories, for people resent us even more: we lie and waste their time with Stories that are lies. Trust. It matters. Below are four factors that influence trust and inform us whether to Tell Stories. (And if you think the issue isn't really *trust*, but *latitude*, you're right – Figure 15.1 explains.)

Factor 1: us as the presenter (obviously...). Do audiences believe we're knowledgeable? Honest? Credibility changes over time too – at the start, audiences don't know us, so Telling Stories is risky. But after a while, they trust us a bit, so we could try a Story. Credibility is fragile though, it shatters easily. If we make six decent statements, audiences like us. If we then add one dodgy comment, they loathe us.

Factor 2: our audience. If people have been let down before – by us or others – trust is low. Also, how much effort do they make to *acquire* the Story and its tips and advice? If something is free, people value it less, and that includes advice: if we go to the effort of buying a how-to book or going to a training event, we want our effort to be rewarded. We root for the book or event to be good. We stick with it for longer before giving up on it as rubbish. This is *cognitive dissonance* – Figure 15.2 explains more.

Factor 3: our audience's bosses. Imagine I'm trying to sell a widget. My Story persuades Pat, a manager, but when she tells it to her bosses – for they must approve the purchase – it's rambling. Unconvincing. Pat's not good at Telling Stories – but what's that to do with trust? Answer: Pat's bosses are suspicious. They stress-test proposals to ensure that company money is well spent. Also, some bosses enjoy saying *No*. When Pat Tells my Story, she encounters a problem we saw in Chapter 9 (*Outcomes*) – her bosses say: "You didn't fall for *that*, did you?".

Factor 4: the Story. We trust more if it's **provable, trivial, permanent**.

1. **Provable**: far-fetched claims undermine trust. If someone says their new logo caused profits to double, I'm unnerved. Profits might have doubled for 1,001 other reasons.

Figure 15.1
A pedants' corner aside
Actually, it's more than trust, it's latitude... let me explain. We may not particularly trust someone – or may not know them well enough to either trust or distrust them – but for a variety of reasons, we still give them a chance. We listen to them for a bit to see how it goes.

In other words, we give them *latitude*. And it's this latitude – the amount our audiences give us – that determines whether we Tell Stories.

However, let's keep it simple and talk instead about *trust*.

Figure 15.2
Cognitive dissonance
Imagine buying tickets to see a play that transpires to be rubbish. It's uncomfortable on several levels – a waste of time, a waste of money, plus it clashes with a belief we have about ourselves: that we make good decisions ("I'm good at deciding which plays to see"). The way out of this clash? We convince ourselves the play wasn't that bad after all.

That's cognitive dissonance. And the more we spend, the more we cognitively dissonate. Imagine we see the same play as our neighbours, but our tickets cost twice as much. Because they spent less, they're more likely than us to criticise the bad play.

2. **Trivial**: if a Story is a witty aside, people hardly care if it's exaggerated or even fictional. However, if it encourages people to do something that might get them in trouble (e.g. whistleblow or try shock-jock tactics with clients), the Story's authenticity matters more.

3. **Permanent**: spoken words are ephemeral and have deniability. Written words are less so, hence we attach more honesty to them.

This last point takes us into a new area: written Stories. Until now, I've said that Telling Stories is for leaders who use the spoken word to inspire. Yet there are people out there who aren't leaders and who don't present. They Tell brilliant Stories though. Written ones. Copywriters. By seeing what they do, we better understand when to Tell written Stories.

Telling Stories in writing

Imagine we want to buy a fancy Patek Philippe watch. Bosses would never sanction such a purchase, but no worries, we're buying it not with company money, but with our own. We needn't justify the purchase to anyone other than ourself (OK, maybe we've a husband, wife, partner, etc, but let's not go into those muddy waters). Justifying it to ourself is easy, we merely cite the copywriters' spiel: "I'm looking after it for the next generation," we surmise. And: "It's a *chronometer*". Also, the watch helps when we next scuba-dive to 50 metres(!). With these words, we rationalise our purchase and delude ourselves we're being logical. We're not. We're buying with the heart, not the head, and copywriting trickery helps in our delusion. And, boy, there's trickery. Emotion. Ego. Imagery.

And Stories. "Pat was desperate," the newspaper ad tells us. "She always picked stocks that bombed, and asked a friend how to declare herself bankrupt. The friend instead lent Pat a book. It changed Pat's life. Forever. She now has a chalet in a ski resort and yachts in the harbour." What a story! Crammed with roadblocks. Someone digging deeper. A rosy outcome. Such Stories entice us to buy the new stock-picking method – and help us understand why copywriters' Stories can work so well: they're for consumer purchases and are read by the decision-maker. At work though, salespeople often pitch middle managers who then ask bosses to approve the purchase. Bosses hear the salesperson's Story secondhand, and we've seen the problems this creates. Also, middle managers are often reluctant to overhype to bosses, for it creates dangerously high expectations that can backfire and harm careers. Compare that to copywriters' hype: if it entices us to buy a fancy watch that then disappoints, yes, we waste money, but we haven't damaged our career. Anyway, we can always cognitively dissonate and convince ourselves the watch wasn't that bad after all.

Of course, sometimes there are no salespeople. Sometimes it's an internal pitch, e.g. Pat wants to recruit two staff and bosses must sanction it. Pat could Tell a Story, and it would be heard by the decision-makers, so wouldn't lose anything in translation. But bosses are unlikely to want to spend time listening to Pat's Story – and would be suspicious of it anyway. Imagine: "I wasn't sure what to do about our increased workload," Pat says, "we can't take advantage of market opportunities. Then I remembered what my Dad told me when I was eight... he said: 'Listen'...", etc... Yes, roadblocks, a hero transformed, etc. And arguably OK if told by bosses to underlings. Or politicians to voters. Or raconteurs in the pub. But unsuitable when told by underlings to bosses.

Finally, here's one last reason why Stories work for copywriters: they're good at writing copy (that figures). They've an aptitude for it that they've sharpened with training and years of experience. They learn tricks of the trade, e.g. how to craft arresting openings. "SEX!" Or: "*Don't* read this". As for us: we're good at what we do (IT, Sales, HR, etc), but we aren't copywriters. When we write Stories, they're clunky, verbose, unconvincing. Pessimistic? No. Realistic. It would be great if we could all write compelling Stories, but the odds are stacked against it. Dispiriting, maybe, but better to realise it than not.

Drawing threads together

There are many ways to persuade. Imagine we wish to convince others to buy our book on picking stocks. Push to one side the copywriting trickery (fancy openings, etc), and instead think of the general direction we want our persuasion to go. We could try these:

1. List features ("My book shows a new method to invest"). Dull.
2. List benefits ("My book helps people pick better stocks"). So-so.
3. Refer to outcomes ("My book makes people rich"). Better.
4. Personalise outcomes ("This book will make you rich"). Better still.
5. Introduce imagery ("What's your dream? Own a yacht? Invest in your kids' education? Retire and travel?"). Neat.
6. Tell a Story ("Pat was a rubbish investor, bought my book and now owns a yacht"). Telling Stories personalises and introduces imagery.

I'm sure there are more ways, but these six are enough. The last three are better than the first three. Arguably, the final way – Telling Stories – is best... assuming it's right to Tell Stories. Which neatly encapsulates the conundrum: Tell Stories when we shouldn't and we damage our credibility. But fail to Tell Stories when we should and we don't persuade or

Figure 15.3

Do people
trust us?

      No

Yes

Internal or
external to
our firm?

Internal | External

To people
senior or
junior to us?

Consumer or
business
purchase?

Junior | Senior   Business | Consumer

Tell
Story

Don't
Tell Story

Do we pitch
the decision-
maker
(CEO, etc)?

No | Yes

Don't
Tell Story   Tell Story   Don't
Tell Story

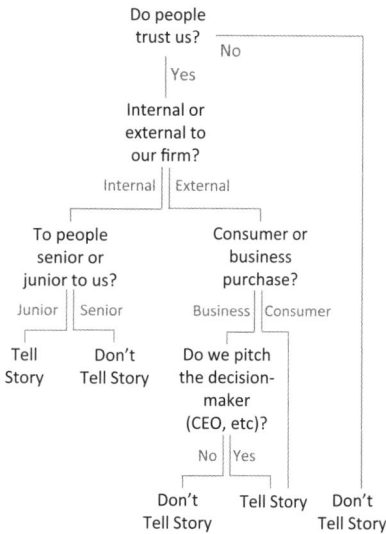

inspire as much as we could. To Tell or not to Tell, that is the question. As we've seen, there are many factors to consider, albeit the big ones are trust and audience. Here are questions to ask ourselves if thinking of Telling Stories.

1. **Do people trust us?** If they don't, Stories hinder, not help.
2. **Who are we pitching?**
   - If an internal pitch, is it to people junior than us? If *Yes*, maybe try a Story. But if pitching to bosses, take care. Think back to out-takes: fun for lead actors, career threatening for extras.
   - If an external pitch, is it a consumer purchase? Or, if a business pitch, do we pitch to the ultimate decision-maker (CEO, etc)? If *Yes* to either, then maybe try a Story. If *No*, our Story will struggle.

If that confused you, try the decision tree instead (Figure 15.3). Chapter 32 explains when to do trees, and this is one such occasion.

Next are more myths. Also, Figure 15.4 looks at Stories in newspapers.

Popping myths

Most myths below arose in articles that exhort us to Tell Stories.

We crave Stories, we've been telling them for 2,000 years	We've craved alcohol, sex and chocolate for years, but don't put any in reports and talks.
Stories are how we remember. Also, we love to be entertained – or even seduced – whilst being enlightened	We can achieve all that without Stories, e.g. to remember something, use acronyms, repetition, etc. Also, there are many ways to seduce, so the issue isn't: "Do Stories achieve these aims?". It's: "How best can we achieve our aims?".
Stories against villains help us seem exciting	Then again, maybe they help others see us as a moaner, exaggerator, etc.
Stories of tough times ahead keep people with us and help them see us as honest	Often, Stories of tough times make people flee for the hills. And anyway, we don't need to Tell a Story to be seen as honest.

Stories are more honest than PR boilerplate spin, better than bulleted lists, etc	If we compare something to a sufficiently bad alternative, it looks good. That doesn't make it the best alternative.
Everyone has a story to tell	Let's be blunt: not every story is worth telling.

There's much sophistry on Story-Telling. And irony too. Articles on Story-Telling don't practise what they preach – they don't Tell Stories about Telling Stories ("I tried to do (A), but always failed … then had an epiphany and now do it by Telling Stories – and it works"). Or they mention Stories that others Tell, but which are unconvincing. One article gave an illustrative example of how to pitch investors: it said the CEO could create a story: "… regulators initially rejected our product… tests failed… money almost ran out… a key boss set up in competition", and so on. Apparently, this creates *suspense* – investors fear an unhappy ending and 'are on the edges of their seats' (yeah, right). The CEO would then say: "But we beat our competitors and are going public" – and bankers would then throw money at the company. Really?!

I also read that someone worked with a dozen companies to refine Stories they told Wall Street, and all 12 got money. But had the companies tried – and failed – to get money *before* having their Stories 'refined'? Maybe they'd foolishly said that their products worked first time and thereby ruined suspense. Finally, was it boom time, with banks giving money to anyone with a plan? It's like the definition of politics: find something that'll inevitably happen, then take credit when it does.

If you still want to Tell Stories

Buy a book or two on Telling Stories	I've little to add to roadblocks and inciting events that is new or takes the thinking further.
Don't make it *linear*	When people Tell Stories, they think: "I need a plot", and so ponder a beginning, middle, end. Soon, the talk is: objectives, method, analysis, conclusions. Which is dull.
Edit viciously – don't waste people's time	And stick to the script. Only extemporise if you're a raconteur. Few are.
Don't make it contrived	Good guys, bad guys, plot twists – fine for movies, not fine for IT updates to bosses and procedure roll-outs.
Avoid spurious claims, people are cynical	"I was rubbish at my job, but learnt Six Steps to Being Great and am now a major CEO!". Yeah, yeah.

Figure 15.4

Stories in newspapers' articles and adverts

First, their articles. When a new tax rule leaves some people worse off, journalists give a human face to the news: "Les cares for his ill father, and doesn't like the rules. 'They're bad,' he says", etc. It personalises, but there aren't roadblocks or inciting events, so – according to Story-Telling 'experts' – it's not a proper Story. But it still works.

Then there are the adverts for, say, charities. They personalise with the plight of a sick child. Sometimes there's no redemption (so it's a story), other times the child gets better and becomes an engineer (so it's a Story). Either way, it *works*. It's written by a copywriter for a consumer purchase (a donation), plus we trust charities more than companies. The ingredients are there. So telling the story works.

If tempted to Tell a Story in reports, maybe put it in a text box to de-emphasise and seem less indulgent. If it doesn't pack the punch we hope, readers can ignore it or dismiss it as a casual aside.

Time for Final Thoughts. I almost ditched this Chapter. I couldn't get it to work. Then a mate told me a great Six Step Way for Chapters, and now it'll earn me a Pulitzer…

Telling Stories is a hot topic. When people discuss draft reports, someone usually asks: "But what Story do we wish to Tell?". It misses the point. Reports and talks aren't about Telling Stories. They're about messages we wish to convey and outcomes we wish to achieve. The Story is a means to an end. One of many. And if we Tell Stories when we shouldn't, it's unproductive. Or counterproductive.

Finally, don't confuse Story-Telling with something people often do – they use, say, a graph to "tell a story". Page 263 explains more.

> ### Applying this Chapter's ideas to reality
>
> Let's apply them to me. Or rather, my books, emails, Courses, website. They're a nice mix – the book is written, the Courses are spoken. The book is more for consumers, the Courses more for corporates. My website is for both. When do I Tell Stories? When do I not?
>
> **My book – it starts with one** ("I once helped a confused CEO"): the book is in writing, so the Story is more believable than if spoken. Also, you spent money on the book, so you want it to be good.
>
> **My website – no stories**: my website is free to visit, so you root for it less. Instead, at the start I make you feel something ("Imagine doing work people praise and envy"). I could chance a Story elsewhere on my site, but instead have something more believable. Other people's stories. Testimonials.
>
> **My Courses – not at the start, but later in the day**: delegates make an effort to attend, so I could risk one at the start. I don't. It would be verbal, so less believable, and delegates may think I'm exaggerating. Not a good start to the day. Instead, I show how my stuff helps – I show the WiT-based CV. Later, after I've earned delegates' trust a bit, I chance a Story.
>
> **Emails to potential clients – no stories**: people contact me to find out about an in-house Course, we speak, then I send a half-page email that they can forward to bosses, HR, staff, etc. The email has a bit on the Course and me, links to my website, testimonials, etc. But no Stories. Courses often need sign-off from cynical bosses, and so a Story might backfire.

More on writing

These Chapters can be read in any order. The first three look at WiT in more detail. Chapter 16 is **other layouts** and **problems**, and 17 is **mistakes, FAQ, concerns**. As for Chapter 18, it's brief and for those who prepare WiT (**formatting tips**).

If your reports are more than, say, six pages, read Chapter 19 (**big reports**). Chapter 20 (**writing – advanced**) has editing tips to help you comply with word or page limits. Also, you see why rhythm isn't just for poets and musicians. Much **technical writing** is impenetrable because people don't know the principles and techniques. Chapter 21 reveals all. It also looks at **jargon** – when it's good, when it's not.

Bosses sometimes ask us to create particular documents, e.g. manuals, plans, etc. Hence Chapter 22 (**specific reports**). It doesn't look at management accounts, KPIs, dashboards though – that's Chapter 33.

Decks are reports written in PowerPoint, then emailed to people for them to read at their desk. They're popular, yet most are bad. Chapter 23 has tips to improve them – and save time too. Finally, on its last two pages is a great new cartoon character… Enjoy.

16 WiT – other layouts; problems

Figure 16.1

This Chapter looks at different types of WiT, plus problems people encounter when they create WiT. First, we see Triple-WiT, a great alternative to the dreaded sub-sub-bullet.

We're helping the housing problem

Lorem ipsum est gloriatur expetendis an. Congue con ten tiones consequuntur et eos, autem.

The indicators show it's bad

House prices falling	Agam conceptam mel cu, eum et porro recteque inter esset. Ex ius idque corrumpit democritum,
House building stalling	Ea fugit ullum assentior duo, euripidis repu diandae quo cu eum choro blandit consectetuer.
Repossessions rising	Eu sit cetero appareat accusata. Per et dicam tem por praesent, eripuit nonummy volumus cu.

We're taking action

We've met mortgage lenders	Per tantas altera praesent in, nam assum recteque disp utationi ut. Te nominavi deserunt qui.
We're helping first-time buyers	Summo copiosae mea ex, doctus eleifend in sea. Mea ne elit iusto. Id corpora salutatus usu, eirmod.
We're helping improve liquidity	No natum eripuit lobortis sit, vel lucilius expetendis cu, ei possit persequeris mel.

We've some key actions still to do

	Eum luptatum contentiones cu, eu mei fabellas medio critatem. Vivendo antiopam nec te, malis.
Show we're on people's side	Graeco virtute detracto sit ei, mea sonet dicant et. Mei ad huc fabulas et, qui ex zzril postea.
Plan in case things get worse	Mei cu dolore volumus volutpat, illum tamquam san ctus ex est. Eum ad sumo invenire, nec falli inimicus at, mel delenit conclusionemque et.
Prepare for the upturn	Vidit corpora ad mea, in altera accusamus quo. Id pri posse idque harum. · Prima pertinacia - Facilisis intellegat · Adipiscing vel

Triple-WiT: for sub-sub-bullets

Figure 16.1 is a one-page note on problems in the housing market. Assume it's a briefing note for, say, a politician. Some comments are a bit empty and don't pass the *Not* test (e.g. "Show we're on people's side"…) but let's not worry about that for the moment. Rather, notice it's a WiT, so we've the usual benefits. Points leap from the page. Readers easily navigate and skim and scan. Narrow rows make it easier to read. Also, it's easy to see if it's in the order we want – and if it isn't, it's easy to reorder it, e.g. if we want action points at the top, not the bottom, no worries: move them.

It's different to previous WiTs. 'Normal' WiT has just two parts to it (left and right columns) – let's call it 'Basic-WiT'. Figure 16.1 has three parts – left and right columns, plus sub-heads (*"We're taking action"*). It's a repeating pattern of three: sub-head, then rows of text on left and right; another sub-head, then more rows of text on left and right, and so on. I call it Triple-WiT (TWiT?). And its typography is different:

Left column: *right*-aligned in Triple-WiT	Compare that to Basic-WiT which *left*-aligns it (as in this Basic-WiT that you are now reading).
Horizontal rules: often absent	They're at sub-head level only, and only on the right. In Basic-WiT, they go far left to far right for every row – again, as in this WiT.
A comment that's not summarised on the left – the first lines of text of the third section ("Eum luptatum etc")	That's fine. If a section needs a lead-in comment – but one not worthy of summarising on the left – put it under the sub-head. Notice the lead-in comment is shunted to the right half of the page.

Study the sub-heads (*"The indicators show it's bad"*). They're headlines, not headings. Also, they're on the right half of the page, left-aligned. Finally, the page does the stuff we saw in earlier Chapters. It has bullets for lists of brief items. It justifies text where possible. There are serifs for detail and sans serifs for summary – and Arial Black in small doses.

The layout works. Triple-WIT looks sharp. Compare it to how we usually show such stuff: as sub-bullets, sub-sub-bullets, etc – see Figure 16.2, which is the last section of the Triple-WiT redone in bullets. It's all a bit ragged, plus it suffers from 'trapped white space' (the text box explains what this is).

However, Triple-WiT is more than just a pretty face. It's great for presenters. That's the next section.

Figure 16.2

Trapped white space

Figure 16.3 is a typical bunch of sub-sub-sub-bullets. Its content isn't important and much is in Latin. I've shaded the areas where there are no words. Much of it is trapped white space – it's the space that arises between lines of text that stretch across the page. Pages need white space, of course, but not this sort. This sort is small. Ineffective. Ugly. Compare that to WiT. It uses its white space more effectively. It has big slugs of dominant white space between summary points down its left side. Much better.

Figure 16.3

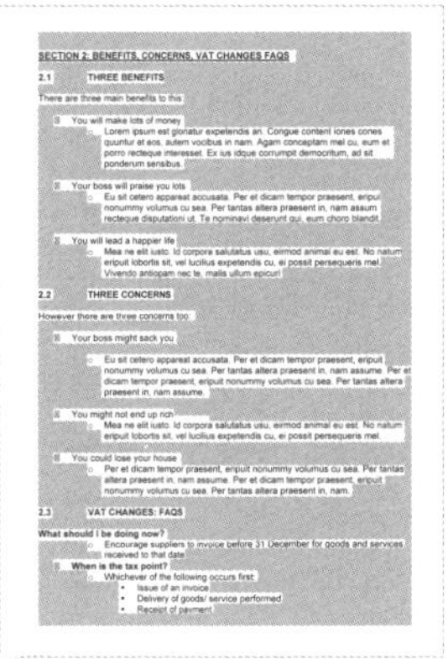

Triple-WiT: great for presenters

Imagine we must talk through Figure 16.1 (the 'housing problem' page) to bosses. With Triple-WiT, we've a great script to read from. Simply read the page heading, the bit in Latin under it, then the sub-heads and text down the left:

"We're helping the housing problem," then some Latin (ignore it please): "Lorem ipsum est gloriatur expetendis an. Congue con ten tiones consequuntur et eos, autem," followed by: "The indicators show it's bad – house prices are falling, house building stalling and repossessions rising. We're taking action though: we've met mortgage lenders, we're helping first-time buyers, and helping improve liquidity. But we've still some key actions to do… show we're on people's side. Plan in case things get worse. Prepare for the upturn."

If anyone then asks a question ("Can you tell me more about house prices falling?"), we dive to the right of that row and read it out. Easy. And if we want to give people a handout, simply circulate the Triple-WiT page. It's a great take-away for delegates. But what slides would we show? Simple:

Figure 16.4
WiT and grammar

Chapter 1 says WiT helps make grammar consistent – and the 'housing problem' page demonstrates this. In Figure 16.1, study the words down the left. All comments within the first sub-head finish with '*ing*' (falling, stalling, etc). All within the second sub-head start with '*we*' (we're, we've, etc). The third are all imperatives (show, plan, etc). This consistency within sections gives it more impact when we read it aloud in a talk. Much better.

Figure 16.5

Some heading up here

Vel in prompta singulis eloquentiam, viderer mediocrem incorrupte ne his, audiam nonummy sed in. Ea eum debet quaerendum. Mel at erant decore, mea id vitae postulant necessitatibus. Ne nam eros doming legimus, sit in quando altera. Menandri periculis vix no.

9 A new section here

Vel in prompta singulis eloquentiam, viderer mediocrem incorrupte ne his, audiam nonummy sed in. Ea eum debet quaerendum. Mel at erant decore, mea id vitae postulant necessitatibus. Ne nam eros doming legimus, sit in quando altera. Menandri periculis vix no. Dicam detraxit voluptatum est id.

Lorem ipsum est gloriatur

Congue contentiones conse quuntur	Agam conceptam mel cu, eum et porro recteque inter esset. Ex ius idque corrumpit democritum, ad sit ponderum sensibus.
Eu sit cetero appar eat accusata	Per et dicam tempor praesent, eripuit nonummy volu mus cu sea. Per tantas altera praesent in.

Menandri periculis vix

Graeco virtute detracto sit ei	Mea sonet dicant et. Mei adhuc fabulas et, qui ex zzril postea posidonium. Per et dicam tempor praesent, eripuit nonummy.
Nec eu dico reque docend	Eum ad sumo invenire, nec falli inimicus at, mel delenit con clusionemque. viderer.
Vidit corpora ad mea in altera	Id corpora salutatus usu, eirmod animal eu est. No natum eripuit lobortis sit, vel lucilius expetendis cu. Per et dicam tempor praeuit.

Vel in prompta singulis eloquentiam, viderer mediocrem incorrupte ne his, audiam nonummy sed in. Ea eum debet quaerendum. Mel at erant decore, mea id vitae postulant necessitatibus. Ne nam eros doming legimus, sit in quando.

---

none. Why show any? Just talk. It's what we did before PowerPoint and what we do outside work. We don't sit in the pub and say to mates: "I played soccer on Monday – this slide helps you grasp what I just said".

Triple-WiTs are fantastic for one- or two-page notes we must present or discuss in meetings. Or even Cabinet meetings. Which is where the 'housing problem' page actually came from. In May 2008, the UK Housing Minister, Caroline Flint, was strolling along Downing Street to a Cabinet meeting, clutching a bullet-riddled Briefing Paper in a see-through envelope. The press took a photograph, read the Paper, and criticised the government for what the Paper said. They criticised its empty statements. They criticised its assessment of the housing market and the actions taken to kick-start it.

I didn't criticise. Rather, I redid it as the Triple-WiT we saw earlier — Figure 16.1 is an abbreviated version of my redo, albeit with Latin on the right rather than the original's words. Then I criticised. In just eight bullets and a concluding sentence, the original had ten mistakes. Not typos either. Rather, its comments were incomplete, in the wrong order, and much more. WiT helps highlight and correct it all. However, my redo also shows how WiT really helps solve one particular problem: inconsistent grammar. Figure 16.4 explains. To see the original and redo, visit my website's *Home* page (the redo is in MS Word, so you can adopt and adapt). Notice how tough it would be to present from the original in a meeting. Or a Cabinet meeting.

However, a word of warning on Triple-WiTs: typographically, they can struggle to fit within longer reports' sections and sub-sections. After all, study this book. You constantly see Basic-WiTs, but rarely see Triple-WiTs. Triple-WiTs are a bit intricate with several moving parts – left bit, right bit, sub-head, maybe numbers in the middle, and even introductory text shunted to the right. Typographically, these moving parts can sometimes jar with the rest of the report. Don't get me wrong, Triple-WiTs can fit in (Figure 16.5), but often they're not entirely comfortable when they do.

The next section looks at another WiT layout, one that's great for reference documents. Before then, the text box shows how to number the sections within Triple-WiT.

Numbering a Triple-WiT

If discussing a Triple-WiT page in a meeting, it helps to number points. In Basic-WiT, numbering is easy: add a column on the left and put numbers in it. With Triple-WiT, it's not so obvious where to put numbers. I've tested various places

– on the left, the right, etc – and the most popular by far is in the middle (Figure 16.6; it just shows part of the page). Insert a middle column and put numbers in grey and a smaller font. The numbers are there when we need them, not in the way when we don't.

If we insert numbers, will readers mistakenly think our comments are in order of priority? No. Readers quickly realise that numbers are not to prioritise, but to aid cross-referencing.

To number sections as well as points, see Figure 16.7 (it just shows section 1 and a bit of section 2). To number sections only, take the unnumbered Triple-WiT, and add a section number to the cell that's on the left of each sub-head. You get the idea. MS Word won't automatically add numbers to WiTs, it's a manual intervention.

WiT-in-columns: for reference documents

Many reports contain boring lists. Such as terms and conditions. Or audit tests. Or steps for using an IT system. Such reports are reference documents and hence benefit from really narrow lines of text (as opposed to text that stretches across the full width of a page).

So do WiT-in-columns (WiT squared, perhaps). Divide the page into two columns and within each, do a mix of WiT and text (Figure 16.8 – overleaf). Readers easily skim and scan. The font is Calibri Light, it's great for dull stuff: light on the eye, compact on the page. Note that continuous text is justified, as are the words in the right column of the WiT. Take care though – if text isn't wide enough to justify, we get visually distracting gaps between words.

WiT-in-columns helps keep dull stuff to as few pages as possible – for three reasons, we can squeeze lots in:

1. **We reduce font size**: with narrow lines of text, smaller fonts are preferable, and with really narrow lines, we can get away with really rather small fonts.
2. **We reduce line spacing**: line spacing of 1.0× is fine with narrow lines.
3. **We reduce the number of orphans**: if the word *orphans* makes sense, good – and WiT-in-columns helps cut down on the wasted space they create. If it doesn't make sense, Chapter 18 explains the term.

Figure 16.6

Figure 16.7

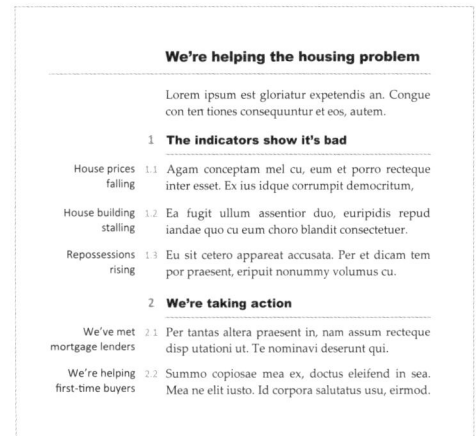

Figure 16.8

A headline, not a heading

A2 Intro, then sub-sub-sections

Id erant scaevola suscipiantur sit, id eam amet fabu las. Sea te error tibique, pro eu novum. Per et dicam tem por praesent, eripuit nonumny volumus cu sea. Graeco virtute detracto sit ei, mea sonet dicant et. Mei adhuc fabulas et, qui ex zzril postea.

A2.1 Text, then WiT

Graeco virtute detracto sit ei, mea sonet dicant et. Mei adhuc fabulas et, qui ex zzril postea. Per et dicam tempor praesent, eripuit nonumny volumus cu sea. Per tantas altera praesent in, nam assum.

Lorem ipsum est gloriatur	Congue contentiones conse quuntur et eos, autem vocibus in nam. Agam concept tam mel cu, eum et porro.
Mea ne elit iusto	Per et dicam tempor praesent, eripuit non ummy volumus cu sea. Per tantas alt era prae sent in, nam assum rect.
Ex ius idque corrumpit	Id erant scaevola suscipiantur sit, id eam amet erant fabulas. Sea te error tib ique, pro eu novum.

Id erant scaevola suscipiantur sit, id eam amet erant fabu las. Sea te error tibique, pro eu novum. Per et dicam tem por praesent, eripuit nonumny volumus.

A2.2 WiT, then text, then numbered list

Per et dicam tempor	Graeco virtute detracto sit ei, mea sonet dicant et. Mei adhuc fabulas et,
Mea ne elit iusto	Per et dicam tempor praesent, eripuit non ummy volumus cu sea. Per tantas alt era prae sent in, nam assum rectque.

Id erant scaevola suscipiantur sit, id eam amet erant fabu las. Sea te error tibique, pro eu novum. Per et dicam tem por praesent, eripuit nonumny volumus.

1. Per tantas altera praesent in, nam assum
2. Disputationi graeco virtute detracto sit ei, mea
3. Dicant et mei adhuc fabulas et, qui ex zzril
4. Per et dicam tempor praesent, eripuit

Vivimus cu sea per tantas altera praesent in.

A3 Text, plus list of brief items

Graeco virtute detracto sit ei, mea sonet dicant et. Mei adhuc fabulas et, qui ex zzril postea. Per et dicam tempor praesent, eripuit nonumny volumus cu sea. Per tantas altera praesent in, nam assum rectque.

- Id eam amet erant
- Fabu las sea te
- Error tibique
- Pro eu novum
- Cu sea erant
- Et et dicam tem
- Por praesent, eripuit
- Nonumny volumus
- Eam amet
- Eripuit nonummy

A4 Lots of text, then WiT

Id erant scaevola suscipiantur sit, id eam amet erant fabu las. Sea te error tibique, pro eu novum. Per et dicam tem por praesent, eripuit nonumny volumus cu sea. Per tantas altera praesent in, nam assum.

Graeco virtute detracto sit ei, mea sonet dicant et. Mei adhuc fabulas et, qui ex zzril postea. Per et dicam tempor praesent, eripuit nonumny volumus cu sea. Per tantas altera praesent in, nam assum rectque.

Id erant scaevola suscipiantur sit, id eam amet erant fabu las. Sea te error tibique, pro eu novum. Per et dicam tem por praesent, eripuit nonumny volumus.

Lorem ipsum est gloriatur	Congue contentiones conse quuntur et eos, autem vocibus in nam. Agam concept tam mel cu, eum et porro.
Mea ne elit iusto	Per et dicam tempor praesent, eripuit non ummy volumus cu sea. Per tantas alt era prae sent in, nam assum rec teque.
Ex ius idque corrumpit	Id erant scaevola suscipiantur sit, id eam amet erant fabulas. Sea te error tib ique, pro eu novum.

Graeco virtute detracto sit ei, mea sonet dicant et. Mei adhuc fabulas et, qui ex zzril postea. Per et dicam tempor praesent, eripuit nonumny volumus.

Figure 16.9

1 Simple numbering

Id erant scaevola suscipiantur sit, id eam amet erant fabu las. Sea te error tibique.

Lorem ipsum est gloriatur	Congue contentiones con se quuntur et eos, autem vocibus.

2 Reversed fonts for numbers

Id erant scaevola suscipiantur sit, id eam amet erant fabu las. Sea te error tibique.

Lorem ipsum est gloriatur	Congue contentiones con se quuntur et eos, autem vocibus.

3 Indents

Id erant scaevola suscipiantur sit, id eam amet erant fabu las. Sea te error tibique.

Lorem ipsum est gloriatur	Congue contentiones con se quuntur et eos, autem vocibus.

4 Indents with reversed fonts

Id erant scaevola suscipiantur sit, id eam amet erant fabu las. Sea te error tibique.

Lorem ipsum est gloriatur	Congue contentiones con se quuntur et eos, autem vocibus.

Nothing

Id erant scaevola suscipiantur sit, id eam amet erant fabu las. Sea te error tibique.

Lorem ipsum est gloriatur	Congue contentiones con se quuntur et eos, autem vocibus.

Figure 16.8 has section numbering. Figure 16.9 looks at ways to number items. Section 1 is as per Figure 16.8 – let's call it Simple Numbering. Section 2 uses Reversed Fonts, whilst Section 3 Indents the text that follows the numbers. Section 4 Indents with Reversed Fonts, and the last has Nothing, i.e. no numbering. Here's which I use when:

Simple Numbering: fine if the page is fairly routine – a mix of text and WiT.

Reversed Fonts: good if the page has lots on it (graphs, tables, text, bullets, etc). Reversed fonts have visual prominence, and this gives shape to what can all too easily look a messy and random page. Chapter 33 has examples.

Indents (with or without reversed fonts): my least favourite. Space greedy.

Nothing: fine if we don't think people will want to refer to items. I use this one a lot in this book.

Finally, Figure 16.10 is another WIT-in-columns layout. In columns, yes. But no longer a mix of WiT and text. This one is 100% WiT. Or – to be precise – Triple-WiT-in-columns. Study its typography. Sub-heads. Grids only occasionally. Etc. This layout is great for, say, a one-page leave-behind after a talk. And it uses its white space wonderfully.

WiT with straplines

Assume we have four areas on which we must briefly report each month: IT, Compliance, Staff, New Business. Figure 16.11 is how we normally show it on a page – stuff laid out one under the other (heading, text, heading, text, etc). It's inelegant, plus points don't lift from the page. Each bit is a brief section, so we could WiT it – but we'd then just have headings down the left: IT, Compliance, etc. Uninformative. Instead, try Figure 16.12: WiT with straplines. It retains the corporate headings (IT, Compliance, etc), but now has straplines that summarise ("Had a great month," etc). Readers see key points on the left – it gives them choice – plus the page has all the other benefits of WiT too.

Notice the fonts. Arial Black can visually overwhelm, but is fine for headings that are just one or two words (e.g. **IT**). The straplines have more words and would overwhelm if in Arial Black, so they're in a more subdued sans serif font.

To conclude, there are several types of WiT – we recap them later in the Chapter. But there's a problem with them all: they're not realistic. All rows are roughly the same size, as are all sections. How convenient. Reality is messier. Next we see what happens when WiT meets reality. And it gets detailed.

Figure 16.10

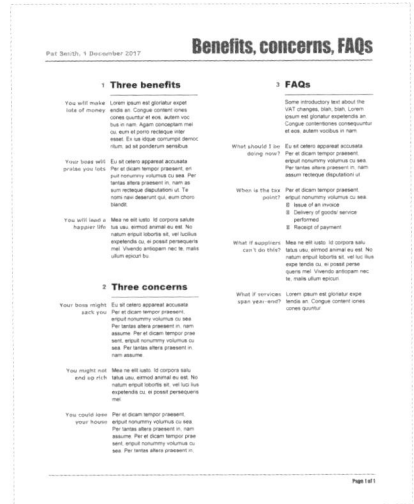

Problems: when WiT meets reality

This section looks at problems that arise when people use WiT. In particular, what if we've lots to say in one row? Or little to say? Or have 12 points we wish to make?

We've lots to say in one row

In a project update, assume we've four topics to comment on: A, B, C and D. Assume A, B and C are each two or three lines, but D is four paragraphs. If D is in a WiT with the other points, its last row goes on too long. The WiT looks odd. Imbalanced (Figure 16.13). We could strip D from the WiT and show as continuous text underneath. However, this creates a disconnect between D and the other points, plus it makes D less visible. So, try these:

Do Triple-WiT: Figure 16.14 has two sections. The first has A, B and C, and the second is just D. Also, D is chopped into four separate rows – one for each of its four paragraphs. Do a decent sub-head, of course, not: "Long point, put in four rows". Do a headline.

Keep as Basic-WiT, but keep D last, brief and introductory: for instance, on the left of D's row, we write a brief headline, then on the right, we add: "This is a big topic, we look at it in more detail below". The four paragraphs are then under the WiT. This keeps D visible and connected to the other three points, but doesn't unbalance the WiT. I use this workaround a lot in this book.

Figure 16.11

Figure 16.12

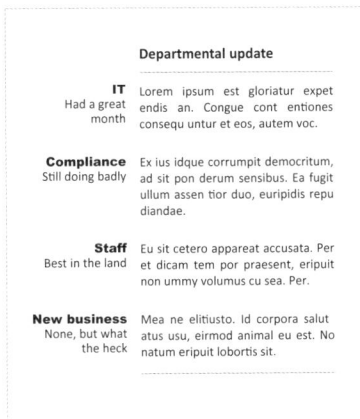

Figure 16.13

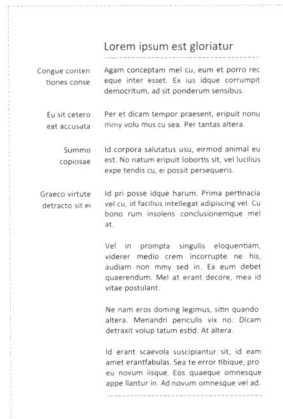

Figure 16.14

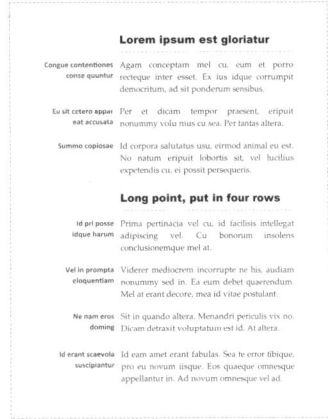

Figure 16.15

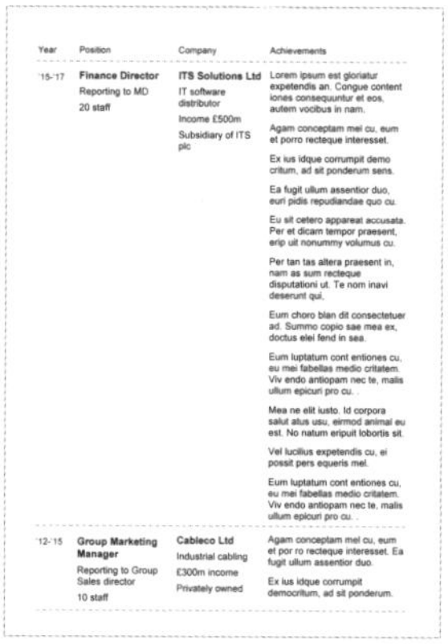

Year	Position	Company	Achievements
'15-'17	**Finance Director** Reporting to MD 20 staff	**ITS Solutions Ltd** IT software distributor Income £500m Subsidiary of ITS plc	Lorem ipsum est gloriatur expetendis an. Congue content iones consequuntur et eos, autem vocibus in nam. Agam conceptam mei cu, eum et porro recteque interesset. Ex ius idque corrumpit demo critum, ad sit ponderum sens. Ea fugit ullum assentior duo, euri pidis repudiandae quo cu. Eu sit cetero appareat accusata. Per et dicam tempor praesent, erip uit nonummy volumus cu. Per tan tas altera praesent in, nam as sum recteque disputationi ut. Te nom inavi deserunt qui. Eum choro blan dit consectetuer ad. Summo copio sae mea ex, doctus elei fend in sea. Eum luptatum cont entiones cu, eu mei fabellas medio critatem. Viv endo antiopam nec te, malis ullum epicuri pro cu. . Mea ne elit iusto. Id corpora salut atus usu, eirmod animal eu est. No natum eripuit lobortis sit. Vel lucilius expetendis cu, ei possit pers equeris mel. Eum luptatum cont entiones cu, eu mei fabellas medio critatem. Viv endo antiopam nec te, malis ullum epicuri pro cu. .
'12-'15	**Group Marketing Manager** Reporting to Group Sales director 10 staff	**Cableco Ltd** Industrial cabling £300m income Privately owned	Agam conceptam mel cu, eum et por ro recteque interesset. Ea fugit ullum assentior duo. Ex ius idque corrumpit democritum, ad sit ponderum.

Edit violently: sounds obvious? Maybe not. People tell me their WiT-based CV looks imbalanced because they've 15 achievements from one job (Figure 16.15). The obvious retort is: don't list 15 achievements – no-one wants to read that many. Choose your top three or four. Our CV isn't to document our life, or even get a job. It's to get us an interview. Tell enough so people want to meet us to find out more.

That's if we've lots to say on a point. What if we've little to say?

We've little to say in one row

Imagine in one row of our WiT, we write on the left: "The new IT is to be in the boss's favourite colour: blue". Ignore the dumbness of the remark, and instead ponder what to write on the right. Not much really, we've pretty much said it all. Result: an empty cell on the right. It looks odd and unnerves readers. "Did you forget to write something?" they ponder.

We could instead retain a bit of the comment for the right side, e.g. the left says: "The new IT is to be in the boss's favourite colour", and the right adds: "Blue". Now, the right isn't empty… but unbalanced. Summary is longer than detail. The left spills onto a second line of text, the right is just one word. Weird. We could live with it – it's not a disaster – and sometimes we can't do much about it. Here though, we can:

1. Redistribute words to improve balance, e.g. on the left: "The new IT must be blue," and on the right: "This is the boss's favourite colour".
2. Widen the left column a bit so the WiT is less imbalanced. However, avoid 'bad' column widths, as Chapter 18 explains.
3. Add words to the right to improve balance, e.g. "Bosses dislike our existing red IT", or "This is per their memo to the CIO, 16 Feb 2015", etc. Adding unnecessary words is never ideal, but I do it sometimes.

If this sounds detailed or contrived, keep it in perspective. Yes, avoid empty cells, but, no, don't obsess about the occasional imbalance. As I said earlier, it's not a disaster. Also, it takes just a few seconds to resolve them.

Figure 16.16

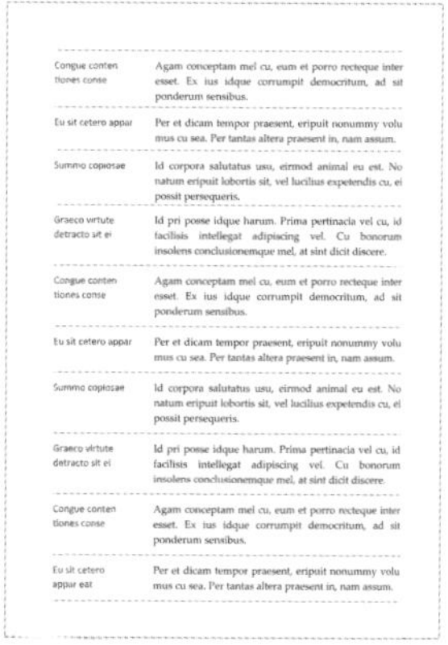

Congue conten tiones conse	Agam conceptam mel cu, eum et porro recteque inter esset. Ex ius idque corrumpit democritum, ad sit ponderum sensibus.
Eu sit cetero appar	Per et dicam tempor praesent, eripuit nonummy volu mus cu sea. Per tantas altera praesent in, nam assum.
Summo copiosae	Id corpora salutatus usu, eirmod animal eu est. No natum eripuit lobortis sit, vel lucilius expetendis cu, ei possit persequeris.
Graeco virtute detracto sit ei	Id pri posse idque harum. Prima pertinacia vel cu, id facilisis intellegat adipiscing vel. Cu bonorum insolens conclusionemque mel, at sint dicit discere.
Congue conten tiones conse	Agam conceptam mel cu, eum et porro recteque inter esset. Ex ius idque corrumpit democritum, ad sit ponderum sensibus.
Eu sit cetero appar	Per et dicam tempor praesent, eripuit nonummy volu mus cu sea. Per tantas altera praesent in, nam assum.
Summo copiosae	Id corpora salutatus usu, eirmod animal eu est. No natum eripuit lobortis sit, vel lucilius expetendis cu, ei possit persequeris.
Graeco virtute detracto sit ei	Id pri posse idque harum. Prima pertinacia vel cu, id facilisis intellegat adipiscing vel. Cu bonorum insolens conclusionemque mel, at sint dicit discere.
Congue conten tiones conse	Agam conceptam mel cu, eum et porro recteque inter esset. Ex ius idque corrumpit democritum, ad sit ponderum sensibus.
Eu sit cetero appar eat	Per et dicam tempor praesent, eripuit nonummy volu mus cu sea. Per tantas altera praesent in, nam assum.

We've 12 points we wish to make

Is there a limit to the number of WiT rows? As ever, the answer is: it depends. In Basic-WiT, avoid more than five or six rows on the trot, for we struggle to take in that many points unless they're grouped. Also, the page starts to look a bit uninteresting (Figure 16.16) – all the horizontal lines make it look like a spreadsheet. Not nice. We could remove the lines, but it looks a bit naked. Take my word for it, or try it yourself. But what to do instead?

Firstly, group items. Then what we do next depends on how briefly we can convey grouping. Sometimes, we can convey it very briefly, e.g. this book has several long WiTs where I group lots of points into *do's* and *don'ts*. The first few rows each start with **Do** in bold, then the rest each start with **Don't** (e.g. page 91). Readers easily see the grouping, plus the contrast helps create visual interest.

If we can't convey groupings that briefly, do Triple-WiT. Use the sub-head to convey grouping ("Some less material bad points" – that sort of thing). With Triple-WiT, 15 rows are fine if they're grouped into, say, three groups of five, each with a sub-head that summarises.

Figure 16.17

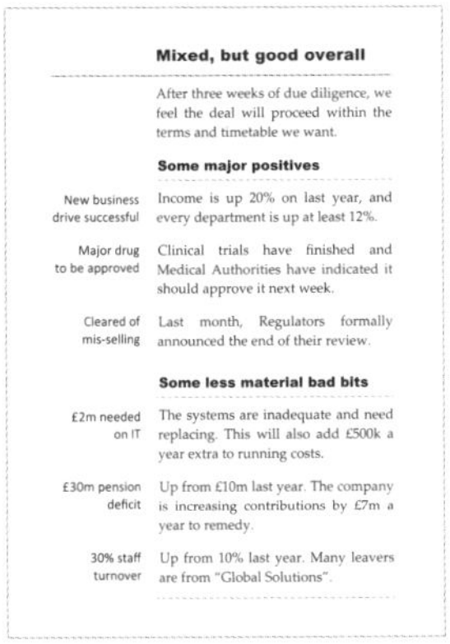

Mixed, but good overall

After three weeks of due diligence, we feel the deal will proceed within the terms and timetable we want.

Some major positives

New business drive successful	Income is up 20% on last year, and every department is up at least 12%.
Major drug to be approved	Clinical trials have finished and Medical Authorities have indicated it should approve it next week.
Cleared of mis-selling	Last month, Regulators formally announced the end of their review.

Some less material bad bits

£2m needed on IT	The systems are inadequate and need replacing. This will also add £500k a year extra to running costs.
£30m pension deficit	Up from £10m last year. The company is increasing contributions by £7m a year to remedy.
30% staff turnover	Up from 10% last year. Many leavers are from "Global Solutions".

Let's recap. We've seen several WiT variations (see the thumbnails below):

1. Triple-WiT: great for a presenter's script.
2. WiT-in-columns: great for reference documents.
3. Triple-WiT-in-columns: great as a one-page leave-behind after a talk.
4. WiT with straplines: great for standard corporate headings.

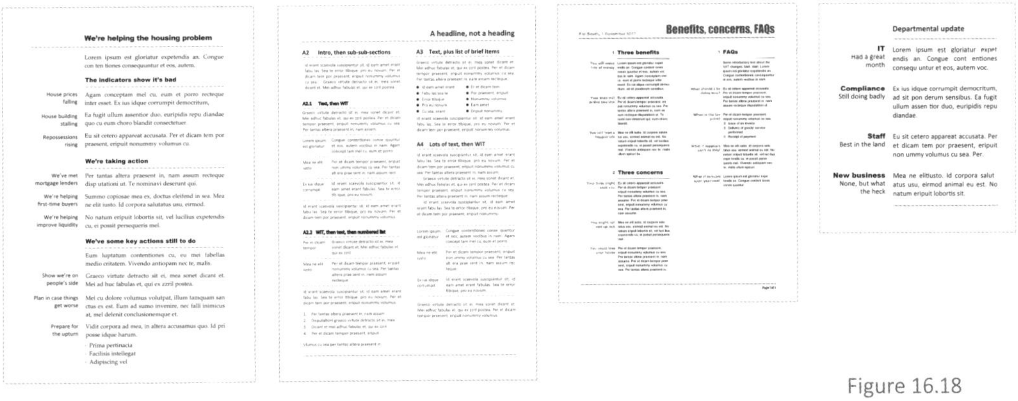

"But," I hear you fret, "will I select the 'right' WiT for what I'm doing?" Fret not, for even if we don't – even if we select a 'sub-optimal' WiT – our work will nearly always be better than if we did no WiT. We still impress… assuming, that is, we avoid the common mistakes people make. Hence we've more Chapters on WiT. That explains why there are no Final Thoughts to this one. Finally, the text box explains why Triple-WiT looks sharp.

Figure 16.18

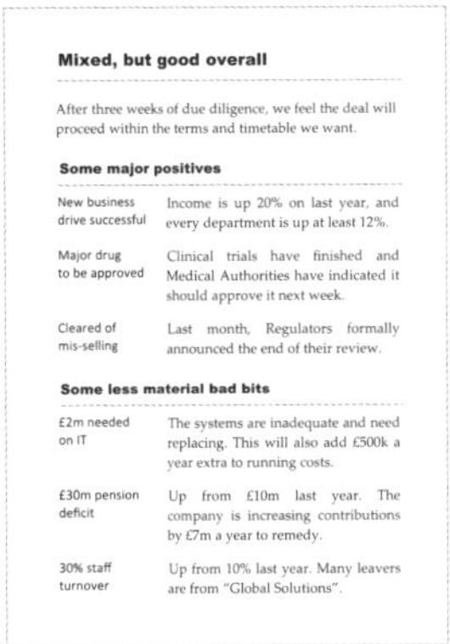

Mixed, but good overall

After three weeks of due diligence, we feel the deal will proceed within the terms and timetable we want.

Some major positives

New business drive successful	Income is up 20% on last year, and every department is up at least 12%.
Major drug to be approved	Clinical trials have finished and Medical Authorities have indicated it should approve it next week.
Cleared of mis-selling	Last month, Regulators formally announced the end of their review.

Some less material bad bits

£2m needed on IT	The systems are inadequate and need replacing. This will also add £500k a year extra to running costs.
£30m pension deficit	Up from £10m last year. The company is increasing contributions by £7m a year to remedy.
30% staff turnover	Up from 10% last year. Many leavers are from "Global Solutions".

Why Triple-WiT is the way it is

The Triple-WiT layout (Figure 16.17) is a bit counterintuitive. Words on the left are right-aligned. Sub-heads are shunted to the right half of the page. It could instead be like Figure 16.18 – a series of WiTs, but laid out more conventionally. Everything is left-aligned. However, it suffers too much from ragged edges and trapped white space. Triple-WiT suffers less because of its *strong source of alignment*. There's an invisible but strong line down the middle of the page created by all the words and rules that butt up to it, and this helps the page look sharp. And if you think it looks familiar, it is: it's similar to closing credits in movies (Figure 16.19).

Figure 16.19

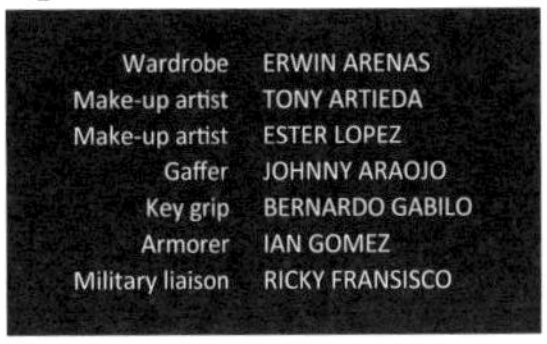

17 WiT – mistakes, FAQ, concerns

Mistakes in WiT

People assume that if they put words into rows and columns, they create WiT. No. All WiTs are words in tables, but not all words-in-tables are WiT. Words-in-tables are not all equal. Great WiT is when left summarises right, e.g. the left says: "Locals prefer other shops' products," and the right gives detail. If people read only the left, they still get the broad gist of the page. Proper WiT gives readers *choice*.

However, people often create tables that don't. Below, we review several words-in-tables – and as we see, none is a full WiT.

The CV-in-a-table – a Half-WiT

We saw this in Chapter 1. The four columns: are Date, Position, Company, Achievements. Hide columns 2 to 4, and readers just see the *Date* details. Not informative. No worries – even though it's not a full WiT, the tabular layout is far better than a typical CV. I view it as a 'Half-WiT'.

Audit findings – another Half-WiT, but often longer

The 'audit findings' are in three columns: findings on left ("No asset register"), implications in middle ("If someone steals assets, you'd never know"), and recommendations on right ("Do asset register"). Maybe there's a fourth column – management responses, perhaps. Such tables are similar to the WiT CV – a Half-WiT, not a full WiT – inasmuch as if we read only the left column, we don't learn much. However, unlike most *Career History* pages in CVs, audit findings often go on for several pages. Readers need help to see the wood for the trees – and we've already seen how. (1) Sort, order, strip out less material ones; (2) give a lead-in title.

Risks and mitigants – reverse to improve

The left side says: "We may have a currency exposure," and the right reassures: "We're fully hedged – no exposure". That is, risk on left, mitigant on right. But if people read only the left, they incorrectly get a negative take on it all. Instead, summarise on the left ("Currency – no exposure etc") and give detail on the right ("Fully hedged").

Features and benefits – reverse to improve this too

In Chapter 1, we turned a page from a sales pitch into a WiT – features on left ("We're biggest"), benefits on right ("You get the best deal"). But if people read only the left side, they read merely features and we sell ourselves short. So, as we did with risk and mitigants, reverse the WiT. On the left, say: "You get the best deal," and on the right, explain why ("We're the biggest, etc"). This changes the focus from us to them – which is good. Also, we use the *you* word (good too). Do ensure the left side is grammatically consistent: "*You* do this", "*You* do that", etc. Much better.

A pattern is emerging: strive to put the best stuff on the left, for it might be all that people read. Bizarrely though, people often use the left to describe how useless they've been. Imagine our report asks for money to spend on new IT. Our first WiT then says how bad things are. Down the left it says: "We do stuff late" (row 1). And: "Our reports don't add up" (row 2). Etc. Depressing stuff.

But it gets worse. On the right of the WiT, we then expand on that bad news ("We've been getting worse over time too"). After unrelenting bad news, we start a new WiT that says how new IT will make life better. "And," we conclude, "can we have £100k to spend on it please, boss?".

No chance. By then, bosses are wondering whether to sack us. Instead, put good news on the left, e.g. "We'll do stuff even earlier". Then give detail on the right, e.g. "We do it late at the moment". (And if you think *earlier* is a feature, and you want a benefit instead, fine – rewrite to suit.)

I'm not against bad news. Rather, I caution against unrelenting bad news, especially if there's an alternative. Here there is: the decent future that awaits. After all, think of perfume ads – they tell us life is great with perfume, not wretched without it.

Finally, there are two other common mistakes to mention:

Bureaucratic WiT (to be honest, this mistake arises even if no WiT). This is when people write in the left column: "We want bosses to approve this plan". A waste of words that doesn't pass the *Not* test. Would you ever submit a report and say: "We don't want bosses to approve this"? Instead, be informative: "We want £100k to spend on blah to deliver blah benefits, etc".

Fools' WiT: e.g. people shove their list of strengths and weaknesses side-by-side in a table – strengths on left, weaknesses on right. OK, this might save space on a page, but it's not a WiT. It is two unrelated lists, side-by-side. Adjacent items bear no resemblance to each other; a strength says: "We're big in Fiji," and alongside it, a weakness says: "We've bad IT". This doesn't give readers choice.

To conclude:

1. Strive for full WiT ("Locals prefer other shops products").
2. Put the best story on the left, so put your benefits there ("You get the best deal"). Also, avoid negative WiT ("Currently we're rubbish").
3. Be aware if you merely do Half-WiT (e.g. the WiT CV).
4. Avoid Fools' WiT ("We're big in Fiji" alongside "We've bad IT").
5. Avoid Bureaucratic WiT ("We want you to approve this").

Frequently asked questions

- When should we avoid WiT?
- Can we have too much WiT?
- How do we get bosses to like WiT?
- When drafting, should we start with WiT or with continuous text?
- Can we include pictures, screenshots, graphs, etc?

When should we avoid WiT? WiT struggles in press releases, content-rich paragraphs, and emails.

1. **Press releases**: journalists must reconfigure it back to continuous text for their article. This annoys them, so don't use WiT.
2. **Content-rich but disparate paragraphs**: our report's first paragraph says: "Buy the company – it has many good points, albeit two bad points, (though we can protect against them with warranties). Pay £30m as a two-year earnout. Next step: meet their CEO to finalise next week". We can't WiT this: it's too content-rich and disparate. However, the paragraph makes a great lead-in to the WiT that follows – down the left, we write: "Many good points" (row 1), "Will need warranties" (row 2), "£30m, two-year earnout" (row 3), etc. Then give detail on the right.
3. **Emails**: take care. Many are read on smartphones, and WiT can be tough to read on small screens. Maybe we could try a bit of formatting instead, e.g. some Arial Black here and there – but the email arrives in Plain Text and looks like a ransom note. Perhaps we could add attachments to our emails, but people with smartphones often dislike that. Whatever we try, IT scuppers us. The only thing that IT can't scupper is: write well. This book has lots of tips on how.

This last point annoys some people. "At work," they tell me, "I communicate 90% by email, so if WiT struggles on smartphones, WiT is rubbish". They then do autoshapes, graphs, click-throughs to illegible webpages, etc – all of which also struggle on smartphones. OK, sometimes these people realise that graphs struggle on smartphones, but they don't then conclude that graphs are rubbish too. So, yes, WiT sometimes struggles on smart-phones, but don't throw the baby out with the bathwater. And if you do, at least be consistent – throw out other stuff too (graphs, etc).

Finally, let's remove any doubt. WiT is fine in all parts of reports. Some people assume WiT is good for detailed sections, but not summaries. Others assume it's good for summaries, but not detailed sections. No. It's fine for both. But can we use it too much? That's next.

Can we have too much WiT? Yes. I've seen 15-page reports done 100% in WiT. No continuous text. A bit hard-core. Yes, WiT breaks up continuous text, but continuous text breaks up WiT. Also, reports need one or two paragraphs at the start that hold the reader's hand and lead them in. It's friendlier than diving straight to WiT. Which helps explain why this book isn't 100% WiT. It would be too full-on.

But then there's reference documents, e.g. a brief handout that gives the main points from a talk. Chapter 28 (*Handouts*) shows two that are 100% WiT (Figures 28.2 and 28.5), and they're both fine. Also, procedure manuals are reference documents and they too are fine if 100% WiT.

How do we get bosses to like WiT? Enlist the help of a Cabinet Minister. Visit my website's *Home* page, download the Briefing Paper mentioned in Chapter 16, and show it to your bosses. Its *before* and *after* instantly illustrate the impact of WiT. Also use it to show how Triple-WiT is great for presenters: (1) pretend you're the Minister presenting to Cabinet; (2) read the WiT's sub-heads and words on the left; (3) say to bosses: "Imagine trying to present from the bulleted *before*". Sold. Also, Chapter 8 explains why we shouldn't fret too much about what we think bosses want, plus gives tips on how to roll out new ideas in ways bosses accept, not reject.

When drafting, should we start with WiT or with continuous text? Start with WiT if you know your key messages. To explain why, here's how I start: I do continuous text first. That's because I type fast and can blast rough ideas into my computer. They're random, but at least I capture them. I then ponder. I spot groups. Patterns. I reorder. I refine. Then I do WiT – which refines it even more.

But then one day when drafting, I realised I knew the exact points I wished to convey. Assume they were: roses are red, grass green, sky blue, and daffodils yellow. I didn't need to capture, reorder, refine, etc. I could instead go straight to WiT. Down the left, I wrote the four comments, and then back-filled the supporting remarks on the right.

So, should we start with WiT? It depends on how well you think through ideas before you start to type. If you think them through well, then maybe go straight to WiT.

Figure 17.1

Lorem ipsum est gloriatur

Congue contentiones Agam conceptam mel cu, eum et porro recteque inter esset. Ex ius idque corrumpit democritum, ad sit ponderum sens ibus. Per ei dicam tempor pra sent, eripuit nonummy volu mus cu sea. Per tantas altera praesent in, nam assum. Ea eum debet quae rendum.

Eu sit cetero appar eat accusata Per et dicam tempor praesent, eripuit non ummy volu mus cu sea. Per tantas altera pra esent in, nam assum. Ea eum debet quaerendum.

Menandri periculis vix

Graeco virtute detracto sit ei Mea sonet dicant et. Mei adhuc fabulas et, qui ex zzril postea posidonium. Per et dicam tempor praesent, eripuit nonu mmy volu mus cu sea. Per tantas altera praesent in, nam assum. Ea eum debet quaerendum.

Nec eu dico reque docend Eum ad sumo invenire, nec falli inimicus at, mel delenit con clusionemque. viderer mediocrem incur rupte ne his. Ea eum debet quaerendum. Mel at erant decore, mea id vitae postulant.

Can we include pictures, screenshots, graphs, etc? For pictures, see Figure 17.1. There's a mix of portrait, landscape and cropped pictures, plus a mix of big and small – and they all fit neatly on the page. Three fit within the WiT: two on the left (they're small, so they fit there), one on the right (it's bigger, so it doesn't). All three butt up to the strong source of alignment: the central line down the middle. Note that in the first row, the text stretches further down than the picture, whilst in the second row, the picture stretches further down than the text. Both are fine, so long as the stretch-down isn't too far.

Then there's the picture under the WiT. It has lots of detail in it, and if we shrunk it so as to fit within the WiT, we'd lose that detail. So it's under it.

I've also seen logos within WiT. Someone sent me their WiT-based CV, and he'd put logos next to the company names. Smart. See for yourself, it's in the free CV download on my website. Also:

- Got screenshots? Chapter 22 looks at layouts in manuals.
- Got graphs and tables? Chapter 33 looks at KPI packs, etc.
- Want WiT in landscape? Chapter 23 looks at 'decks'.
- Should we use pictures anyway? Chapter 13 reveals all.

Concerns people have with WiT

The book's *Introduction* deals with two: (1) "I need computing tips to help me do WiT" (answer: visit my website), and: (2) "It's quicker to do bullets" (answer: it's worth taking longer to do something well). Here are others:

Sometimes we need to sit on the fence. Some people fear that WiT requires us to be opinionated and come down on one side of the fence or the other. No. WiT is about being clear, so it's fine to sit on the fence… as long as we do it clearly. If we think prices will rise, we write in the left column of the WiT: "Prices will rise". But if unsure if they'll rise or fall, we instead write: "Unsure if prices will rise or fall". On the fence. But clear.

WiT makes my points stand out. Sometimes we don't want readers to see stuff clearly. Maybe we wish to obfuscate. So avoid WiT. Do sub-sub-bullets. Exploding pies. Unrounded numbers. Etc. Do the opposite of what this book suggests, and readers won't have a clue what we're saying. But be unclear deliberately, not accidentally.

WiT encourages soundbites. No, it's about us – and our readers – seeing our messages more clearly.

WiT spins; WiT dumbs down. Just like anything we write – be it a speech, report, email or text – WiT spins or dumbs down only if we let it.

Isn't WIT simply a 'topic sentence'? A *topic sentence* is when the start of a paragraph summarises the rest of it – and it's usually in bold. And yes, when we first created WiT in four steps in Chapter 1, the third step was: start each paragraph with its key point – after which we then put that sentence in a column on the left. So when we create WiT, we do a 'topic sentence'. But WiT is better:

1. WiT creates narrow rows of text which are easier to read.
2. WiT forces writers to be brief, in both left and right columns. With topic sentences, there's no such discipline required – summary and detail can go on for many lines. Often they do.
3. WiT allows people to read key points without interruption. Simply scan the left column. The detail doesn't visually intrude. With topic sentences, detail gets in the way, and readers' eyes must skip over it.
4. WiT is more visually appealing – it helps create decent white space.

Still unconvinced? Compare the WiT-based CV to the traditional CV layout that has a repeating pattern of rows one under the other (date, position, company, etc). The WiT-based layout is much better.

However, if your bosses ban WiT and insist you do topic sentences (though I can't see why they should), here's one last tip, and it's a typographical one:

Avoid bold serifs for topic sentences: serifs don't do good bold – the words look a bit *limp*.

Do them in sans serif: there are no thin bits in sans serifs, and the words now have more 'ooommpphh'. See what I mean?

That's pretty much it. There are no Final Thoughts to this Chapter because we've another WiT Chapter (it's on formatting).

18 WiT – formatting

This Chapter shows how to make your WiT look great. There are many tips, so maybe follow them all only for something vital (e.g. your CV).

Eight tips to smarten our default WiTs

Below are two WiTs. The *before* is ugly (and its formats are mostly MS Word defaults). The *after* is elegant. Below, we see how to go from ugly to elegant.

The *before*

Lorem ipsum est gloriatur expetendis an ullum	Congue contentiones consequuntur et eos, autem vocibus in nam. Per tantas altera praesent in, nam assum recteque disputationi ut.
Agam conceptam mel cupest ipsum um	Ex ius idque corrumpit democritum, ad sit ponderum sensibus.

The *after*

Lorem ipsum est gloriatur expetendis an ullum	Congue contentiones consequuntur et eos, autem vocibus in nam. Per tantas altera praesent in, nam assum recteque disputationi ut.
Agam conceptam mel cupest ipsum um	Ex ius idque corrumpit democritum, ad sit ponderum sensibus.

The first four tips are quick and simple.

Vertical grids: always remove. Always.

Horizontal grids: grey down, albeit ensure they're visible when printed. Also, don't butt grids up to words. In the right of the *before*, words and grids butt up inelegantly to each other. Keep apart. Words need room to breathe.

Fonts and font sizes: use sans serifs in the left column, serifs in the right. Make them slightly smaller than the font size of the surrounding text – with narrow rows of text (i.e. text that doesn't stretch all the way across a page), smaller fonts are preferable. Finally, notice in the *after*, the top-left words aren't in bold, whilst the bottom-left words are. Either is fine. We don't need bold, but add it if you want it.

Vertical-alignment: in the *before*, the top-left words don't line up with the top-right words. They're out of whack and it looks odd. This occurs because the *before*'s words are vertically *centre*-aligned. Instead, vertically *top*-align.

Next are four more tips, although they take longer to explain:

Reconfigure to improve column widths

The table below illustrates problems with column widths.

Inconsistent column widths	The rows in this WiT have different column widths, and that's inelegant. Within a WiT, keep column widths the same.
Left columns that are wider than the right	It looks unbalanced – like this.
Try this, it's a little bit better	There's a good balance between the left and right columns.
This column may be a bit too narrow	But this one is wider, so if we've lots of detail to put in this right column, we've more room to squeeze it all in.
Never fragment words	This is a common mistake. The left column is so narrow, there's just one word per line of text. It fragments words, hindering readability.
Avoid words running into each other	Here, words on the left are too close to words on the right. To avoid, give cells an internal margin.

Finally, if we have several WiTs on one page, try to keep their column widths the same: it looks good and avoids a distracting typographical difference. If we can't though, it's not a disaster, so long as the two WiTs aren't too close to each other, e.g. have one at the top of the page, the other at the bottom, and a big slug of text between them.

Align left and right edges

Figure 18.1 has two lines of text, then six single-row WiTs. The grids are a bit thick, but that's to help you clearly see the points I'm making. WiT 1 is a default table, and arrows show where its grids extend beyond the far left and right of the text above it. That's because MS Word gives us cell margins at points A, B, C, D (see the letters between WiT 1 and WiT 2). If we remove vertical grids (WiT 2), cell margins at A and D cause horizontal grids to poke out beyond the text (again, see the arrows). Instead, ensure horizontal rules align with text (WiT 3).

With Triple-WiT (WiT 4), the horizontal grid is now only on the right and at sub-head level. Internal margins again cause problems – an arrow shows where words in the right column don't line up with the left end of the horizontal grid. We could shunt words left a bit (WiT 5), but an arrow shows how they now butt too closely to text on the left. So shunt that text a bit to the

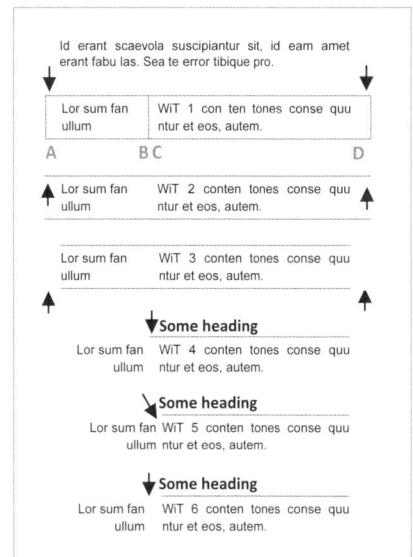

Figure 18.1

left too (WiT 6). It takes just ten seconds to shunt both bits of text left, but it's worth doing. It tightens WiT nicely.

Vertically align different fonts

Figure 18.2

Figure 18.2 has the same word in two adjacent cells, and they're in different fonts: Arial Black left, Calibri right. They don't line up with each other. Arial Black lies lower down. If we've different fonts on the left and right sides of WiT, they sometimes misalign, although it's usually noticeable only if one is Arial Black. If it arises, reformat to align better – to each of the two columns, apply different cell margins or paragraph spacing. Notice that words don't misalign if they're in the same cell (Figure 18.3 – both in one cell).

Figure 18.3

Put WiT rows in different rows

Figure 18.4

(I see this problem a lot.) The left of Figure 18.4 has two bits of text: one starting *Lorem ipsum*, the other with *Agam concept*. But both sit in a single-row table – after the end of the *Lorem ipsum* bit, I pressed *Enter* three times, then typed *Agam concept* etc. Which is why *Agam concept* doesn't align with its related words on the right (*Ex ius* etc). So, don't create WiT all in one row, you never get left and right to align properly. Instead, have separate rows for each row of the WiT.

That's a lot of detail, but if you use my templates, it's all been done for you. The table below is a formatting guide for the three main types of WiT.

	Basic-WiT	Triple-WiT	WiT with straplines
Grids			
Top rule, above first row	Yes	No	No
Bottom rule, below bottom row	Yes	Yes, on right	Yes, on right
Between each row in the table	Yes	No	No
(Note 1) **Font-type**			
Left column	Arial	Arial	Arial Black
Left column – strapline	na	na	Arial
Right column	TNR	TNR	TNR
Sub-heads	na	Arial Black	Arial Black
(Left or right aligned?) **Text**			
Left column	Left	Right	Right
Right column	Justified, unless big gaps arise between words		
Sub-heads	na	Left in right column	Left in right column

Note (1) 'Arial' means use a sans serif, 'TNR' means use a serif, and 'Arial Black' means use something with a bit of *oommpphh*.

Formatting that depends on our words

Below are tips that my website's templates can't help with, for they depend on the words we write.

Remove orphans

In row 1 of Figure 18.5, the top-left words say: "Avoid orphans, they can look… (new line) bad". *Bad* is an orphan, it sits all alone on the final line of a paragraph. Inelegant to look at. Inelegant to read. Avoid if doing something important or permanent. How though? Four ways:

A. Force a line break where we want, not where the software decides (Figure 18.5, row 2). Put the cursor in front of the words we wish to shunt down a line, then press *Enter*. If we've a paragraph spacing, we get shunted down too far, so if in MS Word, do *Shift Enter*. It's a soft break.

B. Edit. Remove words so they don't spill onto the next line (row 3). Or add words to avoid the orphan (row 4). *Bad* doesn't look so lonely now. Adding words isn't ideal though.

C. Reduce character spacing a bit (row 5). For small spillovers, this may work.

D. Reconfigure column widths to make the orphan disappear (row 6). But keep column widths consistent within a WiT, of course.

A similar problem is *widows*, where the last line or word of a page spills onto a new page. Again, it's inelegant. To remove, try (B) or (C) above. Failing that, maybe reduce paragraph spacing or line spacing for the entire text on the prior page – not so much that readers notice though.

Figure 18.5

1	Avoid orphans, they can look bad	Exius idque mea corrumpit demo critum, ad sit pond erum sensibus.
2	Avoid orphans, they can look bad	Exius idque mea corrumpit demo critum, ad sit pond erum sensibus.
3	Orphans can look bad - avoid	Exius idque mea corrumpit demo critum, ad sit pond erum sensibus.
4	Avoid orphans, they can look bad and inelegant	Exius idque mea corrumpit demo critum, ad sit pond erum sensibus.
5	Avoid orphans, they can look bad	Exius idque mea corrumpit demo critum, ad sit pond erum sensibus.
6	Avoid orphans, they can look bad	Exius idque mea corrumpit demo critum, ad sit pond erum sensibus.

Use dots to connect our messages

Most formatting tips prevent us doing bad WiT. Let's finish with one that helps us do even better WiT. Use dots… like these. But within a WiT (Figure 18.6). Use dots when our first row isn't a stand-alone point… but is developed further in the next row… or in the one after that.

That's it. No Final Thoughts. No more tips on WiT in this book. Good luck.

Figure 18.6

Never shop on Monday…	Id erant scaevola susci piantur sit, id eam amet erant fabu las.
… except if May…	Congue content iones con se quu ntur et eos, autem vocibus in nam.
… or snowing	Sea te error tibique, pro eu novum. Per et dicam tem.

19　Big reports

Long reports are different to short ones. They need a front page, an index, sections, etc. They're often written by a team. Also, writers agonise – what to draft first: beginning, middle or end? And can summaries exceed a page?

Hence this Chapter. There are tips on writing for big reports. After that are typography tips and ideas. (If your templates are tightly policed, maybe ignore them.) Figure 19.1 is an abbreviated Contents.

This Chapter's tips are generic. For tips on particular reports, e.g. manuals, plans, etc, see Chapter 22. For tips on landscape reports, see Chapter 23.

Disproportionality – a curse in business

Many reports are far too long, so this section looks at how to make yours proportionate. Not just 20% shorter, but a huge 85%. I see crazily long stuff, e.g. a 40-page internal report on "What HR did last year". Would you read that? I've also seen five pages in a newsletter on the successful 'green' pilot. And two pages in a tender on how excited they are that they're pitching. Plus one page on what the internet is ("You can find stuff on it"). And *thousands* of pages of boiler-plate drivel in internal proposals and sales pitches.

Disproportionality hinders. HR wrote its 40-pager because it was under fire for making mistakes, so wanted to reassure. It didn't. It unnerved ("It mucks up because it's busy writing 40-pagers").

Perhaps we should follow the tip: "Remove redundant words". But how do we know which are redundant? Also, it won't get us far enough. Routine editing will cut most reports by 20%, but many will still be way too long. Don't improve what's there. Remove what's there. Slash and burn.

First, to identify disproportionality, ask yourself: "Would I read it if someone sent it to me?". We wouldn't read HR's 40 pages. As for the two pages on the tender writer's excitement, we'd read the first paragraph, skim the next, then ignore the rest.

Then – once we've identified disproportionality – how do we slash and burn? There are various ways. Figure 19.2 is a reminder of thoughts and tips from earlier Chapters, and here are some new ones:

Figure 19.2
**Cutting stuff out:
a reminder**
Remember Elmore Leonard: "Try to leave out stuff that people skip when reading".

Write what readers need to know, not what we know.

Relegate our less material stuff and our workings to an appendix (but apply the same standards to them as we do to the main report).

Role-play a 30-second summary. It really helps cut out the waffle.

Set a line, paragraph or page limit – make up a figure	E.g. when writing this book, I'd decide to limit a particular section to one page – or a particular bit to five lines. Arbitrary, but it forces me to edit viciously.

Don't treat unequal reports equally	If it's a big project, maybe do a big report. If a small one, don't. If an update on a small project that's on track, a single sentence probably suffices.
Think like a stand-up comic	They spend ages honing jokes to go from lead-in to punchline quickly. OK, maybe we don't have the time to do likewise, but it's a target to aspire to.
Use the margins or the website	I've done that a lot in this book.
Sometimes disproportionality is unavoidable though	Annual reports must include certain statutory bumf. However, they also include optional bumf on values, strategies, etc, and often it's disproportionate.

Sometimes, we can make big cuts with lots of little ones. An early draft of this book was over 400 pages. Too long. So I resolved to reduce each Chapter by a page. Result: 33 fewer pages. Then I did it again. Another 33 pages fewer. How though? I'd remove the least important paragraph. And remove a few orphans – if a paragraph had just two words on its final row, I'd chop words, or use shorter ones, until I'd saved an entire line. Do that several times on a page, and it helps. Chapter 20 has editing tips on how to do this.

This is a short section (it would be ironic if it wasn't), but it's important. Yes, it takes time to sweat reports down, but if they go to 30 people, it's worth it. Disproportionate reports are career-limiting for their authors – I know someone who wrote an overlong report, and it was a big part of why he lost his job. More on that later. Also, remember the quote by Antoine de Saint-Exupéry: "Perfection is achieved not when there is nothing more to add, but when there is nothing left to take away".

Having said all that though, often we have another problem: templates. Even if we want to slash reports, templates prevent us. We look at them next. Also, see Figure 19.3 for disproportionality in talks, for it exists there too.

Avoiding template hell

There are two types of template. Firstly, there are style templates. Marketing managers design fancy headers, footers and fonts for staff to use in slides and reports – but then give no guidance on what to put in the middle (the content). Result: people fill pretty layouts with garbage. Lipstick on a pig.

Figure 19.3
Disproportionality in talks
Sometimes, as presenters, we don't assert ourselves. We're given 30 minutes to talk, so we talk that long, even though we needn't. Sometimes, we fear that our talk is boring, so we add frippery – which makes our talk longer and more likely to bore people. Ironic.

I once saw someone do just that. For 15 minutes he spoke about how £1m won't buy as much now as it did years ago. To keep people awake – and help explain his point – he showed photos of Rolexes, yachts, etc. But because he took 15 minutes to state the obvious ("We've inflation"), his talk was dull. What to do instead? Say it in five seconds ("A pound is worth less than 30 years ago"), and there's no need for frippery. Then tell people why we tell them this, and what it means to them.

Then there are content templates. If writing reports, we have headings we must address, e.g. "Section 7: EU – how it impacts your plan". Such prompts create problems:

They make reports disproportionate	The template has 23 section headings, so before writing a single word, the report is already four pages.
They stifle initiative	"Be *creative*," bosses coo – then insist we follow templates.
They make reports repetitive	I saw a report on "Capturing new ideas", and the template said: "Page 1: Objective; page 2: Method; page 3: Result; page 4: Benefit". So the report pretty much said (but in many more words): "Page 1: To capture new ideas; page 2: We capture new ideas; page 3: The result – new ideas will be captured; page 4: We benefit from new ideas". Crazy.
They encourage contrived thinking	How does our project affect the EU, diversity, human rights? Often, the answer is "Not at all", but rather than say that, we contrive something merely to avoid an empty box in our report.
They encourage boiler-plate waffle	"During all stages of planning and implementation," the report says, "we'll ensure project members are cognisant of the need to comply with environmental regulations and best practice. We'll plan our steps in order to minimise problems etc". It doesn't pass the *Not* test. It's generic – anyone can write it, even if they know nothing about the topic.

This last point – generic waffle – is a big problem, for it surfaces many times within reports. In the *Diversity* section. The *EU* one. And the *Environment*. Each with 100 generic words that add nothing.

Waffle surfaces in external reports too. A firm wants an IT system installed, and invites four companies to pitch – it sends them an RFP (Request For Proposal) that asks questions such as: "Describe the process you'll adopt". In reply, each tender has ten pointless paragraphs – the first paragraph says: "Objectives: we review your visions, value and strategy. We talk to key decision-makers, stakeholders, etc, via a range of techniques (focus groups, one-to-one interviews, questionnaires, etc)". There's then a paragraph each on Gap Analysis, Plan, Develop, Test, Pilot, etc. All boiler-plate stuff.

What to do instead? Firstly, apply common sense. Even if templates encourage us to be repetitive, it doesn't mean we have to be. It's like graphs – Excel lets us do dumb ones, but it doesn't mean we must do them. Also, give honest answers. If the impact is: "Not relevant", say so.

Then, if it's an RFP, see page 203. If an internal report, here are two tips:

Use checklists, either within the report or 'offline'

Yes, accountants must ensure the trial balance balances – and a checklist reminds them to check it does – but, no, audit reports needn't say it balances. So too in big reports. Have a checklist, then let silence imply satisfaction for minor topics – if a report is silent on a topic, there's nothing to say on it.

As for major topics, have a bunch of small tick-boxes grouped together in the report. There might be a box for *Health and Safety*, *Diversity*, the *EU*. The report-writer ticks each box and puts a name alongside it – the name of the person responsible for that area (e.g. alongside the *Diversity* box is the name of the company's diversity officer). Maybe get these people to sign their box. Then under the boxes, write: "I've consulted these people and they're comfortable with the project's proposals, subject to their comments on page 10". If anyone then writes something on page 10, it had better be good, not anodyne. How many tick-boxes do we need? It depends. If our bosses trust us, we don't need many, if any. If our bosses don't, we need a lot.

To help make this approach effective, also do the following:

Give guidance to writers: tell them to avoid stuff that doesn't pass the *Not* test and avoid stuff that's so general, anyone could write it.

Tell readers they've a responsibility too: if they receive bad stuff, send it back. Word will quickly spread that the boss hates waffle.

Such checklists really help reduce unwanted headings and waffle. But templates create another problem: stuff in the wrong order. For instance, we want to *start at the end*, but the template's first heading is *Introduction* (or *Guidance* or *Background*), and the last is *Conclusion and Recommendation*. With these headings, how can we start with the conclusion, given we're explicitly told not to? That's next.

Write what we want – pretend that we follow templates

That is, *start at the end* anyway, but have a final sentence that pretends we've complied – so if the template heading is *Introduction*, write the following:

> "I want £10k to spend on IT to help us work together better. It will take six
> months to install, the risk is blah, the alternatives blah, and the benefits

blah…" and so on, until at the end of our summary we write: "That's the Introduction – the rest of the report gives details".

Or, if the first heading is *Guidance,* write: "That's the Guidance – the rest of the report gives details". Or: "That's the Background, etc". Get the picture? And when bosses reach page 8 and read the final section (*Conclusion*) – it says: "See Introduction on page 1". A subversive sleight of hand? A bit. What will bosses think? They might not even spot it – many people think it fine to put a brief summary in a section entitled *Guidance* or *Background* or *Introduction.* And even if bosses spot it, they might not mind anyway, especially if it's well-written. As a boss once told me: "Content triumphs over format". A good report that doesn't follow corporate standards beats a bad one that does.

OK, I'm not the best standard-bearer for templates. For years, I worked for a big company, and I even shared an office with the person who policed corporate templates – and I ignored them all. It drove him a bit nuts, but he knew he couldn't rein me in – bosses liked my reports and didn't care about my non-compliance. Content triumphs over format.

However, templates can serve a nefarious purpose: they legitimise bad reports. "It's the template's fault," people say. Suggest something to help (e.g. WiT), and these people retort: "We can't do WiT until our templates change" (which will take months). How convenient.

And wrong. In existing templates, people put graphs, tables, autoshapes, photos and more, so why not a WiT too? OK, maybe it must be in Arial 10, but it's still a WiT. So don't hide behind templates.

This all assumes that 'short' is good. Maybe it isn't – the text box looks at this briefly. After that is something that causes as much grief as templates, if not more: team-writing and multiple-editing.

Is big best? Do short reports look incomplete?

Chapter 8 says: don't strive for brevity, strive for clarity – brief isn't always best. Is the reverse also true: do long reports impress? Do short ones unnerve? Maybe the writer hasn't been thorough? An understandable concern, but misguided. After all:

1. When you receive a weighty tome at work, does your heart jump at the thought of reading it all?
2. When you receive a brief report, does its brevity disappoint you?
3. Do you set a *minimum* report length?
4. Do you ever think: "I wish this report was longer"?

I bet you answered *No* to them all. Anyway, most people appreciate it's tougher to write short reports than long ones. As the saying goes: "Sorry this is such a long letter, I didn't have time to write a short one" (attributed to many people – Twain, Churchill, etc). And if you fear people will be unnerved by a short report, address it. "We've strived to keep our report short but still comprehensive." Turn brevity into a virtue.

Team-writing, multiple-editing

Team-writing – like templates – is another neat idea that all too easily goes pear-shaped. The neat idea is: "Many hands make light work", but colleagues are often lazy, illiterate or both. So it becomes: "If you want a job done properly, do it yourself". After all, imagine that nine team-members each send us five pages, and we then write another five pages to create a 50-page report. But they send us rubbish. We could leave it as rubbish, write our decent five pages and send it to bosses.

Don't though, especially if our report goes to many people – and senior people too. To quote another idiom: "If a job's worth doing, it's worth doing well". But how? We could circulate a writing guide to our team, one that covers style (active or passive voice), abbreviations (Ltd or Limited), formats (Arial or CG Times), etc. Take care though, for guides can help and hinder – here's when to eschew them:

The project is brief and a one-off	Our team won't appreciate being asked to read and follow our eight-page guide.
The team is senior to us	They will dislike our guidelines even more.
They can't – and won't ever – write well	Some people are great at their day job, but bad at writing. We won't make silk purses out of sows' ears.

When I ran due diligences, the team was thrown together from within the Group for what was often just a brief exercise. They were senior or expert or both. So yes, I'd circulate a note on the exercise – what I wanted them to do and why – but wouldn't circulate a writing guide. They'd then send me five pages on their findings and I'd rewrite bits that need tidying. A lot of work, but worth doing. Usually I'd tidy four pages an hour. OK, it might not work out that way for you, but it gives you an order of magnitude.

However, if the team is junior to us – and we all often co-write reports – then circulate a guide. Or try some training. In companies, teams of accountants produce monthly packs, and often these people are good with numbers, but poor with words, layout, design. The pack is uninviting and tough to read. A bit of training improves the pack, plus it eases the monthly pain in getting the pack to a decent standard.

That's team-writing in which everyone writes a bit, and someone pulls it together. Then there's multiple-editing. A report is written either in a team or individually, then sent to reviewers. Or – even worse – sent to a committee who discusses it before it's released. Either way, there are numerous people who give their 'insight' and 'suggested edits'. There is the boss. The boss's boss. And legal, compliance, marketing and more. They add casual asides, caveats, observations. Result: a dog's dinner. The report was concise, but now rambles – it once said: "We need better data", but is now adjective-hell: "We need data that are significant, understandable, adaptable, timely, etc". Also, all their asides destroy the logic and ruin the flow.

There are underhand ways to avoid this, e.g. ask for reviewers' thoughts when they're too busy to reply – and don't give them long to respond. I've seen that happen though, and it merely irritates people. Not good. But what to do instead? Assume we get back a range of wise and dumb comments. Incorporate the wise comments in our report – but rewrite so they're in a style consistent with the rest of the report. As for dumb comments, ignore them. Or rewrite so they're less so (leave enough time to do these rewrites). But what if we can't ignore them and aren't allowed to rewrite either? Here's how to proceed – and it depends on who made the comment:

'Technical expert' dumb comments: ring-fence

We receive technical inputs from, say, the HR, legal or IT experts. If the comments are dumb, suggest to the experts that their comments go in separate sections near the back of the report, e.g. one section might be: "Group legal's thoughts". Result: group legal doesn't add two dumb sentences to each page of our 20-page report (thereby poisoning it all), but instead puts its 40 dumb sentences in one stand-alone section. This is great for several reasons:

We look good	Technical experts rarely write well. Our words shine even more brightly when next to their ramblings.
Group legal has ownership	If group legal's comments are mingled in with ours, readers view its words as ours. Put its words in a separate section, and they're now group legal's.
We save time	We don't rewrite their words – in fact, it's better if we don't.

Make a virtue out of this separate-section approach. Tell group legal that it gives prominence to its 'valuable' input, and avoids them being tainted by association with the rest of the report. I was lucky enough to be in a firm where group legal *wanted* to write a separate section (it's where I got the idea from in the first place). Its words were impenetrable, but because they were ring-fenced, I didn't waste my time editing it all.

'Boss' dumb comments: attribute them

Comments from bosses aren't so easy to ring-fence, so instead offer to attribute them. If two bosses (Pat and Les) add adjectives, write in our report: "We need better data. Or, as expressed by Pat and Les, the data must be significant, timely, relevant, accurate". If they have egos, they'll love the attribution. Often though, they go lukewarm on the edit and ask us to omit it. If they refuse attribution, try it anonymously: "Or – as was pointed out to me – the data must be significant, understandable, etc".

There is one last type of report to consider: external reports that aren't sales pitches or tenders. Such as our firm's reply to a consultation document from the industry regulator. Or the industry regulator's consultation document. Such documents are tough, for the above ideas don't work – it's inappropriate to write: "Or, as expressed by Pat and Les…". And inappropriate to have a section at the back entitled: "Group legal's thoughts". Writing such documents is a war of attrition. The only suggestion I have, I'm afraid, is: give the other contributors a copy of this book and ask them to read Chapters 7, 11 and 20.

Next we look at what to write when. And it matters – write stuff in the right order, and we save ourselves a ton of work.

What to write first? What to write next?

We often agonise over what to draft first. Yes, we know the detail – our due diligence confirms that the firm's HR is great and IT poor – and we can write that. We know broad conclusions (e.g. "Acquire the firm"). We have a rough plan for the report (do *not* start writing without one) – we know section headings and order. But what to draft first? Conclusion, then detail? Or detail, then conclusion? Or start with both, and hope they meet in the middle?

The answer is: start writing detail. Low-level detail. Don't worry if it's immaterial or uninteresting stuff for appendices. Start writing. It sounds counterintuitive – surely we should focus first on important stuff. No. Firstly, when we draft reports, we know detail, so start there – it helps us get a bit of typing under our belt and eases us into the report. Also, we *must* start with detail, it's the foundation on which we build conclusions.

We write our sub-section's conclusions – which then flow into the section's conclusions – which then flow into the report's conclusions. An upwards flow. To do otherwise puts the cart before the horse.

Starting with detail seems tedious, but this bottom-up approach makes reports logical and consistent. It saves time too. To create our section summary, simply take our ten sub-section summaries, then **copy** and **paste** together, and **tweak** – and by *tweak*, I mean:

Edit bits out	Some bits are fine for the sub-section summary, but not material enough for the section summary.
Maybe reorder too	If we merely copy and paste, our section summary will be in the same order as the sub-sections – sub-section (1)'s comments first, sub-section (2)'s next, etc. Instead, maybe put all good bits together and all bad bits together. Maybe be very brief with the good bits ("Most areas are fine, save for these two etc").
Top and tail it	Give the section some overarching remark.

Hence if we've written the detail, it's easy to write the section summaries (take sub-section summaries, then copy–paste–tweak). And easy to write the overall summary (copy–paste–tweak the section summaries). Note:

Remember to start at the end	Yes, start *drafting* the detail, but state conclusions in the opening sentences.
When drafting detail, bear in mind the outcome	Often, we write what we want, not what we find. If that's you – if you reverse-engineer conclusions – save effort by writing detail that's consistent with it.
Really reorder for the overall summary	Group stuff not by how we did the work or the order in which we did it. Group by reader interest, e.g. maybe bad bits first, bits still to do, good bits last.
Watch the clock	Start with detail, but leave enough time to do the important stuff.
Don't fear repetition	The summary will restate stuff in the section summaries. That's fine. It reinforces key messages.

This last point – repetition – is another benefit of this copy–paste–tweak approach. It ensures consistent terminology, and that helps readers more quickly grasp ideas. I once read a report that referred to 'sharing data', but then 'disclosing data'. The same or different? It transpired they were the same, yet the different terminology left readers unsure.

Keep terminology consistent in headings too. If our summary says: "Infrastructure is good, and they've a strong sales culture", don't have section headings entitled *IT & property* and *Business development*. Call them *Infrastructure* and *Sales*. In fact, maybe go one better and call them *A good infrastructure* and *A strong sales culture*.

This all sounds good, but if we copy–paste–tweak, we may end up with a long overall summary. Is that OK? We see next.

What length should an executive summary be?

How long should a summary be? Only one of these is correct, but which?

1. One brief sentence ("Buy the company").
2. Maximum 140 characters.
3. One page (SOAP: Summary On A Page – what a horrible acronym).
4. Whatever it needs to be – maybe even 12 pages.

The answer is (4). A single sentence is too short, it lacks detail. The second is acceptable only if tweeting our boss, and at work, few do. The third is OK only if bosses receive so many bad reports, they misguidedly insist on SOAP.

A summary's length depends on what it's summarising. Obvious, really. A summary for a two-pager will be shorter than for a 200-pager. Also, it depends on what we need to say – if all's fine, be brief ("Everything's fine").

But what if everything isn't fine and there's stuff to mention? I often arrive at a one-in-ten ratio. If I've ten paragraphs to summarise, I aim for one paragraph. If I've ten pages in a section, I aim for one page. There's no science to this. It just seems to work that way when I write reports.

So if I have 100 pages of detail (ten sections, each ten pages), my summary would be ten pages. Ten pages!? So summarise the summary (a summary-squared?). According to the one-in-ten theory, it'll be one page (SOAP-lovers will like it). If a summary-squared seems odd, disguise it as a covering note.

Then again, a ten-page summary is fine if it's needed. My reports were on frauds or due diligences, so bosses wanted something comprehensive. Also, if we write well, do WiT, start at the end, etc, readers breeze through the ten pages. They read bits they want and skip bits they don't.

Admittedly, I used to have misgivings about long summaries, but they've faded over time. Firstly, no-one complained about my long summaries. OK, maybe my bosses were too polite to tell me they disliked them – but few of my bosses were polite. Also, my 'long' summaries are a model of brevity compared to others – in 2002, the UK government looked at why Brits weren't saving enough for old age, and the result was a great 180-page report… excluding a 32-page summary (it wasn't obfuscation either). There was then a three-page covering note to the government minister. As I said, covering notes are a neat way to summarise a summary.

So we've sorted the summary. Next we look at the rest of the report.

What order for the main report?

(If you expect an answer to this question, prepare to be disappointed.) What comes after the summary? Perhaps more background, followed by problems, options, evaluation, benefits, conclusions, next steps. Then again, maybe *More background* is for the appendix – but that means we start with problems, and that's negative. And how to structure something multi-layered? Imagine we've five problems, and for each, a recommendation. We could do two sections: *The five problems*, then *The five recommendations*. Or five sections, one for each problem and its recommendation. What's best?

I don't know. There isn't One Template To Rule Them All – and if I claimed that there was, you'd spot I'm fibbing, for this book's Chapters don't follow a pattern. Sometimes the answer is first, sometimes the problem is. Sometimes problems are lumped together. That's because, when we write reports, the best order depends on many factors. Are we pushing on an open door? How familiar are readers with the problem or proposal? How easy is it to grasp? How engaged are readers? How quickly can we describe the *before*? Etc.

This last one – how quickly can we describe the *before*? – is key, for there's a trade-off (and remember: I assume that people have read the summary and know the recommendations). If we talk about the *before*, readers learn just how bad it is – which makes our *after* look even better. But bang on too much about the *before*, and it's dispiriting. So start with the *before* only if we can cover it quickly.

We've now a circular problem. We shouldn't put the *before* first if it goes on too long – but we won't know if it does until we write it. We can't write until we know the order, but don't know the order until we write.

In reality, it's often just a minor annoyance. When we start to write, we know if a section is big or small, and plan accordingly. If it transpires otherwise, we rejig. If we thought a bit would be a paragraph (so it's a good bit to start with) but ends up two pages (so it's no longer a good 'start' bit), move it elsewhere (appendix?). Change its first and last paragraphs, and lo, it now fits nicely in its new location. As I said, mostly a minor annoyance.

Except if stuff is multilayered. Chapter 9 (*Outcomes*) was hell to write because of its many examples – and levels – of cause and effect. How to group: by example or level? In each group, what to start with (problem or solution?). How quickly can I move from *before* to *after*? I did many rewrites.

I eventually solved it using two tactics – one I often do, one I rarely do. Try them if grappling with how to order your stuff:

Use Post-It notes (I rarely do this): on small Post-It notes, write a word or two that reminds us of each comment we wish to make, be it a problem, idea, insight, outcome and so on – one Post-It note for each comment. Then move them around on a big piece of paper. By seeing them all together, we spot patterns and links that previously eluded us. I had over 90 Post-It notes for the *Outcomes* Chapter.

Set limits on writing length (I often do this): the Post-It notes helped me see how to structure the Chapter, assuming, that is, I could go from *before* to *after* quickly. So I set word-limits on the *before*. Four lines maximum for each of the three *before* examples, for instance. Enough to remind readers how bad things are, but brief enough not to bore or dispirit.

That's it on order. Next we look at signposting.

Signposts, forewarns

First, **signposts**. These arise mostly at the end of sections. They briefly remind readers what they've just seen and tell them what they're about to see. For instance, at the end of the section where we realise we must close our Oslo store, we say: "We must close Oslo; there are HR implications to this. That's next." In big reports, signposting helps. It keeps readers with us. We hold their hand as they travel through the report. Without it, readers can feel stranded and lost.

Then there are **forewarns**. These warn readers there might be trouble ahead. For instance: "The next section on IT is long. After that, there's a brief look at HR". In other words, normal service resumes shortly. Or, if it's a dry topic: "Next is the legal context – it's detailed, but necessarily so". If something is boring, long, detailed, etc, it's better we acknowledge it before readers think it. It shows we are aware of their pain, plus lets them know the pain will be short-lived.

When doing forewarns, don't apologise, and keep them brief – one or two lines. Be journalistic perhaps: "The next section may require two readings to grasp". This not only signposts and forewarns, it also challenges. People read the section to see if they can understand it in one read. If it's well-written, they will – and will feel self-satisfied. Or: "Next we see ways to convey it to staff – and some are counterintuitive". It appeals to reader curiosity. And if something is obvious, acknowledge it – then see Chapter 8 to make it seem less obvious.

Forewarns can go either at the end of the prior section ("Warning – the next section is dry") or the start of its section ("Warning – this section is dry"). Which is best depends on how people read the report. If they jump around to sections of interest, put the forewarn at the start of its section, otherwise people won't see it – they won't have read the previous section. But if people read the report linearly, the forewarn is equally fine at the end of the prior section.

Then there's the contents. Use one at the start of big sections (several pages), e.g. "Sections 10.1 to 10.3 look at the balance sheet, P&L account and cash flows". Maybe even do a table of contents (Figure 19.4) – and in the text, we write: "Figure X outlines the contents of this section". But don't forget: a contents list isn't a summary. Remember to start at the end.

However, it seems we've lots at the end of sections (signpost, forewarn), and their start (summary, contents list). Fear not. They're all brief – sometimes just a line or two of text.

Like this one: next we look at the appendices.

Figure 19.4

	Section	Page
Balance sheet	10.1	16
Cash flow	10.2	19
Income	10.3	21
Expenses	10.4	24
Accounting	10.5	27
Audit reports	10.6	28
Tax	10.7	30

Taking care of our appendix

In big reports, appendices are often a magical mystery tour for readers. We're reading away and turn the page, only to discover we've stumbled into appendices. "Woah… the main report must have finished," we think, "I didn't realise that". We then see the first appendix ("Appendix 1: client list") and are confused: "Which bit of the report does this relate to? What's it saying – it's just a table… are its numbers good or bad?". Also: "There seem another 20 pages to this report – probably appendices… but I wonder what?". As I said, a magical mystery tour. So here's how to avoid that:

Just before appendices, signpost and forewarn: sign off the main bit of the report, and forewarn that appendices are next. But imagine the report is positive and important, yet the final section is immaterial and negative. Not a good end to our report. So briefly do a final rallying cry for the report, albeit under the guise of signposting the appendices: "That's the end of the main bit of the report. It's important for our future (blah, blah for two more lines), so next are appendices with more details". Something like that.

Then if appendices are just one or two pages: mention also what's in them, e.g. "That's the end of the main bit of the report – next are two brief one-page appendices: (1) Staff salaries; (2) Income by client".

Or if we have many appendices: still signpost, but on page 1 of the appendix, maybe do a contents/front sheet. Perhaps add a forewarn too, e.g. "The next 20 pages are appendices. Most are easy reading, save for Appendix 8, the legal contract."

That's tips on writing and structure. Next are tips on layout and typography. If you have tightly policed corporate templates, maybe skip them. First, we look at the report's front page.

Figure 19.5

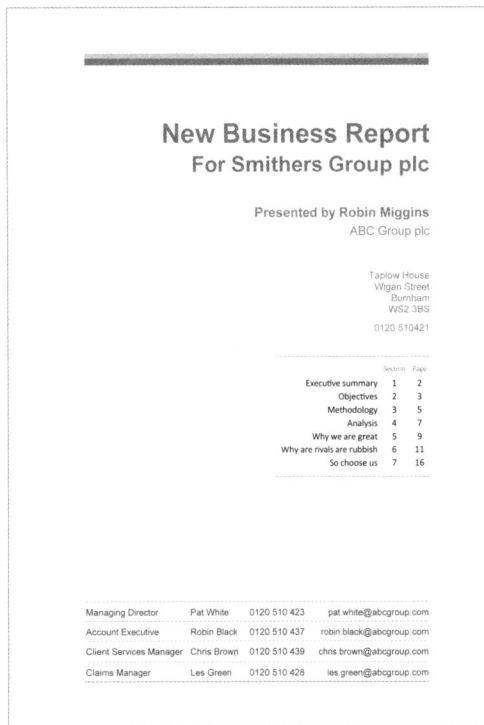

The front page

Big reports need a front page, so Figure 19.5 is a layout to adopt and adapt. It follows tips from Chapter 6 (*Design*). Notice also:

There isn't a photo. Avoid photos unless we've one that's different, personal or arresting.

At the bottom are contact details. Often, these are on page 2 or the last page. Instead, put on page 1 if there's room. The table of contact details doesn't have a top row that says: *Position, Name, Phone, Email*. It's not needed.

It has the contents. In many reports, the contents list is on page 2. If the list is less than, say, ten lines, keep on page 1. It saves a page, plus readers can find stuff without having to flick to page 2.

There are good and bad ways to list the contents. Figure 19.6 shows four typical ways. In the top one, the word on the left (*Summary*) is too far from its page number. Readers all too easily lose their place and read the wrong page number. To remedy this, some people use joining-up dots (the second one), but they're inelegant. The third is better: words and numbers are close to each other. Which is fine until we've a mix of long and short section titles, as we do in the fourth example. *Summary* is short, and *Introduction, methodology* is long. Readers' eyes move big distances to read *Summary*'s page number.

Figure 19.6

Section	Page
Summary	4

Summary............................4	

Summary	4
Introduction	10

Summary	4
Introduction, methodology	10

Figure 19.7

	Section	Page
Executive summary	1	2
Fictional section	2	3
When you use this template	2.1	5
Make this column as narrow as possible	2.2	7
Without a line wrapping over two lines	2.3	9
Another fictional section	3	10
These words are right aligned	3.1	12
Page numbers right align	3.2	14
It creates a neat line down the right	3.3	15
A heading for the first Appendix	A1	20
Another Appendix	A2	22

Figure 19.7 overcomes these problems. Numbers on the right; words on the left and right-aligned. No big gaps between words and numbers. Also, the list of contents is created in tables, not with tabs, so numbers line up with each other. Note that Figure 19.7 is a more complex list of contents than we saw earlier – it has sub-sections and section numbers.

What about section titles? Should we choose brief ones, e.g. "Brands"? Or longer, informative ones, e.g. "Brands doing well this month"? It's a trade-off between comprehension (aided by long titles) and navigation (aided by short, quick-to-read ones). In short reports, navigation is less of an issue – readers easily find their way around – so longer titles are fine. In big reports though, readers struggle more with navigation, so shorter titles are better.

Hence the short Chapter titles in this book, e.g. *Graphs*. *Tables*. The publisher of my first book wanted longer ones (*How to do impactful graphs* and *Wonderful ways to fab tables*, etc), but I felt it wasn't as clear. I also feared I'd run out of adjectives (fab, brill, etc). I also prefer the understatement that comes from calling it just *Graphs*.

That's the front page and contents. Next we look at the main part of reports.

Figure 19.8

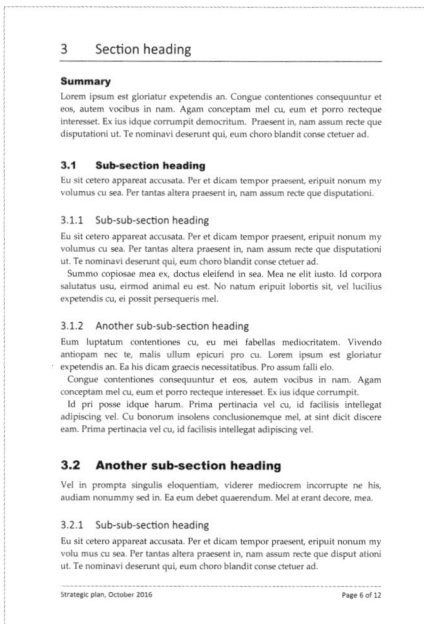

Figure 19.9

Section heading

Sub-section heading

Sub-sub-section heading

Continuous text in a serif font

Sections and sub-sections

Figure 19.8 shows a page with sections, sub-sections, sub-sub-sections, summaries, detail, etc. It has no graphs or tables – see the *KPIs* Chapter for that. The page follows the *Design* Chapter's tips, so let's keep this brief.

1. Headings are sans serifs, text is serif.

2. It has contrast. If you prefer a different mix of typefaces, so be it. Try Figure 19.9.

3. Proximity is good. Sub-section headings are nearer to the text to which they relate than to text in the previous sub-section.

4. First paragraphs aren't indented. People indent paragraphs to signal new ones, but first paragraphs don't need such signals.

5. The footer gives the page number (vital), and report title (optional, but nice to have). The line at the bottom closes the page off nicely. If we've several bits to mention in the footer, maybe separate them with a '|', e.g. Strategic report | Oct 2016 | ABC Group plc | Page 10 of 15.

What about the page that follows? What should we put at the top of it, if it's still sub-sub-section 3.2.1? Most consultants don't have this conundrum, of course – somehow, they shoehorn their thinking into one-page chunks. However, in the real world, sections often stretch beyond a page. In which case, we've two options.

Simply continue writing. Fictional books do this – words just flow on. Edit to avoid orphans though, where the last line of a paragraph (or worse, the last line of an entire section) sits alone atop the next page. Also, edit to avoid widows, where the first line of a paragraph sits all alone on the bottom of a page, with the rest of the paragraph atop the next page. Fix it so the widow starts at the top of the next page.

Repeat some or all of the headings atop the next page. Repeat just sub-sub-section heading. Or include sub-section heading too – or go the whole nine yards and also include section heading. Figure 19.10 illustrates all three options. Notice the word '(cont)' in a smaller font.

Figure 19.10

3.2.1 Sub-sub-section heading (cont)
Blah, blah, the text starts here. You get the picture.

3.1 Another sub-section heading (cont)
3.2.1 Sub-sub-section heading (cont)
Blah, blah, the text starts here. You get the picture.

3 Section heading here (cont)

3.2 Another sub-section heading (cont)
3.2.1 Sub-sub-section heading (cont)
Blah, blah, the text starts here. You get the picture.

The first option (simply continuing writing) uses less space and is easier to edit – if we add a paragraph in the middle of our report at the last minute, it doesn't put section headings out of whack. (To avoid our headings going out of whack, we could, for instance, input section breaks and headers within MS Word – but let's assume we aren't technically able to do that sort of thing. If you are, great.) However, by putting headers at the top, readers more easily grasp where they are in a report, and it looks smarter too. My preference? It depends on how important the report is. If I want to really impress, I put all headers on every page, either manually or by using 'section breaks' in the software package.

Finally on sections, yes, number every table, graph and picture to help us more easily refer to them within the report and in meetings: "In Figure XX, see how etc") – but restart the numbering sequence for each new section. Like in this book. The first Figure in Chapter 5 is Figure 5.1. This saves effort when drafting – if we add a Figure partway through a Section, we need only renumber the rest of the Figures in that Section, not in the entire report.

Final thoughts

Years ago, I got a new boss, an expert in his technical field. But he'd never written a long report, let alone been in charge of a team that wrote one. At the time, I was putting together a 100-page report with contributions from about ten people, who'd each sent me ten pages – and this confused him. He assumed I'd simply put the ten sections together, then write a one-page summary. "One hour to do, surely?" he said to me down the phone. I asked him to hold the line for ten seconds, then head-butted my desk three times out of frustration and disbelief. (This story is 100% true.)

A big report is more than lots of small reports thrown together, so don't treat it as such. After all, big reports are often important. They win business.

Identify fraud. Review acquisitions. Big reports get read by senior people and make reputations, for good and bad.

They also make and break careers. Earlier, I mentioned someone who wrote a disproportionately long report and lost his job fairly soon after. I also know someone who wrote such a good report, he was offered a promotion by a stranger – a director of a big company had no idea that this particular report-writer even existed within the group, yet stumbled across one of his reports in a desk, read it, then rang the person and offered him a promotion.

Two stories. A person who lost his job because of his bad report. Another who was promoted because of his good report. And two post-scripts… Firstly, the two people are the same person. His report-writing had improved a lot in the intervening years.

Secondly, that person was me.

Writing – advanced

20

Need to stay within a word- or page-limit? Want your writing to have *style*? Want to know when you should ask questions? This Chapter reveals all and more. And not once do you read about apostrophes or semi-colons – it's not that sort of Chapter. First are tips on reducing word- and page-count.

Making every word count

Sometimes, we need fewer words or pages. Maybe we've:

- Clients who prescribe word-limits for tenders.
- Bosses who won't read more than one page.
- 'Decks' that allow only one page per topic. (A deck!?! Chapter 23 explains.)
- Sections that spill annoyingly onto the next page.
- WiTs with too many words on the left and too few on the right.
- A list of items, all of which are single rows, yet there's one that annoyingly … isn't.

Also, sometimes we can't remove sentences, we need them all. We must shorten them. Hence this section. Individually, its ideas don't do much. Collectively, they do a lot. They cut reports by 10% easily – and 30% occasionally. Without loss of content. Our writing is more direct too.

First are words we simply remove, no rephrasing needed. Below, remove the words in italics and all we lose is verbosity.

That: "We're sure *that* he'll attend".

Which: "The car *which* I built is fast".

The: "*The* bosses thanked *the* staff for their input".

Possessives: "Edit *your* reports to ensure they have brevity".

And edit a bit more: "Edit reports to ensure *they have* brevity".

Repeating personal pronouns: "We're selling and *we* want to close".

Introductions: "*It should be noted* I like it". Or: "*It must be recognised…*".

Introductions with added emphasis: "*It's most important to note* I like it".

Saying the same thing twice: "It was confusing *and tough to understand*".

Remove 'a': "It's fine even if you're a monk, *a* consultant, *a* manager, *a* boss, or *a* shareholder".

When subjects change in sentences: "They bought our product and *it* saved *them* millions". The subject is *they* in the first half of the sentence, and *it* (*the product*) in the second half.

Those are words we cut, no changes needed. Next are ways to reduce word- or page-count but which require a slight rewrite.

Use contractions: *I'm here*, not *I am here*.

Use the active voice: *Pat did it*, not *it was done by Pat*.

Reverse sentences: *It confused me*, not *I didn't understand it*.

Remove words that end in -ing: *It confused*, not *It was confusing*.

Use better words: *tolerate*, not *put up with*. *Can't*, not *am not able to*.

Combine actions: *I hit walls when jogging*, not *I go jogging and hit walls*.

Use defined terms: *I like the 'graphs' section*, not *I like the section on graphs*.

Remove the obvious: *reports*, not *written reports* (of course it's written…).

Use plurals: *write good reports*, not *write a good report*. This also avoids the *he/she* conundrum when writing:

   With the conundrum: "Be nice to the boss, he/she prefers it".
   Without it: "Be nice to bosses, they prefer it".

Notice in the above list, I use the word *not*, not *instead of*. Or – I suppose – I use *not*, instead of *instead of*.

Short words help us comply with page-limits. For instance, *adopt*, not *implement*. *Start*, not *commence*. Also, if using illustrative names and numbers, choose short ones: "Fiji's six secrets", not "Australia's seven secrets". In this book, I talk about Lincoln, not Martin Luther King. About Pat, not Victoria. About IT and HR, not marketing and compliance. And, if pushed for space, I give three examples, not four ("IT, HR, sales, ~~finance~~").

Also, try truncated sentences, ones without a complete set of subject, verb and object (unless informality is inappropriate). Compare the following:

   "I don't think it's good, and we shouldn't do it."
   "My thoughts? No good. Don't do it."

Try reversing sentences, plus use *so* or "–", not *because*. Compare these:

   "People like it because it's more fun than real work."
   "It's more fun than real work, so people like it."
   "People like it – it's more fun than real work."

Figure 20.1

Same words, fewer rows

Orphans can arise because of a long, polysyllabic word. Reorder words and it's better.

Orphans can arise because of a polysyllabic, long word. Reorder words and it's better.

Finally, reordering words can help. Figure 20.1 shows the same words twice, but in the *after*, I reorder *long* and *polysyllabic* to avoid the orphan and restrict to two rows, not three.

Let's apply some of these tips:

Before: "Imagine the boss had been reading your Australian document and she wasn't able to understand the part that you wrote about beach-huts – she found it confusing and perplexing."

After: "Imagine bosses can't grasp the *beach-huts* part of your Fiji report."

It's 11 words, down from 28. That's 60% fewer. Or 66% fewer lines – it went from three to one. Imagine your ten-page reports shrinking to three pages. The *after* uses 11 ideas we saw above, and the text box lists them.

The *beach-hut* rewrite – the tips it uses

Tip	Before	After (comment in brackets)
Plural, not singular	The boss	Bosses
Shorter titles	Australian	Fiji
Choose better words	Wasn't able to	Can't
Shorter words	Document	Report
	Understand	Grasp
Defined terms	The part about beach-huts	The *beach-huts* part
Remove obvious, part 1	The part that you wrote	(Of course you wrote it)
Remove obvious, part 2	The boss had been reading	(Of course bosses read it)
One adjective, not two	Confusing and perplexing	(Don't need both. In fact, don't need either)
Remove *that*	The report *that* you wrote	The report you wrote
Remove the extra pronoun	And *she* wasn't able to	And wasn't able to

Finally, the *after* is in the present tense, and avoids the *he/she* conundrum.

However, this isn't just about shorter reports. The *after* is also easier to grasp. Remove clutter, and people focus more easily on content. Which means it's great for technical topics. Read this:

> *Before*: "A firm with the most modern IT might make, say, a 5% profit – and if that most modern firm were to upgrade and save costs, the regulator would reduce the prices it can charge in order to keep its profit at 5%."

It shouldn't be tough to read. No long words, a low fog factor. We can remove words though – try this:

> *After*: "Firms with modern IT make, say, 5% profit – and if they upgrade and save costs, the regulator cuts prices they charge to keep profit at 5%."

It's shorter, yes, but more importantly, it's easier to grasp. When we write with brevity, our ideas often have more clarity and impact.

However, there are two last caveats:

Ensure it still makes sense: yes, remove *which* (the car *which* I built) if *which* defines the topic (it's not just any car, it's the one *I* built). Don't remove if it doesn't define the topic, but moves it onwards, e.g. "The car I built is fast, *which* is great". Remove *which* now, and it doesn't make sense.

Don't force readers into double-takes: "Staff know *that* their bosses have a plan." Remove *that* and it says: "Staff know their bosses…". Readers might assume the second half of the sentence goes on to describe what staff think of bosses (e.g. "…and hate them"). It doesn't. The word *that* changes the direction of the sentence – in the second half, the subject is *bosses*, not *staff*. To avoid reader double-takes, leave *that* in.

Why we need rhythm and juxtaposition

"Be fearful when others are greedy, be greedy when others are fearful" – that's Warren Buffett's advice to investors. It has clarity and impact – and that's because it has two elements. Firstly, rhythm. It flows effortlessly. No clunkiness. So it sticks more in people's minds. That's the *impact*. Secondly, juxtaposition. It encapsulates. That's the *clarity*.

When we create rhythm and juxtaposition, it's fantastic. But creating them is tough. Sometimes, we must simply turn ideas over in our heads until we find something. Recently I contrived lots of inelegant phrases for something I was writing. "We send money overseas cheaply!" (Yuk.) "Money sent abroad for not very much." (OK, I didn't dream that up, but it's like a fantastic UK TV ad from the 70s – go to YouTube and enter: "Heineken refreshes the *poets*".) Eventually, I landed on: "Save money when you send money". Much better. OK, it transpires others say it too – but that's because it works.

However, you need more advice than: "Turn ideas over in our heads", so here are ways to help achieve rhythm and juxtaposition.

Use opposites and contrasts (sounds obvious, I know): *less* and *more* – "Eat less, exercise more". *Pessimist* and *optimist* – "A lot of people become pessimists by financing optimists" (CT Jones). *Can* and *can't*, *do* and *don't* – "Many of the things you can count, don't count. Many of the things you can't count, really count" (Einstein), and: "Better they should wonder why you do not speak than why you do" (Disraeli). I'm no Disraeli or Einstein, but I once wrote: "Regulators favour private profit over public health".

Repeat and reverse to create contrast: *doing things right* versus *doing the right thing*, for instance. Or: "Wise men talk because they have something to say; fools, because they have to say something" (Plato). Or: "Don't play squash to get fit. Get fit to play squash" (my squash club). Or: "A place for everything and everything in its place" (my father). And on nuclear weapons: "Better to have them and not need them, than need them and not have them". Regardless of your views on such weapons, the phrase works.

Use rhymes (again, sounds obvious): they needn't be 'perfect' rhymes. Try, for instance, *everything* and *nothing*. "A cynic is someone who knows the price of everything and value of nothing."

Use alliteration: "Save money when you send money". Or: "If you can't convince them, confuse them" (Harry Truman). Then there's the reporter who asked a passer-by if he knew how the two political parties differed. The man replied: "It's the difference between sh*t and sh*te".

Add 'paraprosdokian' perhaps (it's like misdirection – Chapter 8 explains): the following has opposites (big, small), but also the element of surprise: "How do you get a small fortune? Give a financial adviser a big fortune".

Reverse word order to improve flow: sometimes a polysyllabic word is in the wrong place – compare *impact and clarity* (clunky) with *clarity and impact* (elegant). Then again, try these monosyllabic examples: *hate and love; peace and war*. They don't sound right (reading aloud really helps us spot clunkiness). Reverse, and they're better: *love and hate; war and peace*. English football fans are the *red-and-white army*, not the *white-and-red army*. And earlier, we saw a comment about politicians: *sh*t and sh*te* flows, *sh*te and sh*t* less so. Don't change meaning though – compare:

"I'm so poor, I must choose between seeing my son and eating."
"I'm so poor, I must choose between eating and seeing my son."

The second flows better, but implies cannibalism.

Add or subtract a word to change meaning: I once wrote to someone: "I thought you knew better than that. I thought you knew us better than that" – and yes, I wanted to chastise and patronise (that rhymes…).

Keep contrasts close to each other: read this: "Unlike when you've nothing more to add, perfection is achieved when you've nothing left to take away". It doesn't quite work – contrasting elements are too far apart, separated by the words: "Perfection is achieved". Rejig, and we get this: "Perfection is achieved not when there is nothing more to add, but when there is nothing left to take away". It contrasts better. The sentence flows better too – so much so, we don't mind the double negative.

Edit viciously: years ago, the Harvard Business Review had an article on business writing that said: "The simplest way to say it, then, is invariably the best in business writing". What about: "The simplest way is the best way"? Or: "Simplest is best".

Maybe combine ideas. Martin Luther King said: "Our scientific power has outrun our spiritual power. We have guided missiles and misguided men." Wonderful. Next are final thoughts for this section, and after that, we ask: should we ask questions?

This isn't about spin or soundbites	The UK Opposition leader said that the Tories make the rich work harder by making them richer, and make the poor work harder by making them poorer. Fact or fiction? Truth or spin? It depends on your politics – I'm not commenting either way. But it juxtaposes and is memorable.
The first step: see the wood for the trees	Sometimes, outsiders help us better see that wood – remember to role-play the first 30 seconds.
Study song lyrics, they often juxtapose well	"You might not get what you ask for, but if you try sometimes, you just might find you get what you need"
	"It's worse than it was before – if I hadn't seen such riches, I could live with being poor"
	"Everything that kills me makes me feel alive"

Should we ask questions?

Salespeople ask questions to better meet purchasing needs ("How big is your family?" says the car salesperson. "If big, what about a people carrier?"). Also, questions help box people into places where they're more likely to buy. "I can save you money," the salesperson asks, "would you like that?". In particular, cold-callers have two immediate goals: (1) prevent people hanging up, and: (2) get them to say *Yes* a few times. Questions help them do this – and help in mailshots too. They arouse curiosity ("Do you know the secrets to great riches?"). They help readers imagine and connect with benefits ("What would you do if you won £10,000?").

Most business reports aren't cold calls or junk mail though – not even sales reports. Readers *expect* to receive them, so they give them more latitude. Hard-sell sleights are mostly unnecessary and inappropriate. Rather, readers want answers, not questions. Hence avoid the following:

Questions in WiT: avoid questions on the left ("Do locals prefer other products?"). Put answers instead ("Locals prefer other products").

Questions that think aloud: poorly edited reports often pose questions: "So we must ask ourselves a vital question: should we sell our subsidiary or retain it?". It's ponderous, plodding, perambulatory. It arises because authors think through issues as they type. Of course, thinking isn't bad, but don't leave it in the report. Rather, cut straight to the answer: "Sell the subsidiary". It's the answer that's vital, not the question. So give it.

Talks are different again. Mostly, they're not hard-sell, but presenters can indulge in more drama than in reports. They can tell a story, use a quote… or ask a question. Chapter 7 gives an example: "How many of you remember how you felt when you joined this firm?". It connects. However:

1. Do this sparingly, otherwise it becomes devalued.
2. Ensure it suits your style and personality.
3. Avoid overlong pauses, they can sound smug and self-important. What's overlong? Take an *X-Factor* decision pause and halve it. That's overlong.

So, should you ask questions? Now you know. Next are tips on order.

Order, order

Chapter 10 tells us to start at the end. Here are three more tips on order – two quick, one long.

Put the strong word last: compare these:
"For real impact, put the strong word at the end of the sentence."
"Put the strong word at the end of the sentence – it gives it real impact."

Put verbs near the start of sentences: "Iran, Fiji, USA, Peru and Iraq are where we're weak". We read the list without knowing context, until we read "weak"… and then we go back and reread the list. Instead, try this: "We're weak in Iran, Fiji, etc". Also, Figure 20.2 is a real example I once read.

Check thoughts are linear, not circuitous: this is the long tip. Please prevail with it for two reasons: (1) for many people, it's an unknown unknown – many people don't know there's a problem that needs resolving, let alone appreciate how often it arises in writing (it's a weirdly subtle problem); and (2) despite being subtle, our writing improves hugely when we resolve it. On with the tip: yes, review the order of every section, paragraph, list and row within a WiT – are they in the best order? But also check the threads within your words to ensure they're linear, not circuitous. For instance, read the following:

> "Bullets are often incomplete, but WiT resolves this. In bullets, we omit stuff, and don't realise it, whereas with WiT, we spot stuff is missing. That's because bullets give us no clues something's missing, whereas with WiT, we've empty cells. WiT helps ensure completeness."

Its order is bullets, WiT, bullets, WiT, bullets, WiT, WiT. It takes readers back and forth repeatedly – they struggle to keep up with it all. Instead, try this:

Figure 20.2
Putting verbs near the start
Here's how not to do it – I read this in a broadsheet paper, and it's like crime novels that give the reveal right at the end: "A fuel price regulator to keep the price of essential diesel and petrol supplies stable, through a system whereby higher oil prices trigger lower fuel duties (which at the moment make up two-thirds of the price of petrol and diesel), is the obvious solution".

"Bullets are often incomplete – we omit stuff and don't realise it because bullets give us no clues something's missing. With WiT, we spot something's missing because we've empty cells. WiT helps ensure completeness."

Same words, but much easier to follow. Fewer twists and turns – its thread is: bullets, WiT. *Linear*. Not circuitous. "But," I hear you ask, "surely it's easy to spot circuitous or non-linear writing?" Half right. It's easy to spot it in lists, but tougher in written trains of thought. And for several reasons, non-linearity arises in writing constantly:

Most of us start with non-linear thoughts: first-draft stuff is often circuitous.

WiT helps only so much: WiT helps us reorder paragraphs – should the first one instead go last, for instance? But non-linear thinking often arises within paragraphs, as in the above WiT–completeness example.

Short words seduce us into thinking it's all fine: in the WiT–completeness example above, the *before* seems OK at first glance.

Multiple authors hinder too: the boss shoehorns in a last-minute thought, and it dents linearity. Writing by committee rarely works.

Smug authoring hinders too: when writing this book, I'd ache to include a pet phrase, e.g. "Put a pig in a palace, and it's still a pig". Determinedly I'd shove it in, only later to realise it dents linearity.

It's tough to spot: I rarely spot non-linearity. Rather, I spot its outcome: my words just don't seem right. They make me work too hard as a reader.

If your writing makes you work too hard, analyse linearity. Alongside each bit of your text, write a single word that summarises it, e.g. the *before* was bullets, WiT, bullets, WiT, bullets, WiT, WiT. The *after* was bullets, WiT.

How do you know when something is right? Or as good as it can – or needs to – be? The simple answer is: you just know. The longer answer is: as you read it aloud (which really helps), you realise several things:

1. You make hardly any changes – one or two small ones every page.
2. You read effortlessly. It flows. No clunkiness.
3. You instantly grasp individual bits – you don't find yourself rereading sentences to better understand them.
4. You instantly grasp connections. You easily see how different bits compare or contrast. The writing does it all for you.

Of course, the opposite is also true: continue to edit if it doesn't flow, if you don't instantly grasp sentences or spot connections and contrasts. Continue until you get it right. And when you do, it feels *great*. (Notice the *impact* word is at the end of the sentence.)

Time for Final Thoughts. The tips in this Chapter take time to put into practice – and I know that because editing this book took *ages*. So don't get demoralised if you struggle to adopt and apply them all. After all, as the writer's writer, Dr Johnson, said: "What is written without effort is in general read without pleasure." And that's got great rhythm and juxtaposition.

The text box is pedants' corner. It doesn't teach apostrophes though. Nor *fewer* versus *less*. That's because such topics are known unknowns. We know we don't know them and we either carry on regardless or Google the rules. Rather, it looks at what I believe are unknown unknowns.

Rumsfeld's writing mistakes – the unknown unknowns

Only, again, just: "Email me only to clarify" is different to: "Email only me to clarify". And different to: "Only email me to clarify". Take care where you put *only*. Also, rearrange this: "Again I want to just throttle my boss".

Commas: they change meaning. The sign said: "Put the kettle on Paul". A strange hat for Paul, no? Also, remove commas from the following and see the meaning change: "Lawyers, who remove commas, should be shot".

Footnotes: try to avoid, they break up the flow. They send readers to the bottom of the page and back again (note 1). Instead, dovetail the footnote in with the main text. Or maybe lump it – and other similar footnotes – together in an appendix (e.g. put all the bibliography references together in an appendix).

Frequent (plus regular, urgent): avoid, unless a general impression is sufficient. "Write regularly," but is that once a day? Or once a quarter? Halley's comet comes regularly – once every 76 years.

Favourable: but favourable to whom? *The Economist* once took issue with the European Central Bank president who kept saying the outlook for prices was favourable. He meant inflation is falling, but to those who believed that the target inflation rate was too low, *favourable* might imply a rise in inflation.

Pronouns (he, it, they, etc): to whom do they relate? "Lady members have cast off clothing of every kind; they may be seen in the basement today." Also: "Bosses told staff they're great"... but who's great? Staff or bosses?

Used: *Yoozd* or *yoost*? Compare: "Six-month baby used to smuggle drugs", and: "I used to smuggle drugs". I'm guilty, the baby isn't.

(1): see what I mean?

---

21 Technical writing; jargon

This Chapter helps you explain complex stuff to others. If you simplify tough stuff – if you've such mastery of your topic that you can rise above its complexity and explain it well – people will beat a path to your door. First though, let's define terms. I see several types of technical writing:

1. Instruction manuals, i.e. guidance on how to do something.
2. Lists, e.g. the list of IT tasks to complete the database.
3. Explaining something, e.g. what does *stochastic* mean?
4. Explaining several things, e.g. the tax rules for start-ups.
5. Implications, e.g. what's the best age for me to start drawing my pension?

The first two are easy. For instruction manuals, see Chapter 22. For lists, see Figure 21.1. Which leaves the last three. We look at them in turn, plus look at jargon. Throughout, I assume we're writing for non-technical people.

Figure 21.1
The list of IT things to do
To update IT bosses on project progress, IT people list the 40 action points still to do. Previous Chapters show to how improve them: don't just list, but cluster. Cluster between *tough to do* and *easy to do*. Cluster *tough to do* between *critical* and *not critical*. You get the idea. Also, start at the end. Role-play to get a 30-second summary. Think of the *feel* button. Use WiT. Etc.

Explaining something

"Explain *stochastic* to me," the boss asks. Or: "What's an underlying asset currency return?" our client asks. Or: "What is cricket and how is it played?" asks our American mate who's unfamiliar with the game. But to answer such questions, we go about it the wrong way: we deconstruct the complex thing to, say, eight parts and explain each part in turn. To explain cricket to our American mate, we talk about batsmen, bowlers, innings, runs, fielders, etc. To explain stochastic, we take the definition ("A tool to estimate probability distributions of potential outcomes by allowing for random variation in one or more inputs over time"), then talk through each bit in turn. It doesn't work. People can't take it all in. Even if each individual bit makes sense, collectively it's too much. When we reach the sixth bit, we've forgotten the first five.

What to do instead? Start from somewhere else. It's like the punchline to the well known joke: "How do you get to York? Answer: you don't want to start from here". So too with complex stuff: **start with what readers know, then move forward step by step**. To explain cricket to an American, start with baseball. As for *stochastic*, it's to do with the probability of outcomes, so start with betting on horses. Or throwing dice or whatever.

Then there's a slightly different problem. I once read some economic blurb on how governments should reduce public debt – it talked about revenue-based adjustment strategies, recapitalisation, credit expansion, accumulated public debt, expenditure-based strategies, etc. (Eh?!?!) An economist wrote it, but it was so confusing, not even other economists could agree on what it proposed – more on that soon. I rewrote it:

> "Banks are lending less, preferring to rebuild balance sheets. So, if cash-strapped consumers are to spend more, countries must reduce tax burdens on people. Hence for countries to cut public debt after financial crises, they should cut taxes, not public spending."

My rewrite uses words that aren't complex (consumer, crises, debt, etc). It ticks the 'better writing' boxes too. Short words (low fog factor). No jargon. Active voice. But it still takes a couple of reads to grasp, and that's not because it's technical, but because it suffers from variety. There's a lot in quick succession. Banks, lending, balance sheets, consumers, tax, countries, public debt, crises. It's quite a whirlwind of a journey for readers. To help them on that journey, we need to **introduce a recurring phrase or theme**. Like this:

> "People aren't spending, they've lost the pound in their pocket. Banks won't lend them a pound either, preferring to rebuild balance sheets. So, if countries want to cut public debt after financial crises, they should lower taxes and put the pound back in people's pockets. It works better than if they cut public spending."

The theme is the *pound in the pocket*. The phrase is routine. Everyday. Not technical. It links separate bits of the story and provides an accessible constant throughout the narrative. Yes, this final version has a higher word count, but no worries – strive for clarity, not brevity.

Notice that the subject of the sentences changes three times (*people*, then *banks*, then *countries*). I could avoid these changes in subject by using the passive voice ("People aren't being lent a pound") – but the passive voice isn't good. Anyway, these subject changes aren't a problem – when readers move to the next bit of the story, the theme ensures there's still something familiar in it: the pound in the pocket.

Themes also help in bigger articles. I once wrote 1,000 words on: "Should universities make a profit, and if so, how much?". The topic suffered a bit from jargon. Also, there were lots of issues and they jumped about. Result: it wasn't that easy to join dots and spot trade-offs. So I created a theme: Felix and Oscar (from the movie *The Odd Couple*). Felix saved £500 last year, Oscar saved only £50. "But," the article asked, "who is not saving enough?" (it depends, as the article explained). I hung my comments on that theme. To see the article, go to the *Articles* page on my website.

Time to draw threads together. We struggle with cricket because of unfamiliar terms (wicket, innings, etc), whereas with the economic blurb, we struggle not with terms (they're simple), but with variety. Result: the best way to explain stuff depends on whether terms are familiar or unfamiliar:

1. If terms are familiar but variety confuses (e.g. the economic blurb), create themes that help people grasp it all (e.g. the pound in the pocket).
2. If terms are unfamiliar (e.g. cricket), start with a topic that readers know (e.g. baseball), then move forward bit by bit. This automatically creates a theme, of course.

This all might sound obvious, but it isn't. If it were, we wouldn't suffer so many bad explanations of complex stuff.

Before the next section, here's the postscript to my economic rewrites: when I showed them to economists on a training day, they caused quite a debate – did they correctly reflect the *before*? Delegates weren't confused with what I wrote, but with the *before* – what was it saying? My rewrites made them realise they couldn't agree on what it said. As an earlier Chapter says, if we use long words, we don't just confuse readers. We confuse ourselves too.

Explaining several things

Below is part of a real report to the boss of ABC Ltd on the financial implications of ABC buying a property – and then maybe selling it. Warning: it's rather tough going. Also, ignore the fact that its advice might be wrong or out-of-date:

> If ABC's funds are used to acquire the property, it'll diminish ABC's cash reserves. If ABC needs to borrow to fund the purchase, any interest payable to the lender should be tax deductible. This applies equally to loans from a third party or shareholder loans.

> As a trading company, ABC's shares should qualify for 100% Business Property Relief (BPR) exemption from inheritance tax (IHT). As long as the building is used for trading purposes, this can be a useful method to shelter the value of the property from IHT.

> If ABC disposes of the property, corporation tax will be payable on the gain made. Indexation allowance is currently available to offset inflation. Corporation tax rates are currently reducing and from 1 April 2014, this should be a maximum of 22%. The various methodologies of extracting funds from the company are then in point, such as voting dividends, salary, winding the company up, or selling it and taking a capital distribution. Entrepreneurs' Relief, subject to meeting the conditions, would currently result in a 10% rate of tax on a winding up or disposal for a trading company.

It leaves my head spinning. Which is a shame, for there's a lot of good stuff in it. It's content-rich, every sentence packs a punch. Which makes it triple-edged. It should be great advice (there's lots in it), but it's tough to read (there's lots in it), and it's tough to improve (lots needs to be in it). We can't improve by removing stuff, we need it all. We can't reorder it much either, its order is fairly reasonable. As for all those technical terms, surely we can't do much with them either… can we?

Read my redo in Figure 21.2. It's much easier to understand. It has several simple changes, all of which we've seen before:

It groups comments: the *before* looks at two topics – buying, selling – but this isn't clear to readers. The *after* signals this distinction.

It uses *you* and *your*: this makes it a more engaging read.

It uses headlines: the rewrite doesn't just say: "Corporation tax on sale". It says: "You pay corporation tax on any profit etc". Much better.

It's in narrow rows of text: this makes it easier to read.

It avoids too much information: the *before* says the tax rate is falling, yet readers probably don't know what it was, so why say it's falling? Just say what it will be.

It uses consistent terminology: the *before* refers to *acquire* and *purchase*. And to *property* and *buildings*. Same things? Or different? It creates doubt and hinders understanding.

It avoids accounting terms: it avoids the phrase *capital distribution*. It says *cash at bank goes down*, not *diminish cash reserves*. It retains the phrase *Entrepreneurs' Relief* – I felt that readers should probably learn that term.

This last point – fewer technical terms – concerns many technical writers. They're fine with using *buy* instead of *purchase*, but dislike *tax relief* when it should be *tax deductible*. "Surely," technical writers surmise, "advice should be right, not slightly wrong." No. When giving advice to non-experts, trade precision for clarity. As it says earlier in this book, we can be clear or accurate, but not clear and accurate. And if you think people really do want precision or detail – or if you wish to cover your backside – include it at the bottom of the page or in the appendix: "*Tax relief* means it is tax deductible per Section 542 of the 1995 Act" (I made that up).

Finally, there's one other change between the *before* and *after*. It uses not just consistent terminology, but consistent grammar. (In this case, each paragraph starts with *you* or *your*.) This really helps, as I learnt when I was asked to research and write a note that compares UK and US pension accounting. I read lots of guidance notes that taught 'pensions'

Figure 21.2

If you (ABC) buy it:

You buy it with cash or loans: your cash at bank goes down or your loans go up. You get tax relief on any interest you pay on those loans, regardless of whether they're from lenders or shareholders.

Your shareholders avoid inheritance tax on the value of the property: the shares – which include the value of the property – should get a 100% saving on inheritance tax. This is so-called 'Business Property Relief'. If you stop trading though, this could change.

If you then sell it:

You pay corporation tax on any profit on sale: the rate should not exceed 22%. Some of the profit is illusory, arising merely from inflation, so the taxman gives you an allowance for that.

Your shareholders may then wish to extract cash: they could declare a dividend or pay a salary. They could wind the company up or sell it, then distribute what's left to shareholders. Because you had been trading up until the wind-up or sale, shareholders would, subject to meeting certain conditions, be taxed at 10% on what they get – so-called Entrepreneurs' Relief.

double-entry to accountants – but struggled. Their words and grammar were inconsistent. For instance, consider how a firm shows in its accounts the £Xm investment income that's arisen in the year on its £Ym staff pension pot – one US note said (and it's illustrative): "Actual investment return is debited to retained reserves", while a UK note said: "Other income is credited with actual investment return". 'Investment return' is the subject of the sentence in the first note, but not the second – and that made it tougher for me to grasp.

So we've seen how to tidy three paragraphs within a bigger technical report. So far, so good. But often there's a much bigger problem to resolve: how to ensure the technical report makes sense overall. That's next.

Implications and consequences

Two steps: (1) think outcomes, not facts; (2) find tipping points. Let me explain.

Think outcomes, not facts

When bosses read a note on UK and US pension accounting, do they care where items are debited on the balance sheet? Or credited to the profit and loss account? Facts like that are for accountants. Rather, most bosses want to know not facts but overall outcome: "Will my numbers look better, worse, or the same?". So in my report I wrote something like this (again, it's illustrative):

Actual investment return – how it affects profit:

US: profit *un*affected	Whether returns are superb or dreadful, there's no impact on profit – the actual return goes on the balance sheet.
UK: profit affected	The actual return is part of income, so if returns are good, income does well, and if not good, income suffers.

Terminology is simple, comparable and goes straight to outcomes ("Profit is (un)affected"). Grammar is consistent – all in the active voice. The rewrite also refers to *superb* and *dreadful* returns. Exaggerated circumstances really help ram home the effect that actual returns have on US profits: none whatsoever[1].

Sometimes though, it helps to highlight not exaggerated circumstances, but tiny differences. That's the next tip.

(1) Point for pedants: actual returns do affect US profits, but only marginally – but a difference is only a difference if it makes a difference.

Find tipping points to outcomes

We list technical facts. We mention outcomes. But to really shine, we should identify tipping points. The factors upon which decisions hinge. This is what bosses seek. I'm not suggesting we do a decision tree – most topics hinge on just one or two factors, so trees aren't needed. Rather, we say: "If you seek more profit, buy the property; if you seek less tax, rent it" (I made that up). Or: "If you think you'll live beyond 75 years, do A; if not, do B". Or: "If you believe rates will rise, hedge; if you don't, don't".

Again, it sounds obvious, but all too often, technical advice merely lists the facts. I was thinking of taking some cash from my pension pot at the age of 55 (pensions, again) – the UK lets us take 25% tax-free when we hit 55 – but should I? What are the consequences if I do? Taking cash out of a pension pot is known as 'drawdown' – so taking tax-free cash is a type of drawdown. Figure 21.3 is what I was told. Have a quick read.

Individually, each sentence makes sense. Collectively it's tough. I did feel rather proud that, after being told it all by my adviser (and scribbling it down), I stared at my notes for 30 seconds and – surprisingly – spotted the tipping point. See if you can work it out… assuming I think I'll live beyond 75, what should I do? Take cash or not take cash? The answer is in the next paragraph.

Next we look at jargon. And here's the answer to the question: should I take tax-free cash at 55, assuming I reckon I'll live beyond 75? Answer: I should. I get cash tax-free and without any change in outcome – taking cash at 55 changes outcomes only if I die before 75. After all, study the two post-75 outcomes – pre- and post-drawdown. They're the same. That tipping point is not apparent from Figure 21.3; readers must work to find it. That's what happens when we list facts, not identify tipping points.

Figure 21.3
If I die pre-drawdown (i.e. before taking anything out of my pension pot):

a) If I die before 75, my wife gets the lot, but this increases her estate.

b) If I die post-75,
1) My wife can do a drawdown in her own name.
2) Or she can elect to take a lump-sum death benefit, albeit it will be taxed at some high rate (45% to 55%).

If I die post-drawdown:
Pre-75 or post-75 – as per (1) and (2) above.

Jargon

Jargon is often accused of crimes it doesn't commit. The following sentence is tough to read, but see if you can spot the jargon in it:

> "To facilitate enhanced collaboration, we need to upgrade the protocols and functionality in our system – the WiT below explains how… and without sophistry either."

The phrase *facilitate enhanced collaboration* isn't really jargon – it's business-speak. So avoid. The bit from *upgrade* to *system* isn't really jargon either. It's just a bit too much detail – why not simply say: "We must upgrade our system". The word *sophistry* isn't jargon. It's merely a rarely used word. Use such words sparingly. Which means the jargon is *WiT*. WiT means something only to those who read this book. Which is why jargon can be great. If people know it, jargon is a conversational shortcut that saves time. It's easier to say: "Insert a WiT" than: "Put those words in a table, with the summary on the left, detail on the right".

Jargon has brevity – and industries rely on it. The insurance industry couldn't function if it banned words like *facultative* and *retrocessional*. Jargon isn't bad, it's only bad when used badly. Here's how to use it properly:

Surround with short words in short sentences	*Nominalisation* is jargon (Chapter 7), but even if you're sure readers know it, don't say: "We must facilitate the implementation of a reduction in nominalisations". Instead, say: "We must cut out any nominalisations".
Don't use jargon to explain jargon	If *AB624 Upgrade* confuses, it won't help to say it's *a third generation XYZ 747 Protocol*. After all, if people don't know the word *sophistry*, they probably don't know *specious* either.
Don't use a variant of a word to explain that word	"*Price elasticity* is when prices are elastic." Unhelpful, and usually a sign we don't know what it means. It's similar to circular jargon – a website's glossary said that a *syndicate* is something run by a managing agency… and a *managing agency* is something that runs a syndicate.
Don't explain jargon with definitions	Actually, the website said a bit more – a syndicate is: "A member who underwrites insurance business at Lloyd's through… a managing agent… to which a syndicate number is assigned by the Council". It's as useful as saying a company is something to which a number has been assigned by Companies House. Accurate, but useless.

When to introduce the jargon? That depends:

If there's only one bit of jargon, state at the start: "We cost using a Modern Equivalent Asset model", then acknowledge that the jargon might make eyes glaze ("OK, that sounds tough"). Then explain it.

If two or more bits of jargon, state at the end: don't state it upfront: "We use three ways: Modern Equivalent Asset, Anchor Prices, Glide Paths". Eyes glaze, short-term memory struggles, and readers give up. Instead, remember that, to explain cricket to an American, start with baseball. Then at the end, give the jargon almost as an afterthought. Our readers have something on which they can hang those bits of jargon.

Earlier I said to avoid business-speak (*facilitate* etc), but also said that industry jargon is fine (*captive* for insurance). So try this as a summary:

Use the business's jargon, not the jargon of business.

Below is a text box on abbreviations. After that are Final Thoughts.

Abbreviations – TAP (Tips And Principles)

Just like jargon, abbreviations create short cuts and save time. BBC, USA, NATO. But we can go wrong with them. Here are tips to ensure you don't:

First, the obvious: • Don't assume • Define • Do a glossary	*Don't assume* people know what they stand for. Many don't, yet are too embarrassed to ask. Never overestimate people's knowledge (but never underestimate their intelligence). *Define* on first use: "We look at genetically modified products ('GM')". No need to define BBC, USA, etc. *Do a glossary* at the front or back of the report.
Take care if sending stuff overseas	Funding the IRA is OK in America (your Individual Retirement Account), but not in the UK.
A common confusion: 'NA'	Is it *not applicable* or *not available*? It makes a difference – the form asks: "Give details if you've been in prison", and we write 'NA'. Does that mean we haven't been inside? Or we have, but don't have details?
Avoid too many at once	"The NPV under IFRS is £1m, and the IRR of the DCF is 12%…". To an accountant, each acronym is fine individually, but they're tough collectively. HTU (Hard To Understand). After all, no-one ever says: "PUMA" (Please Use More Acronyms…).

Also, avoid polysyllabic abbreviations and ones that are too similar to each other: "The RPPRC will do the RPPR next week". RPPR is the Regional Post Project Review and RPPRC is the committee that does it, but the two abbreviations are too close to each other visually. Readers must concentrate to distinguish between them. Also, when we read them, RPPR is four syllables and RPPRC is five, and that makes the reading clunky and produces a stumble effect. Instead, shorten to PR ("Project Review") and PC ("Project Committee"). Or create defined words. RPPR = "the Review" and RPPRC = "the Committee". The sentence becomes: "The Committee will do the Review next week". No acronyms, decoding, stumbling. It even reads like English. Much better.

Finally, Figure 21.4 is from Robin Williams (the actor). Enjoy.

Figure 21.4
When abbreviations go bad
In the movie *Good Morning, Vietnam*, Robin Williams says: "Seeing as how the VP is such a VIP, shouldn't we keep the PC on the QT? 'Cause if it leaks to the VC he could end up MIA, and then we'd all be put on KP".

Final thoughts

When we read technical reports, we've a responsibility in all this. We need the courage to stand up to the report-writer and confront them with our confusion. Courage to keep asking the same question until we get the clarity we seek. Courage, because we're accusing the report-writer of not being clear. Courage, because our confusion might be our own fault – maybe everyone else understands and we're just, well, being a bit slow.

No. When we're confused, we're not alone. On one training day, a director told other delegates (managers from across his firm) how he spent too many Friday evenings trying to grasp the latest board pack. "I read a sentence three, maybe four times," he said, "but still don't get it". He said he finally confessed to other directors. "Does anyone else," he asked the directors, "struggle with the pack?" A brave question – if no-one else did, he'd look a bit thick. But his question lit a fuse. "Thank goodness you said that," others 'fessed up, "I find them hell too." As I said, when we're confused, we're not alone.

So next time you read: "Credit risk: where there is a risk that the counterparty you have placed an investment with defaults on its obligation to repay all or part of the investment", ask authors to change it. Maybe to something along these lines: "Credit risk – you place money with a firm who then can't afford to give it all back to you when you want it".

Specific reports

22

At work, the boss often hands us a document – a manual, plan, pitch or whatever – and says: "Update it… spruce it up a bit". So we perpetuate errors of the previous one and churn out something bad.

Hence this Chapter. It has tips on content, writing and layout for work that people often bring to my training Courses, i.e.:

1. Forms that get filled in, e.g. when we're compiling a database of clients.
2. Manuals – compliance manuals ("Sign the form") and how-to manuals ("Learn macros and get more from Excel!").
3. Written pitches.
4. Plans, be they marketing, sales, business, strategic.
5. Course outlines for training events.

Skip to whichever ones are of interest to you (if any). Also do note what this Chapter doesn't have:

1. Pilots' or nurses' checklists, etc: no-one has yet brought them to my Courses.
2. Section headings for templates: Chapter 19 explains why there isn't One Template to Rule Them All.
3. Lists: for instance, the *Plans* part of this Chapter could list stuff they should include, e.g. PEST, SWOT, etc. But other books do that (and most plans include them anyway). So I don't. I instead mention what most plans get wrong.

Figure 22.1

Forms that get filled in

Often at work, we fill in forms. Sometimes, we complete them in hard copy, sometimes on screen (I've just done that, it was an Excel expense claim for a client), and sometimes online. Regardless how we do it, many forms are poorly laid out. Uninviting. Hence this section. Assume we're setting up a client database. The database person sends a form to each sales team, and asks their administrator to enter details for each client (location, address, contact name, etc). Figure 22.1 shows one such form, and it's typical. Granted, it could ask more ("Does the client like golf?"), but go with the flow.

It looks amateur. If we don't give our forms some love and attention, others won't either. People won't complete them properly. Also, when forms are poorly designed, it's tricky to spot if all questions have been answered. (As it is, they

Client database

Please complete the following details on your clients and submit to both the Sales Authorisation Department and the Marketing Analysis Department ("SAD and MAD"). Any queries, contact David Smith (0207 8774 777).

Client/ company: Global Solutions Ltd

Type of business: Diversified IT group operating in 100 countries

Size (staff, income, pbt): 4,000 staff, £100m income, £10m profit before tax

Address: 16 High Street, Taplow, Buckinghamshire, England SL1 8GH

Web address: www.abcglobal.com

Holding company: ABC Global Inc, based in Salt Lake City

Income/ length of relationship:

	Income	Length (years)
- Widgets:	150	2
- Gadgets:	-	na
- Solutions:	2500	10
- Services:	20	2
- Total:	2670	

Main client contact: Bert Smith, CBE, ACA, BA, MBA

Job title/ position of contact: Head of Widget purchasing

Previous jobs: Solutions Global plc; Business Global Services Inc

Non-executives held by contact: Solutions Global plc; XYZ conglomerate plc

Telephone: 0207 745 8791

Address: 10 High Street, Little Town, Rutland, England RT10 8BP

Time zone (compared to GMT):

Email: bert_smith@abcglobal.com

Other:

Received by SAD and MAD: .... Date: ....

Details checked: .... Date: ....

Entered into computer: .... Date: ....

Figure 22.2

Main client contact	Bert Smith, CBE, ACA, BA, MBA		
Job title/ position of contact	Head of Widget purchasing		
Previous jobs	Solutions Global plc; Business Global Services Inc		
Non-executives of contact	Solutions Global plc; XYZ conglomerate plc		
Telephone	0207 745 8791		
Address	10 High Street, Little Town, Rutland, England RT10 8BP		
Time zone (compared to GMT)	+ 0 hours	E-mail bert_smith@abcglobal.com	
Other			
	Name	Sign	Date
Received by SAD and MAD			
Details checked			
Entered into computer			

Figure 22.3

Main client contact	Bert Smith, CBE, ACA, BA, MBA		
Job title/ position of contact	Head of Widget purchasing		
Previous jobs	Solutions Global plc; Business Global Services Inc		
Non-executives of contact	Solutions Global plc; XYZ conglomerate plc		
Telephone	0207 745 8791		
Address	10 High Street, Little Town, Rutland, England RT10 8BP		
Time zone (compared to GMT)	+ 0 hours	E-mail bert_smith@abcglobal.com	
Other			
	Name	Sign	Date
Received by SAD and MAD			
Details checked			
Entered into computer			

Figure 22.4

Client database

Please complete the following details on your clients and submit to both the Sales Authorisation Department and the Marketing Analysis Department ("SAD and MAD"). Any queries, contact David Smith (0207 8774 777).

Company information

Client/ company	1	Global Solutions Ltd
Type of business	2	Diversified IT Group operating in 100 countries
Size (staff, income, pot)	3	4,000 staff, £100m income, £10m profit before tax
Address	4	16 High Street, Taplow, Buckinghamshire, England SL7 8GH
Web address	5	www.abcglobal.com
Holding company	6	ABC Global Inc, based in Salt Lake City

Our income with company	7	£k pa	Penetration (£k = Lead £k/unit, Relationship = no pa)
Widgets -		150	2
Gadgets -		-	na
Bondons -		2,500	10
Services -		20	2
Total		2,670	na

Contact details

Main client contact	8	Bert Smith, CBE, ACA, BA, MBA
Job title/ position	9	Head of Widget purchasing
Previous jobs	10	Solutions Global plc; Business Global Services Inc
Non-executives of contact	11	Solutions Global plc; XYZ Conglomerate plc
Telephone	12	0207 745 8791
Address	13	10 High Street, Little Town, Rutland, RT10 8BP
Time zone (compared to GMT)	14	+ 0 hours
Email	15	bert_smith@abcglobal.com
Other	16	None

For H.Q. use

		Name, date	Signed
Received by SAD and MAD	17		
Details checked	18		
Entered into the computer	19		

haven't – review the form and we eventually realise that the *Time Zone* answer is missing.)

Figure 22.1 was created in MS Word. Many people use Excel instead, and produce something like Figure 22.2 (it shows only the bottom half of the form). The default grids are inelegant and visually overwhelm. Also, they're illogical – grids are to highlight or separate cell content, yet many boxed-in cells are empty, so they highlight and separate nothing. Notice there's spare space on the right, so I shoved an input box there (*Email*). Again, forms often do this. Unfortunately, the box is now set apart from others and easy to miss when completing. Figure 22.3 is slightly different – it has grids only for input cells. Better, but still not good.

Figure 22.4 is the *after*. The page is split in two: down the left are captions of stuff to input (in grey), and down the right are inputs. It groups content between *Company information*, *Contact details*, and *For H.Q. use*. This last section is a sign-off area for when Head Office receives the form. Arguably, there should be sign-off areas for those completing the form – two signatures perhaps: sales administrator and local sales manager. It aids accountability and ownership.

Notice it numbers the questions. Numbering is good for big multi-page forms, but less necessary for one-pagers like this.

The layout sacrifices brevity for consistency – let me explain. *Time Zone* (row 14) doesn't need a whole row. Instead, we could put it to the right of *Email* on row 15. The form would be briefer – one row fewer – but inconsistent. Captions are no longer all on the left. The page won't look as clean, plus it's more likely that administrators miss something.

Figure 22.5 is another *after*, but with shading (it shows just the second and third sections of the form). It's even clearer which bits to complete, so is more idiot-proof. Which is better: with or without shading? It depends. Without shading is typographically cleaner, but how idiot-proof does our form need to be?

Compare row numbering in the two *afters*. In Figure 22.4, it goes from 1 to 19, whilst in Figure 22.5, it changes for each section (2.1 to 2.9, then 3.1 on, etc). Either is fine.

Figure 22.5

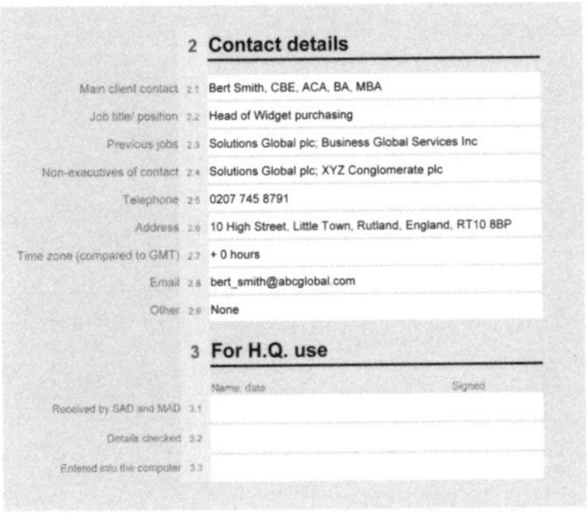

Figure 22.6

This layout – splitting the page down the middle between captions and input – is great for forms that people complete, e.g. expense claims, test assessment forms, etc. It can be in landscape too (Figure 22.6; there's even a space on it bottom left for people to write a paragraph or two).

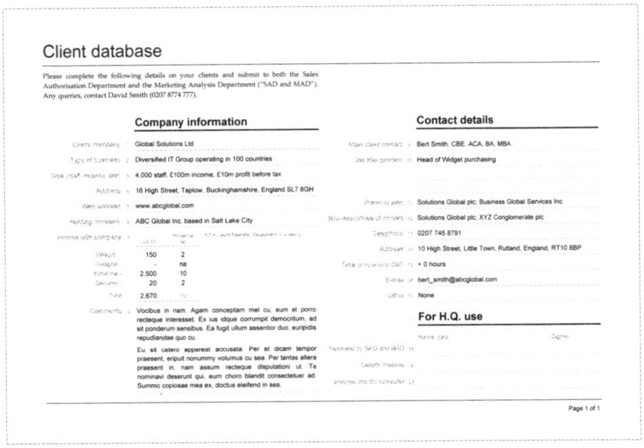

Manuals

There are many types of manual. Compliance manuals describe procedures that ensure we don't fall foul of internal audit. How-to manuals tell us, for instance, how to use our firm's software, and often have screenshots and instructions on which buttons to click when.

Most manuals are written in MS Word by 'topic' experts. HR experts write HR manuals, IT experts write IT manuals, etc. Unfortunately, they aren't experts at writing or layout, so most manuals are badly written and laid out. Hence these tips. First are writing tips, plus layout ideas. After that is something that few manuals have, but most should.

Writing tip (1): use the imperative

Let's start with a typical set of procedures for sending letters:

- Once drafted, it is important that the note is checked.
- It is then vital that the note be sent to the boss for approval.
- It's of the utmost importance that, after sending, it is filed in the client file.

Notice how the author tries to add emphasis ("Vital …hmm. Already said that… how about utmost importance. Bingo"). Let's remove this emphasis:

Figure 22.7

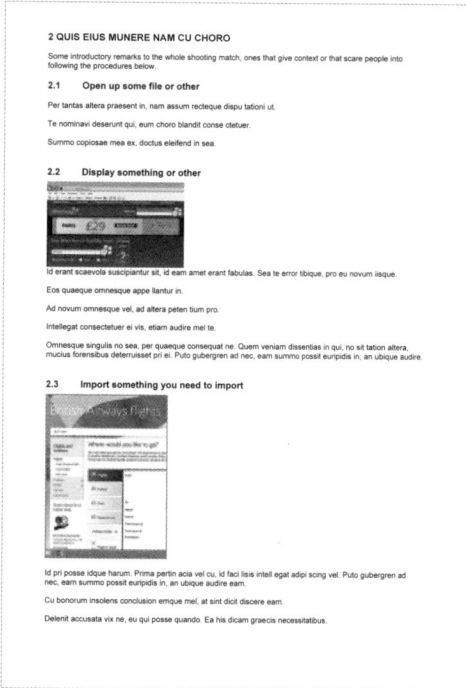

Figure 22.8

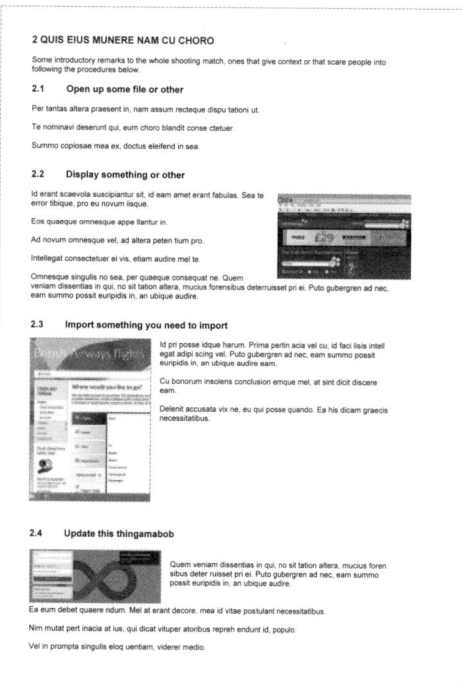

- Once drafted, the note must be checked.
- The note must then be sent to the boss for approval.
- After sending, it should then be filed in the client file.

Better, but try the active voice:

- You must check the note.
- You must send it to the boss for approval.
- After sending, you should file it in the client file.

However, what's this *should* and *must*? Are they different? I can almost hear compliance having debates about them. Instead, use the imperative:

- Check the note.
- Send to the boss for approval.
- After sending, file in the client file.

It's shorter – fewer than half the number of words as the *before*. I once reduced a 100-page office procedures manual to just 25 pages – and more than half the decrease came simply by rewriting in the imperative. However, it's more than just shorter, it's more human too. Compare the following:

"Please ensure bike helmets are removed before entering the room"

"Please remove bike helmets before you enter the room"

The second is more personal. So use the imperative. As I just did.

Writing tip (2): instruct first, explain after

This tip is more for compliance manuals. Imagine a procedure says: "Introduce yourself: tell prospects your name within 30 seconds of meeting them". Imagine this is to: (1) ensure prospects think nicely of us and our firm; and (2) comply with Industry Regulation 5, Part 3.

Unfortunately, many compliance manuals start with rationale (prospects will like us; industry rules insist), then give rule (state your name). The logic is: by putting rationale first, it improves buy-in and compliance.

Dream on. Staff don't read manuals for cheery news and opportunities ("Gosh, this idea helps prospects to like me"). They read them to see what they must do ("Intro-duce myself"). So first and foremost – before anything else – tell staff what they must do. Be didactic. Then if it helps, explain why. As an afterthought. Staff will respect us more. We save them time; they instantly see what to do. We don't indulge in failed attempts at contrived buy-in ("Gosh, if we do this, it improves our image!").

Before looking at layout, here's one last writing tip for manuals, albeit it's brief and obvious: write as simply as possible. No-one ever says: "That manual you wrote … it was a bit easy to understand". How though? Chapters 7 (*Words for reports and talks*), 11 (*Words – specific to writing*) and 21 (*Technical writing; jargon*) explain how.

Layout and typography

Manuals often include screenshots dumped unceremoni-ously on the page – Figure 22.7 is typographically typical of many manuals, and it's uninviting. All in Arial. Occasional upper case. Slightly larger fonts for headings. To make it representative, one section has a small screen-shot, one a larger one, and one no screenshot. (There's no wide screenshot though – we look at that later.) The screenshots are space-greedy. We could instead wrap words around them (Figure 22.8). It wastes less space and we can fit in more stuff at the bottom. The page is still inelegant though.

Instead, try Figure 22.9. It divides the page in two. Screenshots down left, detail down right. If we don't need section numbers (2.1, 2.2, etc) simply delete the middle column. If a screenshot is too wide to fit on the left, put it between two sections or at the bottom of the page (Figure 22.10).

The page looks smarter for reasons we saw in the *Design* Chapter. Contrast. Narrow rows of text. Lack of trapped white space. Not all in Arial. And if you fear that the *after* is too space-greedy because text is only on the right half of the page – if you fear it creates a much longer manual – fear not. The *before* wastes huge amounts of space with half rows of text, empty rows of text, etc. With the *after*, your manual will probably be shorter – or, at the very worst, not much longer.

Figure 22.9

Figure 22.10

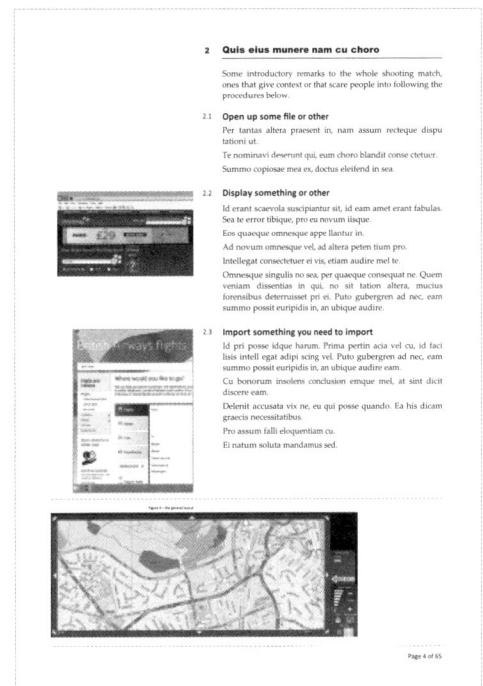

Figure 22.11

Update this thingamabob 2.4 Quem veniam dissentias in qui, no sit tation altera, mucius foren sibus deter ruisset pri ei. Puto gubergren ad nec, eam summo possit euripidis in, an ubique audire.

Ea eum debet quaere ndum. Mel at erant decore, mea id vitae postulant necessitatibus.

Nim mutat pert inacia at ius, qui dicat vituper atoribus repreh endunt id, populo.

Vel in prompta singulis eloq uentiam, viderer medio.

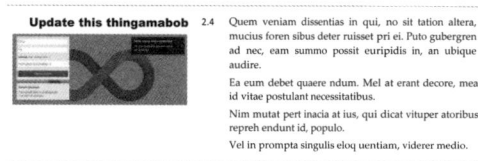

One last point: in the bottom section of Figure 22.9, all words are on the right half. Figure 22.11 shows it again, but this time as a WiT-type layout. The summary point is now on the left. Maybe do your entire manual this way.

That's writing and layout. Next is the final idea for manuals.

Do a schematic overview

Most manuals give ferocious detail, yet readers struggle to see the bigger picture. So try a schematic overview of, for instance, the five main steps (Figure 22.12). The schematic then appears six times in the manual – once near the start, then once at the beginning of each section in the manual. When it appears at the start of each section, grey it down, save for the section to which it relates – as I've done in Figure 22.12. It's similar to what we see at the top of the Amazon screen (Figure 22.13).

Figure 22.12

| **1** Set up client | **2** Collate data | **3** Client approval for data | **4** **Obtain** **quotes** | **5** Confirm & close |

Figure 22.13

WELCOME   ADDRESS   ITEMS   WRAP   DISPATCH   PAY   CONFIRM

These overviews help. They give typographical repetition, which creates a look and feel that runs through the document. They're also similar to the signposting we saw in Chapter 19 – they remind readers what's just happened and forewarn them what's about to happen.

Schematics are great for front-of-file checklists too. Often, compliance create checklists for us to sign when we complete steps and sub-steps. By putting a schematic of steps at the top of the checklist, it not only gives an overview, it helps link the checklist back to the manual.

Some people fear that schematics oversimplify: "A schematic," they say, "pigeonholes stuff where it doesn't exactly fit, and wrongly deconstructs complex processes into just five steps". Exactly. They simplify and clarify. Anyway, all manuals pigeonhole and simplify – they shoehorn everything into five chapters. Amazon simplifies too – there are more bits to buying than just its seven steps. Live with it.

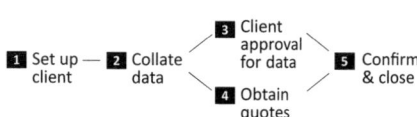

Typographically, there are many ways to do schematics. We can do just words like Amazon (albeit without a shopping cart). Or with each bit numbered in a reversed font, as in Figure 22.12. There is one last way, of course: a simple typed list. However, schematics help show steps that run in parallel (Figure 22.14 – steps 3 and 4 occur at the same time). Also, a typed list is, well, just a list, and most manuals are crawling with lists. A schematic – as the phrase goes – helps break up dull text.

But wait... I object when others use that phrase to justify autoshapes and graphs, so how can I use it to justify schematics? Simple: compliance manuals are different to almost all other documents in business. There's always

Figure 22.14

| **1** Set up client | — | **2** Collate data | **3** Client approval for data | | **5** Confirm & close |
| | | | **4** Obtain quotes | | |

someone who wants to read the tender, information pack, project update, etc. But no-one wants to read compliance manuals. So something brief and visual is almost acceptable. Don't resort to clichéd photos though (e.g. posh pen on watermarked paper).

Figure 22.15

ABC Consolidated in numbers

3	Position in industry
900	Staff
85	Countries in which we trade
4	Restructures in last 5 years
27	Number of FTSE 100 clients
83	Years trading
£2bn	Market value

Written pitches

Just two pages on pitches? Fear not, the rest of this book has more. It has general tips, e.g. WiT, short words, etc. And specific tips, e.g. Chapter 8 showed a table of stats (Figure 22.15). This section has stuff not already mentioned.

Three warnings though. Firstly, as Figure 22.16 explains, people can get defensive about written pitches. So much so, I almost removed this section – but its omission would be odd, given I often train sales teams. Secondly, my tips will probably delight and irritate in equal measure. Finally, dip your toe in the water gently. Try my ideas on small pitches that aren't too critical.

Keep pitches really brief

Take what you're planning to submit, then halve it. Then halve it again. Maybe even halve it again. Then submit. Send in something really brief, and clients will respect, admire and thank you. Make a virtue of it too ("We spent time making this brief to you save time reading it").

Also, imagine procurement's reaction on receiving pitches from two firms (and assume the pitch isn't for some big-ticket project) – a 30-pager from one, a six-pager from the other. The '30-pager' firm looks like they've not much on at the moment – and looks a bit bloated too, replete with designers who tart documents. Also, a 30-pager is probably stuffed with boiler-plate waffle copied from other pitches. As for procurement's reaction to the six-pager, they'll think: "Different…but is it complete?" They then read it (that won't take long) – and assuming it is complete, they're impressed. Much better.

Also, there's a cynical reason to keep pitches brief: many companies know which supplier they want. If that supplier is you, keep pitches brief, otherwise you risk saying something that harms your case. If that supplier isn't you, don't spend long on what's probably a lost cause. Pessimistic? No – I reckon it's realistic. And if you're not the favourite, see the next tip.

If you're the outsider, be different

If you don't have the inside track – if you aren't the preferred candidate – you won't win by being conventional. You win only by doing something that makes readers sit up and go: "Wow!". So remove all boiler-plate waffle and anodyne business-speak that makes you sound like everyone else. Instead,

Figure 22.16

**Pitches
– the perfect storm**
Two reasons why. (1) A lot at stake – a bonus if we succeed, no job if we fail; and (2) poor information – clients don't always give honest feedback. Also, a buyer receives our tender infrequently, so when we pitch again for a three-year contract – but this time we use our New Pitch Approach – did that Approach help or hinder? Who knows? Buyers can't remember what we did three years ago, so can't say if it was better this time.

Result: tenders are the perfect breeding ground for fear, myth, bull. Pitch-writers rattle off long lists as to why things can't or shouldn't change ("No-one complains… it's what clients want… we won our last pitch…"). And spurious boasts too ("My New Way increased our win-rate by 50%"). Really? So it wasn't the new sales boss or ad campaign? Or competitor who went bust? Etc. As I said, pitches are the perfect storm.

be opinionated. Exaggerated. Pin your colours to the mast. Say something that could just as easily delight as annoy. This also helps self-select your clients. If a reader recoils in horror at the colours you pin, it's a doomed relationship anyway, and it's better you both realise it sooner rather than later. You don't waste each other's time. Conversely, if a reader cheers loudly at the colours you fly, you get the "Wow!" you seek, and it could just be "the beginning of a beautiful friendship", as Bogart said.

And overdose on testimonials and quotes too. Ones that sizzle.

Identify and answer the real questions

Yes, answer clients' questions – and in the order they ask them. But look beneath the surface and identify the real question. When clients ask: "How would you design our new system?", they aren't that interested in our comments about stakeholder engagement, interviews, blah, blah. No-one ever said: "Let's choose them, they said they'd engage stakeholders". Instead focus on the real question – which is: "Have you done this sort of job before?". In which case, briefly say: "We'd adopt the five-step plan we've used in over 100 previous IT roll-outs. In brief, they're… (then list the five steps)." Put a bit more detail in the appendix, or even leave out and instead offer to send details if they're wanted. In other words, be brief. Save space for a more important question. And when answering that question, go for it. Really persuade. Chapter 9 shows how.

Plans – marketing, sales, business, strategic

Numerous planning books tell us about SWOT, PEST, Five Forces, the Five Ps, the Seven Ss, the six Ns, etc – so I won't. Instead, here are tips to remedy mistakes I often see (below, I say *plans* when I mean *plans and strategies*).

Ensure plans connect with analysis: many plans have lots of lists (strengths, weakness, Five Forces, etc)… which then get ignored, e.g. "We're big in the UK, but have bad IT. Strategy: do a rebrand." Where did that come from?! It doesn't address weaknesses or threats and doesn't capitalise on strengths or opportunities. The plan is one big disconnect.

Ensure statements pass the *Not* test: the plan says: "We'll invest to build our business". Would anyone say they wouldn't? Also: "We'll be innovative". Maybe we will be, but when we say it that way, it lacks credibility.

Don't confuse strategy with target or wish-list: "Be in the top three of markets in which we compete". This isn't a strategy, it's the outcome of a strategy, a by-product, a target. Similarly, don't say: "Grow profit 10% per annum".

Avoid vague statements: "We will grow organically, unless we get a chance to do bolt-on or strategic deals at acceptable risk–reward ratios". OK, it passes the *Not* test inasmuch as it could say the opposite: "We'll grow by acquisition". However, it's a cop-out because it's so vague. In reality, it says: "We won't do deals unless we feel like it". Strategy statements are road maps that help bosses and staff make decisions and choose between alternatives – so be specific.

Avoid statements that conflict: "We'll provide the best service and be cheapest." But what to do in the event of a clash between these two? Bosses struggle to make choices between alternative courses of action. If you must list stuff that clashes, state which takes precedence – and for a neat example of this (albeit it's on something different), Figure 22.17 has the three rules of robotics according to Isaac Asimov, the science fiction writer.

Don't delude yourself with weak sensitivity analysis (this one's more for start-ups): accountants crunch numbers at, say, 85% and 70% of forecast income – and discover that lower forecasts make little difference to cash. That's because, in early months of trading, forecast income is nil, and 70% of nil is nil. In later trading, forecast income is magnificent, and 70% of magnificent is still magnificent. Result: cash seems reassuringly insensitive to lower income. No… trying lagging numbers: what if income arrives four months later than forecast? Or eight months later? Much more enlightening.

Manners maketh man – but headings don't maketh plan: plans are more than merely following standard headings in a template.

Try stating what you won't do: e.g. "We won't acquire in countries whose fraud ranking per Transparency International is 50 or more". Enlightening.

When rolling it out, don't assume staff are idiots: it's strange – bosses stride down from Mount Strategai with Tablets in hand and unveil them… only for people to roll their eyes cynically. Staff seem impervious to statements such as: "To better meet client needs, we'll organise ourselves by product – the Boss of Asia is now Boss of Widgets, and the Boss of America is now Boss of Gadgets". That's because five years earlier, they were told it's better to organise the other way round – by territory. Staff aren't dumb. It's not enough to explain what we'll do, then justify it with a soundbite ("To better meet client needs"). Instead, see the section in Chapter 8 on *Be positive*, and in particular the part on addressing concerns and its construct *What it isn't, what it is*. Address contrarians. And see Figure 22.18 for some cynicism about reshuffles.

Figure 22.17
Precedence if a clash

1. A robot may not injure a human being or, through inaction, allow a human being to come to harm.
2. A robot must obey the orders given it by human beings, except where such orders would conflict with the First Law.
3. A robot must protect its own existence as long as such protection does not conflict with the First or Second Laws.

Figure 22.18
Three reasons why reshuffles often underwhelm

When I was in corporate life and 'reshuffle' memos arrived, a colleague would sing: "They were only playing leapfrog" (from the movie *Oh! What a Lovely War* – the song is on YouTube).

In the *Carry On* movies, they have the same actors and actresses, regardless of whether it's about Caesar, Vikings, or the Wild West. So too with business – the same cast gets shuffled around.

My parents went to the Arctic Circle and brought me back a paperweight sporting a picture of a dog-sledge team and a quote: "Unless you're the lead dog, the view never changes".

Course outlines for training events

To entice people to sign up for training courses, training managers write one-page course outlines. But they rarely entice. For a course on how to inspire and influence in reports, a training company wrote: "Find out how to improve the quality and effectiveness of reporting to decision-making authorities such as boards of directors." It's so anodyne and abstract. Apparently, the course helps us inspire and influence, yet ironically its outline doesn't.

Templates are partly to blame. They stifle panache. Imagine a *Managing Staff* course for people who manage staff for the first time – the person who drafts the course outline aches to write: "I'm a manager, get me out of here", and add: "How to avoid the impostor syndrome". But the template says: "Who to attend", and so he instead writes: "For those in their first managerial position". Informative. Accurate. Dull.

So strive to ignore templates. Here are four other tips to make your outlines entice. OK, maybe your courses are compulsory, so maybe it doesn't matter if your outline bores. But why bore when you can impress?

Think about what we want people to feel. Address concerns, hopes, fears, and more	Don't focus on what we know. Yes, we know the course timetable, but don't send it to delegates beforehand, it merely unnerves them ("An hour on bullets – is this for real?"). Don't think about delegate objectives either – see page 81 for how people agonise over objectives.
Don't just list the day's topics – think like a journalist	If the sixth bit of the day is 'problem staff', don't say: "(6) Dealing with problem staff". Try: "(6) The Five Steps for dealing with problem staff". Maybe use a negative: "(6) Problem staff: what not to do". Or a challenge: "Problem staff: the five most common mistakes managers make".
Address fears with testimonials – and make them sizzle	People fear that my Course is dull, so I've testimonials that say: "Fantastic!". For a course on managing, delegates worry about the staff they must manage – so try this: "I'm now ready for my staff – bring 'em on!". Neither testimonial talks about the ultimate outcome, but at the end of a training day, it's too soon for people to write: "I'm now a better boss". OK, they might instead say: "I believe I will manage better" – but that sounds dull. It lacks pizzazz.

Also, of course, follow other tips in this book	Avoid wide rows of text. Read the *Outcomes* Chapter. Remember tips in the *Writing* Chapters – avoid adjectives ("exciting tips!"), avoid abstract nouns ("hindrance"), use verbs ("hinder"), strive for juxtaposition and rhythm ("help, not hinder"), strive for high-impact words ("entice") – and put them at the end of sentences for the greatest… impact.

The point above about pizzazz is important. A client of mine has a feedback form that asks: "What will you do differently tomorrow?". Delegates then write dull stuff. "I'll look at reports to see how to change them". It's tough to answer a dull question with exciting rhetoric. The trick though is to ask not an exciting question, but an open one: "Comments?". It gives people free rein to express, emote, vent spleen, or whatever they wish to do.

Finally, here's one last tip: if writing an outline for a course that competes with mine, ignore all the above. Write something dull instead.

There are no Final Thoughts to this Chapter, as it's a hotchpotch of stuff. Do check my website, there are brief tip-sheets on other specific reports, e.g. market-research findings. I'll add more over time, so sign up to receive my newsletters – they'll let you know when I upload new stuff. Also, see my website for why this Chapter doesn't mention annual reports.

23   Decks

Figure 23.1

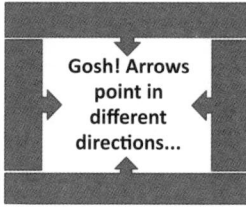

Decks are reports created in PowerPoint and emailed to people for them to read at their desks. If you've not seen one, it might sound strange – surely PowerPoint creates slides we show in talks, not email for others to read. But many people do decks for bespoke reports. Bankers and consultants do decks for strategy papers to CEOs. Accountants do decks for due-diligence reports to boards. Media agencies do decks for campaign updates to marketing. Result: junior people see this 'deck' behaviour and do likewise. They do decks for brief procedure roll-outs and project updates.

As for a deck's layout, it's a broad church. At one end of the spectrum, some are akin to long reports, albeit in landscape – a thousand words in font size 10, plus graphs, tables, etc. At the other end, some are akin to slides – two or three lines of text per page in font size 25, plus many visuals. OK, maybe someone talks through the deck in a meeting and maybe even shines its pages on screen, but don't be fooled. When its pages are on screen, it's mostly for decoration. Delegates got the deck two days earlier as a 'pre-read'.

Figure 23.2

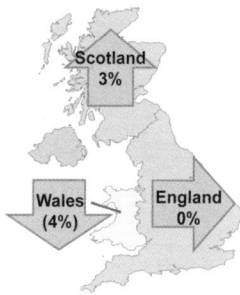

That's decks. If it confuses you, ignore this Chapter and move on. You obviously don't encounter them, and don't need to. If it resonates, read on.

Finally, maybe you do routine monthly packs. In landscape, with funky colours and maybe lots of graphs and tables – and a few words. In which case see Chapter 33 (*KPI packs (and variances)*), it has tips on them.

If it quacks and looks like a deck

Figure 23.3

Figure 23.4

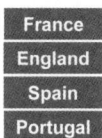

Decks have a number of characteristics. Or – as I call them – faults. This section looks at 15. The first nine arise from *frippery*. Such as **autoshapes**, **photos**, **arrows** (e.g. Figure 23.1's arrows): Chapter 13 explains why they're bad. Yet deck-lovers think otherwise – Figure 23.2 shows growth by country, and deck-lovers say its arrows 'help' convey if it's up, down or the same. I guess it also 'helps' if people don't know where Scotland is ("Look! *That's* where it is!"). Decks often have **colour** too. Lots of it. Result: readers discuss colours, not content. Then there's **chevrons** and **boxes**: don't just list items, *enclose* them (Figures 23.3, 23.4). Which creates **reversed fonts** (Figure 23.5 – white font on dark background). Tough to read, plus it guzzles toner. And **heavy branding** too – huge branded headers and footers that leave little room for content. Finally, there's the **fancy front page**. It's usually adorned with photos too.

Figure 23.5

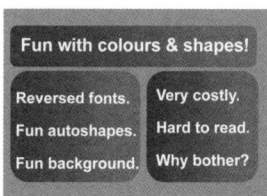

That's nine bits of frippery. And frippery wastes so much time. It wastes deck-writers' time when creating decks ("Which photo," the deck-writing team debate *en masse*, "to put on the front?"). It wastes readers' time – it's tough to read pages crammed with distracting stuff.

But we've more. Faults 10 to 15 are on layout, structure and typography:

10. **Misaligned stuff**. PowerPoint lets us shove things anywhere (much more so than MS Word), so we do. Many decks are messy.

11. **One page per topic**. We give too much space to stuff that doesn't need it and too little space to stuff that does, e.g. assume we've 1.5 pages of material for our *Benefits* section. With decks, we must either: (1) delete half a page of stuff (which means we let format wrongly dictate content); or (2) squeeze it all in with a smaller font (crazy). We don't do this down the pub: "Folks, we've ten topics to discuss in the next hour – some major, some minor – so let's spend six minutes on each…".

12. **Random font sizes**. These arise because: (1) PowerPoint *autofits* words to fit text boxes. Result: boxes with many words have tiny fonts, whilst boxes with few words have big fonts. And (2) writers change font sizes to ensure one page per topic. Result: readers struggle because of the random font sizes. (To disable autofit on my version of PowerPoint, see Figure 23.6; I can't promise it works on yours.)

13. **Wide rows of text** (often 20 words or more on a row). It hinders readability, looks ugly because it creates trapped white space, and is space-greedy too – if some rows of text have orphans, we don't get many words on a page.

Also, decks are wrongly inconsistent – and wrongly consistent. Let me explain:

14. **Wrongly inconsistent – a different layout on every page**. Deck-writers love variety. Each page is a new creation. Result: readers must acclimatise to each page when they first see it. Study Figure 23.7, it's a typical page from a deck that's akin to a long report. When readers' eyes first land on it, where do they start reading? Then where do they go after that? Every page is a journey of discovery for readers that wastes their time. (Notice also in Figure 23.7, some words are sideways and tough to read.)

15. **Wrongly consistent – every page in landscape**. Often, that's inappropriate though. Result: deck-writers split a 60-row table over two pages so it fits. They snake flowcharts to fit too (Figure 23.8).

Study the 15 faults. If you read decks, it probably resonates. If you write decks, it maybe irritates, for many deck-writers are in denial. They recognise faults in other decks, but not their own. They nitpick about differences, and don't recognise similarities. "OK… bad decks have lots of colour," they surmise, "but my deck only has four – and doesn't have one of the other

Figure 23.6
Disabling autofit
In PowerPoint, select *Tools, AutoCorrect Options, AutoFormat As You Type*, then untick *AutoFit title next to placeholders* and *AutoFit body text to placeholder*.

Figure 23.7

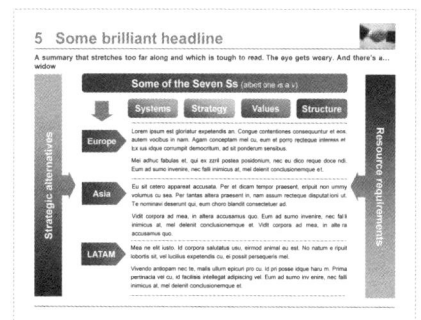

Figure 23.8

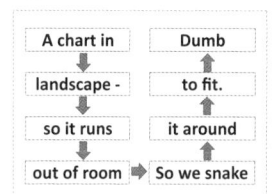

faults – so it's fine…" Please avoid denial. If it quacks and looks like a duck, it probably is a duck. Or rather, a deck.

Of course, decks often suffer from other faults, e.g. their summaries introduce instead of summarise; they use business-speak, etc. However, such faults don't arise because it's a deck, for they also occur in reports done in MS Word. Compare that to the above list of faults: they arise *because* reports are done as decks, and come up far less often in reports done in MS Word.

So far, so bad. But we've not yet seen decks' biggest faults. They're next. It's two pages of negative stuff – but we need to cover it in order to see what to do instead.

The big faults: silo-thinking; lazy lists

Step back. First, consider how we create decks. You, Pat and I must write a report. Two months ago, bosses asked us to review our firm's structure, and since then, we've sent them two reports (both were decks): (1) our Project Plan; (2) an Interim report. We must now write our Final report – so we divide up the task. We'll each write, say, one slide on each of two topics – you'll write *Background* and *Objectives*, Pat the *Current Situation* and *Problems*, I'll do *Proposals* and *Benefits*. Demarcation. Much easier… so long as we follow the First Rule of Deck Club: *one topic per page*. Six topics on six pages.

And that Rule is vital because PowerPoint lets us easily stitch together slides in its slide sorter. And easily add ten more pages too. That is: (1) front page (with photos); (2) contents; (3) summary; (4)–(9) a front page for each of the six sections (e.g. a whole page that says: *Section 2: Objectives*); (10) back page that has closing credits or says: "Any Questions". Easy. Job done. Also, our report has grown to 16 pages. Impressive, huh! As a deck-writer once told me, it's easier to do a 30-page deck than a three-page report.

Also, we take shortcuts. Don't create new slides – that's time-consuming. No. Recycle ones from previous decks, for PowerPoint makes it easy to do this. Our section needs a slide on *Objectives*, so simply copy across one from our *Interim* report. Quick, easy, and it helps bulk out our report. With decks, slides live on.

To recap, here's how we – with PowerPoint's connivance – blast out a deck: (1) carve up the task; (2) ban more than one topic per page; (3) recycle old slides; (4) stitch together in slide sorter; (5) add a cover, index, etc. We do this for strategy reviews. Marketing plans. Project updates. And it creates huge problems. Firstly, consider the one-topic-per-page policy:

It creates content-thin pages and overlong reports	Assume we're writing a project update – even if we've only one paragraph to write on each of three topics (e.g. Objectives, Plan, Progress), we must still spread it over three pages. Stupid, really.
Which fragments information and hinders understanding	To compare Objectives to Plan, and Plan to Progress, readers must flick back and forth between pages. They struggle to compare and join dots.
And might explain why decks are often full of autoshapes	They prevent pages from looking so empty. Also, deck-writers sometimes *add* unnecessary words just to pad out empty pages.

It gets worse though. Because we carve up the task, then stitch it all together in slide-sorter, **we write in silos**. On separate pages, we show your *Current Situation* (the *before*) and my *Proposals* (the *after*). You recycle a slide to show existing controls (eight of them). I then recycle the same slide, but edit it to show the proposed controls (now nine). OK, it's linear (where we are, where we want to be), but unhelpful. Readers flick back and forth between pages, playing a game of spot-the-difference ("Eight rules before, nine now…," they ponder: "seems like we keep five, ditch three, and add four… I think"). Of course, we could add more pages – ones that compare *before* and *after* – but most deck-writers don't. We write in silos.

And **we think in silos**. There's often a disconnect between analysis and recommendations. On pages 4 to 6, a deck might give details on our good IT and bad sales, etc, yet then solemnly states on page 7: "Conclusion: enter the Chinese market". Where's that come from?!?

Of course, disconnects happen in MS Word too. But in MS Word, at least they tend to be easier to spot and avoid because thinking is less fragmented. Analysis and conclusions are often on the same page. Or even the same paragraph, as was the case in a 2011 report which said (and I paraphrase): (1) many problems in the 70s and 80s when safeguards were poor; (2) hardly any problems since then – when safeguards were much better; (3) conclusion: we must change governance. Illogical. Thankfully though, it was all in one paragraph, so readers easily spotted the disconnect.

But it gets worse still. With decks, we **write in lists**. PowerPoint almost encourages us to do so. So we do page after page of them. As Chapter 32 explains in more detail, lists often seem beguilingly evolved ("Gosh, the deck-writer has distilled this complex topic to just three pages and three issues per page. How helpful!"). Yet when people discuss it, they struggle to compare lists on separate pages. Also, lists don't identify the hierarchy of issues nor relate them to outcomes. In effect, it says to bosses: "Work it out yourselves". I once saw a 'strategy' deck that showed four ways the market might evolve, but for each way, it didn't say what to do, or which firm wins or loses. Lazy.

Deck-lovers make several retorts, of course.

MS Word isn't so good for team-writing	In other words, deck-writers choose software that makes their lives easier and readers' lives tougher. Not clever.
One-topic-per-page means it's easier for bosses to grasp (part 1)	How do bosses cope when they read newspapers?!? Broadsheets have several stories on their front page. Then again, tabloids often have just one. Conclusion: decks are the business equivalent of a tabloid.
One-topic-per-page means it's easier for bosses to grasp (part 2)	In other words, either: (1) our bosses are dim; or (2) we can't think and write clearly. I'd put money on (2) being correct.
Decks are 'discussion-documents'	No, often they are 'to-be-explained documents'. When someone talks through a deck, it's because the deck didn't make sense and needs explanation.
Decks are to prompt discussion	We can do this many other ways. With a brief memo. A scribbled flipchart. Post-It notes. Etc. The problem with decks is: they prompt low-quality discussion (lazy lists, silos, etc) at high cost (decks aren't cheap to create).
Decks are good because bosses are short of time	But with all that frippery – and stuff in silos – reading takes longer. It also takes longer to think it all through.
Decks impose a discipline – one-page-per-topic	Eh? With decks, people add words and visuals to fill almost empty pages, and spread 12 paragraphs over 10 pages. If that's disciplined, I'd hate to see ill-disciplined.
Decks let me see the headline at the top of the page	Because decks' pages are often randomly laid out, this retort actually has some validity – if the heading is at the top, at least readers know where something is on the page. Then again, use MS Word, it also lets us put a headline at the top. And do a WiT too, and we see several headlines per page. Down the left. More insight.

This last comment – use MS Word – draws another retort from deck-lovers: "But silo-thinking also arises if working in MS Word". We mentioned this earlier, but there's more on this topic. You see, with PowerPoint, deck-writers are more *distracted*. They succumb to the siren lure of frippery far more than if in MS Word. It's more fun to muck about with photos and colour than spot connections between silos. Given all this, no wonder good decks are exceedingly rare, for it takes great self-discipline to resist the lure and do a decent one. I don't blame PowerPoint though. If we write badly, we don't blame the biro. Admittedly, PowerPoint is more pernicious than a biro, it's an enticing mistress. But if we succumb to its lures, it's our fault.

There are other flawed reasons people like decks, e.g. "The boss asked me to limit my deck to eight pages, and it was a good deck – so decks are good". But we've seen enough problems and flawed logic. Let's see how to overcome these problems.

To improve decks, use MS Word

The obvious way to improve decks is: avoid the above faults. Avoid autoshapes, photos, arrows, too many colours, chevrons, boxes, reversed fonts, too much branding, fancy front pages, and misaligned stuff. Avoid one page per topic, random fonts, wide rows of text, inconsistent layouts. Avoid all pages in landscape – use a mix of landscape and portrait, depending on which is best for a given page. Avoid silo thinking, lazy lists.

And the easiest way to do all that is use MS Word. It's great if we have words (hence its name…). It aligns stuff automatically (it has 'margins'). It tempts us less with frippery. It's easier to keep fonts consistent. Readers no longer suffer a journey of discovery – when they turn to a new page, they know where to start (top left), and finish (bottom right). Also, in MS Word we follow rules intelligently, not slavishly. Yes, we mostly do stuff in portrait, but if we've a wide table, we do it in landscape.

At this point, deck-lovers often retort: "But if we put a landscape page in the middle of a portrait report, readers must rotate their report". Hmmm – which is better: to spend one second rotating a report? Or 30 seconds trying to read a wide table wrongly forced onto a portrait page by using a tiny font?

Back to MS Word. In it, we edit intelligently. Many of us edit words to avoid the last line of a section spilling inelegantly onto the next page – but what if we've three paragraphs that spill over? In MS Word, we think: "So be it" and let the section spill over. In PowerPoint, we chop the three paragraphs – or reduce font size so it fits. Both are bad.

However, some people raise objections to creating reports in MS Word.

In MS Word, it's tough to add graphs, pictures, visuals. A somewhat circular argument. Because people use PowerPoint, they often crave – or feel obliged – to add graphs, pictures, visuals. They then rationalise: "Lucky it's in PowerPoint, I can more easily add them". Yet if it wasn't in PowerPoint, they'd add far fewer, if any.

In MS Word, pictures suffer poltergeist-like experiences. That is, pictures and graphs sometimes move around on their own accord, or even disappear. True, but to avoid that, see Figure 23.9 (it's a techie tip).

MS Word is tougher to read on screen. Landscape decks are easier to read on landscape screens – readers can see a page in one go. In MS Word though, readers must scroll down to see the bottom half of the page. I can see this argument, albeit with one caveat: tablets. They change orientation, and so allow readers to see MS Word pages all in one go.

Which means: if our readers don't print reports and don't use tablets, then decks have a reason to live. However, only once has someone (an avid deck-lover) told me that nobody in his firm ever prints anything. "So decks are fine!!" he concluded. His boss then told me afterwards: "Not true – loads of people print stuff. Including him". I learnt a lesson that day: some deck-lovers defend decks not with their lives, but with their lies.

To conclude, do decks in **MS Word and mostly in portrait**, not in PowerPoint and landscape. We save a lot of time, and how much we save depends on our type of deck. Cast your mind back to the start of the Chapter where I said decks are a 'broad church'. Are our decks akin to wordy presentation slides? Or lengthy reports but in PowerPoint? We look at each in turn. After that, we've tips for those who must use PowerPoint for their decks.

Decks that are akin to wordy presentation slides

These are when people stretch 12 brief paragraphs over 12 pages in font size 20 (it sounds daft, but people do it a lot). Yet in MS Word, they become one-page notes in font size 10. Readers more easily take it in. We save time too. We prepare reports not 20% faster, but 80% faster. When people realise they can replace their decks with one or two pages, it liberates. They wonder why they overcomplicated the simple.

And really go for it. Don't tinker, as some people do. They take their 15-page content-thin deck with just 12 paragraphs – and edit it to… 13 pages. They change a font or two. They merge two pages. Or split one into two. No. Slash and burn. It's great when we do. We nearly always cut it down to two or three pages. Or just one. Occasionally, we cut it to one sentence – we realise our nine-page deck merely says: "The project is on track".

Decks that are reports in landscape

I refer to these as 'Landscape Reports', and they often have lots in them. Whilst not as bloated as overgrown one-page notes, most are still poor. Some aren't though. A tiny few are great, albeit their authors need Herculean self-discipline to resist the lures that PowerPoint entices them with.

Which is why it really helps to do them in MS Word and mostly in portrait. We save time and money, and can employ ordinary people, not Herculean ones. And as for how to write big reports, see Chapter 19 (*Big reports*).

But we've now a problem. Some bosses insist their staff create Landscape Reports and in PowerPoint. So how to do decent ones? That's next.

Decent Landscape Reports in PowerPoint

Figure 23.10   🖳

Figure 23.11

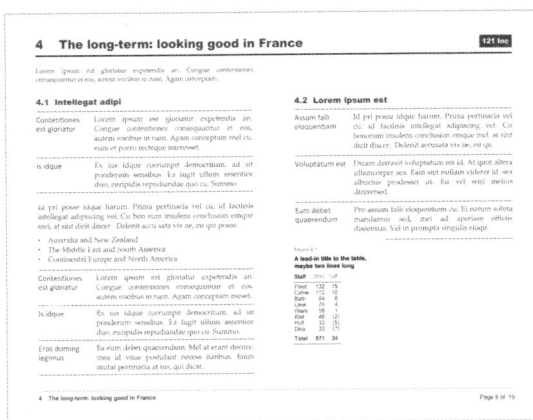
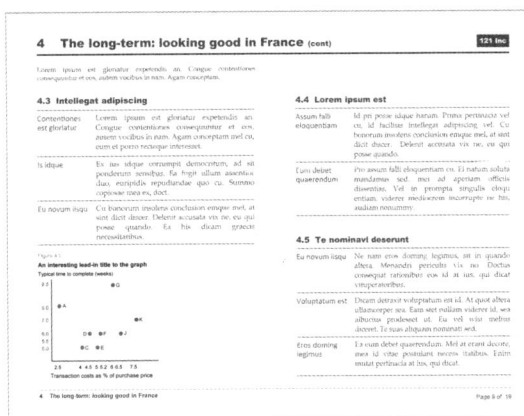

(Remember, this section isn't on overgrown one-page notes.) Figures 23.10 and 23.11 are consecutive pages from section 4 of a 19-page Landscape Report. The pages avoid the mistakes we saw earlier, e.g. misaligned content, frippery, etc. No need to repeat them all. Also:

Its sections are numbered	People can more easily refer to stuff in meetings.
It has WiT-in-columns	In font size 10 or sò, it all fits easily on a landscape page, plus is less space greedy – orphans waste far less space.
It has headlines	They reinforce messages. Avoid headings.
It follows Robin Williams' principles	All pages are aligned tightly and have contrast. There's also a look and feel that runs through them. Repetition.

Its page heading is repeated bottom left	Because Landscape Reports are often bound along their top edge, page titles are tucked in by the binding and hard to spot when flicking through it all. To help readers navigate around, repeat the page titles at the bottom in a smaller font.
It has just one colour (see the Figure on my website)	Choose one colour – your corporate colour – and use just that. Juxtapose it with grey. Grey goes well with most colours (grey and red, grey and blue, etc). Also, see Appendix 1 for tips on colour.

Each page has a graph or table. It's to illustrate how to put them on the page – I'd find somewhere the graph or table can fit, then align one of its edges with something else on the page. So in Figure 23.11, the left edge of the graph aligns with the left edge of the left column of text, whilst in Figure 23.10, the left edge of the table aligns with the left edge of the *right* column. I tried shunting the table right so its right edge lined up with the far right margin – but it didn't work as well. There's no right or wrong way (other than random alignment or centred, which are wrong), so long as charts and tables line up with something. Experiment, and trust your eyes.

Both graph and table are compact. I didn't s—t—r—e—t—c—h them to make them as wide as the text that sits above them. That would look dumb.

And the benefit of all these little changes? The pages look smart. Orderly. People can read them in a logical, grown-up way, undistracted by frippery. Also, they more quickly acclimatise to a new page – when they turn to it, it looks like the page they've just read. They also know where to start when they turn to it (top left), and where to finish (bottom right). Easy. There are fewer pages too (there's no pointless, space-wasting autoshapes), and that'll please your bosses. All in all, much better.

Landscape Reports need a front page too (Figure 23.12). No photos. The list of contents is there – put it on page 1, unless it's too long to fit.

However, we've a problem: Figures 23.10 and 23.11 are conveniently tidy. Everything fits neatly on a page. But consider Section 4.1 in Figure 23.10 – if the WiT on the left is two lines longer, it spills over to the top of the right column – and in turn, the table under Section 4.2 spills onto the next page. Messy.

But what to do? We could reduce the font size until it fits, but inconsistent font sizes are bad. Instead, try this:

Figure 23.12

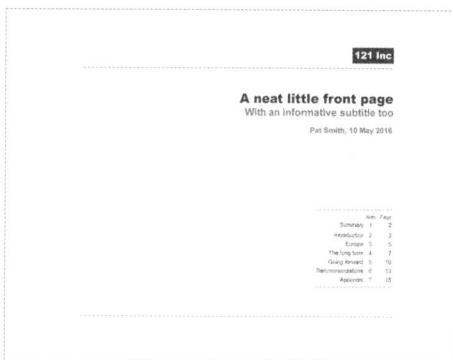

A neat little front page
With an informative subtitle too

Pat Smith, 10 May 2016

Edit words so it all fits	But we can't always edit enough to make it fit.
Reduce character spacing	This works only if the overflow isn't much, i.e. one line, not one paragraph.
Accept spillovers within a page, but not across separate pages	Allow Section 4.1 to spill to the right column, but start Section 4.2 on a new page. We get more white space on each page (arguably better), but more pages in our report (rarely good).
Do in portrait	In portrait in MS Word we accept spillovers much more than in landscape in PowerPoint.

We're near the end, albeit I must address some more strange remarks spouted by deck-lovers. I've already addressed many in this Chapter and book (e.g. "A concise deck is better than a dense 100-page report") – but below are some more. After that is a text box that looks at why some companies love decks, then there's Final Thoughts.

Bosses are visual	Where's that come from?! If they are, use WiT.
Bosses prefer landscape	Really? Bosses are fine reading books, newspapers and magazines – all portrait. As are annual reports.
Bosses like colour Bosses engage more with PowerPoint than with MS Word	Maybe that's because in MS Word, reports are often confusing, ugly and wordy, whereas in PowerPoint, they're confusing and quite ugly, but also colourful and less wordy. Which isn't a reason to do decks. Rather, it's a reason to learn to do better reports.
Bosses like to be bored, they find it reassuring	Someone said this to me in order to justify their unnecessarily long deck... Bizarre.

If decks are so flawed, why are they so popular?

I blame investment banks and consultancies. They throw huge resources at doing decks (and sometimes do good ones), then present them to admiring CEOs. Word then spreads amongst the CEOs' staffers: "The boss likes decks," so decks become the Next Big Thing, as clans of fawning in-house analysts and staffers pump out decks for bosses.

These deck-producing clans are an exclusive bunch too – "Our reports are for the CEO". Decks bestow status on authors. They magically transform bespectacled middle manager into *Deckman*, the new corporate superhero (Figure 23.13).

Figure 23.13

DECKMAN!

Deckman basks in reflected glory – "Bankers and consultants do decks and they're clever, so if I do decks, I'm clever". Also, decks are funky, contemporary, cool. Compared to shabby MS Word reports, decks seem so... *sophisticated*.

There's more though. Fun stuff is often risky or comes with consequences – think beer, fast cars, cream buns. Not decks though. They're an elusive, but winning combination: risk-free fun. Fun, for pimping pages beats doing real work. Risk-free: no-one can say ours don't follow best practice, *for there seemingly is none*. There are thousands of books on writing reports or preparing slides, but you'll struggle to find even one on how to do decks. (I've tried to find one, and when I think I have, it's yet another book on how to pimp slides.) Hence deck-writers can claim without fear of contradiction that theirs are great and follow best practice. It adds mystique too – decks are such a dark art, there's not even books on them. The skill is handed down from master to disciple. We don't own deck-skills, we look after them for the next generation.

Which is why this Chapter was the toughest to write. Other Chapters don't bestow status – everyone does bullets, graphs, tables, etc – hence people object less if I wade into them. Decks do though, so proponents defend them with their lives. And lies.

Final thoughts

Maybe this Chapter would be better as a deck. After all, maybe you're short of time. Or like visual information. Also, it would 'impose a discipline' on me, and help 'prompt discussion'. Etc. No. Self-serving nonsense.

Let's summarise. If at all possible, do your reports in MS Word, and lay them out in portrait for pages that are best in portrait, and landscape for pages that are best in landscape. If you must do Landscape Reports in PowerPoint, keep them simple. Also, avoid silo-thinking, silo-writing and lazy lists. It is possible to do really good Landscape Reports, but it takes discipline.

Finally, a confession: in corporate life, I sometimes did decks. For nefarious reasons. For box-ticking exercises that bosses didn't care for. I'd quickly blast out eight pages of brief, inconclusive lists ("Look how much work I've done! Eight pages!!"). If a boss criticised my silo-thinking, I'd reply: "But it's just a discussion document". Also, I'd do decks for one particular boss who had an unhealthy admiration for consultants and bankers. My decks made me look like one, and fooled him into thinking I'd done a thorough job. Sometimes, decks can serve a purpose.

More on talks

This Part is unlike others in this book, for it needs an introductory Chapter – so it's next. It also tells you what is – and what isn't – in this Part.

24 Introduction

I once helped a middle manager prepare a 15-minute talk he was to deliver throughout his firm. It was on a dull topic – the industry's new procedures. Let's call it 'New Procedures'.

However, it gets worse. He had to present the dull part of a dull topic: the detail of New Procedures. He wasn't some boss trotting out formulaic, big-picture stuff ("Pace of change quickening… global competition … change to survive"). Rather, he had to get down to nitty-gritty detail. Tough.

And when I went through his draft talk, it showed. The slides, handout, words, structure – it was bland. OK, it informed, but no-one would stay awake long enough to hear it. In his defence, most talks are bland. Also, he hadn't tried to make it bland. He just didn't know how not to.

We talked for two hours, then I left. A day later, we met again. He now had just four slides, and they'd completely changed (we briefly see how in a later Chapter). Now, they were a bit *basic* – there wasn't much to them – and didn't make sense on their own. No worries, for when he talked me through his accompanying commentary, I realised his talk worked. It was informative. Detailed. Even entertaining. It sizzled. His boss thought so too, as did his colleagues. His talk impressed.

Decent talks get results. The skills and techniques are transferable too – if the ideas in this Part can make New Procedures sizzle, just think what they can do for your talks. You'll *shine*. Which, to be honest, isn't that hard to do, given that most talks are poor. Next we see why they're poor.

Why so many talks are poor

We've all seen bad talks and most of us have seen good ones too. But why is one bad and the other good? Firstly, there's the obvious problem: too many bullet points. They're awful, and most of us realise this. Yet when we give talks, we do bullets ourselves. We see the mistakes of others, but repeat them. There's a herd mentality at play, a fear of doing something different.

Some people realise bullets are bad, and instead follow 'advice' for good talks. "No more than three points – or 15 words – on a slide." Or: "A slide every two minutes", and so on. But to no avail. Our talks are still poor.

Some people believe that presenting can't be taught. You've got it or you haven't. Understandable… but unnecessarily fatalistic. OK, unless you've a knack for presenting, you may never be truly exceptional. But still strive to improve, because, with the right advice, almost everyone can impress.

Some people attend courses and read books. They learn to do slides that are sophisticated. Minimalist. And probably fine for conference speakers. Most of us aren't though. Our audiences want information, not arty slides.

Some people believe they should tell stories. Or – in the vernacular of Chapter 15 – Tell Stories. Or show autoshapes. Visuals. Photos. But as explained in earlier Chapters, such ideas rarely help and often hinder.

Some people believe it's about personal style. They project their voice. Make eye contact. Power-dress. And yes, they look the part, but if their talk's content is poor, they merely put lipstick on a pig.

But what to do instead? This Part tells you. Next, we see what's in it.

Content, warnings

First, what should go on a slide – and what shouldn't? Chapter 25 (**slides**) reveals all. It takes you from reading slides to presenting. Chapter 26 (**the Slide Rule**) takes you further – from presenting to achieving outcomes.

Ever agonised over how to give your talk **coherence** and a **theme**? Need it to have a bit of style, panache… even levity? Chapter 27 is for you.

Handouts are usually bad – how many do you refer to afterwards? Chapter 28 shows how to do ones that impress. Chapter 29 gives tips on **presenting**. It includes a tip I learnt many years ago that instantly cured me of the nerves from which I suffered. I loved that tip.

That's what's in this Part. However, perhaps surprisingly, there's stuff that isn't. For instance, there's hardly any slide mock-ups. As we explain later, slides aren't that important, so we don't see how to pimp them – although if you do want to pimp yours, see Chapter 6 (*Design*) and page 126 on photos. Also, we don't ponder if we should do a talk – maybe a phone call would be better, for instance. Then again, often we've no choice. Bosses insist we give a talk.

Now for a warning: adopt this Part's tips and ideas only if they're appropriate. If we're presenting to bosses, they might object if we chuck around a toy dog or show a frog photo (these are ideas you briefly see later).

Will the tips save you time? Yes and no, several times over. Yes, you spend less time preparing slides – you do talks with fewer or even no slides. No, you spend more time thinking. But yes, this thinking time needn't eat into your working day, you can do it 'off-line' in trains or cars. Or when cleaning teeth or making tea. But no, you spend more time doing a proper handout – you no longer merely print your slides and circulate. Overall? You save time. And your talks are much better. A double bonus.

Figure 24.1
High-end fancy talks
(Or: if only we were
Al or Steve)
Al Gore tells us to save the
planet. Steve Jobs launches
the iPad. And we listen.
One's an ex-Vice President
and the other was, well,
Steve Jobs. We defer to
them. Their delegates don't
interrupt and say: "I've a
meeting in 5 minutes –
hurry up". Also, their topics
are interesting. The planet.
The iPad.

But there's more. They've
big budgets. They get
people to mock up story-
boards (cool!) and create
slick events. Delegates expect an event too, they'd be
fine with dry ice and a rock
soundtrack. Al and Steve are
big people with big budgets
presenting big topics.

For us, it's different.
Delegates arrive late,
then text and interrupt.
Our topics are duller – HR
updates, IT training. As for
budgets, most of us have
none and wouldn't want
one. Imagine delivering
IT updates to the tune of
Simply the Best with dry ice
billowing over our shoes.
We'd be sacked.

I'm sure Al and Steve
could have done great talks
on New Procedures – and
appropriate ones too (no
dry ice or rock soundtrack).
But they didn't have to.
We do. So this book is for
you, not them – and never
mentions them again.

Why there's not much technology here

I've read that delegates "expect sophisticated multi-media talks". Which is like saying that cinema audiences expect computer-generated images (CGI). No. They expect to be entertained, to see a good film. If CGI helps entertain and is relevant to the plot, they get CGI. But if CGI isn't relevant and doesn't help, they don't. Cinema audiences don't care which techniques movie-makers use, so long as it's a good film.

So too with talks: presenters can use movie clips, dry ice, and more – yet we don't care which they use, so long as it's a good talk. We don't expect sophisticated multi-media. We expect to be informed. Or persuaded. Maybe entertained. Or whatever it is that caused us to attend in the first place.

Having said that, some people use multi-media, and others might want to, so maybe this book should look at it. It doesn't. Firstly, talks are about people and communication, not IT wizardry. Secondly, this book isn't aimed at those that deliver high-end, all-singing, all-dancing talks (think Oscar ceremonies, political rallies, iPad launches, etc). It's aimed at the other 99% of talks, where it's neither necessary nor appropriate to get too fancy (think HR updates, New Procedure rollouts, etc). And if you want more on why this book ignores high-end, fancy talks, see Figure 24.1.

Then there's PowerPoint. It evokes strong reactions – "PowerPointless", "Death by PowerPoint", etc. Perhaps PowerPoint should be banned. No. We don't blame pens if people write badly. Anyway, PowerPoint is like most things in life: a force for good or evil. Like cars. Drive well, and they help. Drive badly, and they kill. We don't ban cars though. We ban bad drivers. Or force them to learn how to drive well. So too with PowerPoint. Don't ban it. Instead, present well with – or without – it. Many people do.

You can too. After all, it's in our nature to talk. We do it in pubs, coffee bars, canteens. We enjoy it. Or – at least – we do, until we're asked to do it at work. This Part takes us back to what we enjoy and what we're natural at: *talking*. It helps every type of talk too. Board updates. Sales pitches. Lunch-and-learns. Conference talks. Training events. It also helps when presenting reports to bosses. Which is the next Chapter.

Slides 25

This Chapter looks at different ways to convey information on slides. Along the way, we expose flaws in conventional wisdom, e.g. "No more than three points on a slide". Throughout, assume that we strive for clarity – do we convey information clearly? OK, in talks we've other goals to achieve – give delegates unprompted recall perhaps. Or persuade them. But Chapter 9 covers those.

Let's set the scene. Imagine we write a report to help bosses decide whether to buy a company. The report outlines what we found, then gives thoughts on price, post-deal structure, synergies, etc. Figure 25.1 is a page from it – the eight main findings. Please don't feel you must read it. Rather, appreciate that, because we saw it in Chapter 1, it follows some of that Chapter's tips, i.e. it groups items and starts at the end.

However, bosses want us to present our report to them in a talk. Assume that bosses don't read the report before we talk. Assume we're to talk for 15 minutes and the eight findings take up three of them. How might we show the eight on a slide? That's the scene set. Let's start.

Figure 25.1

> ## Summary of the findings
>
> There were mixed findings, but overall the company seems in good shape.
>
> **Good findings**
>
> - Its new business initiative has been a success and income is up 20% on last year. Every department has increased income by at least 12%.
> - It's finished clinical trials on the major new drug and Medical Authorities have indicated it should approve it next week.
> - Last month, Regulators formally announced the company has been cleared of the mis-selling accusations that hung over it for the last 2 years.
> - The market value of their Leeds site is worth £3m more than shown on its balance sheet.
>
> **Bad findings**
>
> - Its pension deficit has worsened in the year from £10m to £30m. The company is increasing contributions by £7m a year to remedy.
> - Because of its lack of hedging, the dollar weakness will hit profit by £3m next year. It has recently recruited a new Treasurer.
> - There has been a problem with staff turnover – 30% of staff left last year, up 10% from the prior year. Many leavers were from "Global Solutions" department.
> - Its computer system is inadequate and needs replacing at a cost of £2m. This will also add £500k a year extra to running costs.

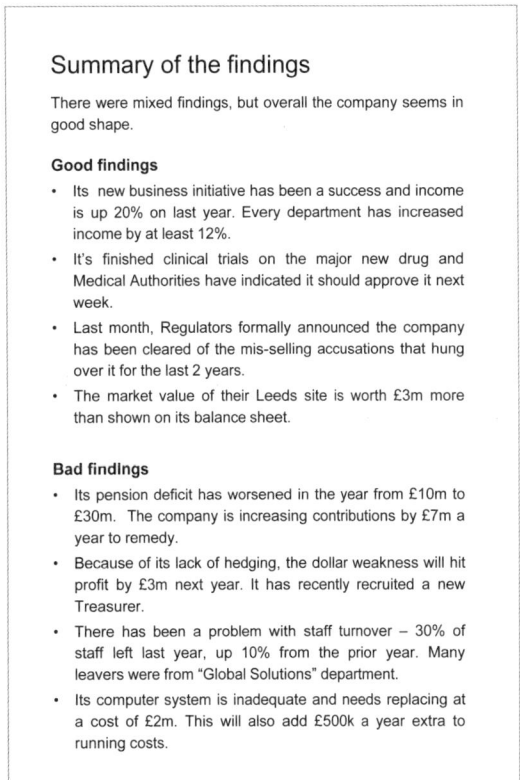

Turning a page from a report into a slide

Firstly, we could write the findings in full on a slide. Don't. It makes talks intensely tedious. Also, it creates conflict: do delegates read words or listen to presenters? If they read words, delegates and presenters get out of sync – people are faster at reading than speaking. Finally, if all words are on screen, why bother with the talk? Presenters could instead simply email the report to bosses for them to read in their own time.

We could redo the eight findings in a WiT. It's better, but delegates still have the quandary: read slide or listen to presenter? And if they read, presenter and delegates get out of sync. So what to do? Here are three ideas:

1. **Reveal findings one by one on a single slide**. OK, it keeps presenter and delegates more in sync, but it's agony to sit through. It drip-feeds information to delegates in frustratingly small chunks.

2. **Break the slide in two**, i.e. good findings on one slide, bad findings on another. Yes, fewer words on each slide. But overall, no, not fewer words on slides. Don't do it.

3. **Edit**. Read Figure 25.2. It has only 39 words. Much better. Its words are no longer a major distraction. Delegates scan them in a few seconds, and then *listen*. Which they must do, for the slide doesn't say that much.

Figure 25.2

Mixed findings, but good overall	
Good findings	**Bad findings**
New business drive successful	£30m pension deficit
Major drug to be approved	£3m 'forex' hit next year
Cleared of mis-selling	30% staff turnover
Property £3m undervalued	£2m needed on IT

The slide heading is better too. Previously it said: "Summary of the findings". Now it's: "Mixed findings, but good overall". Don't do headings, do headlines. Use them to reinforce and give insight.

Notice in Figure 25.2, I have managed to strip out any redundant words wherever I could. Or rather: "*I removed redundant words*". The heading isn't: "There were mixed findings, but overall it's good". It's: "Mixed findings, but good overall". OK, it's only three words less, but that's 37.5% fewer words. Slides improve with every word we remove.

Figure 25.2 has just 39 words, but don't conclude that slides should have 39 words maximum. However, I know a presenter who limits himself to five words per bullet or line of text. It ensures he edits viciously.

Back to our slide. We could spread the eight points over eight slides. Yes, it declutters, there's less on each slide, but it fragments information and hinders comparability. Also, it can drive delegates nuts. Click… click… click… click. What often kills delegates isn't the slides or their number – I've seen great talks with 50 slides. Rather, it's their rhythm. Constant, repetitive, metronomic. It sends out a debilitating signal – that the talk is so orchestrated, there's no place within it to participate or interact, even if we want to. So be mindful of your slides' rhythm. Mix up their pace a bit – a few short ones, a few long ones.

And mix them up with 'non-slide' stuff. Even great slides bore delegates eventually. So have something in your talk you can scribble on a flipchart or whiteboard. Maybe it's a trend line or key number – whatever it is, delegates see it emerge on a flipchart over a few seconds, instead of, yet again, seeing it instantly click on screen. You *create* – and in front of delegates too. It introduces an element of suspense and animation: "What's he drawing?" they ponder. It helps ring the changes – and that's good. On training days, I show a graph to convey that City have 9 points, Rovers 10 (I show it to mock graphs). But I don't instantly click to a slide of the graph, pre-prepared in Excel defaults, then copied into PowerPoint. Rather, I draw it on a flipchart, talking through it as I do so (Figure 25.3). Much more impact.

Figure 25.3

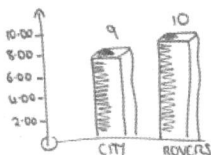

Back to our eight findings. We can do more. That's next.

Even fewer words

Our slide now has 39 words. Let's reduce that bit by bit:

Edit the topics: "New business drive successful" – that's four words. Try: "New business drive" (three). Or: "Business development" (two). Or: "Sales" (one). "Sales" doesn't mean much on its own, but in the talk, we *explain* it. We could replace all findings with eight words: Sales, Patents, Legal, Property, Pension, Forex, Staff, IT. Delegates read them in two seconds.

Just a heading: try: "Good and bad findings". Or: "Findings". Or: "Good overall". The slide now has just one or two words (font size 80). They're 'visual anchors', and they remind delegates what we're talking about if their minds wander a bit. The next Chapter looks more at visual anchors.

Nothing: simply ditch the slide and just talk bosses through the findings. Without slides, we communicate better. And engage more.

What about the other stuff we wish to cover in our talk? Well, we could just talk. Without slides. We could also ditch the slide that shows agenda and timings. And ditch the first slide too (title of talk, presenter's name).

But can it be possible? Life without slides? Without words on slides? Definitely. Firstly, imagine it's pre-1980s when PowerPoint didn't exist, and you must give a talk. Would you type out bits of your script on pieces of paper in a big font, then show them one by one to delegates as you speak? Secondly, after you give talks, does anyone ever say to you: "I wish you'd put more words on screen"? Do you ever say it to others?

Ditching slides is a seriously neat trick, and the next Chapter explores life without slides in more detail. Before then, we've one last section: slide advice to ignore.

Slide advice to ignore

How many people does it take to mock up slides for talks? Two. One to toil over slides, and one to sit behind and give dumb advice on how to do slides. "Never have more than three points on a slide." I've even read that five points are better than four, because they look better on slides(!). Such pseudo-science is bad advice, as we see from these examples:

No more than five numbers on a slide. *Rubbish*: we've all seen bad slides with 50 numbers on them, but not all slides with 50 numbers are bad. If I'm

Figure 25.4
When reading words on screen is fine
Imagine we train call centre staff and want them to answer calls with the phrase: "This is RSB Bank, how can I help?". Try this: show the words on screen, then read them aloud word-for-word. Then do it again. It emphasises. However, do this infrequently and with short phrases.

Also, there's another counterintuitive oddity that's great when used sparingly: get delegates to read a slide. To themselves. In silence. Let me explain: after you finish a section of your talk, show a *20-second recap* slide that recaps what you just covered. You keep quiet. Delegates read it and get a break from listening to you. It reinforces. After 20 seconds, maybe comment on, or further reinforce, a particular point. Simple. Effective.

a soccer pundit talking to soccer fans, I could show the Premier League on screen (over 200 numbers) then talk for 20 minutes. I'd highlight how City is above United on goal difference because City whipped Rovers 5–0 last week. I'd talk about last year's promoted teams. The table on screen would act as a reference point for my comments, and delegates would be fine with it. Sometimes 200 numbers is fine. Sometimes eight is too many.

No more than three points per slide. *Rubbish*: think of Moses' Ten Commandments – if he'd been limited to three points per tablet, he'd struggle to cart four tablets down the mountain, so would stop at nine commandments to avoid injury. Which means we could covet our neighbour's wife, servant, ox. Also, Robin Williams' design acronym would be a bit dull if she had just three points per slide: Contrast, Repetition and Alignment (slide 1); Proximity (slide 2)…

A slide every two minutes. *Rubbish*: a 'visual anchor' slide might be on screen for five minutes if we've lots to mention. There's no right or wrong number of slides per minute, it depends on us, our material and audience. At conferences, I show 40 slides in an hour – some slides for 15 seconds, and one for eight minutes (I warn delegates we spend that long on it). And it's fine.

Unfortunately with pseudo-science, people believe it. Just as drowning people cling to driftwood in the hope it saves their lives, so people cling to pseudo-science in the hope it saves their talks. Driftwood won't hinder and might help. Pseudo-science is less benign though:

It helps the few truly terrible presenters	It spares them from their worst atrocities, such as showing entire scripts on screen.
It's irrelevant to the few great presenters	They ignore 'rules' anyway – they know rules can be broken, and they break them.
It hinders the huge swathe of average presenters	The 'rules' dumb down by encouraging presenters to drip-feed information to delegates in small chunks.

But the internet makes it worse. It propagates these 'rules' and so legitimises them. The 'rules' become the accepted norm from which it's difficult to wriggle free. We must wriggle free though. Good talks don't come from following 'rules' and pseudo-science. They come from thinking about messages to convey and outcomes to achieve.

The Slide Rule 26

The Slide Rule focuses presenters away from slides and onto outcomes. It transforms every type of talk. We think more about what to say. We save time for us and our audiences. First though, let's imagine… think back to the good and bad findings we saw in the last Chapter – they're part of a report on a company we might buy, and we must prepare a talk on the report. This is how many of us proceed: first, we fire up PowerPoint and mock up slides. We do the front slide – we put a photo of widgets on it (the company makes them). We do a *contents* page: (1) Introduction; (2) Company; (3) Industry; (4) Methodology, etc. We put in facts, figures, bullets.

And why not? Surely talks need slides, so let's mock some up. Also, slides help us marshal our thoughts, *for we aren't yet sure what we'll say*. Which neatly exposes the fault-line in all this. If we don't know what we'll say, how can we mock up slides to help us say it? It's putting the cart before the horse. Instead, work out what to say, then do slides if they help us say it better.

Also, when we mock up random slides for 20 minutes, we get a false sense of progress ("Hey, I've done six slides"). We mistakenly believe if we do slides, we're getting ready. And if they're *foxy* slides, we're really ready. The slides, not the talk, become our goal.

Let's start again. We must still prepare and present the same talk, but this time, slides are banned. Now, with no slides to mock up, we can't hide behind a 'displacement activity'. Ban slides, and all we can do is *think*. About what to say. About outcomes to achieve. Which is great, because it's words, not slides, that make the talk. There's an IT phrase: *WYSIWYG* (pronounced *wizzy-wig*) – What You See Is What You Get. I use it for talks, but change it to: What You *Say* Is What You Get. After all, what separates good talks from bad ones? Not the slides. Bad talks often have bad slides, but they'd still be bad even with good slides. Good slides won't save a bad talk. (Of course, maybe good slides make good talks even better – we look at that later.) When preparing talks, we often ask ourselves: "What slides do we need?". Perhaps we should instead ask: "Do we need slides?" – but this isn't quite right either. Our goal isn't to ditch pointless slides. It's to achieve outcomes. Which is where the Slide Rule comes in. It's next.

The Slide Rule

It's just six words: "Achieve our outcomes before doing slides". Let's look at each bit in turn.

Achieve our outcomes before doing slides

It doesn't say: "*Think* about our outcomes" – it's not enough to think about them. Nor: "What outcomes do we wish to achieve?" Posing a question merely encourages us to write lists – and on its own, writing lists gets us nowhere. It says: "Achieve our outcomes". Also, don't confuse *achieve* with *pimp*. Flash slides don't achieve outcomes, unless our desired outcome is to look flash. And be specific, not vague. If we want to manage expectations – if we want delegates to be patient with teething troubles – try the cartoon we saw in Chapter 9 (*Outcomes*). See Figure 26.1. Notice the steps we followed:

Figure 26.1

"What do you mean… 'it's a bit muddy'?"

Step 1: identify outcome (to manage expectations);
Step 2: decide how to achieve it (use the *Moses* cartoon);
Step 3: do slide if it helps (and in this case, it does).

Unfortunately, people often omit step (2) and go straight to step (3). That is, we think: "I'm unsure how to achieve the outcome – to manage expectations – but I'm sure I'll find a cartoon that'll do it… let's insert a blank slide, ready for when I find one". This is wrong for several reasons:

We close our mind to better ways	We decide a cartoon is best even if though it might not be.
We lull ourselves into a false sense of security	We mistakenly believe we're further along with drafting our talk than we actually are.
The night before the talk, we see lots of empty slides	So we panic and cram stuff on them that underwhelms and doesn't achieve outcomes.
We waste time	If we decide not to show a cartoon, we mock up a template we don't use.

So don't just think about our outcomes. Don't just list them. Don't be vague in how we achieve them. Rather, *achieve* them. And yes, I know we achieve outcomes not by identifying cartoons but by showing them to delegates, so perhaps the Slide Rule should say: "Before doing any slides, identify the specific way in which we will aim to achieve our outcomes when we present to delegates"… but it doesn't. I trade precision for punchiness.

That's the word **achieve**. Next, we look at the **our** word.

Achieve *our* outcomes before doing slides

There's a reasonably well known phrase: What's In it For Me? *WIFM*. Delegates think *WIFM* when listening to talks, so surely presenters should think not about their own outcomes, but instead target delegate self-interest. It's not always possible though. If we show the *Moses* slide and ask delegates for patience on our project, we don't meet their needs. We ask for their altruism. Also, sometimes self-interest isn't clear-cut – if we're in sales, what's in our best interest: attend a course on selling? Or spend the day selling? Then there's bad news – if sacking people, we can't meet delegates' needs. What we say isn't what they want to hear, so all we can do is achieve our outcome whilst being mindful of their predicaments and feelings.

So the Rule refers to *our* outcomes. Yes, they often overlap with delegates' needs – for instance, salespeople often achieve their outcomes by meeting delegates' needs. But it's our talk. And our outcomes. They've primacy.

That's the first two words of the Slide Rule. As for the other four words:

Achieve our **outcomes** before doing slides	As Chapter 9 (*Outcomes*) explains, think about angles, the *feel* button, accessible logic, repeatability. Also, we've probably several outcomes – some are critical (spend time on these, hit them hard), others are hygiene factors (reassure, then move on).
Achieve our outcomes **before doing slides**	This reinforces the point: work out how to achieve our outcomes, then do slides if they help. Don't do them if they don't.

That's the Slide Rule. As an aside – and so as to avoid any confusion – please don't assume there's a 'one-to-one' relationship between outcomes and slides. We don't need a slide for each outcome. Nor need an outcome for each slide. Rather, we have slides if they help us achieve our outcomes.

And talking of outcomes, the outcome of the Slide Rule is great. It *transforms* talks and meetings. Here are two examples of it in action. Neither looks at the benefits of the Slide Rule – we see them later.

The approval procedures: a manager had 12 slides on approval procedures to present to the management team. There were flowcharts, visuals (interlocking wheels with cogs…) and more. I asked him what he was trying to achieve. "Approval procedures," he said, "are too complex… low-value stuff is reviewed by five committees and six sub-committees – and it's worse for high-value stuff. I want the team to agree we simplify them." His words were clear and concise – far more so than the slides – so in his talk, he ditched the slides and said the words instead.

The accounting losses: an accountant had ten slides for his management team – analyses, tables, words and more. He told me an accounting issue had created small profits and losses on expense claims – some staff were out of pocket by a few pounds, others better off by a few pounds. He wanted the team to agree to draw a line under the small differences, and to sanction new procedures to avoid them recurring. His words were clear and concise – far more so than the slides – so in his talk, he ditched the slides and said the words instead.

In both examples, I asked the presenters to summarise their talk. That is, we role-played – we saw this in Chapter 12 – and when we did, we realised we could achieve our outcomes without slides. Also in both examples, presenters were pushing on an open door. They proposed ideas that were uncontroversial. Uncontentious. But isn't it deceitful of me to illustrate the Slide Rule with 'open door' examples? No. At work, the door is often open – so don't waste people's time by talking through it for 20 minutes. And if it isn't open, we won't prise it open by presenting lots of slides. Rather, we're more likely to lock it shut. Boring our audience into submission rarely works.

Here's one last example of the Slide Rule, but it's not from business. It's the teenager from Chapter 13 (*Visuals*) who's lazy, dishonest, disrespectful. His parents must prepare a pep talk, but haven't heard of the Slide Rule. No worries, they do what most parents do in this situation: they think of sticks and carrots. A reward if the boy bucks up, a punishment if he doesn't.

Let's analyse it. Firstly, the parents know the *outcomes* they seek: that the boy shows more effort, honesty, respect. They then decide how to *achieve* that outcome: sticks and carrots that connect in ways the boy *feels*. All pretty obvious. We apply the Slide Rule at home without even thinking about it. Yet at work, we fire up PowerPoint and blast out slides in the mistaken belief they give talks more impact.

The benefits of fewer – or even no – slides

We've already seen some:

1. We think more about what we say – *WYSIWYG*.
2. We strive to achieve outcomes, not produce slides.
3. We engage more with delegates – they look at us, not our screen.
4. We are more focused. Result: people waste less time in meetings. This is a huge benefit.

Here are more benefits:

We save 'prep' time	Which is quicker to do? Prepare slides? Or prepare no slides? It's a no-brainer.

We more easily make last-minute changes	Imagine something happens just before our talk, and we must edit our script. A pain – but so be it. But at least we're spared the task of editing slides. We don't have any to edit.
We're not at the mercy of IT	Our talk no longer depends on electricity, projectors, laptops, memory sticks. It depends on us as presenter, and what we say. We're now in control.
We look more senior	There's something confident, almost cocky, about talking without the security blanket of slides. It creates an air of seniority (and that helps a lot if you actually are senior).

Also, we stand out more. A corporate buyer told me that, when he put his business out to tender, potential suppliers all hoofed up with slides… except one who brought along another client's file (doctored to preserve anonymity). The buyer and supplier then spent an hour going through the file, talking about how they'd work together – asking questions, raising concerns, etc. They had a conversation. The person won the business. I also heard about a conference chairperson who, when introducing the next talk, said the presenter had no slides. The room burst into spontaneous applause.

There's one last big benefit to ditching slides: if we don't do slides, *we can't circulate them as a handout to delegates*. Which is great news. When it comes to handouts, having no slides doesn't create a problem. It avoids one. It prevents presenters from circulating copies of slides. Slides and handouts serve different needs, and it's almost impossible to create something that meets both – we create something too detailed to be decent slides and not detailed enough to be a decent handout. We fail on both counts. Out of all the slide packs you've received over the years, how many did you look at afterwards? Not many, I guess. How many do you still refer to? Almost none. (OK, you might look at packs of slides that aren't actually slides; they're reports done in PowerPoint. Chapter 23 looks at these.)

To conclude, if you do slides, never hand them out. Instead, create two documents. Slides. And a handout. However, when preparing talks, most of us barely have enough time to prepare slides, let alone a separate handout. But that's because we concertina all the prep work into the day before our talk, whereas with better planning, we'd have time to do a proper handout. It's worth spending that time too – we do slides that work as slides and a handout that works as a handout. A good target to aspire to. And, of course, if our slides are visual anchors (e.g. "Findings"), they won't take long to prepare. Chapter 28 covers how to do decent handouts.

Figure 26.2
Bosses demand my slides
People regularly tell me: "When I present to bosses, they insist I hand out my slides". When people say this, I ask: "What do you give bosses besides slides?". "Nothing", they reply.

Bingo! Bosses demand slides because we've given them nothing else. Give them a decent handout and they will no longer crave our slides.

The benefits of ditching slides apply equally to visual anchors. Except one. We still depend on IT, albeit we cope better if it fails. If we can't show our visual anchors, it won't affect our talk much. We can still talk without them.

However, despite all these benefits, people have concerns with fewer – or even no – slides. We address them next.

The concerns of ditching slides

How will I keep delegates' attention if I've no slides? How will I remember what to say? How can I show detail? Understandable concerns… but as we soon see, unfounded.

How will I keep people's attention if I've no slides?
Answer: we keep their attention more if we've no slides

Apparently, slides help retain people's attention – delegates can stare at them when bored. No. Most slides don't prevent people getting bored. Slides are why they're bored. Admittedly that's because most slides are bad... so surely we just get rid of bad slides, no? Not quite, for it misses the point. It gives too much credit to slides. When slides help, it's not because they're slides. It's because of the *thinking behind the slides*. Perhaps our slide shows a graph that gives people new insight. Yes, a slide is the mechanism by which they see the graph, but no, it's not the slide that keeps people awake. Rather, we do, with the thinking behind our graph. It sounds pedantic, but it's critical: slides are a by-product of our thinking. Previously, I said we don't blame biros if people write badly. The reverse is also true: we don't credit biros if people write well. So don't credit slides if people like our talks. Rather, credit ourselves. Slides don't keep people's attention. We do.

How will I remember what to say if I've no slides?
Answer: not an issue, we don't have to remember

It's said that politicians use statistics like drunkards use streetlamps: for support, not illumination. So too with slides. All too often, they help presenters, not illuminate delegates. They remind presenters what to say. In which case, can we edit them too much or dispense with them altogether? Without words on screen, presenters must remember the script. Whilst this might be OK for trainers who often give the same talk, is it practical for one-off talks to, say, prospects?

Life with fewer words on screen needn't be a problem though. I'm not asking you to deliver talks from memory. Rather, I'm saying: don't put your script on screen. Instead, keep it in your hand. It's called 'Speaker Notes'… Do this and it changes the dynamic between presenter and delegates. They don't stare at a screen. They look at and listen to you. You engage.

Figure 26.3
Can bad slides ruin talks?
Yes, if really bad. Let me explain. Talks are made up of many things. A commentary. An audience. A presenter. Maybe slides. Each can hit or miss the mark – does the commentary resonate? Are delegates friendly? Are slides good? And if slides aren't good, yes, it creates a poor first impression.

However, if there's a following wind for everything else – a decent presenter, friendly audience, etc – everyone quickly realises the slides are an aberration and ignores their poor quality. Delegates listen to an engaging presenter give a compelling commentary.

But avoid slides that are really bad, for delegates might not pay attention long enough to spot the following wind for everything else. Hence bad slides might not matter that much, but really bad slides can be fatal.

But maybe slides help nervous presenters. It's like the riddle: "What can you hide behind by standing in front of?" Answer: slides. Many presenters view slides as a safety net that prevents them from delivering bad talks.

It's flawed thinking for two reasons. Firstly, if you want to hide, at least hide behind something that provides decent cover. Most slides don't. Secondly, as doctors know, it's better to cure problems than mask symptoms. By which I mean: do something to improve confidence and reduce nerves – such as follow the tips and ideas in this book. OK, yes, it can be intimidating when we first abandon our slide-heavy talks. But it's also hugely liberating, for both us and our audiences. And a virtuous circle. The more we do it, the more we crave doing it again. Once the genie is out the bottle, once contact has been made with the audience, it's difficult to go back to how it was.

How can I show detail if I've no slides?
Answer: we show detail better with no slides

There are two issues. Firstly, should presenters show detail? Answer: yes, if it's appropriate. If delegates expect and want it – and if presenters can talk about it without getting too bogged down – detail is fine in talks. Unfortunately, as presenters, we often give too much detail… and that's *because we have slides*. Slides enable us to show everything, even if delegates don't want it. A finance director showed me a 'cash forecast' slide he'd done for the board – and it had a lot on it. About 200 words. A graph with three trend lines over 12 months, and a legend too. Two arrows to highlight gaps here and there. Call-out boxes to comment on bits of the graph.

Legible? Yes – everything could be read. Simple to grasp? No. There was a lot to take in, and it was spread all over the place. So I asked him to explain it to me. He said: "I want to pay an £80m dividend next March – that will leave us £40m in the bank. OK?". That's it. No slides needed. No graphs, legends, arrows, etc. Note the following:

1. If the board trusts the director, the slide isn't needed – and actually hinders. It entices people to ask about irrelevant detail ("Why's there a blip in June's numbers?"). And if the board doesn't trust the director, the slide unnerves ("The guy can't rise above detail…").

2. Without the slide, the debate moves from background and workings ("Here are trend lines") to consequences and outcomes ("Is £40m in the bank enough? Or too much?"). Much better.

3. I asked the director to give me a 30-second summary. Turned out it was a seven-second summary.

Detail is fine in talks, yet all too often, slides lure us into showing too much. We show what we know, not what delegates need to know.

Then there's the second issue we saw above: do slides show detail well? Answer: no. Often, detail is illegibly small. To squeeze, say, a table with

(1) I know 80 pieces of Paper isn't 'green', but neither is the travel to get people to the conference. Nor are all the fab lunches laid on for delegates, and pastries and coffee too. If conference organisers really cared about the environment, they'd scrap fancy lunches or even entire conferences. When they refuse to circulate handouts, it's not because they're green. Often, it's because they're lazy, penny-pinching or both.

many rows on a slide, presenters use tiny font sizes. Or they chop the table in half and spread over two slides. Both are, of course, nuts. Also, maybe we wish to convey elegance – we want people to see our smart new template. Showing it on screen won't do it justice, for the resolution of most projectors isn't good. Instead, use this thing called 'Paper'. It's great for detail. And – unlike slides – it comes in two fantastic orientations. Landscape *and* portrait. Neat. Portrait's great for stuff that's too long to fit on screen, such as tall tables. Also, Paper's image quality is better than a projector's, and so does justice to our smart new templates.

There's a downside though: Paper creates work, especially in conferences. It's an effort to circulate 80 bits of Paper to 80 delegates – but surely it's worth it. We've taken time to prepare our talk. And 80 people travel to – and attend – it. We then waste that effort because someone won't print 80 pieces of paper and put one on each delegate's chair. False economy[1].

What if we've something we wish to show, such as the graph in Figure 26.4 (we saw it originally in Chapter 13 (*Visuals*))? Simple: show it on a slide. As I said, do a slide if it helps. But what if this graph is all we wish to show? Should we fire up a computer and projector just for one slide? It depends. If others present before or after us – maybe we're at a conference – the IT is set up, so it's easy to show just one slide. In fact, it's great – our talk stands out. Also, if we've just one slide, we do it well. We won't do 50 slides to the same standard as just one.

However, if we're the only presenter, it's odd to talk without slides and then suddenly ping a scattergram on screen. So instead, draw it on a flipchart (which is what I do when I talk about Figure 26.4 on training days). It won't take long, and we talk through it as we draw. Our scribbled graph isn't perfect, but is fit for purpose – it conveys that Company A is an outlier.

OK, the scattergram is easy to draw, but what if we want to show columns and pies on our slides? We'll struggle to draw them – but reread Chapter 2, and you'll no longer want to show those sorts of graphs.

What if we've something that we can't scribble out quickly, such as a photo or cartoon? We've options: (1) distribute a copy to everyone; (2) show it on screen – the only slide in our talk; (3) omit it. I recommend (3), unless it's critical to our talk. By showing it – and showing only it – we hype it, so it had better be really good, or it's a damp squib. A cartoon that brings a wry smile to delegates' faces is acceptable if one of many slides. It's a let-down if it has a unique position in our talk: the only slide we show.

Depending on what we wish to show, there are other ways around this one-slide conundrum, e.g. before delegates arrive, put a hard copy of it on the wall in the room. Or scribble it out on page 2 of a flipchart and keep it hidden until it's time to show it. This second approach retains the element of reveal, plus doesn't hype it too much.

Figure 26.4

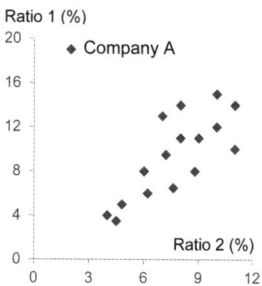

Of course we could omit the slide, and instead describe it. Radio 4 presenters often talk through cartoons and it's fine. Also, as a presenter I often find it's better to describe a diagram than show it. There's a wonderful decision tree of the lyrics to the song *You're the One that I Want* from the movie *Grease*. It has boxes that run down the page – do you have chills? Are they multiplying? Are you losing control? And if you answer *No* to any question, arrows take you bottom-left to a box (*You're not the one that I want*), and if you answer *Yes*, arrows take you bottom-right to a different box (*You are the one that I want*). In the past, I showed the tree on a slide, and it got a smile. Now, I just describe it instead – and it gets a laugh. I guess that when I describe it, its punchline has more surprise.

Which brings us to a question posed earlier: can good slides make good talks even better? Of course. Sometimes. Don't forget: *I'm not against slides*. I'm against slides that don't help us achieve outcomes. But – as I said earlier – when slides do help, don't credit the slides. Credit the thinking behind the slides. And if our thinking is so spot-on, there's a good chance it will have even more impact without slides.

Time to summarise, albeit here's one last concern people have: "If I've no slides, how will I ensure delegates remember what I say?" If that's the outcome you seek, see Chapter 9 (*Outcomes*), and in particular page 85.

Final thoughts

A few years ago, I went on a great tour of the BBC in London. Two guides enthralled us with history, background, anecdotes – and all without slides. None of my fellow visitors noticed the lack of slides, let alone complained about it. Also, think about TV newsreaders – they shovel information out to us and do it perfectly well without slides. Their words don't appear behind them on screen (although they often use visual anchors such as a picture of whatever they're talking about). Then there are radio commentators who communicate brilliantly without slides or even visual anchors.

In fact, this last example – radio commentators – got me thinking. I almost renamed the Slide Rule as the Radio Rule: "*First achieve our outcomes as if on the radio*". It encapsulates everything in the Slide Rule… except handouts. Yes, handouts are often available on a radio station's website, but radio pundits must assume that listeners can't access them whilst tuning in. Hence a Radio Rule wrongly implies that as presenters, we should avoid handouts. Notwithstanding, the Radio Rule is almost the complete article. Most of us can think of radio presenters we admire because they bring topics to life through the words they say. Which is what talks should be: bringing topics to life through the words we say. *WYSIWYG*. What You Say Is What You Get.

27   Coherence, themes

Lunch-and-learns, conference talks, training events, etc. Tricky for us as presenters for two reasons. Firstly, our delegates want more than dry facts – they want a bit of levity, maybe even humour or intrigue. Secondly, we want to give our delegates more than just disparate facts. We must tie content together and create something coherent. The talks need a theme.

This Chapter has five ideas to achieve all this. Four are hooks on which to hang your talks' content. They work for entire talks or just bits of them – and for most types of talk too. As for the fifth idea, it's, well, *different*. As unique as you. First, note the following about the ideas in this Chapter:

1.   They work. I used them in the New Procedures talk mentioned in this Part's Introduction. They made that talk sizzle. We see how later.
2.   They don't resort to contrived business-book science ("For great talks, remember to R-A-V-E: Repeatedly Add Value Everywhere").
3.   Some require slides (the first does). Remember: I'm not against slides. I'm against bad slides. Use slides if they help us achieve our outcomes.

Theme 1: Just Pictures

(If you've read Chapter 13 (*Visuals and photos*), you'll know this story.) When a Sales Director had to give a lunch-and-learn to staff on Sales, he set himself a goal: no words on slides. So at the start, he showed a screen-filling photo of a frog. Delegates were intrigued. "Sales," he said, "is like kissing frogs. We must kiss lots of frogs to find a prince". Bang. It woke delegates up because it was memorable. A bit irreverent. He then showed more photos throughout his talk. They created a theme which united a list of otherwise isolated remarks.

But doesn't this fall foul of 'advice' on how to do talks? Apparently, delegates should see a talk's logic merely by looking at slide thumbnails – and if we show just pictures, they can't. It doesn't mean pictures are bad. It means the 'advice' is bad. Thumbnails help presenters prepare slides, not help delegates see a talk's logic. Our slide shows '15%' – or Dalmatians and a bloke in a spotty suit – and its logic isn't clear until we bring it to life with our words.

Figure 27.1

Try not just photos, but cartoons too. Not clipart, of course – never use it. If describing something that might transpire to be heaven or hell – or that people might view as heaven or hell – try Figure 27.1. It's either an elegant lady or a witch. It conveys our point in a slightly quirky way ("Do you see beauty or beast?"). Also, I once saw a great cartoon of arrows raining down on a medieval King and his knights, whilst a man in a suit stands behind clutching an AK47 – and the King shouts at his 'Chief of Staff': "I've no time to see some crazy salesman, can't you see I've a battle to fight?". In other words, if we step back from the day-to-day, we might spot a better way.

Over the years, I built up a library of cartoons, be they on compliance, change, or whatever. When giving a talk in corporate life, I always used one or two, yet (and this is quite telling) I now don't use any. Back then, my talks were one-offs, and the words I spoke were… *OK*. Cartoons helped. Now, I do the same talk repeatedly and have refined my words so they're better than any cartoons I'd show. If I show cartoons now, they underwhelm. So I don't show any. Conclusion: whilst cartoons can help, good words are often better. After all, few stand-up comics show cartoons.

Revisiting the $220m typing error

Chapter 9 talks of a $220m typing error and says the story is great for talks that launch our shiny new quality initiative. The story doesn't need a slide, it works fine without one. However, maybe our talk has a *Just Pictures* theme. Or we have an *urge* to show a slide. So here are ideas for what to show:

An arresting photo	Show a screen-filling image of a depressed stockbroker – or maybe even an invite to the Christmas party, but with the word *Cancelled* stamped over it (remember: bosses cancelled the party because of the $220m loss).
A visual anchor	Show the section title on screen in, say, font size 80 (e.g. "Why we must avoid errors").
A 'big font' – it helps unprompted recall	Show *$220m* in font size 140. Delegates think: "What's that about?" We then explain.
A Post-It note (Figure 27.2)	I bought the image from www.istockphoto.com.

Figure 27.2

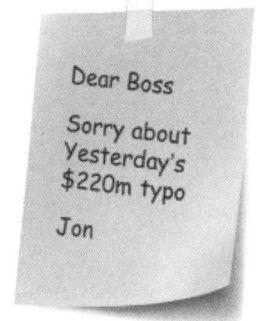

Dear Boss

Sorry about Yesterday's $220m typo

Jon

Theme 2: Lists

As Chapter 8 explains, lists are great for talks, e.g. the six myths of HR. Lists are great for an entire talk, or just bits of it – and don't need slides either. But if we feel slides will help, maybe just show a series of numbers. As we start our third point, show a massive '3' on screen. Or combine *Just Pictures* and *Lists*, and show a photo for each point. If our third point is:

"Ian uses four staples a day" (Chapter 8 explains this), show a screen-filling picture of a stapler. It intrigues. Avoid clichéd photos (rowing eights, etc).

Or try *Randomly Splattered Numbers*. Imagine we're talking at an internal conference, and wish to mention our industry position (third), forecast industry growth (5%), last year's profit (£200m), customer base (1,000 subscribers), and acquisition war chest (£500m). We could simply say it all, but if we want a slide, try Figure 27.3. Numbers are random in order, alignment, typography, and that adds to their intrigue and visual interest.

Randomly Splattered Numbers also stops us from filling slides with unnecessary bumf – and to understand why, take a step back. To tell delegates that profit is £200m: we type on a slide: "Profit £200m"… then get nervous. The slide looks empty. Also, we like to show our workings, so we then fill the slide with the profit and loss account, plus comparatives too. Twenty numbers on screen, plus associated labels ("Profit before goodwill and exceptional items"), just to convey one number: £200m. *Randomly Splattered Numbers* prevents this – we haven't room to cram stuff on, so we don't. We keep it simple. Which helps us and our audience.

When we talk through the numbers in Figure 27.3, refer to them in our preferred order, whatever that is. If we don't have a preferred order, let delegates decide. Ask a delegate to read out a number, then after we've talked through it, ask someone else to select another number, etc. It helps engage delegates. Also, we look good. It seems paradoxical, but when we let others take control, we seem even more in control. That is, we're so on top of our topic, we let them select what's next, yet still cope magnificently.

Maybe also adopt this approach for words. Imagine that new rules alter how companies assess risk in six of their back-office areas – HR, cash, IT, etc. If presenting these, try *Randomly Splattered Words*. Type the words randomly around the page and in a variety of fonts. You get the idea.

Figure 27.3

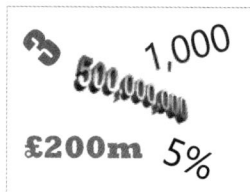

Themes 3 and 4: Deck of Cards; What It Isn't

Years ago, there was a cheesy song called *Deck of Cards* that tells of a soldier who – when arrested for looking at cards in church – said in his defence that the deck was his Bible. The Ace reminds him there is one God, the Deuce reminds him the Bible is divided in two (Old and New Testaments), the Three represents the Father, Son and Holy Ghost, and so on.

I've used this construct in several talks. One was to launch an internal programme – I explained that: "The programme is like a deck of cards". "The Two," I said, "is the two key changes needed for success" – and talked through them. "The Eight is the eight minutes a day I need you to devote to it all" (cue more comments). The song didn't mention the Joker, but I did ("The person who thinks we shouldn't do the programme"). Talking of jokers, you needn't be the office clown to carry off this theme, you aren't playing guitar or doing magic. It's fairly unintimidating to deliver. Also, you needn't run through the 'deck' in the right order (one, two, three, etc). Rather, run through in the order that suits (no pun intended). As for slides:

Keep them simple	Maybe show a screen with vacant spots for all the cards, then, as you talk about a card, click the mouse and show that card filling up the relevant spot.
Or avoid slides and have a real deck of cards	Once, I physically put cards on an easel as I talked through them. It's more tactile than slides – and more memorable too.
Or have nothing at all	I've used it for sports speeches ("Our team is like a deck of cards"), reunion speeches ("Our MBA was like a deck of cards") – and without slides or props.

That's it on *Deck of Cards*. The fourth idea to create coherence is one we saw in Myth 4 of Chapter 8: *What It Isn't, What It Is* (Figure 27.4). Enough said. Next is the fifth idea, and it's as unique as you.

Figure 27.4

The myths of budgeting	
What it isn't	What it is
The profit	A profit
Cast in stone	Evolving
The way we compute bonuses	An input into bonuses
Etc, etc	Etc, etc

Theme 5...

When I was at college, a law lecturer made the topic fizz with excitement. He regaled us with bizarre court stories or comments on cases in the media. His anecdotes didn't help us learn our material, but they breathed life into the topic of law. Also, he'd fire questions at us – and these did help us learn. Without warning, he'd stop mid-sentence, point at someone and shout "IF...". As students, we quickly learnt to reply: "IF... a wrong is done to a company, the proper plaintiff is the company". He was fantastic.

He had a truly unique theme. Him. He was the theme. His style ran through his talks more strongly than any corporate branding. It ensured we hung onto his every word. And that's the 'idea' in this section – that a person can be the theme. It sounds odd, but makes sense. Delegates are there to listen to us, and if we engage and are interesting, we create the coherence and thread that runs through the talk.

OK, this lecturer was particularly gifted... but so what? If you present, you perform. Accept it. It's especially true if you teach or train. School teachers know that the best training tool isn't their whiteboards or DVDs.

It's their imagination. To teach *one* to *twenty* in French, my son's teacher chucks a toy dog around the class. Which sounds all well and good, but two last points on this. Firstly, ensure what you do is appropriate. Yes, chuck a toy dog around a junior school, but not around a board room. And secondly, how to perform? Entertain? Engage? Chapter 29 explores how.

How not to create themes

There are two popular but dreadful ideas for creating themes. Firstly, there's the contrived metaphor. Once, I was part of a team drafting a talk on how to win business, and a team member suggested we adopt a cricket theme ("We *defend* existing clients and *attack* competitors' clients"). It spiralled out of control as we struggled to stick to the metaphor – for instance, some quick tips on compliance became contrived comments about umpires. Thankfully, we realised how pear-shaped it had gone, ditched the metaphor, and instead simply talked through our findings. Much better.

Secondly, avoid contrived visuals. Step back and think about design: slides benefit from repetition, a look that runs throughout and creates a visual theme. But don't take it too far. One book suggests putting a lemon-related image on every slide "to give the talk dimension and dynamic continuity". It then has examples – alongside a few bullets, slide 1 has a picture of a line of lemons, slide 2 has a peeled lemon, slide 3 a lemon peel, slide 4 a lemon with sunglasses, and so on. Also, some websites offer us templates to give our slides, say, a marbles theme (as in the kids' game, not the bathroom floor). Yes, it's groovy and creates interest, but in a way that's distracting. When we talk, what do we want people to remember and ask questions about? Our messages? Or our lemons? "Why lemons...?!?!" everyone will think. Am I being inconsistent though? If a picture of a frog is OK, why not lemons? Simple: the frog is relevant and a one-off, whereas lemons are contrived and irrelevant. And lots of them add insult to injury.

For Final Thoughts, think back to the New Procedures talk. We redid it with *Randomly Splattered Numbers* and *What It Isn't*. These themes ran through a large part of the talk, and addressed delegates' concerns. Also, with fewer slides, the presenter engaged with delegates. Finally, we used two ideas from earlier Chapters: the *Moses* cartoon and *$220m typo*. The talk was coherent, memorable, persuasive. Impressive, really, given it was such a boring topic.

Handouts   28

Good handouts impress and influence, so this Chapter shows how to make yours good. First, let's define terms. This Chapter is on handouts that summarise talks. Don't confuse this with talks that summarise reports, i.e. an author circulates a report to people as a pre-read, then talks through it at a meeting. *That's not a handout*. It's a report. This Chapter doesn't look at them.

Also, sometimes we can't follow this Chapter's tips. Maybe convention or regulation won't allow it, e.g. I say: "Don't hand out slides", but CEOs must circulate them when they present results to investment analysts.

Let's start. First we see whether to do a handout.

Should presenters do a handout?

Handouts do a lot, both good and bad. First, the good. Handouts **reinforce** a talk's ideas. They **liberate**, because delegates listen, rather than take notes. They **impress**, as fancy artwork often looks much better in high-resolution handouts than when shown on screen. They **inform** – they provide notes on stuff there isn't time to mention in the talk. They **influence** key non-attendees who would otherwise miss the talk's messages. They **reassure** delegates' bosses ("Look, boss, a handout! The talk was worthwhile"). They can even **entice** and drum up business for presenters ("Gosh," the boss replies, "I'll attend next time!"). They **brand** presenters' work, and might **protect** them if a dispute arises.

Now the bad news. Handouts **create work** – presenters must prepare them (assuming they don't merely print off their slides). Handouts can **disengage** – delegates might switch off if they know it's all in the handout. They **formalise**, and that can be bad. If we put our sales forecast in a handout, bosses can more easily hold our feet to the fire if we don't deliver. Also, our sales prospects may be confidential.

Finally, handouts can **deaden**. If you're charismatic, it's hard to list stuff on paper in a way that does justice to your rhetoric. Think of stand-up comics – they don't do a handout of jokes.

Hence with handouts, we won't please all the people all the time. Attendees may prefer a brief handout, non-attendees a comprehensive one. Then there's us as presenter. A short handout might entice potential clients – it doesn't give too much away, so others must attend our talks to learn more. A longer one might better protect our intellectual property, for it's a hard-copy proof of our ideas. It's a trade-off: "Will handouts help achieve our outcome without harming our cause?". Maybe not, in which case don't do one. The default position is no longer: "What can we circulate?" but: "Should we do a handout?". Do one if upsides outweigh downsides. And if we decide to do one, we've another decision to make: whose needs do we strive to meet? Proceed as follows:

1.   Impress everyone. Whatever you do, do it well.
2.   In the event of a trade-off, do a handout that caters for those who bothered to attend, not those who didn't.
3.   The exception: key non-attendees. If three bosses couldn't attend our talk – or if many staff couldn't attend our *New Initiative* launch – then a detailed handout may be better. Then again, maybe see the bosses one-on-one (if they let us). And run another 'launch' talk for staff who couldn't make the first. This saves us trying to turn our rhetoric into an inspiring, convincing, complete handout.

As for what to hand out, don't just think about pieces of paper that linearly summarise the talk. Assume we've something we want people to remember. Maybe it's an acronym ("Skills, Attitude, Knowledge"). Or a series of steps, e.g. The Five Steps for Tables. Depending on budget, the options are endless. We could put it on a mouse mat, mug, Rubik's Cube, pen, ruler, calendar, keyring, poster, app, and so on. And we can fit a lot into a small space. A colleague and I once put 260 different parking rules on one side of a credit-card-sized piece of plastic.

Even if our handout is a piece of paper, it needn't all be in Arial font size 10. Instead, to emphasise something:

"try different fonts"

If we want our leave-behind to be useful – if we want people to keep it and refer to it – make it *special*. Later we see how to do decent written handouts, but before then, we see when to circulate handouts.

When to circulate handouts

Firstly, what not to do: don't circulate a day or two before the talk. Without our accompanying words, they won't mean anything. (Remember: this Chapter isn't on pre-reads sent around in advance of talks, such as board packs.) Rather, circulate at the talk – but when? Before we start? After we finish? There are two theories:

1.   **Circulate at the start**: delegates can make notes on them as we speak. Also, once they see that topics are summarised in our handout, they realise they needn't take notes and instead concentrate on what we say.

2. **Don't circulate at the start**: delegates flick through it and spoil any big reveal we might have. Also, people get out of sync and ask questions about topic 6, even though we're on topic 3.

Which is correct? It depends. On convention. On the relationship between us and our delegates. On the number of delegates. On our style. On the topic. Let me explain. Sometimes, we've no choice. If delegates are senior to us and want handouts at the start, we must go with the flow. Also, convention might demand it – as I said earlier, investment analysts get handouts at the start.

What if we circulate at the start, but don't want them to fast-forward through it? We could ask them not to, and if we're their boss, they might obey. If they're our boss, they might just ignore our request. They'll fast-forward if they wish. They may hijack our talk and impose their idea of order on it: "Topic 6 looks intriguing".

Interruptions are less likely with big groups. People are reluctant to shout out thoughts in front of many people, they're nervous of saying something foolish. I get few delegate interruptions from big groups, but lots from small ones. It's tougher to control 12 delegates than 312.

Then there's us as presenter. If we're engaging and likeable, delegates are less likely to fast-forward, they're too busy listening. Finally, there's the topic. If delegates know we've a big reveal at the end, it won't remain a big reveal for long if we circulate a handout – they'll flick through and find it.

My preference is to hand out at the start, but then try to impose some order ("If it's OK, please don't flick ahead because blah, blah"). If I've a reveal, I don't put it in the handout. But this approach works for me and my style, topic, delegates. As for you, think through the issues explored above, then tailor what you do accordingly.

Finally, there is another alternative: distribute handouts neither at the start nor end, but during the talk. Trainers do this – part-way through a Course, they distribute an exercise, and afterwards hand out the answers. That's fine.

Ideas for written handouts

If the handout is long, it goes by another name: a written report – and other Chapters look at those. Often, handouts are much shorter – maybe just a page or two of reference material or key points – so here are ideas. Try WiT (Figure 28.1 – it's a thumbnail reminder of what we saw earlier in the book). Or WiT-in-columns (Figure 28.2). If not comfortable doing WiT, try simple columns with no WiT (Figure 28.3 – it's a layout we've not seen before in this book). All these layouts put words in narrow rows of text, which makes them easier to read

Figure 28.1

Figure 28.2

Figure 28.3

Figure 28.4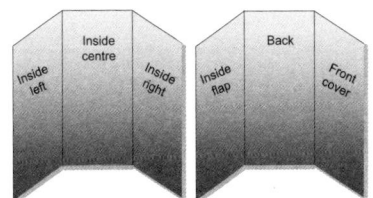

Figure 28.5

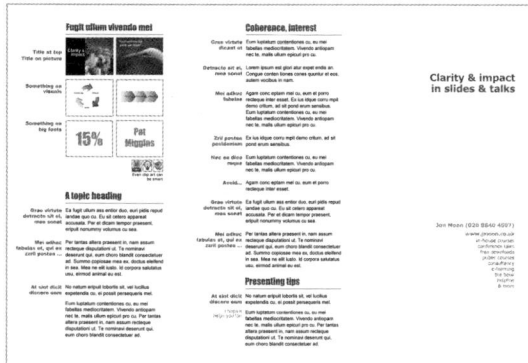

Figure 28.6

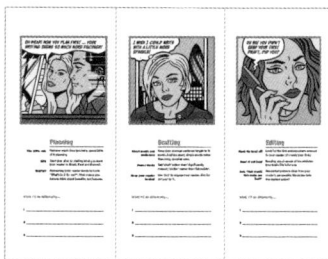

Figure 28.7

Conference speaking

Take care, for many conference organisers like to upload your talk's slides to a website so that non-attendees can see them. Also, so the logic goes, delegates can refer back to them. If you're asked to send in slides to upload, refuse. Firstly, slides make a poor handout, so they don't help attendees. Instead, do a separate handout and give that to the conference organiser. As for non-attendees, if any are critical to you, contact them afterwards. Or do a bespoke note for the conference website, one that works for them.

and are good for reference documents. Which is what handouts are: something to refer back to.

Or try Figure 28.4, a single sheet of A4, printed double-sided, then folded twice. It's a reminder of the main points of the talk, and fits neatly in a jacket pocket or unobtrusively on a desk. Figure 28.5 is an example of one, albeit it's in Latin. It's the inside flap, back and front cover.

For something more posh and durable, print on thicker paper, e.g. 200gsm bright, white coated card (check your printer can cope with that thickness) – but don't then fold manually. Instead, use a 'manual creasing machine'. It's not some electronic gadget (it's as hi-tech as a hole punch), but it makes the handout much smarter. Compared to getting a local print company to print and fold pamphlets for you, it pays for itself after about 150 handouts. Finally, if you work for a company that's big enough to have its own print unit to do all this, lucky you.

To do Figure 28.5, you need to create three columns in landscape – but fear not, for my website has a download that's done it for you. People adopt it for many different topics. Their departmental *Style Guide*. Or: *Department XYZ: What We Do*. Or: *The Steps for Reporting Fraud*. And so on.

Your folded handouts can be more than just words. Include anything that's appropriate – graphs, flowcharts… even pop art. I mentioned Andy Maslen in Chapter 9 (*Outcomes*), and Figure 28.6 is the handout from his course. Cool. He downloaded my template, then commissioned an artist to do the drawings. Thanks to Andy for letting me show it.

Time for Final Thoughts. Many presenters treat their handouts with the same casual indifference as they would their business card. No. Treat it like you'd treat your CV. With CVs, people think about what to include (achievements) and what to exclude (how they did those achievements – leave potential employers keen to meet you to find out more). They think about their direct audience (manager who has vacancy), and indirect ones too (manager's manager, recruitment agent, etc). They think about the CV's layout. With CVs, people *think*. They want the CV to inform, impress, entice, remind.

Which is what handouts should do. Give yours the same care and attention as you would your CV. Yes, it takes longer than robotically clicking on your keyboard and letting the computer turn your slides into a handout. But you've worked hard on your talk, so don't spoil the ship for a halfpenny-worth of tar. Do a decent handout. One to be proud of.

And if you speak at conferences, see Figure 28.7.

Presenting　　29

Here are tips on presenting. They aren't exhaustive, e.g. they don't say: "Check projector bulbs". Or: "Wear deodorant". Other books cover that, so I don't. Also, I don't repeat stuff I've covered elsewhere, e.g. start at the end.

　This Chapter has six parts. Preparing. Delivering. Questions and answers. Uninterested people. Dealing with nerves. After the talk. We also pop myths, e.g. "93% of impact comes not from what we say, but from how we say it". At the end are Final Thoughts to this Part of the book.

Preparing – seven tips

Write a speech, not a memo	Writing and speaking styles are different. In his famous speech, Churchill kept saying: "We shall… we shall…" (Figure 29.1). It's emphatic. In a written note, it's repetitive.	**Figure 29.1** **Winston Churchill's speech to Parliament, 1940** "We shall go on to the end. We shall fight in France, we shall fight on the seas and oceans, we shall fight with growing confidence and growing strength in the air, we shall defend our island, whatever the cost may be. We shall fight on the beaches, we shall fight on the landing grounds, we shall fight in the fields and in the streets, we shall fight in the hills; we shall never surrender."
Plan to finish early	Nobody will complain if you do.	
Don't plan to read your speech	In particular, memorise the first 30 seconds. You can't connect with delegates if staring at a piece of paper.	
But don't memorise it all word-for-word either	It can sound like a script. Also, you risk panicking if your memory fails you on the day. Instead, master your material and have notes to refer to.	
Plan for an occasional light intermission if your talk is more than, say, 30 minutes	I've heard that delegates' attention wanes after 30 minutes. Don't limit talks to 30 minutes though. Rather, have an occasional wake-up call. During my Courses, I have 20-second intermissions. I show a funny graph or two. It lightens the mood and gives everyone a break.	
But avoid contrived breaks – delegates spot phonies	"OK, Group A is to spend five minutes flipcharting what they want from HR, Group B on what they don't want – then we talk about it". Delegates see this for what it often is: a trainer's desperate attempt to keep people awake or pad the day. Instead, shorten the event or make it more interesting.	
What will you ask delegates to do?	If you've gone to the trouble of preparing a talk, I reckon you've the right to make a request of delegates, even if just a small one. "Mention this to two people in your unit." Or: "Make a note to review this in six months". PS: the exception: don't make a request in a job interview.	

Delivering

First, a myth: "93% of our impact comes from not what we say, but from how we say it". The figure is irrelevant and misquoted. Albert Mehrabian, a Professor at UCLA, did experiments in the 1960s on the importance of the spoken word in face-to-face communication. So far, so good. However, participants said just one word at a time (e.g. "terrible"), the only variation being the tone with which they said the word. Albert never suggested that non-verbal factors (e.g. body language) are more important than what we say, and for years has tried to stop people misquoting his findings. However, if you train people in body language, why let facts get in the way of a good stat?

Anyway, it's illogical for only 7% of impact to come from what we say. Imagine we're presenting to bosses. We don a smart outfit, authoritatively stride to the front, and say in a rich timbre: "I'm Les, and you're all idiots", then walk out. Will bosses give us a 93% satisfaction score…? With thanks to my 12-year-old nephew Robert for painting this scenario for me.

That's the wrongly misquoted advice. Now for some better advice:

Maintain eye contact	Don't present to the screen, floor or ceiling.
Talk to all delegates	Don't focus on just one person or one section of the audience. Focus on different people in turn, long enough to pull them into the talk (a second or two will do it). Make all delegates feel involved. The one person you never look at may well be the decision-maker.
Avoid speaking when looking at your notes	Don't let notes come between you and delegates. Instead, pause, look down briefly, then look up and speak directly to delegates. The 'look-down' time may seem like ages to you, but it takes just a second, and delegates will be glad for the chance to relax.
Clear the screen when not needed	If you do something in your talk that doesn't need slides (e.g. you scribble on a flipchart or talk offline for a bit), spare delegates from staring at a slide that's no longer relevant by pressing *B* on your keyboard (if you're in the *Slide Show* mode in PowerPoint). The screen turns black. Press *B* again to return to slides. *W* turns the screen white.
Pitch, pace – and pace… a bit	Vary the pitch and pace of your voice. To emphasise something… speak softly. Don't stay rooted to the spot, but don't stride up and down too much either. Use gestures.

Be a bit... *lively*	If you want people to be enthusiastic about your ideas, present them enthusiastically – or as enthusiastically as possible within the constraints of your topic, style and personality. Don't adopt a style that's inconsistent with who you are. Also, remember the ABC and XYZ of presenting: Always Be Cheerful and eXamine Your Zipper.
If there's a lectern, don't grip it like it's a pinball machine or as if your life depends on it	I find the lectern creates a barrier between me and those with whom I strive to connect: delegates. So I try not to stand behind it. At conferences, I often step off the platform and walk among the first rows of the audience – it suits my style. To do this, you'll need a walk-around mic.

Then there's… silence. Use it briefly every now and then (but take care, for too many – and overlong – pauses make you seem a bit affected). Use it:

Before your punchline. It builds anticipation. Don't overegg it though.

After your punchline. "This year, we doubled profits" (pause). It adds impact and gives delegates a chance to digest the message.

To help mock the ludicrous. I pause when describing a graph mentioned in Chapter 25: City 9 points, Rovers 10 (Figure 29.2). Graph-lovers believe that, because the right column is bigger, the graph helps those who aren't good with numbers: "It helps," I say, "people see that *10* (pause) is bigger than (pause) *9*". The pauses make the comment seem even more ludicrous.

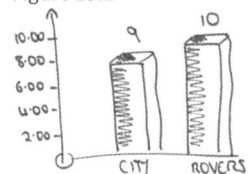

Figure 29.2

In rhetorical questions. We saw one in an earlier Chapter: "How many of you remember how you felt when you joined this firm? (Pause)". The pause gives delegates a chance to reminisce and internalise.

To get people's attention. Teachers know this. If kids are talking and not looking at the teacher, he or she just waits. In silence. Eventually, the kids shut up and look up. If presenting and someone spends the entire time looking at their mobile, stay silent for several seconds. They eventually look up at you. Guiltily. It's quite fun when this happens (unless the texter is your boss).

But if people text, maybe we should plan our talk better so they don't. Maybe ask more questions ("Why do you think plan A won't work?"). Or have more break-out sessions. *Involve* delegates, surely, and we keep their attention, no?

No. Don't confuse the verb to *involve* with the verb to *engage*. As delegates, we all want to be engaged, but many of us don't want to be involved. We don't want to answer questions that are often just contrived attempts to get us talking. We don't want to stand at flipcharts. We don't want to play along with the presenter's lame game. We don't want to feel uncomfortable.

We don't want to risk looking dumb. So don't strive to involve. Strive to engage. Don't get people talking. Get them *thinking*. And we've seen how in this book. Use angles. Think like a journalist. Etc.

Or – to return to the topic of silence – use pauses and rhetorical questions. Years ago, I saw a presenter deliver the same talk many times, and each time he used silence and rhetorical questions to keep delegates' attention. Mid-talk, he'd pause, sit on a chair and mutter to himself: "What's the day? Wednesday?". Delegates help him out: "Tuesday". "OK…" – his voice lowers, and he pauses… "Here's what I want you to do by next Tuesday". He then takes ten seconds saying what he wants – and looks in turn at as many delegates as he can, plus repeatedly says *you* and *your*. Then the rhetorical question: "And do you know what you find when you do this?". Another brief pause. Delegates almost lean forward in anticipation. He then gives the answer. Delegates are *engaged*.

Finally, on *involved* versus *engaged*: don't contrive to relate everything to delegates' social interests. For instance, if delegates like astronomy, don't create lots of astronomy-related examples. Firstly, it can sound patronising. Secondly, comparisons backfire if your facts are wrong – a delegate says: "You said that management reporting is like full moons because we get one a month… but some months have two moons – they're called blue moons". Lastly, it's not even necessary. If you make your thoughts easy to grasp, use simple language, etc, you'll be fine. In this book, I often talk about stuff outside work, e.g. losing weight, chastising teenagers, etc. I've no idea if you do them, but hopefully the examples resonate and get you thinking.

Questions and answers – 12 tips

If you genuinely want questions, make it an open invitation	Don't say: "Any questions?" but: "What questions do you have?". Raise your hand as you say this, it gives delegates a lead and encourages those who may be shy. It helps keep order too – people raise hands rather than yell out.
Repeat delegates' questions	Others may not have heard them. They may be long, complex multi-part questions. Restating them ensures you're clear about what's being asked. It also gives you breathing space to ponder your answer, should you need it.
Start with the punchline	It gives context to your explanatory comments that follow.
Avoid clichés	E.g.: "That's a good question, I'm glad you asked that".

Unless you want to create doubt, avoid saying: "I believe…"	"We'll hit our targets" sounds more confident than: "I believe we'll hit our targets". Also avoid: "I hope…". And "I'd like to think …".
Keep a consistent style	Keep the style the same as when you present. If different, people read something into it.
Admit if you don't know	Maybe even throw the question over to delegates: "I don't know the government's forecast. Can anyone else here help with that question?".
Involve all delegates	Don't focus exclusively on the person who asked the question, they might not appreciate the attention. Also, other delegates might feel excluded.
Don't humiliate	Spare people's blushes – but don't let errors stick.
Don't be afraid of silence	When you've made your point, don't repeat yourself. When you've made your point, don't repeat yourself.
Hostile, tricky, loaded questions?	Keep cool. Stick to issues, not personalities. Ask an open question back, you find out more about their concerns and it gives you thinking time. Example: "Which sections do you feel are poor?". Don't sound defensive though.
If someone disagrees with you, maybe throw it back out to others – they might counter the comment for you	If you say: "Do ABC, not XYZ", and a delegate counters: "My boss prefers XYZ", throw the question out: "Interesting…. what do others find with their bosses?". Others might side with you and argue against the dissenting delegate. Which helps you. Then again, they may side with the dissenting delegate, but at least you know that before you give your thoughts.

Uninterested people

What if one or two delegates look bored and exude 'negative waves'? On the one hand, don't ignore valid feedback. "Dull!" they think – so you should at least ponder why. Then again, their bored faces may have nothing to do with your talk. Maybe they're resigning next week. Or got drunk last night. Or been up with their newborn. Here are ideas for what to do.

Talk to them offline – maybe they aren't bored	If there's a coffee break in your talk, chat to them – maybe you've misread the signals. Often, seemingly disengaged delegates aren't bored, but on board. It turns out they're fine.

Don't let the squeaky wheel get the grease (assuming it isn't the most important wheel, i.e. the boss)	As presenters, it's tempting to focus on getting a smile or reaction from the bored ones. Maybe you look at them a lot, or talk louder and indulge in more histrionics than normal. Don't. If your normal approach works for 95% of delegates, don't change it to try to connect with the other 5% – you risk losing the 95% you have.
Give them something to fill their time	I find an excuse to briefly tell everyone about a neat puzzle. The bored delegate then ponders it. This may distract other delegates who might also ponder it, but if the person's 'negative waves' are bringing down the whole room, I must do something.

Dealing with nerves

Many people are understandably nervous when they present. They're in front of people and fear looking foolish. As the saying goes: "Better to remain silent and be thought a fool, than open your mouth and remove any doubt".

When we present, nerves can help – but for many of us, they hinder. We don't come across well. So we're more nervous next time – and come across even worse. Eventually we don't get asked to present and avoid presenting even if asked to. A vicious circle. If we could overcome our nerves, it would be a virtuous circle – we come across well and enjoy it. We want to present more – and others want us to too – and we get even better.

So how to go from vicious to virtuous circle? There are dozens of ideas on how to overcome nerves. Some are rather obvious, e.g. "Practise". Or: "Be prepared". Both are 100% true, but hardly necessary to state. Some are a bit bizarre, e.g. "Imagine delegates are naked – they won't seem so daunting, and you feel more confident". Weird, but if it works for you, why not? Rather than list the obvious and weird, here are tips that worked for me. The first took me instantly from quivering wreck to confident presenter.

Pause right at the start	Try a five-second pause at the start, and scan delegates' faces as you do. As we saw above, this grabs their attention – but it does more. To my surprise, when I first tried pausing at the start, I felt much more relaxed. In control of the event. I loved this tip. Before I read it, I hadn't liked presenting; after, I was fine.

Don't panic if you forget something (unless it's critical)	Most talks have lots of nice-to-have stuff, but little must-have stuff. So fear not if you miss something out or get the order wrong – delegates don't know what you planned to say anyway. A liberating thought.
Be yourself	Don't adopt a style that isn't you. If you strive to be funny, angry or passionate when that's not you, it looks horrible.

Also, don't get hung up on 'rules' of presenting (we've seen some in this Chapter and also in Chapter 25 (*Slides*)). Many are rubbish, and even good ones are made to be broken. I break loads, but most people are fine with it. Also, think of presenters you look up to. They probably break many 'rules'.

If you are nervous, keep trying different tips and techniques until you find one that works for you. Maybe try Toastmasters International, a not-for-profit entity that develops speaking skills. It has branches all over the world, and most meet one evening a week. It gives people a safe environment in which to try out their stuff and practise their techniques. I hear it's fun too.

After the talk

Review how things went. Make notes as soon as possible – what worked, what didn't. Don't leave it a week, you forget details by then.

Seek feedback too. Seek it from delegates. Get them to complete a feedback form. The text box overleaf looks at feedback forms and why you should treat comments with caution. Ask delegates to complete the form before they leave the room whilst your talk is fresh in their minds. Intranet-based feedback forms might save paper, but many delegates don't complete them when back at their desks – they're too distracted by their day-to-day jobs.

Sometimes it's inappropriate to seek feedback from delegates – maybe you're telling staff they're redundant. Instead, talk to a co-presenter or colleague who sat in and listened. Get their thoughts on how it went.

Also, analyse other talks you hear – their words, slides, handouts, etc. What worked and why? What didn't? Be a magpie, steal good ideas.

Time for Final Thoughts. This is the last Chapter of the *Talks* Part, so here are six brief thoughts for you to ponder next time you give a talk.

1. Good slides won't save a bad talk, bad slides won't ruin a good talk.
2. *WYSIWYG* – it's not what you show, it's what you say.
3. Don't show slides. Achieve outcomes. And imagine you're on the radio.
4. Don't hand out slides. Do a proper handout if it helps you.
5. No-one says: "I wish you had more words on your slides".
6. Lists are great – but use cautiously if presenting to bosses.

Feedback forms

Keep them simple and short	My form has just one 'tick box' question: "The Course overall?", then there are six boxes from *Excellent* to *Very Poor*. There's also an area for delegate comments – whatever they want to write.
Don't ask about the room, sarnies, etc.	If these matter to delegates, they'll write about them. If these matter to you, ask about them in casual conversation.
Don't unwittingly limit delegates' answers	If your form says: "Describe how the course will change what you do", delegates write: "I'll do my talks differently" (if it's a *Talks* course). Not informative. Instead, give free rein with an open question – just ask "Overall?", and they'll say: "Fab". Or: "Rubbish". Or: "Interesting but irrelevant", etc. They'll also tell you why. Much more useful.
Look for patterns in the feedback	You can't please all the people all the time. Some will say your talk's too long, some that it's too short. So instead, look for patterns and themes – overall, are people satisfied or annoyed? – and tweak your talk accordingly.
Appreciate that things aren't always as they seem	I suspect some people hate my Course. Their boss forces them to attend and they resent it – yet they tick the box that says "Excellent" because it saves hassle from HR afterwards. Others excitedly eulogise about the Course in the coffee break, then tick on the feedback form "Good", not "Very good" or "Excellent"...?

My feedback form has nothing on learning objectives or meeting expectations. People's expectations are diverse, and, for a variety of reasons, can be misguided. Asking about them is of historic interest – it gives insight into how well delegates were briefed by someone in their company before attending, or how attentively delegates read the Course outline and joining instructions. These don't help me much. Rather, I want to know what delegates felt about the Course, so I ask about that. I suspect that HR managers disagree with this approach.

More on charts, numbers

Whilst Chapter 2 reviews routine graphs, Chapter 30 (**graphs – more**) reviews less routine ones. Scattergrams, histograms, waterfalls, etc. Find out which to use when.

There are many ways to **signal performance** ('RAGs', smiley faces, 'Harvey Balls', etc). Chapter 31 explains – then assesses – them. Find out why you should avoid RAGs unless you're Gordon Gekko or Homer Simpson.

Then there's organisation charts, flowcharts and decision trees. Chapter 32 (**other diagrams**) has tips on how and when to do them.

Finally, many people shove lots of graphs and tables on a single page and call it a KPI or dashboard. Usually, it's dreadful. Chapter 33 (**KPIs (and variances)**) ensures yours is fantastic.

What?!? No big data?
Journalists write about big data a lot, yet there's nothing in this book on the subject. That's because I've never had a Course delegate ask me about it, so I assume it's not of interest to people who attend my Courses – and hence won't be of interest to people who read my book.

30 Graphs – more

Better sensitivity analysis – isobars 💻

Consider how sensitivity analysis is normally done. Imagine we're forecasting profit for our new product – and it mainly depends on two things: the price we sell it at, and the market penetration it achieves. What profit do we forecast if we price the product at £15 and achieve market penetration of 4%? And what penetration for £20m profit if price is £20? And so on. For each scenario, we churn out a printout of numbers, and eventually, we've 16 printouts for 16 scenarios – and when we submit a report to bosses seeking approval for the new product, we shove them in an appendix.

But comparable numbers are spread over 16 pages, so bosses flick back and forth constantly to compare the comparable. Not good.

Sometimes, we give bosses a table of numbers. Figure 30.1 shows the penetration we need for different levels of profit and price. For example, read along the row starting 15 – at £15 price, profit is £5m if penetration is 6.7%.

The table is better than printouts. It shows what bosses need (summary figures), not what we know (workings). It's all on one page too, so is comparable. But bosses struggle to find answers to other scenarios – try working out penetration for £13m profit at £17.50 price. It shouldn't be tricky, the table has lots of numbers, so surely we find some that are close to that scenario, then adjust up or down a bit. It's not easy though: "Now," we say to ourselves, "we've penetration at prices of £15 and £20, and at profit of £10m and £15m… so penetration for £17.50 price and £13m profit is somewhere between the numbers in the middle: 8.0%, 10.0%, 9.7%, 11.7% – but is it nearer the biggest (11.7%) or smallest (8.0%)?" Tricky.

Time for isobars (Figure 30.2). Let's explain it (and this isn't fixing the test, I also talked through the table above). Each line represents points that give the same profit. Look along the x-axis (price). When price is £20, travel up until you hit the top line labelled £20m – point A. Now go left until you hit the y-axis (penetration). It's about 11.5%. That is, to get £20m profit, we need 11.5% penetration at £20 price. Point B is also on the £20m line – if price is £15 and we get 13% penetration, we again make £20m.

So far, so good. Next we see why isobars are my favourite graph.

The isobars show trends better than the table

The graph shows several patterns, so bosses spend a few seconds understanding them – and in so doing, they grasp the numbers better. For instance,

Figure 30.1

Price per unit	Penetration for these profits			
	£5m	£10m	£15m	£20m
£	%	%	%	%
25	4.0	7.0	9.0	10.5
20	5.0	8.0	10.0	11.5
15	6.7	9.7	11.7	13.2
10	10.0	13.0	15.0	16.5

Figure 30.2

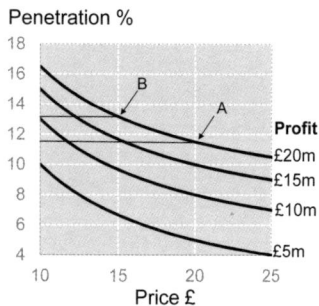

Penetration %

Price £

each line is a mix of penetration and unit price that equates to a given profit, and lines curve downward from left to right. That is, to get a given profit, we need high penetration, low price, or low penetration, high price. Yup. That figures. First bit of internalisation done.

Also, bosses notice that as we move up from one line to the next, the profit alongside each line increases. In other words, if penetration or price increases, so does profit. Again, that figures. Second bit of internalisation done.

Thirdly, as we move out and up, lines get closer to each other. That is, to get the same increase in profit, we need smaller increases in penetration or price. This arises from two effects: the learning curve (the more times we do something, the more efficiently we do it), and economies of scale (fixed costs are spread over more units of output). Third bit of internalisation done – and bosses have a feel for numbers far beyond what they'd get from the table.

The isobars show detail better than the table

Let's revisit the question we asked earlier: what penetration for £13m profit at £17.50 price? Easy – £13m profit is just over halfway between £10m and £15m. A £17.50 price is halfway between £15 and £20. Follow imaginary lines, and required penetration is about 10%. With the graph, interpolation is easy. The graph is better at detail than the table. It seems counterintuitive – surely tables are better at detail than graphs – but not here.

Back to our bosses. With isobars, they can work out scenarios themselves. Which is great when forecasting, because everyone has their own view on price and penetration, and wants to know the profit that they produce. Rather than scurrying to the person with the spreadsheet, bosses use the graph to compute it themselves: "I reckon we'll get 8% penetration at £15 price – that gives us about (study graph for five seconds) £7m profit".

This is the huge benefit of isobars: they make decision-makers self-sufficient. Numbers are no longer something that emerge from an analyst's spreadsheet. Rather, they're something that bosses can play around with. They easily see the consequences of different scenarios. They have more informed conversations amongst themselves, and more easily reach better decisions.

Do you ever do a surface graph (Figure 30.3 – engineers sometimes do them)? Figure 30.4 redoes it as isobars. Much better. Isobars – my favourite type of graph. For several more pages of material on them, see my website (including how to do them).

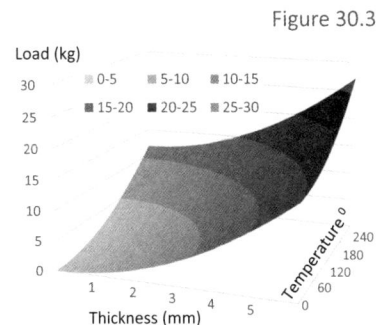

Figure 30.3

Figure 30.4

Figure 30.5

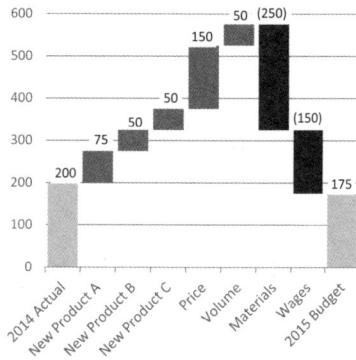

How to do better waterfall graphs

Waterfall graphs show the main differences between two numbers, e.g. the differences between this year's *actual* and *budget*. Or last year's *actual* and this year's *budget* (Figure 30.5). The left column is 2014 actual profit (£200k), the far right column is 2015 budget profit (£175k), and the seven columns in between are how we get from £200k to £175k. Five of the seven are increases in profit from New Products A, B, C, and higher Prices and Volumes. Two of the seven are decreases from higher costs for Materials and Wages. These two are a different colour because they're negative. Some people call these graphs 'floating bricks', so below I refer to the 'difference' columns as *bricks*.

Waterfalls suffer from several problems:

They're not easy to read	Their x-axis labels are often written sideways. Result: readers crane necks to read labels.
They're space-greedy	They take a lot of space to show not very much.
They often force readers' eyes to move big distances	It's all too easy to scan down from brick to x-axis and land on the wrong label. Also, it's difficult to see detail ("Which of those two tiny bricks is bigger?").
They fragment numbers	Numbers are on top of bricks. It's a badly laid out table.
They often distort reality	To shorten distances between bricks and x-axis, many waterfalls don't start the y-axis at zero. But we gauge columns by their height. In Figure 30.6, the right column looks five times bigger than the left, but the y-axis doesn't start at zero. It's actually 9% bigger.
They're often riddled with errors	Creating them often requires much manual intervention – and that leads to errors.
Bricks are often in the wrong order	In Figure 30.7, bricks are in descending order (good) but this causes the graph to rise high, then sink low (bad – too much wasted space, too big a distance between labels and numbers). Waterfall-lovers 'solve' this by reordering bricks almost randomly (Figure 30.8). Crazy. PS. Figure 30.8 really existed – and when I recreated it for this book, I found two errors in its original.

Figure 30.6

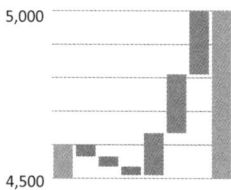

Figure 30.7

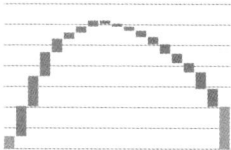

Figure 30.8

The last reason – bricks in the wrong order – deserves further comment. Waterfall-lovers say bricks *help us see which is biggest*. A circular argument. *Because* bricks aren't in descending order, we need help seeing the biggest. Eschew waterfalls though – do a table in strict descending order instead – and we no longer need help to spot which is biggest (it's the top row…).

Also, ask yourself this: would you do a waterfall at home? Imagine I want my partner to move in with me, and to convince her, I show how much we collectively save from cohabiting (not romantic, but go with the flow). I could do a waterfall (Figure 30.9) – it shows what we spend every month if living separately (left column), what we spend if living together (right column), and the differences (we save her rent, utilities (gas, electricity, etc), food, but lose child benefit, spend more on booze (swilling wine at home) and need a slightly bigger place). But if I showed Figure 30.9 to my partner, she wouldn't move in. She'd think I'd gone nuts.

Instead, do a table. One that reconciles last year's actual profit to this year's budget (you see it shortly). Or what we spend apart to what we spend together – Figure 30.10 is my Post-It note analysis on cohabiting, and to be more romantic, I doodled a heart and roses on it, and would stick it on a box of choccies. Don't do that with the profit reconciliation for bosses though.

What if bosses insist on waterfalls? Simple – have bricks not side by side, but one under the other. *Stack* the bricks. Figure 30.11 is my redo (the *after*) of a waterfall we saw earlier, shown again in Figure 30.12 (the *before*). Stacked waterfalls resolve many of the problems we've seen. They don't take much space. They're easy to read. There aren't big distances between labels and numbers. They show numbers well. In the *after*, bricks aren't in descending order, but that's to keep it comparable to the *before*. All in all, the stacked waterfall is better, albeit it still distorts if the axis doesn't start at zero. Also, note three other points. Firstly, if someone needs 'help' seeing the biggest number, no worries – they merely look for the longest horizontal line.

Secondly, try this: in the *after*, cover the bricks. Lo, it's a table of numbers (and tables cope easily with wide ranges of numbers – £10m to £10 if need be). Thirdly, the *after* is roughly the same size as its *before* (shown again, Figure 30.12), yet it's much more legible. The *before* is very space-greedy.

Now for the techie bit: I create the horizontal version in Excel using the REPT and CONCATENATE functions. See my website for the spreadsheet, along with instructions. It creates only simple waterfalls, not ones with sub-total columns in the middle (I haven't discussed these – let's not go there).

Figure 30.9

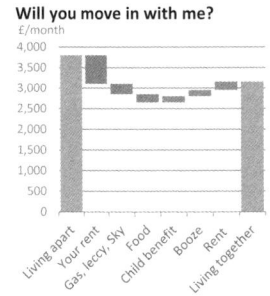

Will you move in with me?
£/month

Figure 30.10

Figure 30.11

Variances	£k 0		575
2014 Actual	**200**		
New Product A	75		
New Product B	50		
New Product C	50		
Price	150		
Volume	50		
Materials	(250)		
Wages	(150)		
2015 Budget	**175**		

Figure 30.12

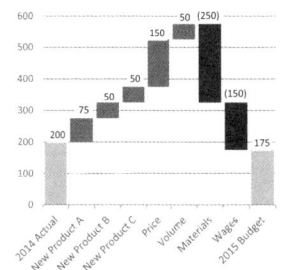

Figure 30.13

Why bosses like waterfalls

Blame bankers. They do waterfalls to 'prove' value accretion on acquisitions they peddle – and their waterfalls are very similar to the cohabit waterfall: "Here we are apart, then bricks float to where we're together – and lo, we're worth more".

A chain reaction then occurs (and we saw something like it in the *Decks* Chapter): bosses like bankers' ideas, bosses associate waterfalls with bankers and so like them, and so ask staff to do them. Hence, staff do them. Often reluctantly.

That's it on waterfalls. We're about 35% through this Chapter – the other 65% looks at columns (10%), scattergrams (15%), other graphs (40%). If that last sentence confuses you, maybe a waterfall would help. Also, see Figure 30.13 (overleaf), it looks at why bosses like waterfalls.

Return of columns – when they work

At a conference of IT teachers, the presenter compares the IT exam pass rate with that for 22 other subjects. Delegates hear it's 45% – 10th out of the 23 subjects. But that's not enough. Depending on how pass rates are clustered, IT may be close to plummeting down the rankings or rocketing up them. A table might help, but tables are good if we want exact numbers, and this audience wants an exact number only for IT.

Try Figure 30.14 (other subjects are labelled with letters). It's a series of rectangular boxes. A transposed column chart, I suppose. And it helps. We more easily spot groupings. Results are clustered into three tiers. IT is top of the second, but far removed from the first. IT is unlikely to rise up the rankings, even if it improves a lot, but if it worsens even slightly, it could plummet.

It could easily be a different story for IT though, as illustrated by Figure 30.15. It shows a different set of pass rates, and as before, we've three tiers. Now, the first is just one topic – M is way ahead. IT is now bottom of the second tier, and if it improves slightly, it rockets up to second. But if it worsens, it's unlikely to be overtaken by anyone in the third tier. Arguably, the columns highlight these patterns better than a table.

However, columns are typographically busy – they use a whole column to show just one dot on the page. So instead try Figure 30.16. Not columns but ' I 's. Similar to the stacked waterfall in the previous section, it's created in Excel using REPT and CONCATENATE (as are Figures 30.17 and 30.19). My website has the spreadsheet, along with instructions on how to tailor it, e.g. with limitations, you can have a different icon to ' I '. Or – if you don't mind numbers not lining up one under the other – try Figure 30.17. It doesn't plot ' I ', it plots pass rates (for just a few topics to illustrate).

Then there's Figure 30.18. It plots pass rates, again albeit for just a few topics. Pass rates are now the y-axis. I got the idea from a duff

Figure 30.14

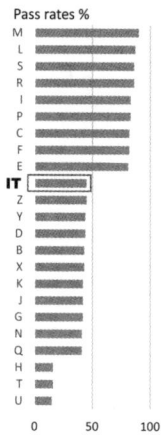

Pass rates %

Figure 30.15

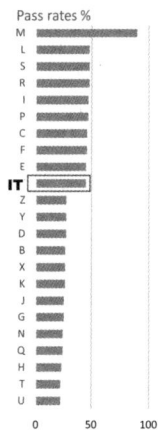

Pass rates %

Figure 30.16

Pass rates %

M	90	I
L	87	I
S	86	I
R	86	I
I	83	I
P	83	I
C	82	I
F	82	I
E	81	I
IT	**45**	I
Z	45	I
Y	44	I
D	44	I
B	43	I
X	43	I
K	42	I
J	42	I
G	42	I
N	41	I
Q	41	I
H	16	I
T	16	I
U	15	I

Figure 30.17

Pass rates %

P	83
C	82
F	82
E	81
IT	45
Z	45
Y	44
D	44
N	41
Q	41
H	16
T	16
U	15

Figure 30.18

83			
	45	41	
			16
P	IT	Q	T

graph I saw whose columns were shaded so lightly – and printed so poorly – they disappeared. All that was visible were numbers on top of each invisible column. I didn't realise it was an accident, and complimented the person on a clever graph – one that plots numbers. She admitted it wasn't deliberate.

I plot Figure 30.18 by doing a column chart in Excel, then making the columns invisible. No fill. No borders. I then get Excel to automatically add the numbers, plus format them to sit neither above nor beneath the columns but precisely atop them (*Format Data Labels, Label Options, Label Position, Center*). Easy.

So we've pass rates that run down the page (Figure 30.17) or along it (Figure 30.18). Note:

1. Don't do such plots with just a few numbers. Figure 30.18 has only four, and with that few, the plot is a bit contrived and unnecessary – readers hardly need a graph to help them see patterns in just four numbers. A table would be fine. Remember: this section started with the premise that we've many numbers – pass rates for 23 subjects.

2. Down-the-page plots (Figure 30.17) are probably preferable to along-the-page ones (Figure 30.18). Firstly, we more easily scan down numbers than along them. Also, when there are many numbers and labels, readers are more likely to scan between label and number correctly. Finally, imagine the graph with proper labels (Chemistry, English Literature, etc) – in Figure 30.18, these longer labels would struggle to fit on the x-axis.

Finally, Figure 30.19 plots not numbers but labels. A bit like a scattergram. They're next.

Scattergrams – the Cinderella of graphs

Scattergrams are great, we should do more of them. I've done them to:

- Negotiate a company sale – it helped accurately forecast the profit.
- Blame accountants for missing a fraud they should have spotted.
- Show how companies use their 'provisions' account to smooth results.
- Forewarn that business in corrupt countries is a white-knuckle ride.

Others use scattergrams to show 'commission bias' – that is, financial advisors sell us products that pay them the highest commission. Professor Porter (strategy guru) used a scattergram to show how mid-sized companies make the worst margins. Scattergrams help us better understand what's happened. They help us better predict – or anticipate – what will happen.

When to do them though? That's easy: do them to help get insight into two sets of data. Rather than show examples of when people do scattergrams, it's

Figure 30.19

Pass rates %	
90	Maths
87	Latin
86	Sport
86	Religion
83	ICT
83	Physics
82	Chemistry
82	French
81	English
45	IT
45	Chinese
44	Politics
44	Drama
43	Ballet
43	Italian
42	Polish
42	Magic
42	Geography
41	Spanish
41	Biology
16	History
16	German
15	Music

Figure 30.20

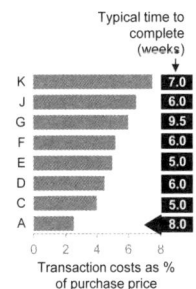

enlightening to see when people don't, but should. Figure 30.20 is a layout I occasionally see – shaded rectangles on left, numbers on right – and it's on house purchases for eight countries (K, J, G, etc). Rectangles are the transaction cost as a percentage of purchase price, and numbers are weeks to complete the sale. Eight countries. Two bits of data for each. And yes, the graph looks funky, with reversed fonts for numbers. It could be even funkier, with chevrons (see its bottom-right number) – and infographic-lovers might even fill it with icons of houses, spivvy estate agents and bank notes.

But Figure 30.20 doesn't work. It doesn't surrender patterns easily. Do quick deals result in higher or lower costs? Which countries do well – i.e. low cost and quick deal – and which don't? The author of the report seemingly didn't know, for the original graph had an uninformative title: "On the move". Figure 30.21 redoes it as a scattergram. Readers more easily see groupings. Winners. Losers. With many data sets, scattergrams can bring order out of chaos. Here, there are just eight, but the scattergram still really helps. Notice the axes of Figure 30.21. They give the numbers for each of the dots (I manually typed

Figure 30.21

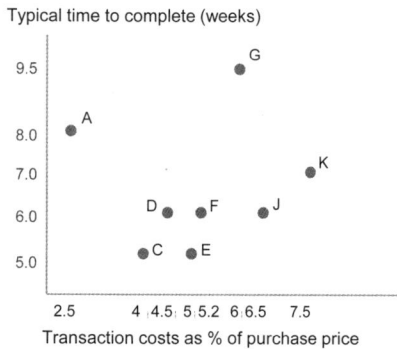

Typical time to complete (weeks)

Transaction costs as % of purchase price

Figure 30.22

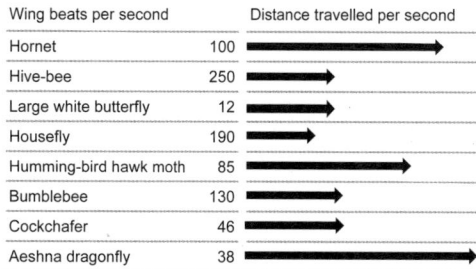

Wing beats per second		Distance travelled per second
Hornet	100	
Hive-bee	250	
Large white butterfly	12	
Housefly	190	
Humming-bird hawk moth	85	
Bumblebee	130	
Cockchafer	46	
Aeshna dragonfly	38	

Figure 30.23

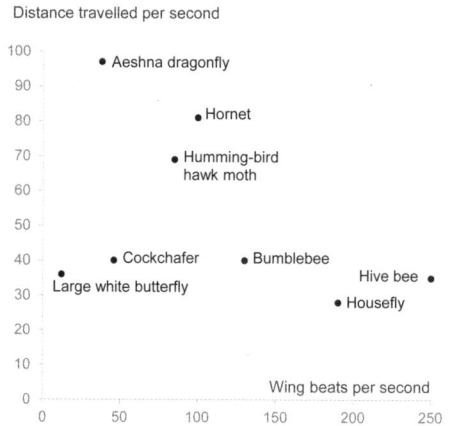

Distance travelled per second

them in). However, take care when doing this if you have lots of dots – your numbers struggle to squeeze in.

Figure 30.22 is another example of when a scattergram would help. It's based on something in the book *Diagrams* mentioned in Chapter 14 (*Infographics*). For eight insects, the graph shows wing beats per second (second column) and distance travelled per second (length of arrow – and I've no idea if the distance is inches, feet, lengths of rope or whatever). Do faster wing beats make you fly faster? A scattergram reveals all (Figure 30.23). With arguably the exception of white butterflies and cockchafers, there's a straight line sloping top left to bottom right. The relationship is inverse – if wings beat fast, you travel slowly; if they beat slowly, you travel fast.

However, take care:

Often, scattergrams change long-term policy, not immediate outcomes	People won't relocate to a country just because it's cheap and quick to move house there, but the graph might cause policy-makers in, say, country G to have a rethink.
If variables are binary, just list the items – no need to plot them	Which kids wear ties and which wear blazers? Both are binary *Yes/No* questions. Don't plot the names of kids. Just do lists. Or a Venn diagram.
Scattergrams help you spot patterns, but aren't always needed to convey them	Often, words convey it perfectly well, e.g. "There's commission bias". Quote figures if it helps ("95% confidence limit", etc). However, if there's an outlier, scattergrams highlight it wonderfully.

Also, check the logic. Does it make sense? Don't confuse correlation and causation. See Figure 30.24 for where people got it wrong – they're from *How to Lie with Statistics*, a great book by Darrell Huff.

Finally on scattergrams, Google *Anscombe's quartet*. It's good.

Sundry graphs

Here are brief topics that aren't that common, including sparklines, population pyramids, spider graphs, histograms and more. Along the way, we find a new rule for when to do graphs.

Sparklines (invented by Edward Tufte)

Sparklines are tiny graphs the size of an Excel cell – and Excel now has add-ins that create them. Figure 30.25 is a sparkline of share price over time. It has no y-axis. Most don't. Which is why I struggle with most sparklines – in Figure 30.25, does share price rise by 1% or 51%? Who knows? Having said that, sparklines can help spot deviations:

1. **Deviations from tolerance limits**: Figure 30.26 shows a patient's temperature, and if it stays within the bands, fine. If it goes outside them, we've a problem. Or, rather, our patient has.
2. **Deviations from others**: Figure 30.27 shows share prices for eight companies. It's easy to see that one had different results to the rest.

Notice that many sparklines are much wider than they are high, and that's fine. For other graphs though, strive to make to make them neither too tall

Figure 30.24
Correlation v causation
Body lice keep us healthy: researchers found that healthy people had body lice, unhealthy people didn't, so – it seems – body lice keep us healthy. Reality: it's the reverse. If we're healthy, lice like to live on us; if we're unhealthy, we're feverish, and uncomfortable for lice, so they leave.

Smoking dulls the brain: researchers found that smokers get worse college grades. Maybe less able people get depressed and start smoking, i.e. causality's reversed. Reality: smoking and grades are linked not to each other, but to a third variable: sociability. Sociable people are more likely to study less, and smoke and party more. Result: worse grades.

Rum prices and Ministers' salaries are linked: mathematically they might be, but it's spurious causality.

Figure 30.25

Figure 30.26

Figure 30.27

and thin, nor too short and wide. Avoid the y-axis being more than about 1.2 times the x-axis, and avoid the x-axis being more than twice the length of the y-axis. Unless our data dictate otherwise, of course.

Pyramids – and a new rule on when to do graphs

Figure 30.28 is a population pyramid for Australia, around the middle of the twentieth century. To see why the graph might be useful in business, Figure 30.29 shows the 2014 and 2015 split of credit ratings for companies in an industry – AAA is best, <A worst (figures illustrative, and '∆' is the change from one year to the next). Credit ratings have rocketed – there are many more well-ranked companies in 2015 than in 2014. Maybe a graph would show it better. Figures 30.30 and 30.31 are the usual suspects (paired columns, pies), and neither works well.

Instead, Figure 30.32 is a 'pyramid' of credit ratings. It produces patterns that we can describe with words: a 2014 pyramid, a 2015 cross. Which means we remember the patterns. It works. The graphs in Figure 30.33 also work – a U-shape, an inverted U, a hockey stick. In other words, if we can describe a graph's shape in words, we remember the graph. It's paradoxical: do a graph (visual) if we can describe it in words (not visual).

Which means we must revisit one of the statements to ponder before we do graphs (we saw it in Chapter 2). We said that a graph helps if "we can't replace the graph with just a few words". Being pedantic, it should have said: "… if we can't replace *the message* of the graph with just a few words". If we can replace the message (e.g. "Income up 10%", or: "Top two accounts are 40% of income"), we don't need the graph. But in this section, we've seen how words help if they can describe *the shape* of the graph (e.g. "Margins are U-shaped" or: "Income is a hockey-stick"). To conclude:

1. If words can replace a graph's message, ditch the graph.
2. If words can describe a graph's shape, keep the graph. The graph helps us remember that shape, and hence reinforces the message. The graph and words work together in harmony.

Finally on pyramids, Figure 30.34 is a 'pyramid' pie chart someone sent me. Check my website's *Fun* page to see it in colour. It's even better.

Adding text, plus thoughts on graph complexity

Is it OK to shove comments onto graphs? To annotate them? The answer is *Yes*, if they convey messages relating to stuff the graph helps highlight. Figure 30.35 shows share price for the last 12 months. The graph highlights two items – shares rose like a rocket and sank like a stone – and the two comments explain why. Also, we can describe the shape in words (it's a bit

Figure 30.28

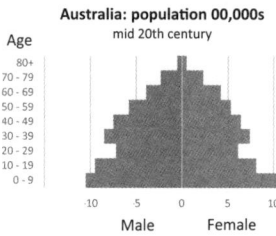
Australia: population 00,000s
mid 20th century

Figure 30.29

%	'15	'14	∆
AAA	8	4	4
AA	64	14	50
A	20	32	(12)
< A	8	50	(42)
Total	100	100	na

Figure 30.30

Figure 30.31

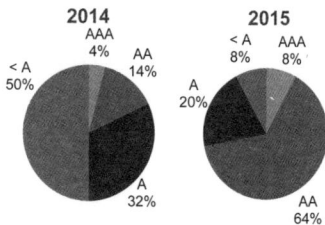

Figure 30.32

2014		
AAA	4	
AA	14	
A	32	
< A	50	

2015		
AAA	8	
AA	64	
A	20	
< A	8	

Figure 30.33

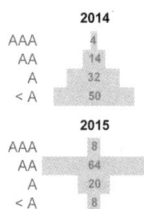

Figure 30.34

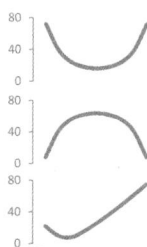

like Bart Simpson's head). Notice that the comments don't have borders – they don't need them.

Problems arise when comments convey messages that the graph doesn't particularly help highlight. This often occurs with (dare I take you back to them?) waterfall graphs. When people use waterfalls to show the differences between, say, last year's profit and this year's, often there are interesting stories behind the differences. But coloured rectangles rarely convey much, so in an attempt to make waterfalls convey something, waterfall-lovers cram in text boxes (Figure 30.36 – it's illustrative, so is 50% of actual size). Messages are unhelpfully splattered around the page, making them tougher to read. Instead, do a table in descending numerical order, with comments alongside each number. Logical, orderly, easy to read.

Such text boxes are symptomatic of a wider problem: people who overcomplicate graphs. This mostly occurs when graph-lovers crawl over hot coals to make them work. Faced with an ineffective graph, they 'improve' it: "If we put a star at the top to highlight the key dot," they say, "then add a second y-axis – and a call-out comment, plus introduce a third colour code to show percentage changes too – then the graph works". They make a bad graph worse – readers take even longer to acclimatise to it.

Which begs the question: what is unnecessarily complex? Isobars are a bit complex – we must talk people through them first – yet I claim they work. Is this double standards? Are other complex graphs bad, but my complex graphs good? No. Remember the statements to ask before doing graphs: "Better than the next best alternative". Isobars are.

Finally, the text box has a bit more on waterfalls and story-telling.

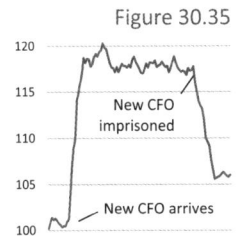

Figure 30.35

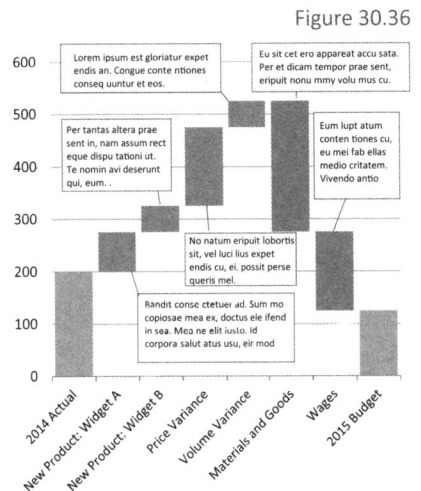

Figure 30.36

"My waterfall tells a story"

People often tell me that their waterfall tells a story, yet as I said above, coloured rectangles rarely tell a decent one. Waterfall-lovers don't give up though: "My waterfall *helps* me tell a story," they say. "*Helps me tell a story*"... such a handy phrase. We can use it to justify almost anything. Such as an infographic ("It helps me tell a story..."). Or a tin of Ronseal (I know someone who used one to help him tell a story). Or even string – to explain something to bosses, I could hold up a bit of string and cut bits off it as I talk. It 'helps' me tell a story.

This doesn't mean string is the latest fad, or that it's the best way to convey stuff to others. After all, when presenters put their script on screen as bullets, yes, it helps them 'tell a story'. But it's agony for delegates. The issue isn't: does something help us tell a story? Rather: does that something help others grasp it and remember it – and is it better than other ways? Ask those questions of waterfalls, and we see that they are useful only if people are so bored, they need colour. Or so innumerate, they need rectangles.

Figure 30.37

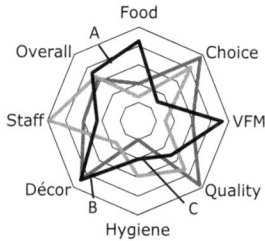

Spider graphs

Figure 30.37 shows people's views on three cafés – what do they think of their food, choice, etc? The further from the centre, the better the score (ignore the lack of legends, it's illustrative). Like most spider graphs, it's a confusing mess. Also, it's not intuitive – consider the 'direction of travel' for the black line. At points A and B, the line goes up as it goes from left to right, yet they each give us different signals – at A, we improve as we go to the right, yet at B, we worsen … until we reach point C, at which point we improve as we move further right. It makes readers think too hard. OK, occasionally numbers conspire to produce a tidy spider graph, but that's rare.

We could do a table of numbers instead, but whilst tables are good for detail, readers must concentrate to divine stuff from them. So instead try a logo chart (we originally saw this in Chapter 2). Figure 30.38 shows the cafés again. Compared to the spider graph, it's easier to grasp, there's no decoding of legends. It's also more intuitive – up is good, down is bad. Patterns stand out more, albeit there don't seem to be any great patterns for the cafés.

Having said that, Figure 30.39 is a table of the cafés' results. It's better than the logo chart if we want detailed numbers – but not as good if we want insight into patterns. With the table, we must scrutinise all columns of numbers, and after 10 or 15 seconds, we conclude: "There's no real pattern". The logo chart surrenders this pattern (or lack of it) much more quickly. The table and logo chart are opposites – the table surrenders detail first, then overview after 10 or 15 seconds. Conversely, the logo chart surrenders overview first, then detail next if we want it. There can be problems with them though: logos sometimes overlap. See the *Overall* and *Décor* columns. Not ideal, but not a disaster either.

Logo charts also work if one variable is time. Imagine we have a plan for each of our 20 brands: in the next four months we'll increase price or decrease pack size (a price increase by another name). Figure 30.40 shows the plan – the graph plots brand names (and each brand is named after a colour). Months are x-axis, and percentage change the y-axis. Dark labels are price increases, light

Figure 30.38

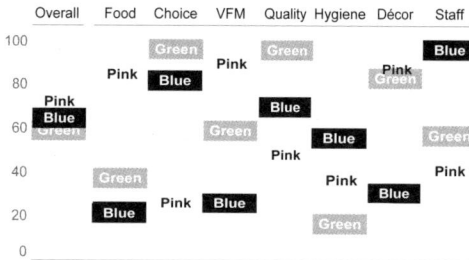

Figure 30.39

	Blue	Pink	Green
Food	26	87	41
Choice	83	30	98
VFM	30	94	61
Quality	74	52	98
Hygiene	60	41	20
Décor	34	91	89
Staff	100	46	61
Overall	**68**	**74**	**64**

Figure 30.40

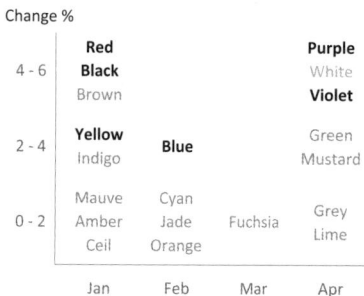

labels pack-size decreases. The chart quickly surrenders patterns. We see that March is a rather quiet month, whilst January and April are much busier. Also, there are more pack-size decreases than price increases, albeit they're mostly small (0% to 2%). Price increases are mostly more material (4% to 6% range).

If we want detail, add it to the labels. For example, **Red** (£5.00 – £5.25) would show Red's price going from £5 to £5.25, and Brown (100 – 95) would show its pack size going from 100 to 95.

The y-axis isn't a continuum, but in ranges – 0% to 2%, 2% to 4%, etc. This helps the chart cope if several brands change by, say, 5% in one month – if the y-axis is a continuum, brand names would stack on top of each other, thereby making only the top one legible. Maybe a range isn't sufficiently accurate for bosses – maybe they want to know if it's 4.5% or 5.5%. In which case put the figure after the brand name, e.g. **Red** 4.7%.

What if we want to show something that changes over time? Firstly, don't use spider charts. Figure 30.41 shows hours worked by two people over weeks 1 to 5, and a *Graphs* book hailed it as a great use of spider graphs. Hmmm. Try a line graph instead (Figure 30.42). Simple, really.

When to truncate axes

Admire the remarkable income growth in Figure 30.43 – the 2016 column is much bigger than 2015's. It's a cheat though. Growth is only 10%, yet looks much more because the y-axis doesn't start at zero. With column charts, people judge them by the columns' height or area, so if we start at non-zero, it distorts. Don't think this doesn't happen – in 2013, a big Scottish football team, Rangers, released a photo of its manager standing next to a graph of season-ticket holders for the last three years. And, my, this year's column of season-ticket holders is 90% bigger than that of two years ago. What a huge increase! Yet the numbers at the top of the columns tell otherwise. Over that period, the number of season tickets increases by just 0.25%. The graph turns 0.25% into 90%. It exaggerates 360-fold. What a cheat. The photo is on my website (under the *Graphs* bit of the *Fun* page).

If you think this only happens with football managers, it doesn't. BAT, the tobacco company, tried something similar… yet failed. In 2013, it did Figure 30.44 to show how earnings per share had grown in the past five years (notice no y-axis…). Growth is 61% (129 to 208), yet looks 18%. I computed that the graph's unlabelled y-axis must start at *minus* 300. Weird. What had BAT been smoking? At least it's not an infographic (cigarettes as columns)…

It's fine to truncate axes for line graphs though. Figure 30.45 shows share price over the past three months – little change, it seems. But that's because

Figure 30.41

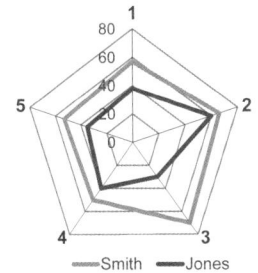

Figure 30.42

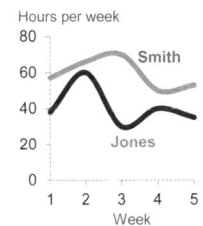

Figure 30.43

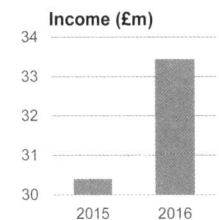

Figure 30.44

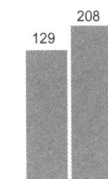

Figure 30.45

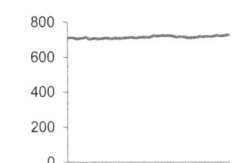

Figure 30.46

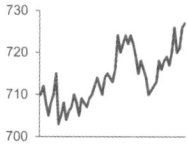

the y-axis starts at zero, so small changes aren't prominent. Start the axis at non-zero, and it's clearer (Figure 30.46).

100% stacked columns

Figure 30.47

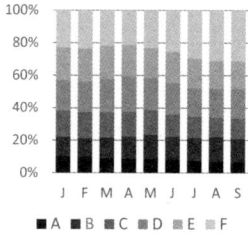

Chapter 2 looked briefly at a stacked column graph – one with just two columns – and concluded it didn't work. However, people don't put just two columns side by side, but lots (Figure 30.47). This one shows asset allocation by month (e.g. A to E are cash, government bonds, corporate bonds, equities, derivatives). And it's dreadful. It struggles to convey detail or overview. I describe such graphs as 'pie charts with corners'. Instead, try small line graphs (Figure 30.48). Much better. To avoid too many criss-crossing lines on one graph, I've spread the six lines over two graphs. But what if numbers conspire to produce a criss-crossing mess, as in Figure 30.49? We could strip lines apart from each other and show one line per graph, but that won't help much. Lines aren't just criss-crossing, they're volatile. Spikey. We'd go from two weird line graphs to six. Perhaps we could show fewer numbers. If people are mostly interested in the change from year-start to now, maybe omit the intervening numbers from February to August, then do a 'China surges' plot (we saw one in Chapter 2).

Figure 30.48

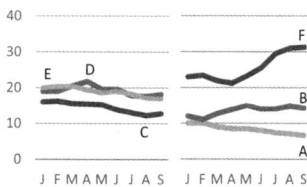

Figure 30.49

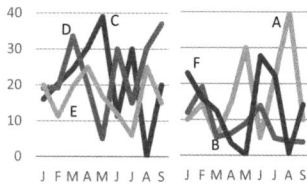

If we need to show all numbers, do a table or a logo chart – and to decide between them, think back to earlier in this Chapter when it said:

"The table and logo chart are opposites – the table surrenders detail first, then overview after 10 or 15 seconds. Conversely, the logo chart surrenders overview first, then detail next if we want it."

Hence do a table if we think people want detail first, overview next. Do a logo chart if we think they want overview first, detail next.

Histograms

Figure 30.50

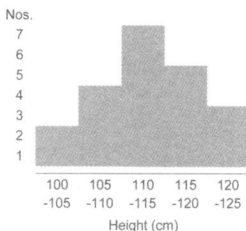

Schoolkids do histograms of heights. In Figure 30.50, two kids were between 100cm and 105cm, four between 105cm and 110cm, and so on. But we can also show children's names (Figure 30.51). We then don't need the columns or outline. The names create a shape that shows distribution. It's similar to train timetables on London Underground (Figure 30.52). Typographically, it's efficient – each hour is mentioned only once. The times create a pattern that show train frequency – most frequent around the rush hour. It also gives detail – important if turning up for a train at two in the afternoon, and less important if heading home at half-past five (trains come often anyway).

Figure 30.51

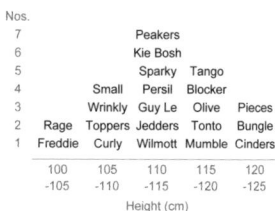

And at work, maybe try a histogram of competitors' profits (Figure 30.53). Or business unit audit scores. Or staff test scores. You get the picture.

Inverting graphs to make more intuitive

We tend to view up as good, down as bad, so sometimes it helps to invert graphs. Imagine a currency weakening from 1.900 to the pound to 1.916. Figure 30.54 is the 'normal' plot, but it gives the wrong impression – up is getting better, no? Figure 30.55 inverts it. It's more intuitive. Figure 30.56 shows a company rising up the FT Global 500 ranking.

Figure 30.57 shows house prices (dark line) and interest rates (light line) over time. They're inversely related. Invert one line to reinforce the relationship (Figure 30.58). Then there's my Unicef chart from the *Graphs* Chapter – Figure 30.59 shows a bit of it, and as currently presented, up is bad, down is good. Maybe invert to make more intuitive.

Figure 30.52

```
14:  00 30
15:  00 15 30 45
16:  00 10 20 30 40 50
17:  00 08 16 24 32 40 48 56
18:  00 10 20 30 40 50
19:  00 15 30 45
20:  00 30
```

Figure 30.53

Nos					
7			South		
6			Brown		
5			AKT	Red	
4		East	KJK	Green	
3		ADW	Pink	Violet	Orange
2	Smith	KLW	AKA	White	Yellow
1	Jones	North	Blue	Black	Indigo
Profit margin	(10%) to (5%)	(5%) to 0%	0% to 5%	5% to 10%	10% to 15%

Figure 30.54

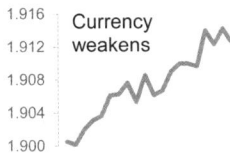

Figure 30.55

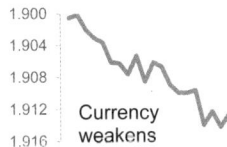

Figure 30.56

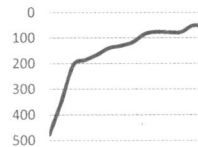

Figure 30.57

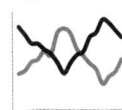

Figure 30.58

Also, invert graphs to help comparability. Imagine ten trend lines on a page of a report, each showing a movement over the past three months. Income. Footfall. Profit. Etc. Then wastage. But with wastage, up is bad, down is good. If all ten trend lines went up, readers would incorrectly feel reassured. Invert the wastage graph so readers correctly feel unnerved. Of course, sometimes it's not clear if up is good or bad. If the police catch more criminals, are they better at catching criminals (which is good) or is total crime rising (which is bad)? Maybe we simply keep the 'catching criminals' graph away from the other graphs so as not to confuse.

All these ideas are similar to the fantastic 'Upside Down' map published in 1998 by a designer called John Sims (Figure 30.60). He inverted the UK road map, surmising it would be easier for driving North to South. A great idea, albeit Sat Nav now renders it obsolete.

Figure 30.59

Figure 30.60

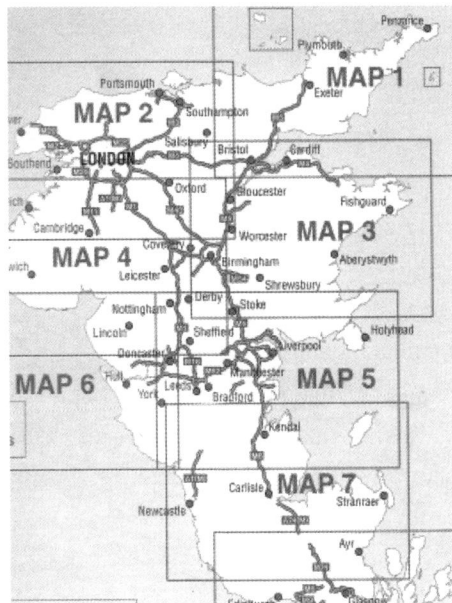

Figure 30.61

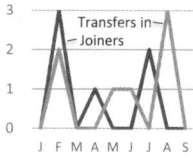

Figure 30.62

	Join-ers	Trans-fers in
Jan	-	-
Feb	3	2
Mar	-	-
Apr	1	-
May	-	1
Jun	-	1
Jul	2	-
Aug	-	3
Sep	-	-
Total	**6**	**7**

When trend lines don't work

Here is when instinct says to plot a trend line, but reality says otherwise:

When our numbers jump about: Figure 30.61 shows the number of staff who joined or transferred during the past nine months. It looks spikey and doesn't work. Anyway, the graph adds little, for its numbers are small and easy to grasp. A table is better (Figure 30.62). It gives the total too.

Figure 30.63 is how Warren Buffett compares his annual return with that of the S&P (his table goes back to 1965). Would it better as a graph? Figure 30.64 plots two of his three data sets. Again, spikey. Not good.

Notice several points about Warren's table. Because numbers are in columns, they're easier to scan. Also, the 1999 figure is shown as 0.5. He used to show it as .5, but in recent years, he's added the leading zero. A shame – I liked it without the 0. (OK, yes, Chapter 3 says to include the leading zero in text ("Exchange rates are 0.85 to the pound"), but Figure 30.63 is a table, not text.) Finally, notice how the table signals the maths for readers: the far right column is: "(1) – (2)".

Figure 30.63

	Annual percentage change		
	in Per-Share Book Value of Berkshire (1)	In S&P 500 with Dividends Included (2)	Relative Results (1)-(2)
1998	48.3	28.6	19.7
1999	0.5	21.0	(20.5)
2000	6.5	(9.1)	15.6
2001	(6.2)	(11.9)	5.7
2002	10.0	(22.1)	32.1
2003	21.0	28.7	(7.7)
2004	10.5	10.9	(0.4)
2005	6.4	4.9	1.5
2006	18.4	15.8	2.6
2007	11.0	5.5	5.5
2008	(9.6)	(37.0)	27.4
2009	19.8	26.5	(6.7)
2010	13.0	15.1	(2.1)
2011	4.6	2.1	2.5
2012	14.4	16.0	(1.6)
2013	18.2	32.4	(14.2)

Figure 30.64

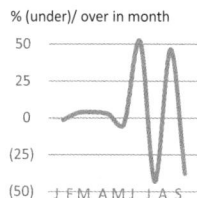

When readers have to squint at tiny gaps: Figure 30.65 compares our actual and budget cumulative sales. As at September, we're £0.5m under budget, yet to spot this shortfall from the graph, readers must squint at a tiny gap between two lines (see the circle). Some people counter that the graph shows history. OK, but when we reach September, do bosses care if we were under or over budget in May? And if something big happened back then – and its effect is still felt four months on – we'd mention it in our commentary, e.g. "Still under because of big client loss in May".

Maybe the graph helps convey how we do against budget each month. Again, no. Figure 30.66 does it better, it's a smoothed curve of the monthly percentage variance versus budget. For five months, we're close to budget every month, then it goes awry. Conclusion: to compare actual with budget, don't plot two lines and ask readers to squint. Plot the difference. Or the percentage difference. Or do a table (Figure 30.67). Sometimes, graphs help us spot patterns, but aren't always the best way to convey them to others.

Figure 30.65

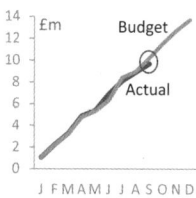

Figure 30.66

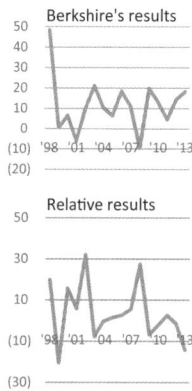

Figure 30.67

	% Over/ (under) in month
Jan	(1)
Feb	4
Mar	4
Apr	3
May	(4)
Jun	52
Jul	(43)
Aug	46
Sep	(38)

However, cumulative-graph-lovers don't give up. "The graph shows," they say, "that cumulative income goes up every month". Hardly front-page news, unless, that is, your firm sometimes reports negative sales in a month. If it does, then maybe cumulative graphs will help…

It gets worse though. Some people show not just actual and budget, but last year too (Figure 30.68). Squint at columns in September and we spot we're £0.5m under budget to date – but that misses the bigger £1.7m possible problem. To see why, Figure 30.69 shows the final four months. The line AB is what we did in the last three months of last year (£2.3m), and the line CD is what we need to do in the last three months of this year if we're to reach budget (£4.0m), i.e. £1.7m more. So, unless we've a good reason why the last three months of this year will be much better than the last three months of last year, we've a £1.7m hole. The cumulative graph (Figure 30.68) fails to convey this clearly (albeit it does have one redeeming feature: its y-axis is on the right, given that we're more interested in later months' figures). Figure 30.69 isn't good either, it's like a trigonometry exam.

Which helps pops another myth about graphs: "The more complex a topic, the more a graph helps". No. Often, it's the reverse. With graphs like Figures 30.68 and 30.69, we've lots to absorb (axes, captions, numbers, etc), plus we don't know where to start. Instead, think back to Chapter 2 – it said that with a complex graph, words are often better *because* the graph is complex. To convey the £1.7m problem, use words (Figure 30.70).

Two other points on cumulative graphs. Firstly, they look odd in the first month of the year; a rolling 12-month graph would be better. And secondly, sometimes they can work. In Figure 30.71, the pattern is obvious – every month, we've been too optimistic, and the gap between actual and budget keeps growing. Then again, Figure 30.72 shows the percentage difference in a table. It shows more clearly than the graph that we got it most wrong in May.

There's another graph I often see that, again, forces readers to squint at tiny gaps. Figure 30.73 shows the percentage of calls answered in the target time. Actual is dark grey, and target light grey. Notice that the target is always 96%, so to help readers(!), such graphs often have a horizontal rule astride the *Target* columns. Which is like rearranging deck chairs on the Titanic. Instead, plot the variance from target, like we did above. Or, if it's too spikey, do a table.

This section begs the question: which is better – a graph or a table? A flawed question. It's like asking if it's better to swim or cycle. The answer to that question, of course, is another question: "Better for what?". Maybe we should instead ask: "When should we do a graph instead of a table, and vice versa?". Again, a flawed question, for it ignores a third alternative: words.

Figure 30.68

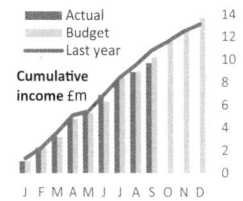

Figure 30.69

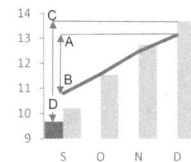

Figure 30.70

Possible £1.7m shortfall?

"About £4.0m income needed by year-end to reach forecast, compared to £2.3m income in last 3 months of last year."

Figure 30.71

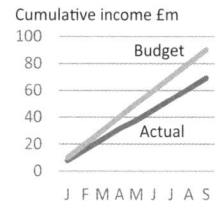

Figure 30.72

	% Under in month
J	22
F	21
M	23
A	22
M	39
J	21
J	19
A	23
S	19

Figure 30.73

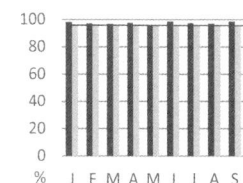

Which is why Chapter 2 lists four questions to ask before doing a graph – and one question is on whether words are better.

Finally on this topic, the text box gives brief details of a 2008 study in which an academic tested whether we make better decisions from graphs or tables. The findings are interesting. But unhelpful.

Graphs v tables – an academic's view

In 2008, a 20-page research paper described how people were shown the same data as either a graph or a table, then asked to make choices from them. It found that accountants made better decisions from the table, whilst non-accountants fared better with the graph. Sounds sensible. Realistic.

Unfortunately, the graph and table were realistic too. They were truly awful. In other words, accountants prefer bad tables to bad graphs, whilst non-accountants prefer bad graphs to bad tables. I wonder how people would fare with good graphs and tables.

Figure 30.74

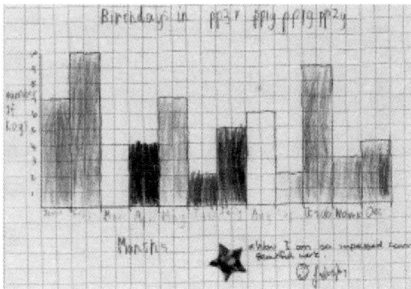

Time for Final Thoughts. There's more we could cover. Hi-lo plots. Bullet graphs. Log graphs. How to cheat with graphs. Let's stop though. This Chapter has been a mix of the good, bad and ugly. Which reinforces that I'm not against graphs. I'm against bad graphs. I love good ones. I've even an all-time favourite graph – it's Figure 30.74, done by my eldest son when he was six. It's a histogram of his schoolmates' birthdays – the first column shows that seven kids had birthdays in January. The teacher gave my boy a gold star, and wrote on the graph: "Wow, I am so impressed, Conor. Beautiful work".

Figure 30.75

And yes, it's good. But could be better. If he'd read the *histogram* bit of this Chapter, he'd have put schoolmates' names on it too. Figure 30.75 shows January and February redone. On that note, let's sign off.

Signalling performance

31

How are our projects doing? Or our business units? Or the risks that we monitor? How have they done this month, and how do they compare to last month? So much to track, but how to track it all?

This Chapter shows how. We look at red-amber-green reports, smiley faces, upward and downward arrows, heat maps and more. We see which work and which don't. Also, towards the end of the Chapter, we look briefly at surveys and benchmarking. Before then, two warnings: (1) you don't see how to put it all together – Chapter 33 shows that; (2) there are no Excel tips.

Red-amber-green reports

Assume we've 15 areas of activity to monitor, all denoted by letters (U, F, I, etc). They could be projects, business units, risks, people, income, costs, profits, etc. For each area, we know how it compares to budget, e.g. U is 2% above, F is 2% under. Also, we group the scores into clusters – good if above budget, so-so if within 5% of it, and poor if more than 5% under.

To show all this, people use colour codes – red for poor, amber for so-so, green for good – and call them 'RAG' reports (Red, Amber, Green). Or Traffic Light reports. And at first glance, they *should* work. They're more colourful than black-and-white spreadsheets, and colour engages people and helps right-brainers, no? Also, RAGs are intuitive. We all know traffic lights.

Flawed logic. Figure 31.1 is a typical RAG for the 15 areas, and it suffers from many problems.

Figure 31.1

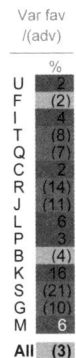

It's a GLGG report (Grey, Light Grey, Grey)	If printed on black-and-white printers or copied on black-and-white copiers, red and green all too easily look similar or the same. Also, 5% to 10% of people are colour blind or deficient. Finally, colour is expensive to print.
It can score only out three and so lacks granularity	In an attempt to remedy this, some people do RDAALAG reports: Red, Dark Amber, Amber, Light Amber, Green. Crazy. As are RAGBBl reports – Red, Amber, Green, Black (not yet started), Blue (finished).
It isn't as intuitive as we think	When we did good work at junior school, did teachers adorn it with coloured blobs? No – they probably drew a smiley face, tick or gold star.

Colour intrudes and impedes readability	To remedy this, some RAGs show numbers in white if a cell is red or green (e.g. see M near the bottom of Figure 31.1). Better, but still not good.
Colour visually dominates in way that lacks charm	It's not how people show information outside business – Figure 31.2 is part of the legend for the London tube map (elegant, easy to read). Figure 31.3 shows it as if in a RAG report (ugly, tricky to read).
It's unattractive	Colours butt up to each other.

Figure 31.2

Central —
District —

Figure 31.3

Central
District

Maybe you're unconvinced. Don't we like information to be visual? Also, fighter pilots and racing drivers use RAGs. I address these and other myths later. Next though, we see how to improve RAGs.

Better RAGs – and better than RAGs

In Figure 31.4, coloured blobs are in a separate column on the right. They no longer visually interfere with numbers. We more easily see detail. Also, the blobs are smaller and more elegant. Colours in adjacent cells still butt up to each other though, but that's easily remedied (Figure 31.5). Much better. (I did this by putting a white border around each shaded cell.) Would the blob be better if circular (also Figure 31.5)? Down to personal choice.

That's how to do a better RAG. But we could do something better than a RAG. Figure 31.6 is a RA layout. Red, Amber. We don't need G (green). RA layouts have less visual distraction than RAGs. Sounds obvious, really. Maybe it's dispiriting to report just poor and so-so stuff, in which case try an AG report (Amber, Green). Or an RG. You get the picture. All are better than RAGs. None are ideal in black and white, of course.

So try ticks, dashes, crosses (Figure 31.7). They work in black-and-white, and can also score out of more than three. To score out of four, do double-tick to double-cross with no dash. To score out of five, do double-tick to double-cross with a dash. They're intuitive too, teachers put them on our homework. Finally, if bosses demand colour, do a red cross, an amber dash and a green tick – and maybe even omit the dash. We need only two of the three indicators.

But there's more. In Figure 31.7, ticks, dashes, crosses are all in the same column, making it trickier to see the wood for the trees. In Figure 31.8, they're in separate columns and no longer visually compete with each other. There are totals at the bottom too – seven ticks, two dashes, six crosses. It gives readers insight and overview.

Figure 31.4   Figure 31.5

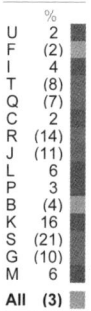
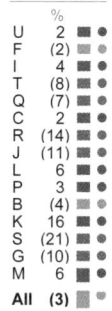

Figure 31.6   Figure 31.7

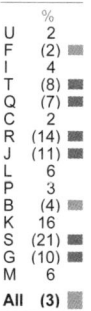
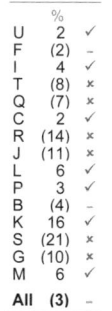

Figure 31.8

We've one last step. Figure 31.9 sorts information between good, so-so and poor. Maybe the right column would be better with ticks and crosses, not rectangular blobs, but now that we've sorted the information, *it doesn't matter*. We don't need the 'blob' column anyway. Cover it and we lose nothing. The three sub-headings spell it out fine.

We've reached the punchline: RAG layouts are often nothing more than badly sorted lists. After all, think what we do when our eyes land on a RAG report. If we're involved in just one of the activities, we want to see how it's doing (assume it's amber), and we then strive to compare it with everyone else. So we reorder it all – good ones together ("Ahhh... seven – my *amber* looks worrying"), so-so ones together ("Just two"), and poor ones together ("Six poor – my *amber* score isn't too bad after all").

If we're involved not with just one but with all – maybe we're the boss who oversees everything – we again want to identify poor performers. And, so the logic goes, RAGs help us do this, for they help stuff pop from the page (assuming the RAG isn't copied or printed in monochrome, and we aren't colour blind…). But if we reorder the list, the poor ones are all together and easy for us to spot. We don't need the blobs.

It sounds so obvious, people invent reasons to object to this 'reorder' idea. They retort: "Figure 31.9 doesn't define *good*, *so-so* and *poor*". But neither did any of Figures 31.4 to 31.8. Remember: we defined clusters at the start, and I assume such definitions would be in the reports in which the tables appear. Also, if you prefer to see *poor* first, fine. Reverse the row order. No problem.

Sometimes we can't lump poor ones together. Maybe activities are overseen by three bosses (Pat, Les, Robin) and we must cluster by boss. No worries, for later we see what to do instead.

Alternative signals to ticks, crosses and coloured blobs

What about smiley or miserable faces (Figure 31.10)? They work in black and white, but are inelegant, and would struggle to rank out of more than three (unless we do double smiley to double miserable – but that's odd). Also, are miserable faces an appropriate way to convey bad news? If HR were sacking you, would you like to see a 'miserable face' icon at the top of their dismissal letter? Finally on faces, information hardly pops from the page. Readers must scrutinise each face to see if it's a frown, smile or neither. Not easy, for the three types of face have a lot in common typographically (eyes, outline) and little that differs (smile or frown). It's like £14,268,492.32 and £14,286,492.32 – because they're similar, we must really concentrate to see how they differ. We could just show smiles or frowns (Figure 31.11). There's less distracting typography (no eyes or outlines). They're a bit silly though.

Figure 31.9

Good	%	
K	16	■
L	6	■
M	6	■
I	4	■
P	3	■
U	2	■
C	2	■
So-so		
F	(2)	■
B	(4)	■
Poor		
Q	(7)	■
T	(8)	■
G	(10)	■
J	(11)	■
R	(14)	■
S	(21)	■
All	**(3)**	■

Figure 31.10

	%	
U	2	☺
F	(2)	☹
I	4	☺
T	(8)	☹
Q	(7)	☹
C	2	☺
R	(14)	☹
J	(11)	☹
L	6	☺
P	3	☺
B	(4)	☹
K	16	☺
S	(21)	☹
G	(10)	☹
M	6	☺
All	**(3)**	☺

Figure 31.11

	%	
U	2	⌣
F	(2)	-
I	4	⌣
T	(8)	⌢
Q	(7)	⌢
C	2	⌣
R	(14)	⌢
J	(11)	⌢
L	6	⌣
P	3	⌣
B	(4)	-
K	16	⌣
S	(21)	⌢
G	(10)	-
M	6	-
All	**(3)**	-

Figure 31.12

	%	
U	2	↑
F	(2)	→
I	4	↑
T	(8)	↓
Q	(7)	↓
C	2	↑
R	(14)	↓
J	(11)	↓
L	6	↑
P	3	↑
B	(4)	↓
K	16	↑
S	(21)	↓
G	(10)	↓
M	6	↑
All	**(3)**	→

Figure 31.13

	%
K	16
L	6
M	6
I	4
P	3
U	2
C	2
F	(2)
B	(4)
Q	(7)
T	(8)
G	(10)
J	(11)
R	(14)
S	(21)
All	(3)

What about arrows (Figure 31.12)? They work in black and white, but are a bit inelegant and struggle to rank out of more than three. OK, we could have double *up* arrows and double *down* ones – after all, I suggest double ticks and crosses. But double arrows seem just a bit weird.

We could use numbers, e.g.: 1 = poor, 2 = so-so, 3 = good. It works in black and white, plus allows us to rank out of 5, 10 or even 100 (1 = worst, 100 = best). As for whether they pop from the page, numbers are on a level with arrows: not bad. They don't pop as much as colours (but remember colour has limitations), but pop more than smiley faces.

Finally, we could just show the data. Figure 31.13 shows our 15 areas in descending numerical order. Simple. Sometimes though, exact figures aren't available, e.g. when giving updates on, say, 15 projects.

Drawing threads together

Time to summarise. Most RAG reports are badly sorted lists. Sort the list and we don't need a separate signal for performance. However, if we still need or want a separate signal, there are alternatives: coloured blobs; ticks and crosses; smiley faces; arrows; numbers. Five different ways. There are more, but we've covered enough for our purposes. And as Figure 31.14 shows, there

Figure 31.14

	Ticks, crosses	Numbers	RAG	Arrows	Smiley faces
	✓=x	1234	■■■	↓↑→	☺☺☺
Intuitive	✓	✓	✓	✓	✓
Works in B&W	✓	✓	✗	✓	✓
Can score > 3	✓	✓	✗	✗	✗
Elegant	✓	–	✓	✗	✗
Pops from page	✓	–	✓	–	✗
Total score	**5**	**3**	**1**	**0**	**(1)**

are pros and cons to them. The five ways are in columns (*Ticks, crosses*; *Numbers*, etc), and the criteria by which we assess them are in rows (Are they intuitive? Do they work in black and white? Etc). Tick for good, cross for bad. *Ticks, crosses* is best (which is why it's the first column). You could say it ticks all the boxes.

The RAG score may surprise you. Somewhat graciously, the table says RAGs are as intuitive as ticks and crosses. It also says that RAGs are elegant – they can be, so long as the coloured blobs are small and don't run into each other.

Note the *Total* row at the bottom of Figure 31.14. It adds insight. Also, columns are in order (best first, worst last – it assumes a tick is +1 and a cross is –1). Maybe we could weight the ranking, e.g. if *Works in B&W* is important, *Arrows* might come before *RAG*.

Figure 31.14 uses ticks and crosses to show its analysis. Rather telling, really. We could instead show it with smiley faces – Figure 31.15 redoes part of it that way, and it's not as good. Stuff doesn't pop from the page. Then there's Figure 31.16. It redoes part of the table again, but this time as a RAG. Again, not as good. It's a kaleidoscope of colour. There's no white border between coloured blobs. That's deliberate. These RAG kaleidoscopes are often referred to as 'heat maps', and they're to help readers see the continuum of colour – and a white border between blobs interrupts

Figure 31.15

	RAG	Arrows	Faces
Intuitive	☺	☺	☺
Works in B&W	☹	☺	☺
Can score > 3	☹	☹	☹
Elegant	☺	☹	☹
Pops from page	☺	☺	☹

Figure 31.16

RAG Arrows Faces

Intuitive
Works in B&W
Can score > 3
Elegant
Pops from page

that continuum. We look at heat maps later. Next we see when RAGs go really bad: when we've two variables.

When RAGs go bad – two variables

Figure 31.17 is the RAG we saw earlier, but it now has arrows to show how activities compare with last month. An *up* arrow means it's improved, *down* means it's worsened, and *horizontal* means no change. Of course, a red area can have an *up* arrow – it's bad this month, but was really bad last month.

Figure 31.17

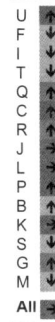

It's useful to compare to last month. Are red areas getting worse or better? But the arrows create puzzles for readers to decode ("Now let's see… we want status-red areas with *down* arrows…"). We chant this in our heads whilst we scan the table ("Red and down, red and down"). It's hard to see patterns – which are there more of: *up* or *down* arrows? It's hard to see groupings too – try finding the *down* amber ones. We must keep a running tally in our head.

Try Figure 31.18 instead (and *All* in the middle is the overall position). The x-axis compares to last month (equivalent to the *up, down, horizontal* arrows), and the y-axis shows current status (equivalent to red, amber, green). Notice the double-tick top right and double-cross bottom left – they make the grid more intuitive for readers.

Figure 31.18

| | | Compared to last month | | |
		Worse	Similar	Better
	Above budget	I, M	L, K	✓✓ U, C, P
Compared to budget	Within 5%	F	**All**	B
	Missing by > 5%	T, S ✗✗	J	Q, R, G

It's easy to spot patterns and groupings. Look top right – three activities are doing well and improving (U, C, P). Also, a quick glance reveals that scores are reasonably balanced. That is, the number of activities above budget is roughly the same as the number beneath it. Also, roughly the same number are getting worse as are getting better.

The grid uses its physical space to help convey information. The layout is logical too: we wish to show two independent scores – compared to budget, and compared to last month – so we plot one variable down one axis, and one along the other.

We can now revisit a conundrum we saw earlier – how to report our 15 activities (U, F, I, etc) that are split between three managers (Pat, Les, Robin). The answer is a three-by-three grid (Figure 31.19). It's Figure 31.18, but with different headings along the top, and no ticks or crosses in the corners. It uses its physical space to help us more easily see patterns and groupings.

Figure 31.19

| | | Manager | | |
		Pat	Les	Robin
	Above budget	I, M	L, K	U, C, P
Compared to budget	Within 5%	F		B
	Missing by > 5%	T, S	J	Q, R, G

We can also use the grid to summarise audit findings. Our audit looked at 15 topics (U, F, I, etc), and some are fine, some bad. Some material, some less so. Good and bad is the y-axis, material and immaterial the x-axis. Easy.

Figure 31.20

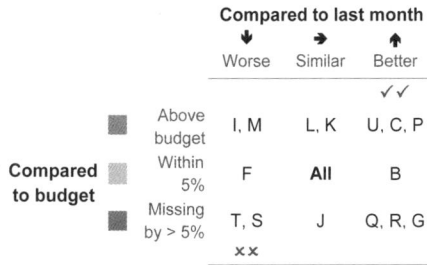

		Compared to last month		
		↓ Worse	→ Similar	↑ Better
				✓✓
Compared to budget	Above budget	I, M	L, K	U, C, P
	Within 5%	F	**All**	B
	Missing by > 5%	T, S	J	Q, R, G
		✗✗		

With two variables, there is another option: 'Harvey Balls'. However, they're neither common nor good. The text box below explains why.

The next section looks at many variables. Before then, here's a final thought: if your bosses struggle to grasp words like *Worse, Similar, Better* – or *Above, Within, Missing by* – or if they can't survive without a bit of colour, try shoving some arrows and blobs on the axes (Figure 31.20). Bosses might find it clearer…

Figure 31.21

Harvey Balls

Figure 31.21 shows Harvey Balls. Circles with blacked-out bits. People use them to denote score, e.g. to show how our 15 areas did against budget, we put alongside each area either a white circle (to denote *Good*), a half-filled circle (*So-so*), or a black circle (*Poor*). When used this way, the balls are reasonably elegant, work in monochrome, are fairly intuitive (not as intuitive as ticks and crosses though), and just about pop from the page. The balls can also rank out of five reasonably well – see the first five of Figure 31.21.

But it goes pear-shaped when people use balls for two variables. The left half of a ball compares to budget, the right half compares to last month. So a blank circle is a good score getting better, a black circle is a bad score getting worse, and a left-sided half moon is a bad score getting better, etc. Readers must decode circles ("Let's see, this one is half filled, albeit it's on the right, not the left… which means…?"). No. Instead, plot labels, as we saw above.

Harvey Balls are good at one thing: denoting phases of the moon (half moon, etc), and given my surname, that's neat. I'm not a fan of them at work though. However, two groups of people seem to favour them: consultants and graduate trainees. Read into that what you want. Finally, here's a weird aside: a consultant called Harvey Poppel is credited with inventing the balls in the 1970s (not weird), whereas smiley faces were invented by someone called…Harvey Ball.

Figure 31.22

Eight Takes on risk

1. Probability of loss: unlikely, possible, likely, very likely.
2. Impact: limited, moderate, significant, very significant.
3. Area: financial, reputational, operational, strategic.
4. Direction of travel: getting worse, staying the same, getting better.
5. Immediacy: short, medium or long term (each was then defined).
6. Number of actions needed: a few, lots, tonnes.
7. Cost of action needed: cheap, so-so, costly.
8. Urgency of action needed: urgent, so-so, not urgent.

Really pear-shaped – too many variables

I once saw a 'Risk' report that looked at 17 areas – political, reputational, social, environmental, etc – and looked at them eight ways (let's call them different 'Takes'). Figure 31.22 has the Takes if you want to read them. To convey it all to bosses, the risk-manager did a four-by-four coloured grid, with 17 differently sized numbered circles, and arrows on each circle. He also did a table with words, arrows (up, down, sideways), two types of colour coding (one was RAG, the other was Blue, Grey, Green, Purple…), and initials (S, M, L). Confusing. But what to do instead? After all, there were 17 areas and eight Takes – each with between three or four scores. A quarter of a million possible combinations.

What to do instead? Answer: don't send bosses all the schedules, areas and Takes, but maybe still wave them around to amaze others with how thorough we've been. Then, to impress them with our thinking, simplify:

Consolidate to create one master table	In the table, show areas in descending order of the overall weighted average risk that we compute from our eight Takes. One table, 17 rows, one score for each area. Much simpler.
Or edit – cut out all Takes except two key ones	Then plot the 17 areas with the two key Takes as the x- and y-axes (e.g. impact and probability). Figure 31.23 illustrates, albeit with country names.
Then summarise	Rise above detail. Do a 30-second role-play. What do bosses need to know? "This month, it's steady as she goes – the usual round of risks our business faces – albeit there's something looming up ahead, etc".

Figure 31.23

Probability	Limited	Moderate	Significant	Very significant
Very likely	Iraq Peru		USA	Iceland Norway
Likely	America		China	Ireland
Possible	Liberia Wales	Canada	Australia	
Unlikely	Fiji France	Bermuda Vietnam		Mexico

Impact

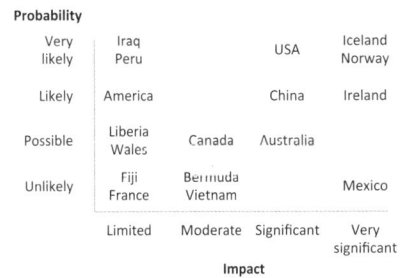

Above, we looked at just two key Takes. If we must have a third Take, signal it with different fonts – we saw this in Chapter 5 (*Making comparisons*).

RAGs with lots of words

Some people do RAG reports that have lots of words. Figure 31.24 (the *before*) shows part of one such report, and its coloured rectangles are inelegant and intrusive. That's because comments on the right stretch beyond one line (fine), so coloured rectangles also stretch beyond one line (not fine). If you must have coloured rectangles, limit their height to just one line – see the first row of Figure 31.25 (the *after*). Ensure they're not too wide either. Make them elegantly compact. Or, for reasons mentioned earlier, remove the rectangles and do ticks and crosses – see rows 2 to 4 of the *after*.

Beyond tidying the rectangles, there are six other changes in the *after*. We've seen them in this book already, so they're listed in Figure 31.26 (overleaf). Each is small, yet collectively they make a huge difference.

Figure 31.24

IT dept		
The boss is rubbish		Lorem ipsum est gloriatur exp etendis an. Congue conte ntiones conseq untur et eos, autem vocibus.
A new one joins soon		Lorem ipsum est gloriatur exp etendis an. Congue conte ntiones conseq untur et eos, autem vocibus.
Staff might hate her		Mea ne elit iusto. Id corp ora salutatus usu, eirm od animal eu est. No natum eripuit lobortis sit.
But staff are rubbish too		Congue conte ntiones conseq untur et eos, autem voci bus in.

Figure 31.25

IT dept		
The boss is rubbish	■	Lorem ipsum est gloriatur exp etendis an. Congue conte ntiones conseq untur et eos, autem vocibus.
A new one joins soon	✓	Lorem ipsum est gloriatur exp etendis an. Congue conte ntiones conseq untur et eos, autem vocibus.
Staff might hate her	-	Mea ne elit iusto. Id corp ora salutatus usu, eirm od animal eu est. No natum eripuit lobortis sit.
But staff are rubbish too	×	Congue conte ntiones conseq untur et eos, autem voci bus in.

Figure 31.26

Changes to Figure 31.24

1. Remove vertical rules.
2. Widen left column a bit to avoid the orphan in the last row.
3. Widen the right column a bit. Rows 1 and 2 are now three lines long, not four.
4. Justify the right column, it's now wide enough to do so.
5. Remove the internal cell margin that MS Word automatically gives.
6. Put a gap between words and horizontal rules.

Figure 31.27

Figure 31.28

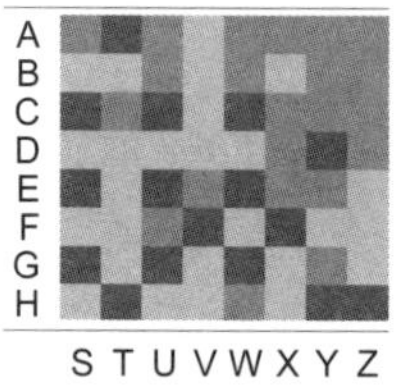

Figure 31.29

Notice what hasn't changed between *before* and *after*. Firstly, the overall table width hasn't changed; that's to keep *before* and *after* comparable. Also, I didn't reorder the rows. Perhaps I should – after all, most RAG reports are badly ordered lists. This one isn't though. Study the words in the left column – they've an order and flow that would be lost if I reordered rows.

Talking of badly ordered lists, next we look at heat maps.

Most heat maps are neither hot nor maps

Maps are great. Maps that overlay information are even better. Police do heat maps to show a city's crime hot-spots. Businesses do maps to show clusters and gaps of, say, a city's tea shops.

So far, so good. Unfortunately, people do heat maps like the one we saw earlier (shown again in Figure 31.27). Or of staff survey findings. Or of risks to the business. Figure 31.28 illustrates – the x-axis is the eight business areas (S to Z), and y-axis the staff survey questions (A: do you like your boss? B: do you like our products?, etc). Red = *No*, amber = *Sort of*, green = *Yes*. Or, if you prefer, the y-axis could be risks (A: *Reputational*, B: *Political*, etc), and red = *Risky*, amber = *So-so*, etc. Obviously, we'd label axes properly, but I've done A to H and S to Z to keep it generic. Also, I've fixed colours so they don't look the same in black and white (which means it's a DGLGG report, for dark grey = red, light grey = amber, grey = green…).

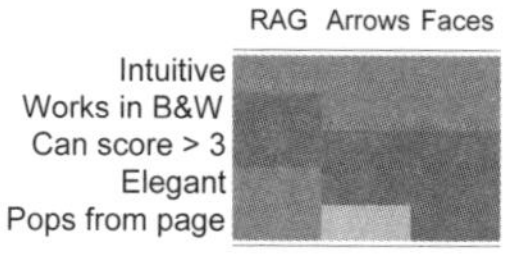

If we give scores (1 = red, 2 = amber, 3 = green), Figure 31.28 is in descending order – bottom left low scores, top right high scores.

People think this layout helps. It doesn't, and to understand why, think back to a city's crime heat map. The bottom-right bit of it shows the South East of the city, and the bit that's next to it on the map is – at the risk of stating the obvious – next to it. *In real life*. Adjacent on the map, and connected in real life. Which is why crime heat maps are good – we spot geographic clusters or gaps: "Look – we've a problem north of centre."

But Figure 31.28 isn't like that. *Products* is next to *Boss*. Their findings are adjacent – but *unconnected*. So too in *risk* maps – *Reputational* findings are next to *Political* ones. Again, adjacent but unconnected. With such 'maps', we don't spot clusters, we spot isolated answers that remain isolated. And sometimes, colours mislead and create wrong answers. In Figure 31.28, we can reorder its columns and rows and create Figure 31.29. There are now four red boxes bottom left. Readers wrongly conclude that problem areas are C, E, G and S, U, W. They'd miss F, H and T, all of which score lower than C, E, W.

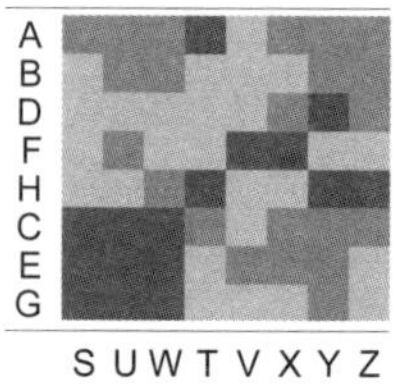

Perhaps we could improve such maps by grouping items. Assume we ask four questions each about our products, staff and service. They're the x-axis of our heat map. Also, we seek client feedback on each of our 12 units

– four units in each of our Widget, Gadget and Gidget divisions. They're our heat map's y-axis. That's 144 coloured blobs, but now with some order to it. Widget's answers are the bottom four rows, Gidget's answers the top four. There is some order that helps us spot clusters. But within each four-by-four block of blobs, we still struggle.

To conclude, most heat maps aren't maps. They're isolated coloured blobs next to other isolated coloured blobs. At best, they identify patterns and clusters that we'd more easily spot if we reordered rows and columns. At worst, colours conspire to convey fake clusters. And I've one last problem with such 'maps': they remind me of the computer game Tetris (Figure 31.30). But what to do instead? That's next.

Figure 31.30

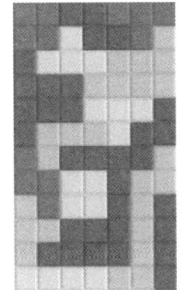

Redo of a typical 'heat map'

Let's not make this too easy for me. Assume that readers want exact numbers as well as overview. Imagine we ask staff why they work for our company, ABC. We ask five questions – is it because we make them feel loved? Or the long holidays? Or good tea? And so on. We've results for ABC as a whole, and for each of our five business units – Chad, UK, Peru, etc. We also have an average score for our rivals (the survey is an industry-wide exercise). Figure 31.31 is the *before*. There are average rows and columns (which is good), plus response numbers (*Replies*) and *Reply rate* (also good). There's a heat map too – red if our score is lower than rivals', green if higher, amber if the same. This is why the *Rivals* column is, somewhat pointlessly, all amber – and if that sounds unbelievable, this layout really existed. Also, the table had more on it: there were ten units, not five. And nine questions, not five.

Figure 31.31

	Average		Our units				
	ABC	Rivals	Chad	UK	Peru	Iran	Fiji
% Avrge score	75	74	70	74	83	69	79
Nos Replies	343	3,973	117	115	24	18	69
% Reply rate	89	72	89	91	96	95	83
% Feel loved	68	70	66	71	71	61	73
% Long hols	51	49	40	44	74	43	54
% Good tea	81	80	80	84	78	74	90
% Fancy PC	94	93	88	91	99	96	95
% Few emails	82	80	78	82	94	72	85

As we saw before, the heat map works only on a superficial level. Yes, colour draws people in, we fairly quickly see that greens are the most common, then reds, then ambers (ignoring the pointless ambers in the rivals' column). But we then struggle. Colour distracts us from detail. Also, to see how units compare to each other, we must mentally reorder each column. We glance at the *before*, but struggle to engage with it. A lead-in title would help, but here, the map's author didn't do one, probably surmising that heat maps are intuitive…

Let's improve it. Firstly, remove the pointless amber on the *Rivals* column. Then add an 'overview' row (Figure 31.32). It tells us: for how many of the five survey questions did we score higher than our rivals? Fiji scores higher five times out of five, and overall, we beat rivals four times out of five.

Figure 31.32

Nos of times we beat rivals

	Average		Our units				
	ABC	Rivals	Chad	UK	Peru	Iran	Fiji
	4	na	-	3	4	1	5

However, there's more:

Transpose the table. We'd expect, say, *Good tea* scores to be similar across units, yet the *before* shows them in rows. Put in columns instead.

Create not one big table, but lots of little ones. We must mentally reorder the *before* to see who's top and bottom. Instead, create several little tables, each in descending order.

Figure 31.33

Some lead-in summary comment
Scores from benchmarking exercise, November 2015, by Pat Miggins

Lorem ipsum est gloriatur expetendis an. Congue conten tiones conseq uuntur et eos, autem vocibus in nam. Agam conceptam mel cu, eum et porro recte que interesset. Ex ius idque corrumpit democritum, ad sit. Congue conten tiones consequuntur et eos, autem vocibus in nam. Agam conc eptam mel cu, eum et porro recte que interesset. Ex ius idque corru mpit democritum, ad sit.

1 Summary stats

Fig 1		Fig 2		Fig 3		Fig 4	
Overall %		How often > rivals		Returns (Nos)		Response %	
Peru	83	Fiji	5	Rivals	4,000	Peru	96
Fiji	79	**ABC**	4	**ABC**	343	Iran	95
ABC	75	Peru	4	Chad	120	UK	91
UK	74	UK	3	UK	115	**ABC**	89
Rivals	74	Iran	1	Fiji	69	Chad	89
Chad	70	Chad	-	Peru	24	Fiji	83
Iran	69			Iran	18	Rivals	72

2 Results by question (%)

Grouped according to rival versus our overall score

Fig 5		Fig 6				Fig 7			
2% worse		**1% better**				**2% better**			
Feel loved		Fancy PC		Good tea		Few emails		Long hols	
Fiji	73	Peru	99	Fiji	90	Peru	94	Peru	74
UK	71	Iran	96	UK	84	Fiji	85	Fiji	54
Peru	71	Fiji	95	**ABC**	81	UK	82	**ABC**	51
Rivals	70	**ABC**	94	**Rivals**	80	**ABC**	82	Rivals	49
ABC	68	**Rivals**	93	Chad	80	**Rivals**	80	UK	44
Chad	66	UK	91	Peru	78	Chad	78	Iran	43
Iran	61	Chad	88	Iran	74	Iran	72	Chad	40

What the figures represent
Eu sit cetero appareat accusata. Per et dicam tempor praesent, eripuit nonu nmy volumus cu sea. Per tantas altera prae sentin, nam assum rect eque dispu tationi ut. Te nom inavi des runt qui, eum choro blandit consec tetuer.

How the stats are shown
Mea ne elitiusto. Id corpora salutatus usu, eirmod animal eu est. No natum eri puit lobortis sit, vel lucilius ex pet endis cu, ei possit persequeris mel. Eum lupt atum contentiones cu, eu mei fabe llas fab ellas mediocritatem.

Page 1 of 1

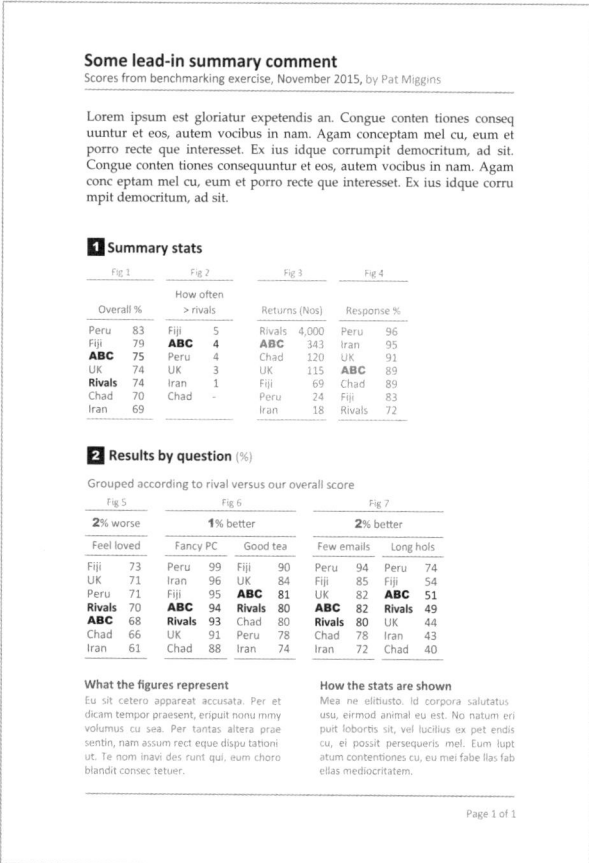

Give a lead-in title. Also, explain what the survey is about and what the page shows, albeit maybe grey it down. People might know it already.

Result: Figure 31.33 (the *after*). It has seven tables, each in descending order. Each highlights our and our rivals' scores so that readers easily see them. At the bottom, words give background context ('What the figures represent', and 'How the stats are shown'). The tables are numbered (Fig 1, Fig 2, etc), so we can more easily refer to them. Study Figures 5 to 7 (see what I mean?) – they're grouped and ordered according to how we've done. Figure 5 is where our overall score is two points worse than our rivals'. Figure 6 is where we're one point better than them, etc. In other words, we not only put rows in order, we put tables in order too.

Figures 3 and 4 are survey stats (returns, response rate). They're within the summary, yet greyed down. It seems contradictory – to highlight and de-emphasise at the same time. However, people are cynical of dodgy surveys based on tiny sample sizes that skew numbers ("80% of people said our shampoo thickened their hair!" screams the ad, and the small print says: "Sample size: 10"). So the survey stats are near the top to reassure readers. However, once reassured, such stats aren't critical. So I grey them down.

The *after* has lots on it. Is that a problem? To answer that, look back at the *before*. In effect it says to readers: "It's not sorted or summarised… work it out yourselves". The *after* is designed to draw readers in. They can easily engage with both its summary and its detail.

However, our redo assumes we can reorder rows and columns. Sometimes we can't. Assume bosses want to see income for each of four products

Figure 31.34

	A	B	C	D
Jan	214	148	130	86
Feb	200	141	130	78
Mar	210	163	132	68
Apr	200	166	118	73
May	199	153	129	71
Jun	202	169	123	69
Jul	205	153	113	86
Aug	216	163	127	88
Sep	216	155	117	75
Oct	210	150	137	65
Nov	198	164	112	87
Dec	198	151	119	73

for each of the past 12 months (I often see such reports, yet wonder why bosses care about what happened 9 months ago). Assume bosses don't want *total* figures, but insist on colour coding: red if a number is more than 5% from budget, amber within 5%, green if on budget (Figure 31.34).

It doesn't work (and that's not because it's in black-and-white – it doesn't work in colour either). Typography overwhelms and obscures detail. But what to do instead? We can't reorder rows and put all *red* months together, all *amber* together, etc – rows are in month order and must stay that way. Instead, try Figure 31.35. Colour codes are gone. Instead, what was green is now grey, and what was red is now Arial Black. Key numbers pop from the page, no longer hidden by intrusive typography. Less important numbers – ones that are fine – are de-emphasised.

One small typographical point. Arial Black comes out bigger, so I did its numbers in a font half a point smaller than the rest of the table.

In this section, we looked at a heat map of a benchmarking survey, and indulged in two bits of table trickery: (1) greyed down numbers; (2) put tables in strict numerical descending order. In the next two sections, we look further at surveys and benchmarking – and see those two bits of trickery in action again. Let's start with surveys.

Figure 31.35

	A	B	C	D
Jan	214	**148**	130	86
Feb	200	**141**	130	78
Mar	210	163	132	**68**
Apr	200	166	**118**	73
May	**199**	153	129	71
Jun	202	169	123	**69**
Jul	205	153	**113**	86
Aug	216	163	127	88
Sep	216	155	**117**	75
Oct	210	150	137	**65**
Nov	**198**	164	**112**	87
Dec	**198**	151	**119**	73

Showing survey findings

Our firm has five levels of staff: boss (grade A) down to dogsbody (grade E) – and for simplicity, assume there are equal numbers of staff in each grade. They anonymously tell us how happy they feel. A score of 100 means ecstatic, and 1 means suicidal. Figure 31.36 shows results by grade for the last 12 months. It has average rows and columns too. Study the formats – low scores are prominent, high scores less so. Readers more easily see key numbers and patterns, e.g. June and July were bad.

Notice that columns A to E aren't in order of, say, the average score for the year, i.e. column C first, and column D last. Rather, it's in order of grade – A to E. But didn't Chapter 4 (*Tables*) discourage alphabetical order, no? Yes, but here it's fine, for it's also order of seniority. We more easily see patterns by grade.

Maybe graphs would be better? Not with these data sets – Figure 31.37 plots four of them, and because scores move a lot from one month to the next, they're spikey and confusing.

Figure 31.38 (overleaf) also greys down numbers. In our survey, staff not only told us their grade, they gave their age too, so the table cross-tabulates the December results (*very* few internal staff surveys cross-tabulate, but they should, for it gives extra insight).

Figure 31.36

%	Avge	A	B	C	D	E
Jan	65	46	53	67	90	70
Feb	68	54	89	93	46	58
Mar	54	**28**	66	73	**32**	71
Apr	37	**21**	**12**	95	**14**	42
May	41	35	36	**24**	48	62
Jun	**27**	38	**12**	**12**	70	**3**
Jul	**28**	35	**19**	**3**	**20**	64
Aug	66	64	64	89	**25**	90
Sep	77	97	76	99	78	34
Oct	51	76	85	56	**16**	**23**
Nov	70	63	82	98	**29**	80
Dec	50	44	50	61	95	**1**
Avge	53	50	54	64	47	50

Figure 31.37

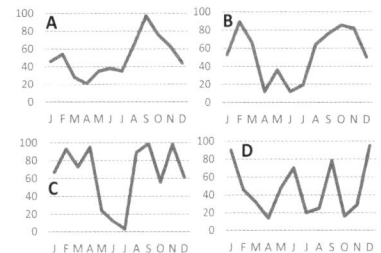

Figure 31.38

Happy?	Avrge	Age range (years)			
		18 - 30	30 - 45	45 - 60	60+
	%	%	%	%	%
Boss	44	90	65	20	1
Manager	50	48	52	54	46
Senior	61	65	33	65	82
Trainee	95	95	95	95	95
Dogsbody	1	1	1	1	1
Average	50	60	49	47	45

Figure 31.39 🖳

	Avrge score	Strongly agree	Agree	Neutral	Dis- agree	Strongly disagree
Max 5, min 1		%	%	%	%	%
Quality	4.5	62	34	3	1	-
Service	4.1	29	59	9	2	1
Adverts	4.0	22	59	19	-	-
Location	3.8	36	25	34	2	3
Website	3.7	3	42	51	3	1
Display	3.7	3	82	12	3	-
Price	3.4	9	47	29	12	3
Range	3.1	5	52	36	4	3
Average	3.8	21	50	24	3	1

Figure 31.40

Don't average averages

I see this a lot... imagine that unit A employs one person who is 100% happy, and unit B employs 99 people who are 0% happy. A's average is 100%, B's 0% – but overall average isn't 50% (the average of 0% and 100%). It's 1%, the weighted average.

Figure 31.41

Fees £m

Fees – growth in year %

Yes, happiness is 50% on average (see bottom left of Figure 31.38), but look – bosses become unhappier with age. Old bosses are suicidal. As are all dogsbodies. Senior staff suffer a mid-life crisis between 30 and 45 years. And trainees are a cheerful lot. Insight. Of course, correlation doesn't mean causation, but it gets grey cells ticking.

Figure 31.39 has findings from a different survey. We asked clients to comment on eight areas (Quality, Service, etc) based on a so-called Likert scale ("Quality is great – do you: (1) strongly disagree?" through to "(5) Strongly agree?"). And again, by greying down stuff, key numbers pop from the page. Notice that good ones pop out, unlike in the previous example in which bad ones pop out. Is this preferable? Your call – is your glass half empty or half full?

The first column of Figure 31.39 shows averages (and if we've historic data, we could also compare to last time or last year). Strictly speaking, averages are statistically invalid for Likert scales, so maybe avoid them for professional publicly-available surveys. However, do them for simple internal staff surveys where 'roughly right' is fine. Also, please don't average the averages. Figure 31.40 explains.

Benchmarking (or: lots of tables)

Imagine we have data for us and 13 competitors. Fees. Fees growth. Profit margin. Etc. People often convey it all in charts (Figure 31.41 has two). OK, they're neat. Compact. But they don't work. We glance at them, but don't engage with them. With graphs, less is more. The more graphs we do, the less impact they have. It's negative marginal returns. None make an impact. Do just one graph though, and it stands out. We notice it.

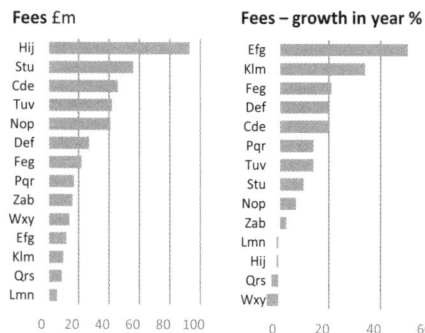

So maybe we should do one graph. Perhaps a logo chart. But with 14 companies, logos would overlap too much, hindering readability. Also, people often want numbers. Perhaps we could put numbers astride the columns in Figure 31.41, but that's just a badly laid-out table. Instead, try Figure 31.42 (the *before*). A well laid-out table. Notice how its three *percentage* columns are labelled. One has a % by the numbers, one has a % once above them, and one (the far right column) has a % by just the top and bottom numbers. Which is better? A close call. If a table is a mix of numbers (£, %, nos, etc), I prefer a % alongside each number – it helps remove doubt as to what the column shows. But if I've lots on my page, I put a % by just the top and bottom numbers. Less typography.

Notice that numbers for a company are on a row. Sounds good. Read the *Nop* row (our company) – fees are £41m, up 7%, and fees per person are £204k, etc. But now we've a problem. When we see growth is 7%, we ask ourselves: "How does that compare to others?" So we reorder the *Growth* column. In our head. Tricky. And to see how our (3%) margin compares, we reorder that column too.

Instead, try Figure 31.43 (the *after*). Each column of numbers is in descending order. OK, there's more typography – company names appear five times. But we engage with it more. We instantly grasp the significance of a number because we see where it is within the distribution. Also, our numbers are easy to spot, for our company's name is in a distinctive font – which is what we did with our heat map redo two sections earlier.

Let's summarise. When benchmarking, don't do one big table with row labels shown just once (Figure 31.42 – the *before*). Instead, do several smaller tables, each in numerical descending order (Figure 31.43 – the *after*). But… is this right though? It adds typography. Also, yes, we can find our firm (Nop) easily enough, for it stands out. But what if it's a table not of competitors, but of the 14 units in our group? We can't highlight a unit. Also, each unit's boss wants to see their unit's numbers, yet the *after* makes them hunt for them. Maybe the *before* is better, given that a unit's numbers are all on one row. No, for bosses still ask themselves: "How do we compare?" So retain descending order for each column. OK, finding a firm's numbers takes a little longer, but as Chapter 4 explains, the benefit of grasping numbers a lot more quickly far outweighs the benefit of finding numbers a little more quickly.

Anyway, it doesn't take long to find stuff. In the *after*, search for, say, Pqr. It takes just seconds – and in so doing, we get insight. In the first two columns, Pqr is near the middle. In the next two, it's near the top, and in the fifth, it's back in the middle. We get a feel for how it's doing.

Or we would if *up* is always good. It is for the first four columns, but not the fifth. High staff turnover is bad. To aid comparability, show staff turnover in ascending order. Or show staff retention in descending order. Either way, KLM would be bottom and Wxy top.

What if we've 140 units? If each column is in descending order, it's tough to find our unit's numbers amongst them all. Yes, but mentally reordering

Figure 31.42

	This year	Growth in year	Per person	Margin	Staff t'over
	£m	%	£k		%
Hij	93	(1%)	98	21	22%
Stu	56	10%	85	9	18
Cde	46	20%	107	16	18
Tuv	42	14%	145	6	21
Nop	41	7%	204	(3)	12
Def	27	20%	77	12	9
Feg	22	21%	108	5	26
Pqr	17	14%	174	17	15
Zab	16	3%	125	(5)	6
Wxy	14	(5%)	103	8	5
Efg	12	51%	117	13	35
Klm	10	34%	112	17	47
Qrs	9	(3%)	88	(4)	14
Lmn	6	(1%)	126	8	16%

Figure 31.43

	This year		Growth in year		Per person		Margin		Staff turnover
A	B	C	D	E	F	G	H	I	J
Hij	£93m	Efg	51%	Nop	£204k	Hij	21%	Klm	47%
Stu	56	Klm	34	Pqr	174	Klm	17	Efg	35
Cde	46	Feg	21	Tuv	145	Pqr	17	Feg	26
Tuv	42	Cde	20	Lmn	126	Cde	16	Hij	22
Nop	41	Def	20	Zab	125	Efg	13	Tuv	21
Def	27	Tuv	14	Efg	117	Def	12	Stu	18
Feg	22	Pqr	14	Klm	112	Stu	9	Cde	18
Pqr	17	Stu	14	Feg	108	Lmn	8	Lmn	16
Zab	16	Nop	7	Cde	107	Wxy	8	Pqr	15
Wxy	14	Zab	3	Wxy	103	Tuv	6	Qrs	14
Efg	12	Hij	(1)	Hij	98	Feg	5	Nop	12
Klm	10	Lmn	(1)	Qrs	88	Nop	(3)	Def	9
Qrs	9	Qrs	(3)	Stu	85	Qrs	(4)	Zab	6
Lmn	£6m	Wxy	(5)%	Def	£77k	Zab	(5)%	Wxy	5%

140 units is far tougher. Perhaps we do the table in alphabetical order (so it's easy to find our unit), then to give context, we add summary stats to the top of each column (top, bottom, average, median, etc). But our eyes must constantly flick back and forth from unit row to summary row. Also, we struggle to spot clusters within it all – maybe we want to study all loss-making units.

So instead, retain descending order for all columns, then do what Chapter 4 suggests for school tables: have a second table in alphabetical order that gives each unit's position for the five data sets ("ABC: 67, 83, 26, 12, 54", i.e. ABC is 67th in Fees, 83rd in Growth, etc). ABC's boss quickly underlines its numbers in the main table, then settles down and compares. Alternatively, let technology help – the boss pings the report on screen, then searches for *ABC*. They're instantly highlighted.

Finally, apply this tip intelligently, not slavishly. Don't reorder all columns of all tables in strict descending order. In sports league tables, only one column is in order – the points to date. That's because it has primacy. And in Figure 31.44, we want to see how costs change over time, and are less interested in how one cost compares to others. So retain the same row order throughout the table. (Having said that, maybe transpose it.) Also, in Figure 31.45 we want to see how each cost compares to budget. Again, retain the same row order throughout the table.

Tables need lead-in titles though

What should we write and where should we put it? It depends on how much we wish to write for each table. If it's just a brief sentence of two, maybe put it under each table (Figure 31.46 (two tables only)); I added a bit of space between the tables to give room for the words. But if we want to write a bit more – say a paragraph or two for each table – we could do a sort of WiT – tables on left, words on right. We see one in Chapter 33 (it's Figure 33.29).

And if we wish to write lots – half a page or more for each – then it's not a benchmarking page. It's a benchmarking report. Say, ten pages long. So do a different section for each table – each section would be between half and one page long. Then at the back in Appendix 1 of our report, put a big master table, like Figure 31.43 that we saw earlier. And its lead-in title? Simple. "There is no summary comment to this table. Rather, it's for your own reference and interest". It removes any ambiguity that readers might have.

Final Thoughts are soon. Before then, we address some more myths that arise on the topic of signalling performance.

Figure 31.44

£	2015	2016	2017
Staff	850	904	956
Travel	894	872	926
Drinks	801	749	773
Rent	846	822	767
Rates	779	790	739
Post	744	708	734
Rates	723	674	649
Tax	617	604	646
Fines	515	489	456

Figure 31.45

£	Act	Bdgt	Fav/ (adv)
Staff	81	75	(6)
Travel	74	76	2
Drinks	71	70	(1)
Rent	69	68	(1)
Rates	65	62	(3)
Phone	60	63	3
Post	57	61	4
Rates	51	53	2
Tax	44	43	(1)
Fines	39	37	(2)

Figure 31.46

This year		Growth	
A	B	C	D
Hij	£93m	Efg	51%
Stu	56	Klm	34
Cde	46	Feg	21
Tuv	42	Cde	20
Nop	41	Def	20
Def	27	Tuv	14
Feg	22	Pqr	14
Pqr	17	Stu	10
Zab	16	**Nop**	7
Wxy	14	Zab	3
Efg	12	Hij	(1)
Klm	10	Lmn	(1)
Qrs	9	Qrs	(3)
Lmn	£6m	Wxy	(5)%

Alas, poor Yorick! I knew him, Horatio: a fellow of infinite jest...

Of most excellent fancy. He hath borne me on his back a thousand times.

The myths

The *Graphs* and *Visuals* Chapters addressed many myths relevant to RAGs and icons, e.g. "We engage with visuals"; "Numbers are dull". Let's address two more: (1) we like to grasp information visually, not numerically; and (2) jet pilots and racing drivers use RAGs. Hmmm. We like to grasp information visually, not numerically eh? Think about radios, thermometers, watches, car speedometers, kitchen and bathroom scales, etc. In days gone by, they were visual (dials, rising mercury, etc), but are now digital. *Numerical*. Surely someone should let their manufacturers know they're doing it wrong.

No. In reports, speedometers don't help, they hinder. They take a lot of space to show very little, and are even more patronising than smiley faces.

"But," people counter, "jet pilots and racing drivers have RAG displays on their dashboards." And, yes, these displays help when we must see if we're seconds from disaster. Such as when oil gushes from cars. Or heat-seeking missiles lock onto fighter planes. Or stockbrokers' screens go red during market crashes. Or Homer Simpson spots a nuclear meltdown. Each requires instant action. Don't worry about details, just *act*. Stop car. Hit eject button. Sell shares. Evacuate plant. NOW. Also, to ensure we spot the problem, the dashboard flashes repeatedly and emits beeping sounds.

A bit like real-life traffic lights. When drivers see the lights go red, they hit the brake. No more info needed. Pedestrians also hear a beeping noise that tells them it's safe to cross.

OK, let's apply this to RAG updates. Are they on topics that show if we're seconds from disaster? Or in reports that take days to prepare? And which people don't read for another day? Also, when bosses see our red icon, do they simply hit the eject button or whatever it is they're primed to do? If our reports are to highlight if we're seconds from disaster and hence prompt us into instant action, then do a RAG. But also add flashing lights and a loud beeping noise too.

Time for Final Thoughts. Here's a question: when I show good and bad ways to do stuff, do I use coloured rectangles? Smiling faces? Arrows? No. And you'd think it crazy if I did.

☺☺☺☺☺***** | **That's an interesting thought on which to end.**

32

Other diagrams

Figure 32.1

Figure 32.1

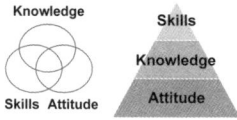

This Chapter looks at a sundry mix of business diagrams. Such as flowcharts. Decision trees – trees are great, so please read. Organisation charts. And 'builds' – in talks, people often show, say, a flowchart that builds bit by bit to the final picture; so we look at them too. Obviously, we don't look at stuff reviewed in other Chapters, e.g. graphs or autoshapes (Figure 32.1). First up are flowcharts.

Figure 32.2

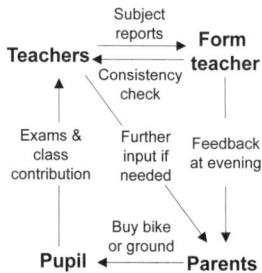

Flowcharts

To explain a parent–teachers' evening to a 9-year-old, we might say: "Your form teacher tells us about your exams and class contribution. He or she finds this out from your other teachers and ensures their comments are consistent. We might speak to these other teachers too. If you're doing well, we buy you a bike. If not, we ground you". That is, we use words.

At work though, people do flowcharts (Figure 32.2). OK, this one is visually elegant – for instance, no unnecessary boxes around words – but like many flowcharts, it suffers from problems. Firstly, where does it start? Where do our eyes go when we first alight on it? Tricky to say, for it's circular.

Figure 32.3

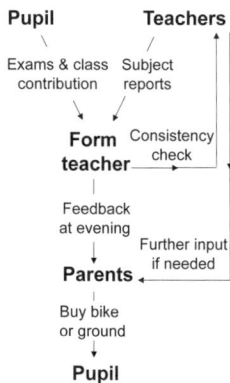

Figure 32.3 remedies this. Not circular. Readers start at the top and go down. OK, I could snake an arrow from *Parents* back up to the top *Pupil* and shove the words *Buy bike or ground* alongside it, but I want the chart to finish with the pupil. It ends with the pupil. Literally and metaphorically.

But it still has a huge problem: hardly any verbs (*buy* and *ground* being notable exceptions). It's like Figure 32.4 – what does it say? That Head Office recharges costs to subsidiaries? Or reimburses subsidiaries' costs? Who knows? Most flowcharts need verbs to make sense... even to the person who created them. Someone once told me: "I did that chart six months ago, and looking at it now, I don't know what it says". Rather telling, really.

Of course, not all flowcharts need verbs. The London Tube map doesn't – but that's because it shows just train stations, so the only verb we might add is *Travel*. Not needed. At work though, flowcharts usually comprise several different parts. They show, say, companies. Committees. Documents. And so on. There are many possible verbs that might apply to each, e.g. to *Document*, the verb could be *write, edit, circulate, read, discuss*, etc.

Figure 32.4

So too with the parent–teachers flowchart. But then again, the chart is all a bit unnecessary anyway. We don't need it. Words are fine instead ("Your form teacher tells us about your exams etc"). Words present the information sequentially. After all, even a 9-year-old understands them.

Sometimes words don't work though. Figure 32.5 (the *before*) shows too much to explain in words (and it really existed). It shows who pays whom in an insurance transaction – and fear not that its words are small, for Figure 32.6 is a labelled version (the *labelled before*). Below, I talk through its hatched area, big letters, and shaded shapes.

Figure 32.5

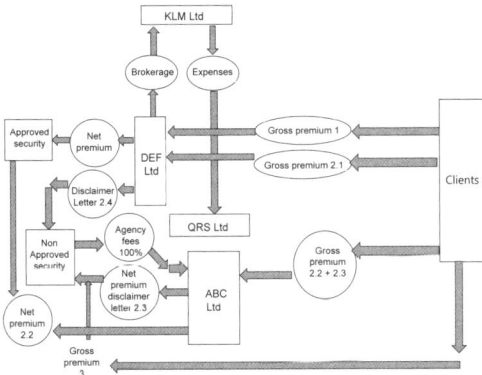

Figure 32.6

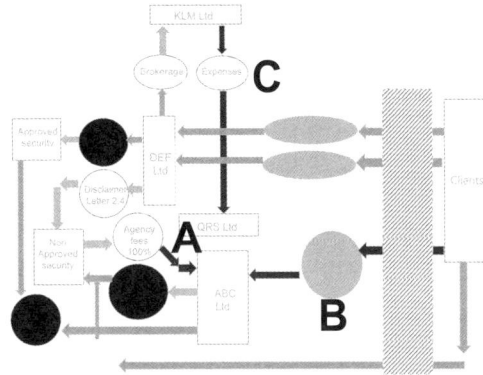

Figure 32.7 is the *after*. Much better. Firstly, it groups items – in the *labelled before*, grey ovals are gross premium, black ovals are net premium, and they're all over the place. The *after* groups them – study the headings along the top: Gross premium, Net premium, Security. Everything under a heading relates to that heading. Because the *after* uses its physical space effectively, we more quickly grasp it all. Also, by grouping items, we avoid intersecting lines. The *before* has three intersects; the *after*, none. Don't get me wrong though – I'm not against intersects. Tube maps have lots. Rather, I'm against unnecessary intersects.

Figure 32.7

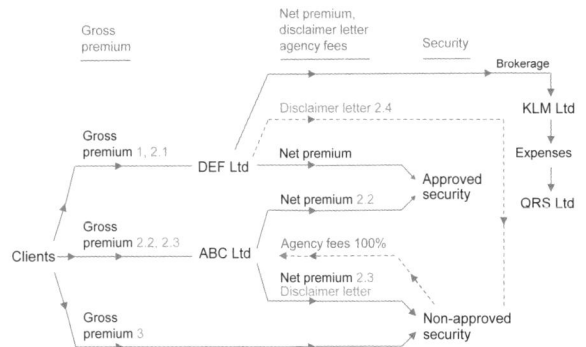

Grouping items is akin to clustering bullets (good items in one list, bad in another) and it really helps. But often it's not done. That's because, when people create flowcharts, they confuse documenting with clarifying. They believe that if a chart shows the flows completely and correctly, then the job is done, even if it's like a Jackson Pollock painting. They believe they've conveyed the flows. No. Don't just document. Document clearly.

Which means elegantly too. To that end, the *after* makes other changes:

Figure 32.8

Kinked   Weird

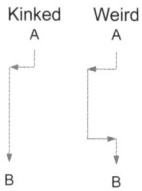

It straightens lines	Point A of the *labelled before* has a kink; the *after* avoids it. I once saw a flowchart on how to do flowcharts, and – ironically – it had several unnecessary kinks, such as those in Figure 32.8.
It keeps lines short – result: it's compact and easy to scan	In the *labelled before*, we can slice out everything in its hatched box, and so shorten lines. This tip is similar to Step 3 for decent tables: "Make compact".
It aligns stuff	At point B of the *labelled before*, arrows either side of the oval don't align. Untidy.
It strives for symmetry and that looks smart	In the *after*, study the lines on the far left – the upward-sloping line is at the same angle as the downward-sloping one.
It avoids clutter	The *after* greys down lines and avoids large arrows. Also, it avoids boxes and ovals around words.

This last point – boxes and ovals – needs further comment. Systems departments create huge flowcharts replete with icons that denote type, e.g. 🗋 around a word if it's a document, ◇ if an action. OK, such charts are to document, not convey. Rigorously and completely. But why not elegantly too? Dispense with icons and use typography instead, e.g. **Arial Black** for invoice and *italic* for payment. It's less clutter. Or try reversed fonts (dark or light), and maybe <u>underlines</u> (albeit only as a last resort). Try to avoid colour codes though, they mean nothing if printed in black and white.

Next we look at decision trees. Before then, we've two last points. Firstly, the top right of the *after* says: KLM Ltd ➔ Expenses ➔ QRS Ltd. No verb?!? The *before* had no verb either (point C). I don't know what verb to add, so didn't add one. Secondly, the text box has more on intersecting lines.

Figure 32.9

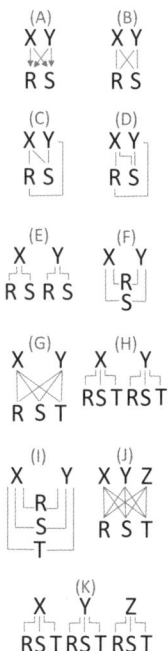

Avoiding intersects – and the 'three utilities' problem

Study Figure 32.9. (A) is the last bit of a bigger flowchart and it shows that X and Y both finish by going to R and S – and (B) shows it again, but without arrows. They aren't significant to the points in this text box, so let's remove them and focus on intersects. And we have one in (B). Layout (C) avoids this, it takes one line on a longer journey – Y joins R by snaking round the outside. However, the X–S line is at 45%, and maybe we prefer right angles. So see (D). But it's asymmetric, so try (E). No intersects. No snaking lines. Just symmetrical right angles. Repetitive though – R and S appear twice. In which case, what about (F)? It stacks S under R. We've symmetry. Right angles. No repetition. Neat.

What if X and Y lead to three outcomes (R, S, T)? Layout (G) is criss-crossing, (H) is the repeating approach (pretty good) and (I) is the stacking approach (neat – no asymmetry, intersects, or repeating labels).

Finally, what if we've 'three to three', i.e. (J) – X, Y, Z to R, S, T? We must then compromise. We can choose intersects but no repetition (J). Or repetition but no intersects (K). But – even if we stack them – we can't avoid both intersects and repetition. It's not possible. (If unconvinced, Google the *three utilities problem*, it's on how to connect gas, water, electricity to three houses without pipes crossing and in two dimensions only.) All we can do is intersect elegantly – and keep lines short, symmetrical, nonintrusive, etc.

Decision trees

Figure 32.10 is a tree from *Diagrams*, a book published in 1969 which I mentioned in Chapter 14. The tree shows pension entitlement, and I've retained its original typography – I explain why later. By answering *Yes* or *No* at each stage of the tree, readers go through successive stages to find their answer. Notice there are only two outcomes (*Pension, No pension*), yet eight end-points (four *Pension*, four *No pension*). No matter. Readers follow the path that suits them, reading only what's relevant to them. They aren't even aware of the repetition.

Trees are great, yet few people do them. Many more should. I did one at a company I'd recently joined and the Group CEO loved it. It made my reputation. This may sound odd – surely trees are for admin. They help us with passport applications. They show us when we can get a pension. They guide us on how to get our investment approved ("Is it a big or small amount?"). Administrative.

Not always. Imagine a CEO can't decide what to do with a non-core subsidiary that's a marginal player in its industry: flog it; hang onto it, but let it carry on unchanged; or give it money to make a big acquisition so it becomes market leader. For simplicity, assume the CEO is new and doesn't care if there's a big loss on disposal: it can be blamed on the previous CEO. (This allows us not to worry about the timing of the disposal – flog now or in a year?) Figure 32.11 puts the issues in order. The CEO and board can clearly see how different assumptions lead to different outcomes. They see tipping points, the points at which decisions hinge. The tree *simplifies*.

Figure 32.10

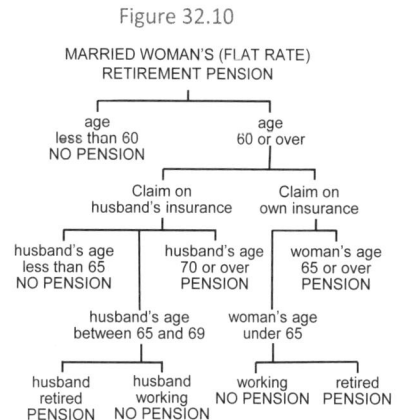

Figure 32.11

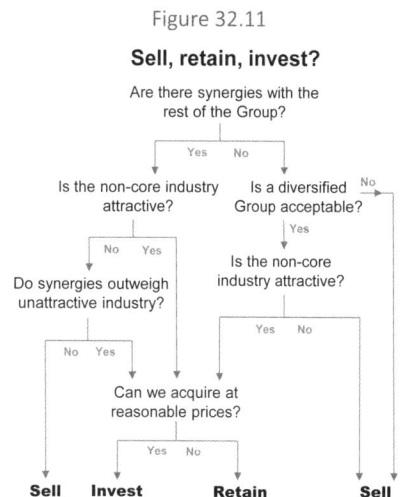

Figure 32.12

Sell, retain or invest?

If we believe a diversified group is acceptable, and if the industry is unattractive, we sell.

If we believe a diversified group is acceptable and if the industry is attractive, we retain the subsidiary – or even invest in it if we can acquire similar companies at reasonable prices.

If we believe there are synergies and if the industry is unattractive, we sell the subsidiary if synergies don't compensate for the unattractiveness of the industry.

Conversely if the industry is unattractive but synergies more than compensate for this unattractiveness, we retain the subsidiary – or even invest in it if we can acquire similar companies at reasonable prices. (Are you still with me?)

If we believe there are synergies and if the industry is attractive, then we retain the subsidiary – or even invest in it if we can acquire similar companies at reasonable prices. (Almost there.)

Finally, we sell the non-core subsidiary if we believe a diversified group is not acceptable, even if the industry is attractive. (Phew, made it.)

If unconvinced, Figure 32.12 shows it in words. Dense, repetitive, confusing, and a huge strain on short-term memory. Readers struggle to follow its endless twists and turns ("If this, then that; if that, then the other"), and may misinterpret its tortuous text as underdeveloped thinking. After all, poor writing often shows poor thinking, and Figure 32.12 seems poorly written. It isn't. Rather, it's the wrong tool for the job. It should be a tree.

However, often bosses get neither tree nor text, but lists. Of 'key issues' (Figure 32.13). And yes, the list might at first impress, it seems simple to grasp ("Gosh, this entire topic, distilled to just 33 words!"). But when bosses discuss it, they quickly realise it's half-baked. It doesn't identify the hierarchy of issues or relate them to outcomes. For instance, if a diversified Group is unacceptable and there aren't synergies, bosses should sell the subsidiary regardless of points 3 and 4 in the list. The list doesn't identify trade-offs either. For instance, do synergies compensate for industry attractiveness? The list is lazy thinking and says to bosses: "Work it out yourselves".

Compare that to the tree: to create it, analysts must grapple properly with issues. What hierarchies? What trade-offs? What outcomes? Which means bosses needn't grapple with them. They spend less time grappling and more time discussing from a position of understanding. Trees *clarify*.

However, some people fear that trees are a sign of indecision. "Isn't it better," people say, "to dispense with a tree of options and instead state a recommendation?" No. Often, the 'best' outcome depends on each individual's values and beliefs. Do they believe there's synergy? Do they believe a diversified group is acceptable? Etc. Often, an analyst doesn't know each boss's values and beliefs – and there isn't consensus anyway. Some bosses think there's synergy, some don't. Some think diversification is bad, some don't. An analyst can't give one recommendation.

Which is why trees are so great – they work for all bosses. They don't give an answer. They give the answers. They aren't underdeveloped thinking. They're exceedingly well-developed thinking, for they think through *everything*. They identify issues, then ask questions in the right order, and for each set of answers, they identify the outcome. They then give the information clearly in a way that's easy to refer to and which doesn't put a strain on short-term memory. They enable everyone to quickly establish the course of action that fits their own assumptions. Which means they cover analysts' backsides far better than giving just one recommendation – no matter what values and beliefs each boss holds, the tree has it covered.

However, there's more: trees crystallise bosses' thinking. To understand why, step back. At home, we *like* something – be it a car, holiday, computer, etc – but often aren't consciously aware why we like it. We just like it. And we don't even think about the assumptions implicit within our preferred choice. So too at work. Often, bosses like a particular course of action, yet might not explicitly know why, nor appreciate the assumptions that subconsciously underpin that preference.

A tree changes that. Bosses see it and ponder: "OK… I feel we should sell the non-core subsidiary – so, as the tree shows, I seemingly assume that synergies don't outweigh industry unattractiveness… but do I really believe that?" The tree is akin to a counselling session – it stress-tests people's assumptions, ones that are often subconscious. Which is *great*.

It's not all good news though

Firstly, in tests, people with an average age of 71 years struggled with trees[1]. Secondly, some people will criticise your trees: "It doesn't mention the subsidiary's great products and IT". Sometimes, such criticisms are valid – after all, whether we retain or sell a subsidiary partly depends on whether it's well run or a basket-case. But to clarify, we must simplify. For bosses to clearly see issues, we assume the subsidiary is doing as well as it could do – and if I were the analyst, I'd tell bosses this assumption. It helps define the agenda, plus explains why the tree doesn't talk about products, IT and so on.

Regardless, some people will still criticise it. "It oversimplifies," they say, "it ignores this, that, the other". But don't pander to complainers by attempting an all-encompassing tree. Firstly, we'll never keep them happy, they'll always find something that's missing ("What about the trainee who just resigned?"). Secondly, our tree becomes so large, we kill the golden goose. By showing everything, we show nothing. It overcomplicates.

Anyway, complainers often object to a tree *because* it's clear. They've agendas to pursue, ones that won't survive close scrutiny, so they undermine anything that shines a light too clearly on issues. Such as a tree. They prefer bulleted lists that help them obfuscate and scrape through duff decisions.

When to do trees

People don't do trees when they should. Analysts don't. As we saw above, they do lists. Governments don't. The *pension* tree that we saw above was created by two doctors to show how text in government pamphlets can be replaced by a diagram. Figure 32.14 shows the text. Tough. And governments seemingly still haven't learnt the lesson. In a recently published book on tax rules, there was a great tree – but it was done not by the government, but by the book's author (Jonquil Lowe) to help us make sense of the rules.

Here's when to do a tree: do one if your text has twists and turns that take readers in many different directions. Look for lots of *if*s ("If this, then that; if

Figure 32.13
Key issues
- Do we believe it acceptable to be diversified?
- Is there synergy between subsidiary and rest of Group?
- Is it in an attractive industry?
- Can we buy competitor companies at reasonable prices?

(1) From *Designing Instructional Text* by J. Hartley

Figure 32.14
The pension tree in words
The earliest age at which a woman can draw a retirement pension is 60. On her own insurance, she can get a pension when she reaches that age, if she has then retired from regular employment. Otherwise, she has to wait until she retires or reaches age 65. At age 65, pension can be paid irrespective of retirement. On her husband's insurance, however, she cannot get a pension, even though she is over 60, until he has reached age 65 and retired from regular employment, or until he is 70 if he does not retire before reaching that age.

Figure 32.15

Who do we let in?

"If you are the spouse or unmarried minor child of a person who has been granted preference classification by the Immigration and Naturalization Service or has applied for preference classification and you are claiming the preference classification, or if you are claiming special immigrant classification as the spouse or unmarried child of a minister of religion who has been accorded or is seeking classification as a special immigrant, submit the following...."

From *Designing Instructional* text by J. Hartley

Figure 32.16

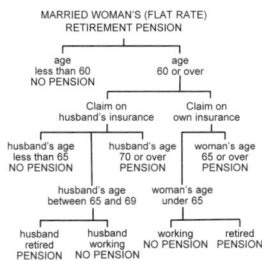

MARRIED WOMAN'S (FLAT RATE) RETIREMENT PENSION

Figure 32.17

Three of the tree's questions are paraphrased from Professor Michael Porter, strategy guru at Harvard Business School. He wrote about the "conditions under which diversification will truly create shareholder value". He calls them the better-off test, the attractiveness test, and the cost-of-entry test. I read about them in Chapter 12 of *Managing the Multibusiness Company*.

that, then the other"). Think back to the *non-core subsidiary* tree. In words, it has 15 *if*s, as we saw earlier in Figure 32.12.

The text version of the *pension* tree has only two *if*s. No worries. It has *or, however, otherwise*. Same difference. Such words arise when we're writing and don't have all the answers. Perhaps the answer differs for each individual. Are you over 65? Do you believe there are synergies? Do you like long or short walks? (This 'walk' question is from the UK Kennel Club and helps people decide which dog is right for them.) Are you claiming special immigrant classification as the spouse or unmarried child of a minister of religion who has been accorded or is seeking classification as a special immigrant? (Eh?!?) This one's on an old form by the US Immigration and Naturalization Service – Figure 32.15 has more. It should be a tree.

Finally, do a tree if you're discussing an analyst's list of issues and you realise you're having to think through:

1. The **hierarchy**: some issues come first, some later.
2. The **trade-offs**: some issues help compensate for others.
3. The **outcomes**: how does each set of issues affect outcomes?

If you're having to work it all out, send the list back and ask the analyst to think it through properly. And to ensure they do a good tree, get them to visit my website. It has tips to ensure your trees are correct. For now, let's conclude by revisiting two trees and briefly looking at three new ones.

The *pension* tree's format, shown again, albeit smaller (Figure 32.16). Study its formats. Short straight lines. No boxed-in words. Compact. Symmetrical … in a manner of speaking. Study the two outcomes in its bottom left corner – they aren't centred along the line above them. Nor are the two outcomes, bottom right. Asymmetric. Yet the two left outcomes mirror the two right ones. Symmetry. OK, the tree uses upper case, but that aside, its format is superb. Especially given how long ago it was created.

The *non-core subsidiary* tree's logic. Some of its logic is from Professor Michael Porter, the strategy guru. Figure 32.17 explains.

Then there are trees with seemingly no branches. Such as on the website of the UK's pension regulator. Successive screens ask questions, e.g. "Are you employed, not employed, self-employed?". If we click *employed*, another screen asks us: "Apart from state pensions, do you have any pension arrangements?". And so on. Collectively, our answers determine the advice we get at the end. We're told we're being taken through a tree, but never see it in full, so aren't intimidated by a huge chart. Very effective.

What about the tree that my Group CEO loved? It wasn't the *non-core subsidiary* one, but was on an initiative to set up an industry-wide trading exchange: should our firm lead the initiative? Or follow someone else's? Or eschew it? Three possible routes, but which to do? Also, it was the year 2000, so the exchange was to be on this new gadget called the 'interweb' – and the world was grappling with how it would change things. My bosses were grappling too. Would it enrich us? Or bankrupt us? Each boss had different views, views underpinned by subconscious assumptions. The CEO asked me for the answer. My report said: "It depends... if this, then that. If that, then the other, etc." But in a tree. Real clarity. After that, the best jobs in the Group landed on my desk. I owe trees a lot.

Finally there's the movie *When Harry Met Sally*, when Meg Ryan orders pie:

Sally: But I'd like the pie heated and I don't want the ice cream on top, I want it on the side and I'd like strawberry instead of vanilla if you have it; if not, then no ice cream, just whipped cream – but only if it's real; if it's out of a can then nothing.

Waitress: Not even the pie?

Sally: No, just the pie, but then not heated.

Confusing. A shame, because Meg had incredibly well defined priorities, but conveyed them the wrong way. A tree would be better (Figure 32.18).

Figure 32.18

When Sally ordered pie

Organisation charts

Figure 32.19 is a typical org chart. It even parodies their poor alignment – on the bottom row, company names don't align. Figure 32.20 redoes it, albeit not top to bottom, but left to right. Group hierarchy is denoted by short grids on the left – ABC Holdings has one subsidiary, DEF, which in turn has four subsidiaries. This layout has room for more information. It shows percentage holdings (greyed down to de-emphasise), directors, notes (e.g. MNO's profit halved in 2015). Show more if you want, e.g. gross profit, EBITDA, etc. Your choice. Such detail might be too much for a slide, but it's great for reports.

Notice that Figure 32.20 follows the formatting tips we saw earlier. It avoids boxes around names, long lines, etc. Also, it's less repetitive than the conventional org chart: it states the word *Income* once, not six times. Then there's Figure 32.21 which shows the chart again, but with slightly different connecting lines. Which do you prefer?

Figure 32.19

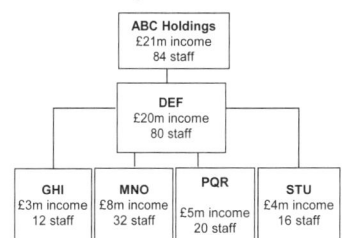

Figure 32.20

(X%) = shares held by Group	Stats		Directors			
	Income	Staff	L Green	P Blue	R Grey	Notes
	£m	Nos				
ABC Holdings	21	84	✓		✓	Registered in Dubai
DEF (100%)	20	80	✓	✓		£5m goodwill
MNO (100%)	8	32	✓	✓		Profit halved in 2015
PQR (80%)	5	20	✓	✓	✓	20% held by o/sider
STU (51%)	4	16	✓	✓		49% held by CEO
GHI (100%)	3	12	✓	✓	✓	Pension hole £10m

Figure 32.21

(X%) = shares held by Group	Stats		Directors			
	Income	Staff	L Green	P Blue	R Grey	Notes
	£m	Nos				
ABC Holdings	21	84	✓		✓	Registered in Dubai
DEF (100%)	20	80	✓	✓		£5m goodwill
MNO (100%)	8	32	✓	✓		Profit halved in 2015
PQR (80%)	5	20	✓	✓	✓	20% held by o/sider
STU (51%)	4	16	✓	✓		49% held by CEO
GHI (100%)	3	12	✓	✓	✓	Pension hole £10m

Figure 32.22

```
Group
  UK and Eire
  Overseas
  Head Office

UK and Eire              Overseas                 Head office
  Solutions Ltd            Asia Pacific             Central
    Service                  Middle East              Central
                             Middle East              Projects
    Risks                    Israel                   Executive
      Financial
      Construction         Far East                 ISJFB
      Insurance              Hong Kong                ISJFB
      Textiles               Singapore                ISJFB UK
      Manufacturing          Asia Pacific             ISJFB ROW
      Breweries              Korea
                             China                  LR
    Banks                                             Romford
      Regional             Pacific Region             Basildon
      Global                 Australia
      Domestic                                      Finance
        North              Europe
        South                Northern Region        HR and payroll
                              Norway                   Payroll
    Sundry                    Finland                  Training
      Other 1                 Iceland                  HR - UK
      Other 2                 Sweden                   HR - ROW
                              Arctic circle
    Other                                            Property
                           Central, West              London
  Supermarkets               Italy                    Romford
    North                    Spain                    Basildon
    South                    Portugal                 Others
    East
    West                   East, CIS                Systems
      Bristol                Ukraine                  FX D2 R10
      Taunton                Latvia                   RS3Y V75
      Bath                   Russia                   Oscar Z20
      Stroud                 Turkey
      Truro                                          Comms
                           The Americas
  Property                   North America          BMS summary
    Manchester                San Fran                 BMS Acton
    Leeds                     Dallas                   BMS Fife
    Bristol                   New York                 Corporate
    Glasgow                   Chicago
                                                    Marketing
  Services Group             Central, LATAM
    Ford                       Brazil               Facilities
    Toyota                     Venezuela              Football
    Vauxhall                   Cuba                   Rugby
    Citroen                    Jamaica                Baseball
      RVPC                     Trinidad               Snooker
      Other                    Tobago                 Rugby
    Lexus                      Antigua                Skating
      HNW                      Chile                  Tennis
                               Peru                   Health
```

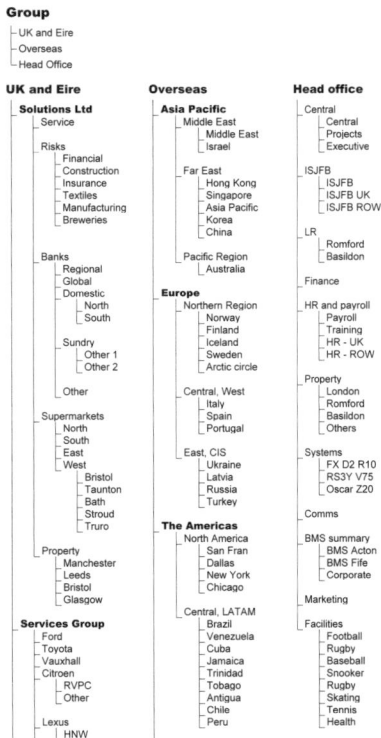

If you don't need extra richness, but want to show just hierarchy, this left-to-right layout is still better, especially if you have lots of entities. Figure 32.22 shows about two-thirds of a big org chart (the complete one has over 180 units spread over six reporting levels), and when printed on A4, the chart is readable, plus has space for more information if you want it. For instance, maybe write each unit's income after its name ("Textiles £1.5m"). Imagine trying to show all that on a conventional chart. I once saw someone try. He spread the chart over ten sheets of A4 – taped together – and at meetings would unfurl it like a tablecloth. Comic, really.

Three final thoughts on this left-to-right layout. Firstly, NATO uses it to show 194 units spread over seven levels of hierarchy – Google *NATO organization structure* to see it. Secondly, I once used it for a family tree. On a single page of A4, there were over 200 names going back to the year 1525. Finally, if the layout looks familiar, it is. It's how Outlook and Windows Explorer show file hierarchy.

Builds

Builds are where presenters reveal something bit by bit to control the pace at which delegates see it. For instance, presenters can talk through a complex flowchart or graph one bit at time before they finally reveal it all in the round. It's like the child's joke: how do you eat an elephant? One chunk at a time. Sounds good, but builds all too easily go bad:

They fragment and so hinder comparison	People wrongly use builds to *compare*. They show something changing over time, but show different versions sequentially, not side-by-side. Delegates struggle to compare.
They put a strain on short-term memory	People wrongly use builds to explain complex stuff that's made up of lots of bits. As we saw in Chapter 21, by the time we explain the last bit of it, everyone's forgotten the first bit. Instead, start with what people know, then move forward from there.
They drip-feed information and drive delegates nuts	People wrongly use builds to explain really simple stuff. It's akin to showing bullets one at a time: annoying. And really annoying if the builds animatedly zoom on screen.

When is it appropriate to use a build? Think back to the *Money flow* chart we saw earlier (Figures 32.23 and 32.24 show the *before* and *after* again, albeit now smaller). To explain it all, the *after* hardly needs a build, it's not complex. Rather, I'd use a build only if I want my delegates to focus on a particular bit – by temporarily removing parts of the whole, I help delegates concentrate on one particular area. As for the *before*, because it's so badly drawn, it's complex enough to warrant a build. A build visually strips apart its overlapping parts, and so aids understanding. In general, the more visual overlaps there are – and there are lots in the *before* – the more a build helps.

Figure 32.23

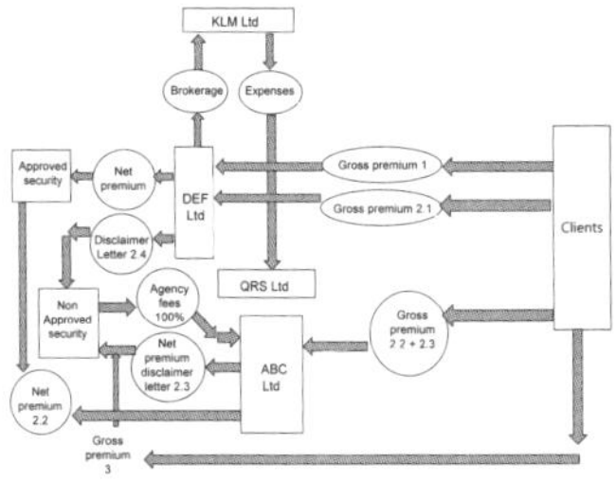

When building, grey down – or remove – the bits we've already shown. It helps delegates instantly see what's new when it appears on screen. Then show the whole thing together at the end.

Should we hand out all our builds or just our complete final picture? It depends on whether the complete picture is sufficient. Think of Lego instructions that build bit by bit to a complete picture – to construct the kit, people need the individual builds. The complete picture isn't sufficient. Then again, assume we're talking through the *Money flow* chart (the *after* version). Even if we decide to explain it to others via a series of builds, people don't need all our builds afterwards. The complete chart shows detail and overview in sufficient clarity to meet people's needs.

Figure 32.24

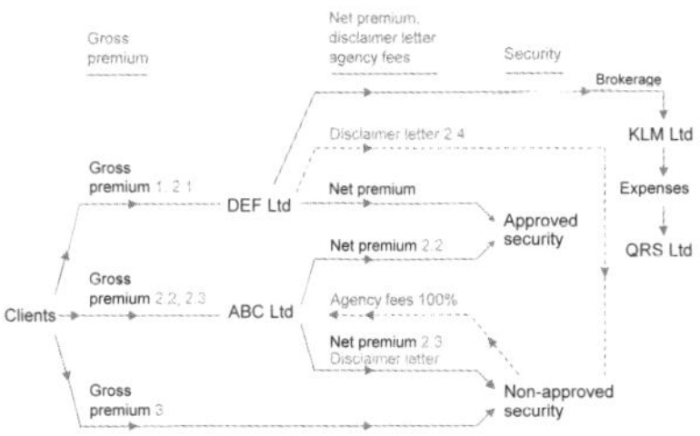

But maybe eschew builds anyway, for there are alternatives.

Our flipchart or whiteboard. Chapter 2 says that, when showing graphs on screen, we should lead delegates into them by explaining their axes first. Alternatively, scribble the graph out on a flipchart, for it gives delegates a break from slides. If our diagram is one we can scribble out quickly – such as a two-by-two grid – try it.

Paper. If we've a big flowchart to show on a slide, we must resort to font size 10 in order to squeeze it all in. Result: our delegates can't read it. So instead circulate a printout, on A3 if need be – and if we've builds, put them on the A3 page too. Lego does with its instructions. Maybe put a faint grid on the page (like a map grid), so that we can more easily talk about bits of it.

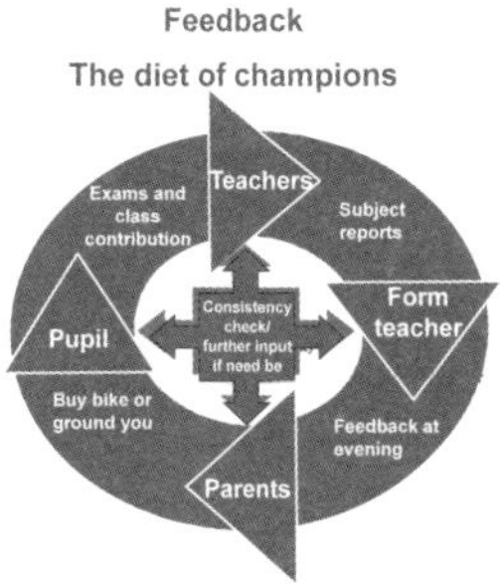

Prezi. It's a presentation software that allows presenters to zoom out and see overview, or zoom in and see detail – which is good for big flowcharts. Take care though, because many people use Prezi in a way that looks cool, but which fragments information and hinders analysis.

That's it for the Chapter. Because it isn't on one topic, there isn't an overall summary. However, let's revisit the parent–teachers chart we saw earlier. Some companies will 'improve' it for us and create Figure 32.25. With

Figure 32.25

Feedback

The diet of champions

chevrons. Shading. Funky circular arrows. A jazzy four-arrowed thing in the middle. Reversed fonts. A motivational headline(!). They'd animate it too, plus add photos (a bike?). One company's website has something just like Figure 3.25, and describes it as a 'brilliant, eye-catching animation'. They're not the words I'd use.

Figure 32.26

What?! Nothing on Gantt charts?

Planners do Gantt charts to show what happens when. The charts help planners spot critical paths, time to complete, and more. Some Gantt charts are big. I once saw one for a £600m project over eight years, and it had 4,000 steps for just the first part of the project. People often do small ones with maybe just 12 steps. When, say, pitching bosses for a new IT system, they create one in Excel or Power-Point (Figure 32.26) and perhaps include some linking arrows. The chart says to bosses: "Look! We've a plan!".

Big and small charts are very similar. Steps. Lines. Linking arrows. And poor at conveying messages, for Gantt charts are our workings. And bosses rarely want to see them. Instead, rise above and *summarise* (use WiT, start at the end, etc).

And the consequence of this? Mostly it's fairly irrelevant how we format and lay out our Gantt charts. There are exceptions though – times when we show Gantt charts to others. Sometimes somebody pins a big Gantt chart on a wall to prompt discussion. People walk up to it, point to a particular point and say: "Hey, see what *that* means!". In which case, tidy it typographically, otherwise people can't have decent conversations – poor layout hinders understanding. How to tidy it? See the flowcharting tips earlier in this Chapter. Also, avoid funky chevrons for all the steps on your chart (Figure 32.27, albeit it's just for part of the plan), for they distract and hinder readability.

Also, maybe we want bosses to see our chart so we can impress them with how complex the project is and how clever we are to grasp it. Should we tidy it though? Perhaps. Keep it untidy and impenetrable, and arguably we look even more amazing for grasping it. Tidy it up though, and we more clearly see it all ourselves – which helps us. Your call.

Finally, if we want to impress bosses with a project's complexity, maybe try words – "£600m spend, 4,000 steps, eight years, a file of A3 printouts, etc".

Figure 32.27

KPI packs (and variances) 33

Dashboards. KPIs. Balanced scorecards. Performance metrics. Whatever you choose to call them, this Chapter has tips to help them all (and the text box on the final page helps variance analysis). To avoid repetition though, I refer throughout to 'KPI packs'. Or 'packs'. And if you do so-called decks, see Figure 33.1.

Now for a huge warning: if you've seen the word *KPI* in the index… if you've fast-forwarded to this Chapter… if you believe you can admire some pretty mock-ups, then create fantastic packs… you can't and you won't. Firstly, this Chapter isn't a parade of arty, page-filling mock-ups ("Look! Five pretty graphs on a page! And this has six graphs and two tables!)". Yes, you see many layouts, but the Chapter is 80% words, 20% layouts. That's because there is a huge variety to KPI packs, and you need to learn which layout to use – and which not to. My words tell you.

Also, doing KPI packs isn't easy. They have lots on each page, so it must all be spot-on, otherwise it's a mess. It's like playing music. Play on our own, and it matters not if we're a little out of time. Play in an orchestra, and we must keep strict time, or chaos ensues. So you must do the following: (1) read earlier Chapters to ensure your packs' graphs, tables and more are spot-on – Figure 33.2 lists which Chapters; and (2) read this Chapter to shove it all together in a way that's spot-on. And reading this Chapter isn't a walk in the park. It's not a breezy read, for it has lots of detail. Then again, if it were easy to do good KPI pages, we'd all be doing them. Most of us don't. Most packs are poor. Very few are fantastic. So if yours are, you'll *shine*. Your packs will impress bosses for many months after. A great KPI pack is the gift that keeps giving.

Finally, two smaller warnings. Firstly, I assume you know the numbers you need to monitor. I help you show them. Secondly, I've heard that KPIs shouldn't be financial. In my mock-ups, many are. So be it.

This Chapter has eight sections. The first four are general tips, the rest look at particular layouts. Variance analysis is a text box at the end.

Sweat the small stuff

First are small tips to remove clutter. Collectively, they make a big difference.

Remove background shading	Don't force content to poke out from rectangular windows (Figure 33.3). Also, see Appendix 1 for tips on colour.

Figure 33.1
Read this Chapter if you do decks
Many KPI packs are created in PowerPoint in landscape. Which means they are decks (albeit thankfully they often eschew photos, autoshapes and frippery). Hence this Chapter sometimes briefly repeats tips from Chapter 23 (*Decks*), e.g. "Avoid big logos". And it's also why this Chapter helps improve decks.

Figure 33.2
Pre-Chapter reading
You need to read Chapters 2 (*Graphs*), 3 (*Numbers*), 4 (*Tables*), 6 (*Design*), 14 (*Infographics*), 30 (*Graphs – more*, other than its first section on isobars), and 31 (*Signalling performance*).

Also, read the second half of Chapter 19 (*Big reports*), it talks about formatting pages. If your packs have more than just a few words in them, read Chapters 1, 16, 17 and 18 (all on *WiT*), and 7 and 11 (both on *writing*). If you worry about what your audience want, read Chapter 8.

In fact, why not just read the whole book?

Figure 33.3

Figure 33.4

Sales
May 2016

Sales   May 2016

Figure 33.5

	Imprss-ions	Clicks
	'm	'000
Wk 1	240	98
2	190	110
3	150	91
4	12	9
5	73	2
6	3	4
7	43	18
8	24	12
9	1	1
10	29	13
Total	**765**	**420**

Figure 33.6

West	Bdgt	Act	Diff
Month	240	214	(26)
Yr to date	942	965	23

North	Act	Bdgt	Diff
Month	151	160	(9)
Yr to date	679	630	49

East	Yr to date	Month
Actual	202	44
Budget	198	43
Diff	4	1

South	Month	Yr to date
Actual	103	382
Budget	95	420
Diff	8	(38)

Avoid big logos	They waste valuable space on the page – you don't need to remind bosses who they work for. Don't put the company name in a huge font either.
Be brief with page titles	One page says: "Fees: actual, budget, variance (month, last year, year to date)". No. Call it: "Fees". Readers more quickly see what the page is about when they first turn to it.
Be brief with row labels in tables	One row says: "Resources invested for staff participation in learning relative to actual payroll". No. Call it: "Learning spend ratio". Maybe define it in a footnote or on the far right of the row to which it relates. In grey too.
Grey down the pack's date	The entire pack shows stuff to May 2016, so grey down that date on all pages other than the first – see Figure 33.4 for two examples.
In fact, grey down anything that's more for reference or is less important	Grey down column headings (we saw this in Chapter 4). Grey down the assumptions and caveats that readers see every month. Grey down smaller numbers (Figure 33.5). In tables, grey down N/A – and make smaller. Show as na.

In other words, be brutal with typography. If we've many dates on a page, don't show them as 21/12/16. Try 21.12.16, or even 21 12 16. On graphs, show labels as Jun 16, not Jun-16. With numbers, try 19 000, not 19,000. In many countries, people show numbers this way.

Then there are tips to ensure our packs help readers and look sharp:

Maybe give the page a lead-in title	E.g. "Fees: a good month". Also, the words *Balanced scorecard* hardly engage. What about: "How we're doing".
Number stuff	Number the sections, graphs, tables, etc. People can more easily talk about them in meetings.
Strive for consistency	Often, each page of a pack looks different to the rest. Different fonts, font sizes, line spacing. The pack looks as if it's been prepared by six people (often it has). It looks incoherent. Amateur. Rather, strive for consistency.
Keep tables structurally consistent	In Figure 33.6, each table is structured differently to the others, so it's tough to see at a glance how each area has done against budget for the month. OK, few tables are this inconsistent, but you get the point. Unless you've a good reason not to, keep table structure consistent within a page – and from one page to the next.

Never align words sideways	In Figure 33.6, *South* is also shown down the side. Sideways. Never do this with your tables, section titles, graph labels. Don't force readers to crane their necks.
Avoid inconsistent font sizes for continuous text	Yes, we sometimes need different font sizes from one table to the next, but for our commentary, keep font sizes consistent. If in PowerPoint, disable its *Autofit* function. As for Excel's *Fit Sheet On One Page*, we look at that later.
Add a horizontal line at the bottom	It brings the page nicely to a close. Without it, readers' eyes reach the bottom of the page, then just… drift off.
Put continuous text in narrow columns	We can use smaller fonts, plus we waste less space with any orphans.

Those are quick tips. The next two take longer to explain.

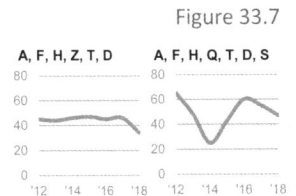

Figure 33.7

Ensure differences are obvious

Here's something I often see, albeit rarely with headings like A, F, H, etc. Figure 33.7 shows two graphs, and because their titles are similar, readers struggle to distinguish between them. As I said in a previous Chapter, it's like £14,268,492.32 and £14,286,492.32 – we must concentrate to see how they differ. Not easy. So, with the graph's headings, straddle what's common across both (Figure 33.8), then above each graph show what's different. Much easier for readers.

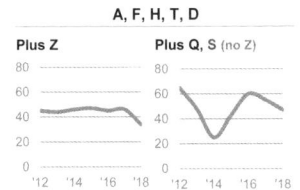

Figure 33.8

Figure 33.9

		North					South					Widgets					Gadgets				
			Projected	Added value				Projected	Added value				Projected	Added value				Projected	Added value		
	Ratio	Sales	Costs	Start	Adj	Ratio	Sales	Costs	Start	Adj	Ratio	Sales	Costs	Start	Adj	Ratio	Sales	Costs	Start	Adj	
	%	$	$	$	%	%	$	$	$	%	%	$	$	$	%	%	$	$	$	%	
AB	3%	600	270	335	7%	10%	462	208	258	4%	9%	356	160	199	1%	7%	274	123	153	1%	AB
CD	8%	420	189	234	(1%)	5%	323	146	180	(5%)	2%	249	112	139	3%	(4%)	192	86	107	10%	CD
EF	6%	330	149	184	10%	9%	254	114	142	1%	4%	196	88	109	(2%)	1%	151	68	84	2%	EF
GH	2%	118	53	66	(5%)	8%	91	41	51	3%	1%	70	31	39	6%	1%	54	24	30	(1%)	GH

Also help readers see differences in tables – in Figure 33.9, the words on the top are in bold. Yes, Chapter 4 tells us to de-emphasise column headings, but when we've many columns – and they're different units and types – a bit of bold helps distinguish the different groupings.

Figure 33.10

Show numbers differently – or show different numbers

Figure 33.10 shows the percentage of calls answered in a target time within a call centre. Column A is how we'd normally show it in a table. In column B, there's a tick for 100%. It's less intrusive. It's greyed down too. Also, the column variably rounds. Some numbers to two digits, some to

	A	B	C	D
Jan	94.0	94	6.0	|||||||
Feb	98.2	98.2	1.8	||
Mar	100.0	✓	-	
Apr	94.8	95	5.2	|||||||
May	98.1	98.1	1.9	|||
Jun	99.2	99.2	.8		
Jul	92.0	92	8.0	||||||||||
Aug	100.0	✓	-	
Sep	91.0	91	9.0	||||||||||

Figure 33.11

Treasury report

"We had £152m on deposit excluding interest earned with ten different banks at 31 October 2016. This compares to the total sum on deposit at 31 October 2015 of £187m, a 19% decrease.

The average closing balance since the start of this year was £167m, and interest earned on these funds was £2.5m, which equates to an average annual deposit rate of 1.80%. This is 0.35% more than the average ECB benchmark of 1.45%."

Figure 33.12

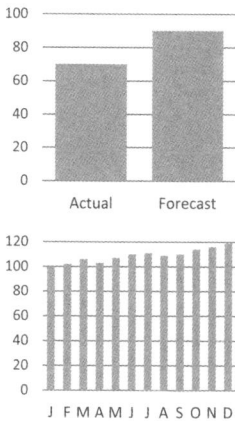

Figure 33.13

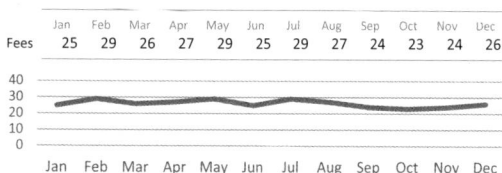

Fees	Jan 25	Feb 29	Mar 26	Apr 27	May 29	Jun 25	Jul 29	Aug 27	Sep 24	Oct 23	Nov 24	Dec 26

ABC Finance monthly pack, Nov 2016   Page 10 of 20

three. Counterintuitively, it rounds small numbers (we usually round big numbers). A score of 92 is far away from 100, so it hardly matters if the score is 92.4 or 91.6. A score of 99 is much closer to 100, and there's a material difference between 99.4 and 98.6. One is more than twice as far from a perfect score as the other. Hence bigger numbers aren't rounded.

Column C shows the amount by which scores are short of target, i.e. it's 100 less column A. Fewer digits. Fewer distractions. Notice June's score. No zero. Then there's column D. It's similar to how iTunes shows volume, and is a rough plot of the numbers in column C. It repeats the letter *I*, based on the number to its left. There aren't six *I*s for January though. Rather, column D proportionalises the numbers in column C (is there such a word?). I'm not a fan of column charts, but these take little space, and if they help innumerate people see which number is biggest, then why not? Finally, Figure 33.10 is in month order, not descending numerical order – and that's fine.

Next are two of Robin Williams' design principles: alignment and proximity. We saw them in Chapter 6, but now need to look at them again. Before then, consider this: when should we create a KPI template? Answer: create one if we have wordy paragraphs with numbers hidden deep within them (Figure 33.11), and we change nothing in it from one month to the next, other than to type over last month's numbers and dates. It's crying out to be put it in a table within a template. How might it look? We see how later.

Sorting out alignment and proximity

First, alignment. Align tightly – but don't force it. Imagine we wish to put two tables and two bar graphs on a page in a two-by-two layout. (Bar graphs?!? Go with the flow.) But one table has five rows, the other ten. One graph has two bars, the other 12. Different dimensions. Force them all to be same size – strive too hard to make them align precisely – and it looks weird. Our five-row table is too spaced out. And one graph is obese, the other anorexic (Figure 33.12).

Also, if you have a graph at the bottom of the page, don't stretch it so it's the same width as the wide table that sits above it (Figure 33.13).

Having said all that, align tightly. A contradiction? No. Figure 33.14 has eight sections – four on its upper row, four on its lower one (the tiny black squares are where its section numbers would be). The page is a mix. Of graphs, tables, words, even WiT. Also, some stuff is big, some small. One table has long and short row labels, so they're right aligned. Finally, it has a header, footer and small logo. As I said, a mix.

But it's aligned tightly. The tops of the upper four sections all line up with each other, as do the tops of the lower four sections. Stuff aligns tightly along the far left edge of the page, as does stuff on the far right. Also, there is equal spacing between sections on the upper row. And equal spacing between sections on the bottom row. It helps bring order out of what could easily be chaos. But study the bottoms of the sections. None align with any others. And it would be wrong for us to force them to do so. Anyway, they don't need to. The page is fine as it is.

In Figure 33.14, I didn't put particular sections next to other ones to make it look any better than 'normal'. Its section order is random. It shows that, if we get the basics right, it doesn't matter what goes next to each other. Which is good, because reality is often messy. Also, maybe we can't control what goes where on a page, for we must stick to a corporate order. Or the bosses' order. Or a logical order (income first, costs next, etc).

Some people put boxes around sections (Figure 33.15 – notice they're nicely greyed down, not visually intrusive). I'm not a fan of boxes though. I feel they add typography and fragment information, hindering readers' ability to float around the page. Also, they draw attention to any lack of alignment, e.g. the second left upper section doesn't align with the second left lower one.

But others say the boxes help compartmentalise stuff, making it easier for readers to focus on one section at a time. I can see that argument, so here's a compromise: if you use boxes, ensure they're aligned tightly, as they are in Figure 33.15 – their tops all align with each other, as do their bottoms. So too do their far left and far right edges. And they're greyed down. A lot.

Figure 33.14

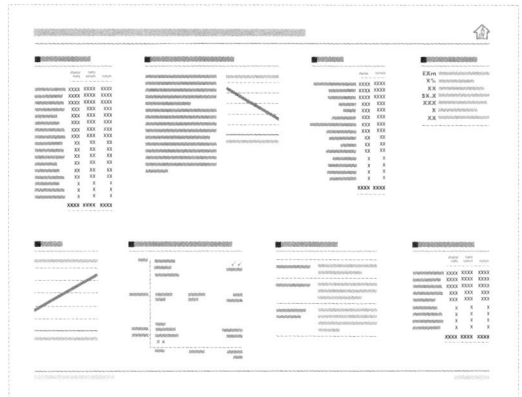

Figure 33.15

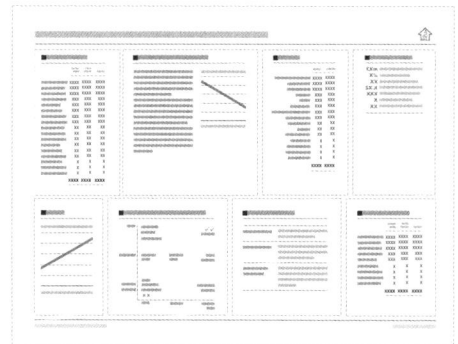

Proximity – poor in many KPI pages

First, a refresher: Chapter 6 (*Design*) said: strive for small gaps between stuff that's related, and bigger gaps between stuff that isn't. It creates visual distinctions between parts of a page and helps readers more easily see structure.

KPI pages often have poor proximity. Gaps when they shouldn't, no gaps when they should. Figure 33.16 (the *before* – overleaf) is a landscape page of just words (and it's realistic inasmuch as I didn't fix its sections to be identically sized). It suffers from poor proximity. Words start at the top and

Figure 33.16

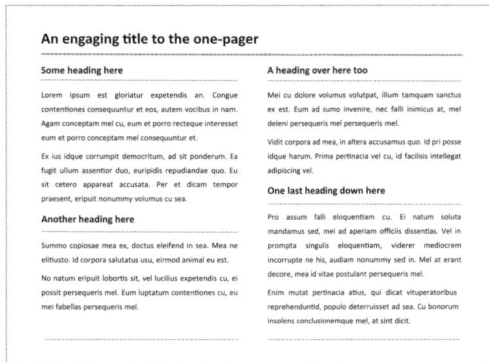

Figure 33.17

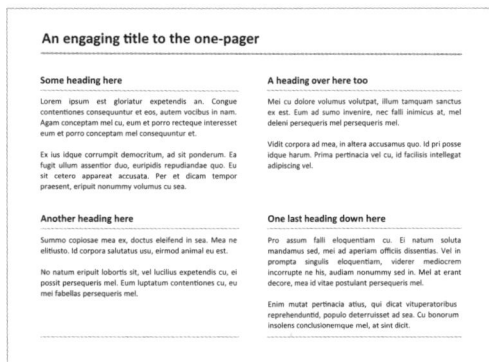

Figure 33.18

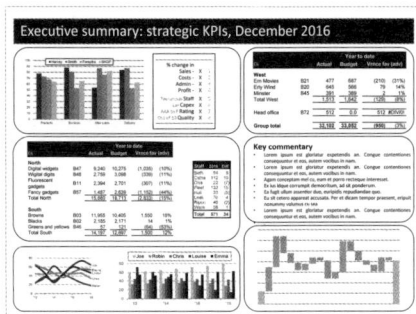

Figure 33.19

% change in sales	X	
% change in costs	X	
% change in profit	X	
% change in return on capital	X	
CPs	X	Average /unit
Capex	X	£m
Rating	X	AAA to E
Quality	X	Out of 5

continue without break until the bottom. A neverending outpouring of text. I see this a lot. Maybe report-writers strive to fill the page. Maybe they fear white space.

Figure 33.17 (the *after*) has the same words on it, so it has the same amount of white space as the *before*. But it uses it better. The *before* has lots of small bits of trapped white space, and no decent slugs of it. The *after* still has lots of small bits – we can't avoid them – but it has decent slugs too, and these help. They look good and create 'breathing space' between sections. In this example, it also creates space for us to align the page better – the bottom two sections now line up with each other, and that helps the page looks smart.

In packs, strive for decent proximity. Scrunch up stuff that's related. Keep stuff apart that isn't. OK, it was easy to do this in Figure 33.17 (the *after*). By reducing line spacing, we create room for decent gaps. But what if we've lots on a page? Surely we can't indulge in decent gaps, and stuff inevitably butts up to each other. As in Figure 33.18 – and it's based closely on a real example. It's neverending – but what can we do about it, given there's so much on it? We see next.

How to avoid tiny fonts

Here's the problem: we put ten tables on a page in Excel in font size 8, then print it as *Fit Sheet On One Page*. Result: illegible font size 5.5. We can't spread it over two pages because our bosses insist on a one-pager, so surely we've no choice but font size 5.5. No. Often, tiny fonts arise not because of too much content, but because of too little effort or ambition. Yes, *Fit Sheet On One Page* is useful, but it's also dangerous. It spares us the tiresome task of *trying*. Study Figure 33.19, it's the *before*. Eight rows of data (and labels are right aligned to avoid big gaps between labels and numbers). Figure 33.20 (the *after*) is almost half the size. Do this to all our tables, and we needn't resort to font size 5.5. Also, the *after* is clearer. Less clutter. Numbers stand out more.

How did I halve it? Not by cheating. I didn't abbreviate words (I could have – I could shorten *average* to *avrge*, and *return on capital* to *ROC*, but I want to keep the *before* and *after* comparable). I didn't scrunch up any unnecessarily wide columns – in the *before*, columns are as narrow as their content permits. Nor did I remove content. In fact, I added stuff – the *after* has a new column, one that numbers the rows (it's greyed down too). No. Here's what I did:

Merged units with labels. In the *before*, the right column lists the units (£m, etc). The *after* puts them in with the row labels, and greys them down.

Avoided repetition in the labels. The *after* puts *% change in* in a row at the top – and that makes the table much narrower. Which sounds good, but this adds an extra row, of course, and doesn't that make the table higher? No. See next point.

Reduced the line spacing, plus improved proximity. The *before* had eight rows that ran down the page without pause or break. The *after* puts rows into two groups of four, with a small empty row separating them. Not a full empty row, but half an empty row. Also, within each group of four, the line spacing is even smaller than in the *before*. Each group of four is compact. It's easier to scan, plus the table uses less space – the *after* is shorter (just) than the *before*, even though it has an extra row at the top and in the middle. (Excel tip: as Chapter 4 (*Tables*) explains, when we've small row heights, bottom-align stuff – paradoxically it makes content sit higher in the cell and so avoids losing the descenders, e.g. the bottom of *g*.)

Also, Figure 33.21 has other ways to scrunch up stuff that we saw in earlier Chapters. And collectively, it all really helps. Clients give me an A3 page in font size 5.5, and I redo it on A4 in font size 7 or 8. It can be done.

To conclude: remove clutter. Follow design principles. Avoid tiny fonts. There's one last common problem to look at. That's next.

Don't make it look like a spreadsheet

It's depressing. We open a PDF and think: "A report", but when it pings on screen, we think: "Damn. A spreadsheet". Numbers in grids. Text in misaligned boxes. So do yourself a big favour: when you create something in Excel to send to others, strive to fool them it isn't a spreadsheet. Here's how (Figure 33.24 overleaf illustrates – and it was done in Excel).

Use serifs for commentaries. We associate serifs more with MS Word than with Excel.

If you can spare the space, use bigger margins. Again, we associate them more with MS Word than Excel.

Figure 33.20

% change in:		
Sales	X	1
Costs	X	2
Profit	X	3
Return on capital	X	4
Average /unit CPs	X	5
£m Capex	X	6
AAA to E Rating	X	7
Out of 5 Quality	X	8

Figure 33.21

Ways to scrunch up stuff – from earlier Chapters

Keep columns narrow: in Figure 33.19 (the *before*), columns were as narrow as possible. In many tables, that's not the case, e.g. Figure 33.22.

Have only an underline: Figure 33.22 isn't compact, but at least its *Total* row has a line under it, but not over it.

Put sub-headings in a separate column (Figure 33.23): this helps if page height is a problem, but page width isn't.

Edit headings (and wordwrap them too): e.g. *Act*, not *Actual*. *This Yr*, not *This Year*. It helps keep columns narrow. However, as we saw in Chapter 4 (*Tables*), avoid *% change over PY CQTD Act 16 v Act 15*.

Make graphs compact: avoid big sprawling ones.

Figure 33.22

North	9
South	7
East	5
West	3
Total	**24**

Figure 33.23

Wales	Holt	23
	Usk	19
	Flint	12
	Risca	11
	Bala	8
	Total	**73**

Figure 33.24

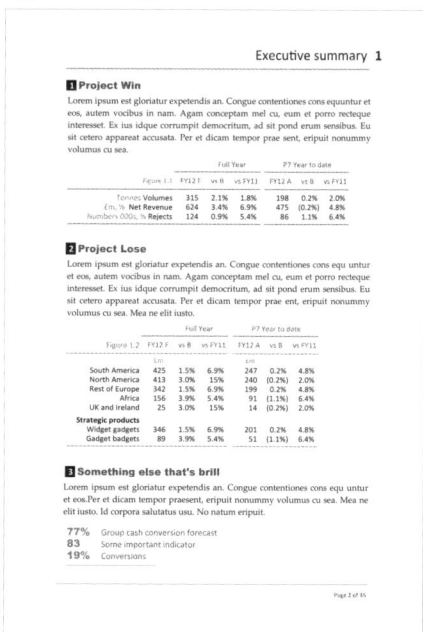

Keep font sizes consistent throughout. Don't let them change randomly from one page to the next. Always print to 100%.

Align tightly. MS Word aligns tightly (it has 'margins'…), so do likewise in spreadsheets. Avoid misaligned text boxes – and remove their borders too.

Have consistent headers and footers. MS Word ensures they're on the same place on each page, so do likewise with your headers and footers in Excel.

In Excel, use its Camera tool. Or copy as 'Pictures' and 'Linked Pictures'. It means you put stuff where you want, not where Excel's cells force you to put it.

That's the last of the general tips, other than the somewhat obsessive text box below. Maybe read it later, for next we look at layouts.

Figure 33.25

How to align column headings

Figure 33.25 shows the same column of numbers eight times. However, their heading (in Latin) and sub-heading (*A*) are aligned eight different ways. Which work? In table (1) the heading and label are left-aligned and hence out of whack with the numbers beneath them. Table (2) is centre-aligned and also doesn't work – stuff is still out of whack. Table (3) is right-aligned and looks good. Seemingly, right-aligned is best.

Not always. In table (4), there's now a negative number. Heading and label – which were fine in table (3) – are back out of whack, i.e. *A* doesn't line up with any numbers. We could revert to centre-alignment (table (5)), but now *A* is too far left. Table (6) looks better, and it's a hybrid. A centre-aligned heading. A right-aligned label, indented by a point. It aligns.

Until we have different numbers. Table (7) has short numbers on the first two rows (0, 7). The headings that are fine in table (6) no longer work – *A* now sits to the left of the '–' and *7* that sit beneath it. Table (8) resolves this (albeit it's contrived). A right-aligned heading (no indent). A centre-aligned label… but with seven spaces before it (i.e. I hit the *Space* bar seven times, then type *A* and *Enter*). Why seven? No great logic, other than it puts the *A* where it looks good.

Let's summarise. Right-align. Unless we've negatives, then centre headings and right-align and indent labels. Except if we've short numbers near the top, then right … Stop. It's getting silly – and it gets worse when we look at a mix of headings (some long, some short). And at long and short numbers. So here's how to proceed with headings and labels:

304

Realise we must compromise	Often, we won't find one format that is perfect for all columns in all tables of our report. Instead, find one that works most of the time.
Then slightly cheat	Strive to align headings consistently within a table – but sneak in a little inconsistency if need be. Add spaces occasionally to individual headings.
Don't give up	For regular reports, it's worth getting them right. When I redo tables, I spend more time on headings than anything else. Sad, but true.

Layouts: starting off simple – symmetrical

Imagine our report looks at five areas. Maybe they're five sales divisions – (1) Widgets; (2) Gadgets; etc to (5). Or they're the answers to five survey questions, e.g. the percentage of respondents who like our (1) Products; (2) Staff; etc to (5). For each area, we have three bits of content: (A) a table that compares now to the last time we reported; (B) a graph that shows changes in the past 12 months; and (C) words that give insight.

To show it all, try Figure 33.26. It's the survey answers, and it has a section for each of the five questions (Products, Staff, Value for money, Décor, Cleanliness). Figure 33.27 is an expanded view of the Staff section. Each section has a trend line on the left, a table in the middle, and comments on the right. On the far right is a number in a big font. More on that later.

The layout effortlessly works at many levels, giving overview (graph), detail (table), and insight (comments). I used this layout to redo a client's survey findings, and replaced its 50-pager with just six pages (it had eight sections to a page – its tables were smaller than those in Figure 33.26). Admittedly the 50-pager was in PowerPoint with one sprawling graph per page, so improving it was like shooting fish in a barrel.

There's a computer icon next to Figure 33.26: it's a free download on my website. However, the download is a 'proper' page, i.e. one that's the 'right' size and has actual numbers, graphs, words, etc.

Figure 33.26

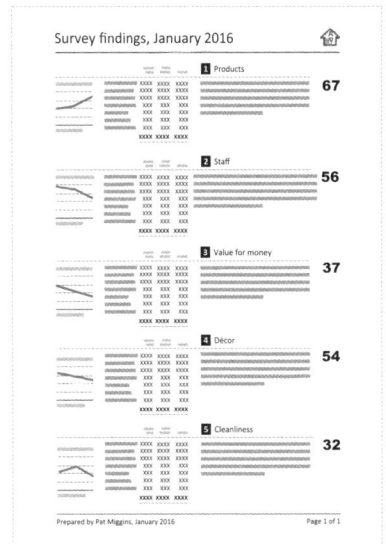

Figure 33.27

Figure 33.28

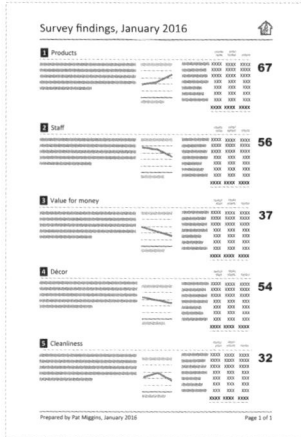

Figure 33.29

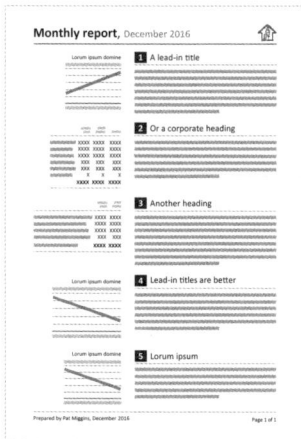

Figure 33.30

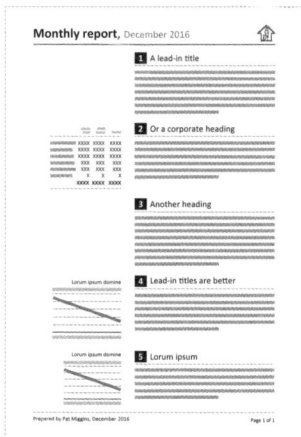

The big numbers down the right

They're the overall score for each of the five questions, e.g. Staff is 56. They're not in descending numerical order. I've assumed that bosses want to retain the order in which questions were asked, i.e. Products first, Cleanliness last. But I want the scores to stand out. I could do a summary table at the top and show the five numbers in descending order. Instead, they're down the right and they pop from the page. OK, readers must still skim down and mentally reorder, but the big numbers create visual interest, and draw readers' eyes. Also, by avoiding a table at the top, the page retains its symmetry – five identically laid-out sections, rather than five sections plus a small table at the top.

The reversed font section numbers down the middle

This is my 'get-out-of-jail' card for design. When I redo a page for a client (or even for this book), here's what often happens: I tidy individual bits – the graphs, tables, words – and then struggle. Yes, each bit is good, but collectively it just doesn't hang together. Then I add reversed font section numbers, and bingo, I'm there. They create a shape to the page. It looks sharp. Many times, I've fallen back on this trick. However, do only the section number in reversed font, not the entire section title. If your corporate colour is dark (e.g. dark blue), use that, e.g. put the section number in white on your dark blue background.

In Figure 33.26, graphs are on the left, tables in middle, words on right, and reversed fonts roughly in the centre. Figure 33.28 reconfigures them. It's fine too, although I prefer the first version. A personal view. But as I said, either way is fine. As are other configurations, e.g. graph, words, reversed fonts, tables.

This layout is great if we've several sections that all have similar content. However, sections often differ. Some have graphs, some don't. Some have big tables, some small tables, some no tables. So next, we see more layouts.

A mix of words, tables and graphs

In Figure 33.29, each section has some comments, along with a supporting graph or table. The graphs and tables aren't all the same size. Notice the layout. A bit like a WiT. Even if we don't have a graph or table to put alongside each comment, the layout still works – in Figure 33.30, two sections are devoid of graphs and tables, and it's fine. If bosses insist on landscape, try Figure 33.31. The same content is laid out across the page in columns – sections 1, 2 and 3 are on the left, and sections 4 and 5 on the right. Rows of text are narrower than in the portrait version; I had to narrow them, otherwise stuff wouldn't fit across the page. To keep overall word count the same, the landscape version has more rows of text.

Let's go back to the portrait layout. What if we have a big table, one that won't fit alongside the text? Easy. Put it at the bottom of the page – we saw how in Chapter 22 with a wide screenshot (see page 201). Or put it at the bottom of the section to which it relates (see the middle of Figure 33.32); arguably it's better, for readers' eyes leap around the page less when they cross-refer between commentary and table.

However, these layouts struggle if we've lots of comments or a table with many rows. So try Figure 33.33, it's in portrait in columns, and it's a bit more flexible. Section 1 (top left) has lots of words, including a WiT. Section 3 (top right) is a table with lots of rows. Section 5 (at the bottom) is a table with many columns. And if a section has both a table and graph, no worries. The layout accommodates it all. It's smart and flexible. It's a bit fiddly to do in MS Word though – every time we type a new line, everything shunts down.

Study Figure 33.33's graph and tables. The graph on the left doesn't stretch to meet the right edge of the column in which it sits. And the table at the bottom doesn't stretch to meet the far right margin. And yet… the table top right is stretched, plus has horizontal grids. That's a breach of the Five Steps for tables, no? I prefer to call it a trade-off. Between readability (a compact table) and look (a stretched table). Yes, avoid tables that stretch too far, e.g. a two-column table that stretches across a sheet of A4. But Figure 33.33 is in columns. The stretch isn't too far, and it helps the page looks smart. For me, it's an acceptable compromise (and one helped by the table's grey horizontal grids). If you view the compromise as unacceptable, have a compact table and no horizontal lines.

Figure 33.33 is portrait. For something in landscape, try Figure 33.34. It's a different mix of graphs and tables to the portrait version, but it illustrates the point. It shows we can have three sections, each with a mix of graphs and

Figure 33.31

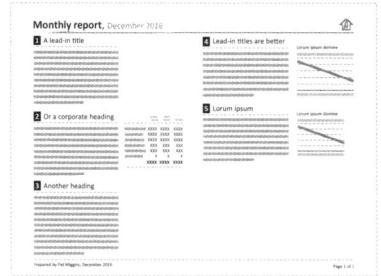

Figure 33.32

Figure 33.33

Figure 33.34

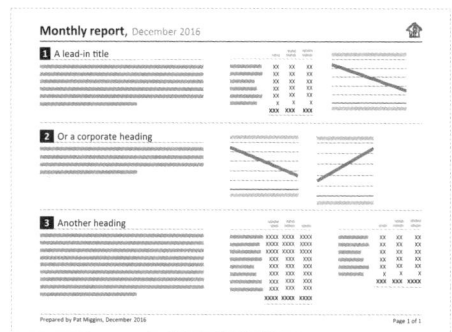

Figure 33.35

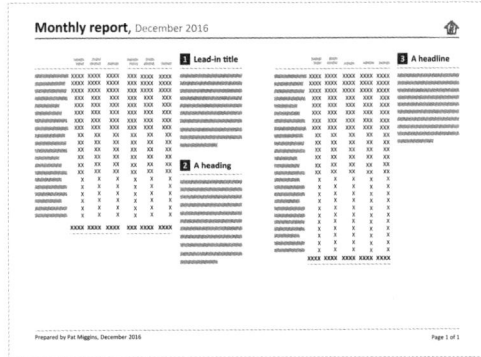

Figure 33.36

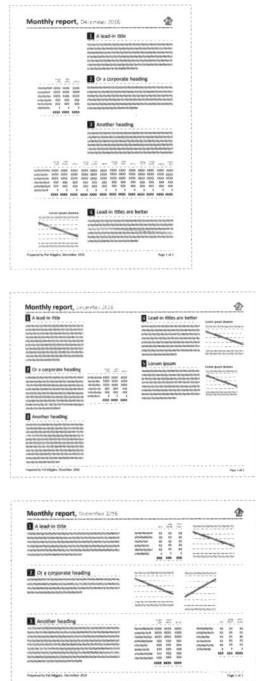

tables, and the page can still look elegant. Figure 33.35 zooms in on one of its section headings, plus it shows how we've done them up to now. In one version, the horizontal line butts up to the reversed font number. In the other, it hovers just beneath it. Slightly different. Either is fine.

Figure 33.34 had small tables and many words. Figure 33.36 has the opposite – big tables, and fewer words. Words are alongside the tables and in narrow rows of text – which makes them even easier to read, of course. And again, the reversed font numbers give shape to the page.

The options are endless. If in portrait, we could put a WiT at the top and a big table underneath. If in landscape, we could put the WiT on the left and a big table on the right. And so on.

Consistent? Or square pegs in round holes?

All this begs the question: should layouts be consistent from one page to the next? E.g. should we fix our pack so that on every page, the graphs and tables are on the left and words on the right? Should we fix it so that words on page 4 stretch as far across the page as words on page 5? Same widths? Or different? The answer is similar to what we found with alignment: yes if possible, but don't force it. Avoid unnecessary differences, but don't shove square pegs in round holes.

And you don't need to either. After all, think of broadsheet newspapers. Every page is different to others. A big article on one page. Three articles on the next. Then a page with ten readers' letters, and the TV schedules after that. Different. But it's fine for two reasons. Firstly, each bit of each page is spot-on. Secondly, there's repetition. There's a look and feel that runs through the paper, one that eclipses individual differences. Yes, the sports page is different to the TV page, but their detailed typography is the same. As is the overall look. And it all looks fine.

So too with packs. Imagine Figures 33.32, 33.31 and 33.34 (shown again on the left) in the middle of a pack. Different. But similar too. And fine.

The next section looks at pages that are just numbers.

If your company does 'Quad' reports, try this tip

A landscape page is divided into four quadrants (Figure 33.37). Each quadrant looks at a different topic (e.g. HR, IT, Sales, etc), and is probably a mix of words, tables, graphs. That's a Quad report, and they can look smart. But in what software package should we create them? Excel is great for numbers, MS Word great for words, and PowerPoint great at neither. Also, if we use MS Word and put stuff in columns, we go through 'word-wrap' hell. If you've experienced it, you know what I mean.

So try this: use MS Word, but create the Quad over four pages, i.e. start each quadrant at the top of a new page. Then save as a PDF, four pages to one. Result: a smart PDF Quad that we can email bosses, one in which quadrants sit neatly in each quarter of the page. And if we add or delete a line, it doesn't affect the position of other quadrants on the printed page (not, that is, unless we add so much, we spill onto the next page).

Obviously we need to use bigger fonts in MS Word — they come out smaller when we save them four pages to one. My download gives tips on this. Also, when saving as a PDF, MS Word asks if we want borders around each quadrant. Say no.

I once saved not four to one, but nine to one. Nine sections per page, done as a three-by-three grid — but in MS Word, each was spread over nine pages. In MS Word, the report was 180 pages. It was 20 pages when printed on A3. And it looked smart.

Figure 33.37

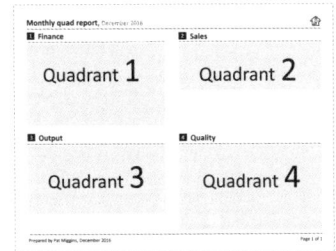

Just a page of numbers

Figure 33.38 is lots of tables. As usual, I've strived to make it realistic. Some tables are short, some long. Some wide, some thin. One section has two tables. 'Normally' we'd align the tables down the left edge of the page. Figure 33.38 doesn't. It shunts them in from the left. It creates decent white space. Visual interest. It helps readers navigate, they can easily scan down the left and find a section that's of interest to them. The layout looks sharp. Study the title of the third section: "Something else as well here". The words don't spread into the column to its right. Instead, they word-wrap within the left column. Smarter. It's what WiT does. In fact, the whole page looks like a WiT. It's Numbers in Tables in Words in Tables. A NiT-WiT, I suppose.

Notice also the table in the third section. It has longer row labels, hence its columns don't line up with other columns on the page. No worries, the page still looks smart. That's because the layout does something similar to a magician's misdirection – a magician draws our eyes to a big move with their right hand so we don't spot the small secret move with their left hand. So too with the page's alignment. Readers' eyes are drawn to the huge line of

Figure 33.38

Figure 33.39

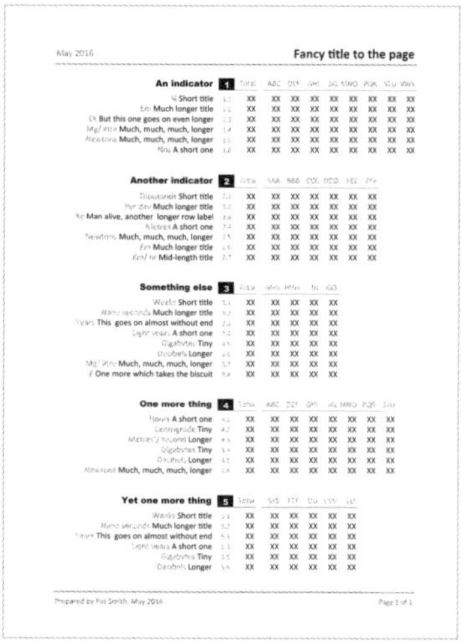

Figure 33.40

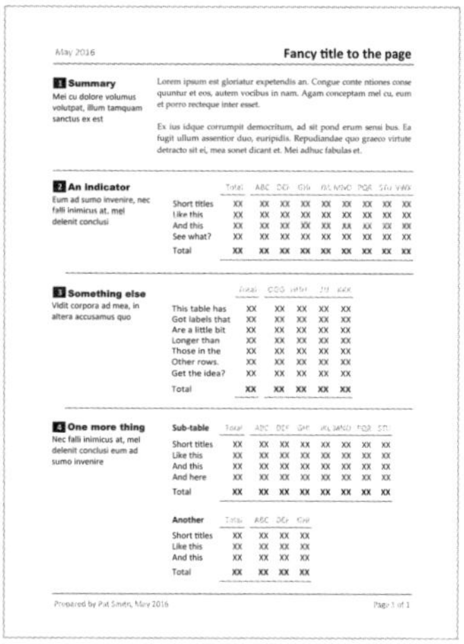

Figure 33.41

alignment created by shunting tables in from the left – which means they hardly notice the smaller matter of these misaligned columns.

Finally on Figure 33.38, a techie tip: the table in the third section is a copied-across picture in Excel.

Figure 33.39 is another bunch of tables, and again I've strived to make it realistic. But this time, its row labels are a mix of long and short, so they're right-aligned in order to better accommodate them. This creates a strong line of alignment down the middle of the page, and that makes the page look good. The reversed font numbers further reinforce that strong line. Each row is numbered too, albeit the numbers are greyed down.

So far, none of this section's layouts have comments or lead-in titles. Add them if you wish, e.g. Figure 33.40 is similar to the Figure we saw earlier, but now with summary comments at the top. Also, there are brief comments down the left under each section title. Each section is numbered too.

We've seen enough layouts. Let's draw threads together. Broadsheet newspapers shove lots on a page, and they look great. Your content-rich pages can too, as we've seen from all the layouts. I tried to do a decision tree to show which layout to use when… but couldn't. There are too many variables at play. Also, I haven't done layouts for every possible scenario. And I won't be able to, for there are too many. Instead, here are the main principles to follow when you create content-rich pages.

- Get each individual graph and table spot-on (of course).
- Align tightly (but don't force it).
- Avoid clutter (grey down the less important).
- Add a bit of contrast (maybe reversed font section numbers).
- Sort out proximity (have gaps between stuff).
- Avoid tiny fonts (often, they arise because of lack of ambition).
- Use narrow rows of text for your words (maybe in WiT).

And don't fear white space. Figure 33.41 has lots of white space because its words are on the right half of the page. It looks smart and is easier to read than if words stretch across the page.

We've three more parts to this Chapter. Below is a text box that ponders which is better: words or tables? Then there are Final Thoughts, and finally there's a text box on variance analysis.

Which is better: words or tables?

Tables are great for numerical lists of similar items. Complaints by office. Costs by activity. Goals scored by player. A table is better than describing in words ("Pat scored most (14 goals), then Les next (11), etc"). But try Figure 33.42. It's not a list, for each row is different to the rest. Which means it's not that easy for readers to grasp. It takes them on a bit of a journey. Maybe words are better (Figure 33.43). Its verbs help readers. "But," people counter, "if readers are familiar with the table, they don't need the verbs." In which case, try Figure 33.44. A table for those familiar with it. Verbs for those that aren't.

And on the topic of words versus tables, there's something called a Word Cloud. A computer counts the frequency with which words appear in a speech or talk (it ignores words like *the* and *and*), then shows it in a funky way. More frequent words are bigger, less frequent words smaller. Figure 33.45 is a Word Cloud of Chapter 1 (*WiT*). Look! WiT is mentioned a lot. Some people are tempted to do Word Clouds at work ("This Word Cloud shows the less offensive words that clients said about us in a survey – look for the bigger words!"). I suppose there is a logic to Word Clouds. After all, apparently our brains process visuals 60,000 times faster than text. Sounds scientific. Authentic. Real. Except no-one seems to know where the stat came from (someone has even offered a reward if anyone can shed light on it).

No. Word Clouds are useless. Figure 33.46 is the English Premier football table, mid-February 2016. Call me old-fashioned, but to show a list of words and numbers (e.g. word frequency in Chapter 1, position in Premier), try a table.

Figure 33.42

£23k behind to date

	£k
Q2 target	442
Q2 actual	402
Over in Q2	(40)
Under to date	(26)
Last yr adjustment	43
Behind to date	(23)

Figure 33.43

£23k behind budget

"We started Q2 £26k under budget, and worsened a further £40k in the quarter (£402k actual for quarter versus £442k target). However, last year's figures have been restated which improves this year's figures by £43k. Result: £23k behind budget to date."

Figure 33.44

£23k behind to date

(26)	**Prior quarters**	We started the quarter £26k under budget
40	**This quarter**	We got £402k this quarter, £40k short of £442k target
43	**Last year**	Last year's figures have been restated which improves this year's figures by £43k
(23)	**Behind target to date**	

Figure 33.45

Figure 33.46

Final thoughts

This Chapter started with warnings, and here is another: when we tidy our packs, bosses will move the goalposts. That's because they no longer waste brain space working out what the pack shows. Instead, they ponder what it means. They then realise they want different numbers. So we give them that – and they then realise they want insight. When bosses do this, some people think it's frustrating. I think it's progress.

KPI packs are a good idea that all too often go wrong. In many firms, committees and sub-committees agonise for months over which KPIs to monitor, but then waste all that effort by giving no thought on how to put it together on a page. And if we do think about that, we get seduced. By funky software ("Hey! A speedometer! Cool…"). By automation ("This IT system lets us create reports 'with just three clicks of a mouse'" – or, rather, with just three clicks, we create ugly, impenetrable reports).

No. Decent packs aren't about IT. They're about layout. Design. Detail. They're about ensuring the individual graphs, tables and words are spot-on, then putting them together in a way that works. When you do that – when you create something special – it feels fantastic.

Figure 33.47

All in £m
ABC Group

Contribution, variances
7 months to June 2016

Summary P&L

Items in bold are analysed below	Year to date Act	Bdgt	Fav/ (adv)	For month Act	Bdgt	Fav/ (adv)
Contribution	63.8	60.0	**3.8**	12.3	10.4	**1.9**
Overheads	(50.3)	(46.0)	**(4.3)**	(12.8)	(7.7)	**(5.1)**
Operating profit	13.5	14.0	(0.5)	(0.5)	2.7	(3.2)

Variances

Contribution	For yr	Month	
North West	2.9	2.6	Two new contracts booked in month - ABC (£1.5m), DEC (£1.1m).
South East	1.8	-	Mainly due to £1.6m extension on Project Smith booked last quarter (+ £1.2m more due in Q4).
Central	-	0.1	On target - small wins and losses. Nothing material.
West and Isles	(0.9)	(0.8)	Contract Xanvier (£0.8m a month) delayed from 1 June start to 1 Sept.
Total contribution	**3.8**	**1.9**	

Overheads	For yr	Month	
IT	2.4	0.8	Project MIS-Development delay - Q1/Q2 to Q3/Q4.
Property	1.2	0.3	Sublet the empty factory on 1 March.
Other, Deprec, T&E	0.1	(0.1)	Minor differences, none material.
Group	(1.4)	(0.7)	Marketing campaign brought forward from Q3 to Q2.
Salaries	(1.6)	(0.4)	New 'Solutions' dept = 40 unbudgeted recruits for 6 months (£0.2m a month). Also, higher than budgeted pay rises (£0.2m a month for last two months).
Legal	(5.0)	(5.0)	Court fine for polluting local river.
Total overheads	**(4.3)**	**(5.1)**	

Page 5 of 15

Figure 33.48

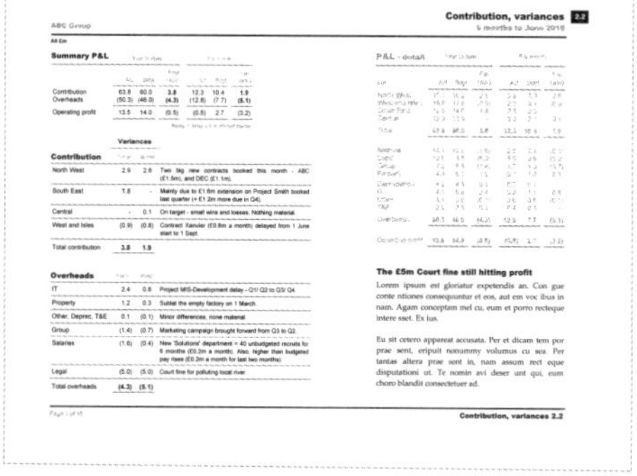

How to do smart variance analysis

Typically, variance analysis is bad. An ugly table at the top of the page. Text boxes of comments underneath. And often, they merely repeat what's in the table ("£Xm above budget, £Ym under") – it lacks insight and is redundant. Also, readers' eyes flick back and forth from table to text. Try Figure 33.47. Study the Contribution table in the middle – it's in descending order of the year-to-date variances. Its comments are in narrow rows of text, so they're easier to read. Also, we've less room to waffle, so we waffle less – we no longer repeat what's in the table. We needn't either – the phrase *North West* is next to 2.9 and 2.6, so we needn't say: "Contribution is up £2.9m for year to date and up £2.6m etc". We cut out words. We go straight to insight.

Typographically, it's smart too. A line at the bottom. A de-emphasised company name top left. A page title top right (readers easily spot it in a bound pack without having to peek in by the bindings). No upper case or italics. It follows the design principles (C-R-A-P). But there's a problem: it doesn't show contribution by unit. There wasn't room to show it, and that's unacceptable.

Try Figure 33.48. What was on the portrait page is now down the left. On the right, there's the full profit and loss account (P&L), plus some overall comments in Latin bottom right – and if you want them to be top left, move them there. The full P&L is in a slightly smaller font and in grey. It sends a signal to readers: "I've analysed it all for you, but here's the P&L in case you want it". All in all, smart.

Finally, my favourites

First, a comment on what might seem oversights. I've hardly mentioned emails or colour, so see Figure 34.1 for emails and Appendix 1 for colour.

Some people tell me this book can be distilled to just three words: Keep It Simple. And yes, we should keep it simple. At work, many of us over-complicate. But if that were all there is to it, this book would be just three words, not many pages. Also, those words don't tell us how to keep it simple. This book does. And here are my favourite bits in it all (numbers in brackets are the relevant Chapters):

1. **Role-play a 30-second summary** (12). It gets us to the nub of it all.
2. **Start at the end** (10). Come out with that nub right at the start.
3. **Aim for repeatability** (9). Logic has a half-life. Instead, strive for arresting angles. Accessible logic. The *feel* button. Start a chain reaction.
4. **Use WiT** (1, 16–18). It gives readers choice. It sharpens writers' thinking.
5. **Keep language simple** (7, 11). It underpins everything. If we do bits (1) to (4), but then use turgid words, we achieve very little.

Figure 34.2

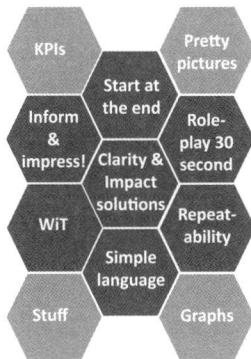

Get these five right, and we convey messages and achieve outcomes. We inform and impress. And Figure 34.2 'helpfully' conveys it all… (it's similar to ones I've unfortunately seen at several clients).

Two of the above five really help talks too. Firstly, the 30-second summary **gives delegates choice** – we don't show our Gantt chart unless they ask to see it. Meetings are much shorter. Secondly, WiT gives presenters a **fantastic script**; it lays it out in a way that's easy to read from.

OK, I've another favourite bit: KPI packs (33). Very few packs are good, so get yours right, and you'll shine. But Chapter 33 builds on up to 15 other Chapters. So, I suppose, one of my favourite bits is those 16 Chapters…

I learnt to deliver reports and talks mostly by trial and error. Yes, a few books helped me, but many more hindered. Even though I experienced highs and lows on the way, it's been a wonderful journey of exploration and discovery. This book is the latest bit of that journey. I hope it helps you experience the highs and avoid the lows, because, when you deliver a report or talk that hits the mark, it's great. Great fun. Great for your career. I hope you have a similarly wonderful journey. Let me know how it goes.

Figure 34.1

Emails – some tips

As Chapter 17 explained, many people read emails on a smartphone, and that scuppers us. Put a WiT in an email, and it can look a right mess on a smartphone. Format an email smartly, and it arrives in Plain Text and looks like a kidnap ransom note. Add an attachment, and smartphone users complain. They don't like attachments.

Result: there's only one thing we can do to our emails that can't be knackered by smartphones, and it's this. Write clearly.

"Holy cow," I hear you ask, "is that it?!". Not exactly. This book has many Chapters to help us write clearly. Three are specifically on writing. Another is on repeatability and the *feel* button. Then there are Chapters that tell us to start at the end, and role-play a 30-second summary. The principles in all those Chapters apply equally to emails.

Which means this book has dozens of pages – and hundreds of tips – that help emails. Job done.

A1 Appendix – colour

First, a confession. One that pins my colours to the mast (no pun intended). When I wrote internal reports in corporate life, I never used colour (assuming, that is, that black and grey aren't colours). I'm not alone either. I once read a 400-page book on document design and it mentioned colour once – and that was to say it wasn't going to mention colour.

I avoided colour because I wanted bosses to discuss my content, not my choice of colour. Too often, I'd ask colleagues what bosses had said about their report, and they'd dispiritingly reply: "Their only comment was: 'Use dark blue, not light blue – it's nicer.'" Everyone has a view on colour. Uninformed, usually. But, heck, why let knowledge get in the way of a good opinion? For both writers and readers, colour is the great time-wasting displacement activity at work today. Writers, don't sweat to improve your report; pimp it. Readers, don't discuss its content; talk about its colours. Much easier. Much more fun.

Which is partly why this book is in black and white and why this topic is an appendix. And there is also an irony and difficulty in writing about colour in a book devoid of it.

Of course, my slides have some colour. Not much though. Enough so they're not too stark. But not so much that people discuss it.

That's the confession. Time for tips. We've seen some already in this book – Figure A1.1 is a reminder. Here are new ones. Firstly, how to survive without colour? Often, we add it to stop our pages from looking so uninteresting and flat. So instead, add **contrast** and grey stuff down. Maybe use **dark grey** and light grey. It creates visual interest and distinctions, and stops our pages from looking so, well, black and white. Also, the design principles in Chapter 6 ensure our pages look good, and that helps us resist the urge to add colour.

But external documents often need a bit of colour. In which case:

Remember that colour distracts	I once saw a bulleted list of brief items (which is fine) but the circular blobs were blue and the text that followed was in black (not fine). I tried to read the list, but my eyes were constantly drawn back to the blue bullets. Not good.
Use just one colour – and use it sparingly	Maybe use your corporate colour, plus grey. My website has examples of this – grey and red, grey and blue, etc. If you don't have a corporate colour, copy one that you like.

Figure A1.1

Tips we've seen before (not in any order)

Use colours people can name, it makes conversations and commentary easier. Avoid ones like auburn. Azure.

Choose muted colours (soft green, orange, blue, etc), not loud and garish ones.

Avoid background colour. It overwhelms, plus soaks up toner.

Avoid reversed fonts other than for very brief bits of text.

Avoid stuff that relies on colour codes. Such as RAG reports and graphs with legends.

Use colours consistently	If doing a series of graphs on unit performance, ensure a unit is the same colour throughout.
Strive to do work that's accessible to colour-blind people	Avoid legends. And when presenting, refer to items by their colour and their location too ("See the red line at the top").
Avoid colours that have connotations	In finance, red often means a loss, so avoid it in financial graphs (unless, of course, you've made a loss). Also, for instance, strong reds and greens together can look like festive wrapping paper – try it and you'll see what I mean.
Be aware of how colours mean different things in different countries	Visit www.informationisbeautiful.net/ visualizations/ colours-in-cultures/ for more. (It's an infographic though, so not that easy to read.)

Even if you use colour, remember that about 5% to 10% of people are colour blind or colour deficient. Also, many people have access only to black-and-white printers or copiers. Finally, to save money, some companies ban colour printing for internal documents.

So ensure your colours work in black and white. Figure A1.2 is the front page of a report, and *The HR update* is in blue (so it stands out), and the author's name is in grey (so as not to seem too egocentric). In black and white though, the name is more prominent than the title, and that's wrong. Instead, choose a lighter grey or a darker blue (Figure A1.3). In other words, focus on contrast, not colours. Designers say that we need to "get it right in black and white".

Time for Final Thoughts. People criticise bad colour, so strive for good colour. But resist the temptation to strive for brilliant colour, because you'll get very few extra brownie points. For most people, colour is a hygiene factor. Which is how it should be. If people talk about the colours you use in your reports and talks, you've got them wrong.

Figure A1.2

The HR update
by Pat Smith

Figure A1.3

The HR update
by Pat Smith

Index

The Contents at the start of this book gives a long list of the Chapters and sections. This index doesn't repeat them all. Rather, it mostly has topics whose location isn't apparent from the Contents (e.g. the *Not* test). Also, it includes topics that are in the Contents but which also appear elsewhere.

First is an index by report type, then an index of myths. Overleaf is an index by category (e.g. movies, people, books, etc). Finally, there's a conventional index.

Page references are as follows:

Heavy bold = Chapter
Bold = first page of a section (or subsection)
Black = a paragraph or two or three
Grey = text box or Figure

1 Report type (alphabetical)

Whole Chapters look at stuff that's common to most reports, i.e. words, numbers, tables, graphs, etc. Below is a list of stuff that's particular to specific reports:

2 Myths

4 Index

For functional areas, e.g. finance, HR, IT, market research, remember also to check Part 1 of this index.